The Criminal's Search for God:
Catholic Reformation of Criminals

By

David H. Lukenbill

1

A Chulu Press Book
Chulu Press First Edition published 2015
IBSN: 978-0-9892429-3-6

Chapter One was formerly published in another form in the book: *The Criminal's Search for God: Criminal Transformation, Catholic Social Teaching, Deep Knowledge Leadership, and Communal Reentry*, by David H. Lukenbill, published in 2006.

Chapter Two was formerly published in another form in the book: *Carceral World, Communal City*, by David H. Lukenbill, published in 2008.

Chapter Three was formerly published in another form in the book: *The Criminal, The Cross & the Church, The Interior Journey*, by David H. Lukenbill, published in 2008.

Chapter Four was formerly published in another form in the book: *Capital Punishment & Catholic Social Teaching: A Tradition of Support*, by David H. Lukenbill, published in 2009.

Chapter Five was formerly published in another form in the book: *Invictus: The Way of the Apostolate*, by David H. Lukenbill, published in 2010.

Chapter Six was formerly published in another form in the book: *The Lampstand Prison Ministry: Constructed on Catholic Social Teaching & the History of the Catholic Church*, by David H. Lukenbill, published in 2011.

The essay, *Hierarchy of Evil* was published in another form in the *Social Justice Review*, Volume 102, NO. 11-12 November-December 2011, (pp. 167-171)

Chapter Seven was formerly published in another form in the book: *The Criminal's Search for God: Sources*, by David H. Lukenbill, published in 2012

Chapter Eight was formerly published in another form in the book: *Catholicism, Communism, & Criminal Reformation*, by David H. Lukenbill, published in 2013.

Chapter Nine was formerly published in another form in the book: *Women in the Church, St. Catherine of Siena, Fr. Teilhard de Chardin, & Criminal Reformation*, by David H. Lukenbill, published in 2014.

Chapter Ten was formerly published in another form in the book: *The Lampstand Foundation: It Takes a Reformed Criminal to Reform Criminals*, by David H. Lukenbill, published in 2014

All scriptural quotes, unless otherwise noted, are from the online *Holy Bible-Knox Translation* at http://www.ncwadvent.org/bible/gen001.htm

All quotes from the *Catechism* are from the Vatican Online edition athttp://www.vatican.va/archive/ENG0015/_INDEX.HTM

All quotes from the Catechism of the Council of Trent are from *The Roman Catechism: Catechism of the Council of Trent*, (McHugh, J.A. & Callan, C.J., Trans.) Rockford, Illinois: Tan Books and Publishers Inc.

We glorify God to attract others to Him

For Marlene & Erika Always

Table of Contents

10

Introduction

The process of forming the Lampstand Foundation, writing ten books, each about various aspects of ministry and reformation of professional criminals—those who commit crimes for money, have served a minimum of five years in a maximum security prison, and are not informers, pedophiles, rapists or serial killers—has been a great learning experience for me.

I began this journey as a Catholic convert, being baptized with my wife in 2004, deeply drawn to the institutional Church and the traditional religious practices—Latin Mass, praying the Rosary, daily mass—to the point I spent several months within the company of Opus Dei to determine if becoming a member of this great devoutly Catholic organization would deepen my Catholicity.

I eventually decided it would not, and took it upon myself to continue and deepen the process of Catholic self-study, prayer and daily mass that I saw as the path to the heart of the Church.

It is a path to the heart of the Church, and I continue still, though transportation logistics preclude daily mass.

As you read the chapters ahead of you dear reader, you will be accompanying me on this journey through the Church, though much I studied has been left unsaid, and unfocused on; such as the sexual abuse within the Church, which I found too painful to write any more than has already been written so magisterially by others that it is an area I only comment on in blogs, and e letters and newsletters to members of the Lampstand Foundation.

The other area I haven't yet wrote much about is the mysticism of two of the greatest Catholic thinkers I have encountered; Fr. Teilhard de Chardin and Fr. Thomas

Merton and how their mysticism shares so much with St. Paul and the Desert Fathers, with the East—the Orthodox mystics, and Zen Buddhists.

It is difficult to write about mysticism as the more you try to describe it the more you miss the reality; but a central practice is living in the moment and in this respect, criminals are attracted to mysticism for we live (in my case, lived) our lives largely in the moment for if we thought too deeply about our criminal actions the impetus and joy criminality offers would dissipate.

This is the heart of the Church, how we live, how we live each hour, each day, how closely we hew to the Great Commandment Christ—and all the mystics in history—gave us, love God, love your neighbor.

As a criminal I ignored God and stole from my neighbor, lied to my neighbor, violating my neighbor in the now understood ridiculousness of satiating myself, when the only fullness of self comes from the path of God, the daily mystical path.

Chapter One
The Criminal's Search for God
Preface
Speaking of Criminals

This book is a reworking of the ten books I have written on criminal reformation, stripping out the voluminous references included in the original books which were meant for my primary readers—criminals in prison—to introduce them to the Catholic sources validating my ideas; leaving only my words and their expansion directed to a broader audience.

The Lampstand Foundation, an apostolate of criminal reformation through Catholic conversion, has grown from what I have learned from my criminal/carceral life, college experience, family life, and transformation within the Catholic Church; proposing that criminal reformation should be conducted by reformed criminals using the supernatural truth of the Catholic Church to trump the secular lies upon which the criminal/carceral world is built.

Speaking of my criminal life is difficult, but what I have learned might be of value to a criminal justice system that has been failing in its public charge of criminal transformation and rehabilitation.

The criminals I speak of are those whose world I was a part; those who commit crimes for money, for whom crime is a way of life—professional criminals—to whom the criminal/carceral world is marked by a subtly defined code of behavior, an ancient tradition, and strong cultural connection.

Professional criminals, who have served time in a maximum security prison, are the only criminals able to transform into transformative leaders.

Those offenders who are pedophiles, rapists, serial killers, or informers; do not possess the criminal/carceral world gravitas to be accepted as transformative leaders.

The criminals of whom I speak are great sinners as was I, but like the prodigal son, are capable of transformation and deserve forgiveness if truly reformed.

I have written this book because as a human being and a Catholic, I owe to humanity and the Church the deepest apostolate work that my experience and knowledge can produce.

I have written this book to expand the ideas I have previously written about to a broader Catholic audience whose current understanding of the criminal/carceral world is too often the limited view of dramatic media, Marxist-oriented theories, and second-hand stories.

Introduction

But God, as he is the supremely good Creator of good natures, so is He of evil wills the most just Ruler; so that, while they make an ill use of good natures, He makes a good use of evil wills. (St. Augustine)

Few human beings are farther from God than criminals, yet the first canonized saint of the Church Christ established on the rock of Peter was the criminal Dismas, the Good Thief, who Christ took with Him from Calvary to heaven, thereby revealing the eternal path to criminal transformation.

This chapter is in three parts. The first is about the criminal world through the prism of my criminal/carceral life—as a thief and robber—lasting for almost twenty years with twelve of them in maximum security prisons, and about my transformation, education, and conversion to Catholicism.

The second and third parts focus on the spiritual and public policy aspects of using transformed criminals to help other criminals transform their lives.

Transformed professional criminals who are devout Catholics with advanced academic degrees and Catholic social teaching knowledge—deep knowledge leaders—working through grassroots community organizations, can help reverse the long-term failure of criminal rehabilitation programs as they possess the elemental experiential knowledge of the criminal/carceral world allowing them authentic access to professional criminals; an access long denied the social worker, psychologist or rehabilitative professional.

The larger issue of how we treat those who have committed crimes against us, who have asked for forgiveness and validated it through their redemptive actions, are thus addressed by an acceptance of their transformation and their help, and an eventual welcome into full communion.

This book is written from a Catholic perspective, seeing crime as sin in the sense described classically through Church teaching.

The prodigal son's return can address the four central criminal justice issues our society struggles with: 1) those of our nation's youth at risk of becoming criminals, 2) the failure of the criminal justice system to rehabilitate, 3) the failure of reentry, and 4) the increasing criminalization of culture.

It is hoped this book will be of help to criminals who are called to transform their lives, restore their connection to the community and help other criminals find the path home to Rome.

It is also hoped it will stimulate among the public, a deeper and more Catholic-informed criminal justice work around the issue of criminal transformation.

Deep spiritual work which the Catholic Church can conduct like no other is vital to transform criminals whose internal life is often governed by ancient and violent spiritually inspired practice.

Part One: A Criminal Life

One's own life has meaning not only because it is earthly but also because in it we decide to be near or far from God, we decide for sin or redemption.
Hannah Arendt (1994). *Essays in understanding: 1930-1954*. New York: Schocken Books. (p. 25)

A Life Far From God

𝕴 was born into the criminal world, far from God, and though well before memory it clearly marked the path I was to walk for many years.

My father was a member of an organized criminal organization and by the time I was two years old we were on the run from the FBI.

They caught up with us and my father was sentenced to twenty years in Leavenworth Federal Penitentiary. Years later when I was sentenced to Leavenworth, I met people who were still serving time from when my father was there, a situation that is unfortunately all too common among many families.

My first criminal act was the theft of a pair of fur-lined leather gloves of another boy in sixth grade. He reported the theft and the teacher had us all stand and face her as she demanded that the thief return the gloves and nothing further would be said. I had put the gloves under my hat where they lay perched on the top of my head, surely sticking up at a strange angle I thought at the time.

Though trembling with barely suppressed fear, and the excitement of dealing with that fear, I never said a word and walking home, hands warm in the gloves; I felt the first joy of gaining something for nothing and the brilliant glow of a risk taken and my fear conquered.

This fear and excitement was always to be present in all of the future crimes I committed.

When I was twelve, my father was released from prison.

My mother had remarried, my step father adopted me and I was raised without any knowledge of my real father and was completely taken by surprise the day he showed up. He knocked on the door and I answered, immediately sensing in his warm "Hello David" someone other than a mere friend of the family.

My father was charming and brought an excitement and worldliness to my life that I had never known. He took me to places I had never been, gave me more money than I had ever had, and let me drive his Cadillac convertible. I deeply love Cadillac's to this very day and for many years drove a pale yellow one that almost perfectly matches the brilliant pale yellow of the Cadillac convertible he was driving the first day he showed up at our door.

I began telling my seventh and eighth grade friends about my father, breathlessly describing what I had been told of his criminal exploits to my wide-eyed friends. I started smoking and drinking as he did, and soon began getting in trouble and became more rebellious at school and home.

My first contact with police came when I stole a pair of diving goggles from a store when I was thirteen. I was caught by the store manager and held for the police. They took me down to the city jail and showed me the juvenile cell where I was told I would wind up if I didn't straighten out. They were trying to scare me straight but it had the opposite effect. I was thrilled. I thought the jail cell and the guys in it were the coolest thing going and could not wait to join them and the world that my father had belonged to.

I began by running away from home on several occasions. One time a friend and I got all the way to Mexico and back—in his chopped and channeled 51 Ford—without getting caught.

After that, another friend and I stole a car—a big red Dodge convertible—and got to Los Angeles before we were caught. Since it was his first offence and his family convinced the judge he was redeemable, he was returned to his family. Since it was not my first offence and my family was not sure if I was redeemable, I was sentenced to a foster youth ranch.

While I was in jail—in the same jail cell I had been shown a year or so earlier—awaiting transfer to the foster youth ranch; I and two others escaped from the jail by jimmying the cell door open. This involved stuffing black paper down the slot the hook dropped into during dinner when the door was open and the guard was distracted, and then lifting the hook off later, (since it wasn't securely down in the slot) with a bent and filed down fork. One of us crept out into the office next to the cell and we called the one guard on duty back to the cell complaining of being sick, and our partner rifled through the office until he found the guard's gun, leading him back into the cell once he had left us. Once he came back we tied him up, and the first time we tied him he was tied too close to the cell door, which was still closed so we couldn't open it, so we had to retie him.

It was three in the morning and we decided to go down the stairs to the basement garage to get out of the city jail building. One of us was in front and slipped out the door and made for the river, but I was hobbling due to a sprained ankle I suffered during a jail fight and my other partner was helping me hop down the stairs. He also had the gun. As we opened the stairwell door into the garage a police officer came through. He recognized my partner and asked what he was doing out of jail. My partner pulled the gun, pointed it at the officer and pulled the trigger. The safety was still on and it did not fire, and how the future of

19

one's life hangs on events that happen so quickly and so decisively.

I was not charged for the escape—though it made the front page of the local paper as the first time anyone had ever escaped from the city jail and the fact that we were juveniles gave it even more news value— and was sent to the youth ranch as planned.

I was warned that if I did not change my behavior the escape would be charged and I would be sent to the state reformatory.

I liked the ranch. We played basketball, did chores, and I might have stayed for my allotted time had I not run into one of my former jail-escape partners, the one who made it to the river and was caught trying to swim across when police on both sides, fired a couple warning shots which brought him out of the frigid water.

One of the duties we had at the ranch was to raise money. We did this by going door-to-door selling stationary, donations for the work of the youth ranch. The counselors would drive us around to the towns in Nevada and we would sell our stationary for three or four hours a day. One day we were selling in my hometown and to my surprise, I knocked on the door of one of my escape partners.

That effectively ended my ranch stay as we took up where we had left off, stealing cars and anything else not bolted down, drinking too much and driving all over creation convinced we were big time outlaws.

I was picked up three weeks later for car theft and promptly sent to the state reformatory in Elko. This was a barren, dusty, and cold place where one of my first chores was fighting the toughest guy there to determine my place in the pecking order.

The reformatory guards refereed the fight which all the other wards watched, circled around me and my protagonist as we slugged it out with boxing gloves in the gym.

I got beat so was relegated to "tough, but not top dog" status.

We spent our days baling hay, feeding cows, and doing pretty much all of the ranch work we were directed to do. The days were much regimented, the weather was extremely cold and I started thinking about escape.

A few months later I rounded up another escape partner and in the late night hours we climbed out the window, over the fence and ran several miles to Elko in our nightshirts and bare feet.

That is how they made us spend the night, away from our clothes and shoes for the express purpose of discouraging escape, but we were determined.

We broke into a church and found money and clothes. We then walked the early dawn streets until we located a car with the keys in it—not hard in the 1950's—and headed east for Salt Lake City. Once there we stole another car from a used car lot, clothes and a shotgun from a sporting goods store, and food from a grocery.

We were brought to earth some hours later after a tire-screaming chase through downtown Salt Lake after I went the wrong way on a one-way street. I drove onto the sidewalk in an attempt to get away but it was not to be.

I came barreling out of the car with the shotgun in my hands, dropping it when I saw several guns pointed at me.

They locked us up in the city jail and our cell mates were the leaders of a riot that had just occurred at the Utah State Prison, Point of the Mountain. They told stories about the riot that had made the news world-wide, and in our criminal pride we basked in the knowledge that we were in the big time.

I had been searching for this ever since I had reached puberty and began to appreciate the world of adventure, excitement, and forbidden things that was represented by my father and I was determined to join that world. Though I lived in a good home and had a good life, there were restrictions, and I was against the imposition of any restriction.

Much of my youthful world, through the music of Elvis Presley, the movies of James Dean, and the fashions from both, provided me with reinforcement that rebellion was cool; rebellion was how you became an adult.

This was a clear counter-choice to the message of living an ordered life that was coming from my mother and step-father.

It was also clear to me from the way people treated my real father that he was admired and respected. That respect flew in the face of the directives to not be like him. He and his world had more potency and vitality than the good and orderly world of my upbringing.

The nature of the ordered life is subtle and quiet, the pleasures serene and soft, and their eternal power was not then, nor for many years, visible to me.

The criminal world pulsated with passion, fear conquered, and deep excitement. I chose to live in the criminal world because I saw it as the world that presented the most value for me, which at that time was to have a good time and live an exciting life; or in the immortal words of criminals everywhere: "Live hard, die young, and leave a good looking corpse."

Prison

Taking the car across the state line during the escape was a federal offense. I pled guilty—setting a pattern of always pleading guilty and accepting responsibility for the crimes I did and was caught for—and was sentenced to the Federal Correctional Institution at Englewood, Colorado, also known as "Little Alcatraz." It was called that for good reason. There were few escapes from Englewood. It was surrounded by a double steel fence topped with rolled barbed wire and several manned gun towers.

Surviving in prison was the most difficult thing I ever did in my life and the most exciting. Prison is a war environment. The threat of death is daily and imminent. It is so intense, the edges are so hard, and the consequences of stupidity are so final and brutal, that the only way to master it is to learn to love it. Mastering war is learning to love war, becoming the ultimate warrior. It is the same in prison, you become the ultimate prisoner.

At that point prison becomes home, with all of its cold warmth and deadly charm, and even though violence and death still stalked daily through the yard and tiers, I eventually felt right at home.

My friends were others like me, who valued the criminal/carceral world values, and accepted the status of criminal, believing it the only path worthy of those—like us—who were men who knew how the world worked and it worked for the strong, it worked for those who knew how to take from it the pleasure and treasure lying abundantly within grasp.

I learned how to project myself beyond myself, how to create a protective space around myself as I walked the halls and yard. In prison the ideal is to be unreachable physically and emotionally. You should not be touched by whatever happens. You should become the strong silent type to the nth degree, and moving beyond that to actually thrive on the chaos and anarchy of prison, to be cold and indifferent when all around you is falling apart, and yet—this is the hardest—to be enjoying the process.

What I saw and felt in prison are what people have been writing about for generations concerning isolation and imprisonment. Reading Viktor Frankl's account from the death camp—*Man's Search for Meaning*— meant much to me, how he found meaning in the suffering. Frankl writes about how he survived the horror of Auschwitz and Dachau. He writes about how after being stripped of all possessions and being isolated with so many values being destroyed, he was still able to find value and meaning in life.

This was built into the criminal/carceral world ethos, the acceptance of suffering caused by our own actions.

I learned about the value of material things in prison and how little power they have over the internal truths we live by. The suffering of punishment rightly delivered—the pain of daily experience—is one of the most comprehensive teachers of all. I learned that in prison. I learned about what I could survive and what I would choose when all choices were closed off.

There is much of the monastery in prison, and the monk Thomas Merton was another author I enjoyed. I used my time in prison to read things I would never have encountered on the outside. During one period, when I spent a year in solitary confinement, I went through the entire dictionary and copied out every mythological proper name and definition into a notebook which became as thick as Grave's *The Greek Myths*. I also went through many of Freud's and Jung's works during this time.

In prison the greatest honor is in protecting yourself, physically and ethically. Any hint of disrespect or violation of criminal/carceral world ethics demands satisfaction.

In a world of predators each revelation was significant. If in defending yourself, it appeared you were close to giving up or appeared to be less than total in your commitment to protecting yourself, you might have to fight again. If the other convicts thought you would kill over a pack of cigarettes, they would be less likely to take your cigarettes.

The cruelty and brutality of the prison is classically evil in the sense that the prisoners are being cruel and brutal consciously. That is the paradigm that works. It is not that there is that much that happens in prison that doesn't happen on the outside, it's just that in prison it is so much more concentrated and undiluted by goodness. Being an evil person is considered good in prison. Being able to hurt others without inner doubt or hesitation is considered high praise.

Honor as it is expressed in prison, is controlled brutality.

As the days spilled into months and years I began to accept the level of terror and alarm that surrounded me as normal. When a few days would go by without a stabbing, fight, or other disturbance, I would find myself getting bored.

The longer you are in prison the more power you acquire. Time builds clout. That first time in prison I did a lot of time in isolation. I was always resisting the guards, stealing, gambling, fighting, getting caught and getting thrown into the hole.

I came to feel a pride in being able to do solitary time. The longest time was the year previously mentioned, getting out of my cell once a week to walk down the tier to the shower.

It was during that period, at the beginning of it when I went on a hunger strike while locked in the stone cell without clothes, or bedding, only receiving a blanket and thin mattress at night, and after 25 days, reading the Bible,

25

remembering studying it when I was a boy in seminary, remembering the happiness of my boyhood, and I broke down, sobbing, asking for forgiveness.

I prayed to God to forgive and protect me and He came to me. I felt such peace and rapture. I felt I was lifted out and walked with Him in a beautiful mountain meadow.

That moment stayed with me for a long time, but could not outweigh what I had to deal with daily, and it was not until almost 30 years later that the power of that moment and that vision became completely evident to me.

I served a little over four years that first time. By the time I got out I had learned to survive in prison, but did not have a clue what to do on the outside.

A few weeks after getting out, while in a bar, someone jostled me, a common occurrence in a bar and yet I found myself snarling a rebuke to the very shocked patron, before I remembered where I was, that I was no longer in prison, and he meant me no harm.

I was out for a very short period. I attempted an armed robbery and within weeks I was back in prison, the attempted robbery plea bargained down to assault with a deadly weapon.

What a relief I thought, and I smiled when I walked back on the prison yard, even though this was a state prison I had never been in, but I felt right at home and was known by reputation. People knew me and I knew how to live here. I was back home.

This return was in the early sixties in California and the prison entry process then was to have every prisoner in the California Youth Authority go through a five week battery of tests designed to discover what made us act as we did and if there were behavioral characteristics peculiar to us as a group.

State prison in California was much more violent than the federal system and the place I was in, Deuel Vocational Institution, or fondly called DVI, in Tracy, California was one of the worst. The racial tension and the gang structure were much more intense. The drug traffic was free-wheeling.

Countering this prison sub-culture was a strong emphasis on rehabilitation, probably the last period until recently that the California penal system focused on it. We had group counseling sessions and needed to complete some type of educational or vocational program prior to being paroled.

I chose to get involved in the dry cleaning vocational training as that put me working in the prison laundry, which was one of the best ways to make extra money while doing time. The regular issue of prison clothing comes out of the laundry all rumpled and wrinkled, but the prisoners who could afford it, paid to have us do their clothing.

This was when the prison gangs were really becoming well organized. The emerging political direction of the various ethnic communities increased the general level of political awareness in the prison at large. There was also more value placed on strategic thinking and building coalitions which helped the first generation of prison gang leaders consolidate their power. As the ethnic groups strategically linked up, broke apart, and remerged, the turf wars increased.

A Criminal Life

I got out of Tracy after about three years and took a job at a dry cleaner. Things began to look okay after a while. I worked hard, up at 5:00 AM, walked to work, put in ten hours or so and was starting to feel pretty good about being a regular citizen.

About this time a new department store opened and advertised for employees. I put in an application, but on the question about ever having been arrested, I lied and said no.

I got the job and for the next six months really started doing something productive. I was working in the men's suits department, wearing nice clothes to work and selling like crazy. I was a natural salesman and led the department in sales for many months.

Then one day the lie caught up with me and two police officers came in, right in front of everybody, and arrested me. There was a local law that made it a misdemeanor to lie on a job application about your criminal record. I was released in just a few days, but the damage was done. My job was lost. I was depressed, angry and hostile and vowed not to go that chump route again.

I spent the next several months riding around the country on a motorcycle I bought with money I stole, supporting myself by stealing from department stores and returning the merchandise, because I knew they would refund the money even without a receipt, and I felt a bit of justice was being accomplished.

After several months I lost my bike, after being held in custody trying to cross the Mexican border with shaky papers. As I was being held, a charge of grand theft came up from the stolen money I used to buy the motorcycle. I managed to talk my way out of the charge and was released but with no transportation.

After a couple of days sleeping on the streets, I ran into a friend from jail walking down the street in front of the state capitol in Sacramento, and he loaned me 'his' car—which was stolen but had a redone ID number and a phony pink slip—so I could resume my wandering and stealing, agreeing to send him money regularly.

After a few months the car broke down and I stole another in Wyoming and took it across the state line into Colorado. Soon after I was caught outside a department store after stealing some clothes and the stolen car charge came up.

This charge was good for another five years. I was considered incorrigible and sent to Leavenworth Federal Penitentiary. I was 23 years old.

Leavenworth is one of the older federal prisons and was where my father had been sent some 18 years previously and as mentioned, I met some people there who had been in with him and were still doing time, never having been released. It was strange talking to them, but made the time in Leavenworth easier as I was part of the family of the old-time convicts, criminals from the 1930's and 40's.

I was eventually transferred to McNeil Island Federal Penitentiary—in the Puget Sound area of Washington State where former Public Enemy #1 Alvin Karpis and his acolyte, Charles Manson, were also doing time—to finish my sentence since I was from the West Coast. This was the hardest and final prison time of my life as I had been out long enough to have discovered a little about living a normal life while working at the dry cleaner and the department store, a way of life I began yearning for.

Even though the relations I had established during this period were short term, there was still enough emotion involved that I began to see and missed the possibilities.

I also began to really think about and study what had happened to me internally that caused me to like being a criminal and not fearing prison, for make no mistake, prison was home to me and though the time was harder this time around, I still felt quite comfortable.
I began reading, deeply, the existential writers, especially Sartre and Colin Wilson, and started expanding my definition of myself. I began to believe that being an outlaw and rebel—an outsider—was an honest intellectual position

to hold. Many of the Vietnam War protesters who were sentenced to prison came to McNeil and the discussions with them seemed to validate my emerging position.

I began to feel that I was of that select group of people who have been blessed to see the world as it really is, and can live with it, even though it is the way it is.

Existentialism is the most incredibly selfish, navel-watching way of thinking devised by cynical man, but in its peculiar and depressing way, it was the beginning of the way out for me.

I was released from prison once again and the Aquarian Age was in full flower. Within a couple of weeks I started doing LSD which was just becoming the drug virtually every one of a certain age and sensibility was doing. Since the heaviest drug I had taken up to that point had been alcohol and marijuana, the LSD had a profound effect on me.

For the next two years I was stoned on it or mescaline and lived in a blue haze of travel, camping out, rock concerts, generally inane living and bubble headed ideas, all surrounded by worn-out levis and a green Chevrolet station wagon that transported me and the entourage I had picked up around the United States and Canada.

I supported myself by writing term papers for college students, advertising in local college newspapers and meeting clients at the college libraries.

It was partly because of my openness in running the business that it came to the attention of college administrators—to the point of one dean meeting me as a prospective client and quizzing me on how I wrote the papers, what I charged, and so forth, before he told me who he was—that it became illegal in California (my favorite client base) shortly thereafter

However, it was a very good living at the time and as I built up a library of papers I resold them around the country.

Then I was arrested for parole violation, deservedly so, and sent back to prison for the final three months of my sentence, which turned out to be a very good thing as it allowed me to begin thinking somewhat clearly again.

I got out for the final time having served a total of twelve years.

College

It took a while to clear my head from the psychedelics, but once I got all the drug influenced nonsense out of my system, I began to think about what I had gone through and what it had made of me. I was 32 years old, had no vocation or profession, and the future did not look too bright.

My previous business writing term papers for college students helped me realize I could go to college, though I thought it impossible with my record until I heard about a program that was helping ex-criminals get into college.

I took advantage of that program and wound up enrolled in college. I majored in criminal justice and psychology and began, for the first time in my life, to learn things that really had mainstream social value.

I learned how the love and admiration for my father and my adolescent nature to rebel led me, a willing participant, into criminal behavior. Being in prison as a result of this behavior, I had to adapt to the prison world to survive in it. I became able to live in that world, but lost, for a time, the ability to live in others.

In college, I learned about the nature of prisons from the perspective of people who build and manage them. I learned about the law and its enforcement by sitting next to cops in the classroom. It was a mind opener beyond anything I had experienced before. I was accepted at college, even in spite of my past, and it allowed me to bloom as people of decency and good will treated me with decency and good will. I began to reach back into my childhood and recover the values that I had been taught by my mother and step-father. I began to see the possibility of becoming something other than a criminal.

College Rehabilitation Program

I got more deeply involved in college, was appointed as a legislative intern with a state senate criminal justice sub-committee, and was hired as a research assistant at the California Department of Corrections on a project that was developing an evaluation model for community-based corrections.

While working on this project, learning about the skill involved in writing grants and managing programs—and having a nice profile written about me in the local newspaper—I developed and had funded, as an action research project, a huge expansion of the self-help program that had helped me.

My successful involvement in college had helped me realize that other criminals could also benefit from college.

As I had studied criminal justice and psychology, I began learning how I had become socialized to be a criminal, and others could also. Once I began to see how things had happened to me, I took the first step towards changing them and I realized that another important step I could take, to help me retain and grow from my new found knowledge, was to show others the way I had found and help them escape the prison and criminal world within which their souls were locked.

In Project Alpha at Sacramento City College—after screening out the sex offenders and drug dealers—we enrolled the students we accepted into a highly structured program of counseling and educational support which was designed to insure that their educational experience was a successful one.

One of the classes we developed was a social survival skills class which all of our students were required to take. This class taught them many of the basics of getting along in society which most people learn from their family and by simple osmosis. But for these students, whose family lives were shattered and blown apart by drug use, abuse, violence, and the constant presence of death, their souls had become wary, predatory, defensive, and dangerous.

After many years in prisons this was amplified, and there were important lessons about living life as a gentle and productive person in a society which they needed to learn if they were ever to reclaim their souls from the stone, steel, and blood of their past.

We taught them things like how to have a normal relationship, open a checking account, how to redirect anger and fear, how to rent an apartment, find a job and be interviewed, and all kinds of things about the basic etiquette of modern living. Other things were folded into the class as students asked questions about various aspects of adult life that confused them and there were many.

I had two full-time staff and ten part-time counselors, who were also students. The staff was 50% former criminals who had been to college and 50% non-criminals who had been to college. Having seen how programs staffed exclusively by either could become unbalanced, I determined to balance the insight, passion, and spiritual insight of the reformed criminals with the academic perspective, moral values, and training of non-criminals.

It worked very well. The program was a tremendous success. During the three years I managed it, the 300 students (at 50 per semester) had an average GPA only one tenth of one percentage point lower than the average GPA of the college. Most significantly, there was not one incident of violence or criminal violation of any kind on campus during that time that was attributed to any of our students.

Many students went on to four year colleges, some pursuing advanced degrees, which has led me to often wonder what has become of their work over the intervening years.

The success of this program led me to work as a consultant with an Office of Economic Opportunity (OEO) funded program providing training and technical assistance to other OEO funded criminal justice programs.

As a government funded program, the tendency to structure the work primarily for the benefit of staff (we were paid very well and had a large budget for our training and conferences) overshadowed the work itself.

Though I felt I was able to provide the clients with some help, assisting many of them over rough times, and giving them new ways to look at the work they were doing, it was ultimately trumped by the needs of the bureaucracy.

The OEO work was an opportunity to share with other organizations some of the tools I'd developed at the college program such as a 50/50 peer to non-peer staffing, and ensuring experiential knowledge was involved in program management.

Private Sector

After this period of several years of relatively intense criminal justice work in the public sector, I felt a respite would be helpful and spent a few years in the private sector—life insurance, long term care insurance, stocks and bonds.

My puttering around in the private sector was restful and I did some property management, some consulting and training seminars, and became very comfortable and serene, at least on the surface.

Internally I struggled with my past and quit sharing with people my turbulent days as a criminal and prisoner and began being accepted just as the person I was rather than the person I had been. Along with this though, I began drinking a lot, writing morbid though often exhilarating poetry, and essentially wallowing in the prison of my past and the bars of my present.

During one brief period of youthful nostalgia, often called a mid-life crisis, I purchased a motorcycle and two weeks later was rammed by a car which took part of my left leg with it. This happened the morning after Halloween, when I had attended a party as the one-legged pirate Long John Silver, play acting what was soon to be a reality even down to the leg and length of amputation.

Many months of adjustment to this new reality followed as I learned to walk in the unsteady, halting nature that my prosthesis required. Walking had always been a consistent pleasure in my life, from circular treks around various prison yards to solitary journeys into the mountains to day-long walks around Sacramento and San Francisco.

Now all that was over, but through it all I realized that I needed to get back to doing what I really loved, helping criminals transform their lives.

Transition

The next several years were spent re-connecting to the public criminal justice sector through focusing on my community. I served as the executive director of an addiction medicine clinic, served as a commissioner on two local governmental commissions, developed my consulting practice and completed my college education by obtaining a Master of Public Administration from the University of San Francisco.

Through all of this work I was beginning to shape the slowly forming realization of the importance of a new type of leadership to operate successful grassroots programs dealing with the transformation of criminals.

In coming to this conclusion, that it was not just about the money, nor management techniques, but ultimately came back to individual leadership and what qualities they were able to bring to their organization; a conclusion reached by the private sector some time before.

The roots of deep knowledge leadership were starting to grow and I began moving into the final preparatory work encompassing my spiritual and intellectual growth.

Becoming Catholic

My search for personal spiritual truth has always been a search for reaching an optimally positive understanding of the four big questions: 1) why are we here, 2) how did we get here, 3) where are we going, and 4) what should we do while we are here. That search has led me through the study and practice of several major religious and philosophical traditions and some attachments to mystics and gurus.

The way the search operates is often by hints and clues dropped by others, picked up through study, and so often a following of one line of work I admire to another connected to it.

For instance, just recently I was led in this way to the works of Blessed Father Charles de Foucauld.

An apostolate founded by a transformed professional criminal after release from prison is founded on the work of Father Charles, and though I read the blog of this apostolate regularly, I had not paid much attention to Father Charles until I noticed that he had been the spiritual forefather of the Little Brothers of Jesus, which happens to be in whose company one of my spiritual mentors, Jacques Maritain, chose to spend the final years of his life and where he wrote one of the best books of his great output, *The Peasant of the Garonne.*

So, this route led to more research on Blessed Father Foucauld, and an ordering of a book of his writings, *Charles de Foucauld (Modern Spiritual Masters)* and in this simple way, my vision expands, expanding my work, continuing my endless path to conversion.

Over the past several years—years of transition— my spiritual path had remained within the Jewish and Christian tradition, ultimately culminating in a conversion to Catholicism which has finally brought me the daily work and internal fulfillment which I had been seeking for so long, often while not even knowing it.

My search for God had ended, and in many ways had just begun.

The religious tradition I was raised in—Mormonism—was enough of an outsider's vision to prepare me admirably for the search ahead. The cornerstone of that tradition was that man entered the world innocent, and the rest of his life would be shaped by the free choices he made; free choice was God's gift and burden.

In my criminal years, I broke completely from the rigidity of that tradition, and began looking at other ways to live that were unconstrained by the morality and spiritual considerations I had been led to believe in.

For many years I didn't think of things in a spiritual way. I committed to being a criminal and lived according to that paradigm, which was primarily hedonistic. I did not pay serious attention to any spiritual reality other than my own pleasure; being young, single, and occasionally free. This worked okay for a while; but something more serious in me always struggled for more meaning.

At some point, deeply embedded within the criminal/carceral world, I began to develop a sense of seriousness, a certain strange liking for dense books about mysterious ideas.

I read voraciously over the next several years about all things spiritual, philosophical, psychological and sociological. I would reach conclusions that I attempted to live by for a time, trying them on to see how they felt in actual living, and succeeded in learning lessons from each brief sojourn.

However, not yet wishing to attach myself to accepting any consequences for my ongoing selfish actions, I adopted the ways of existentialism whose incredibly convoluted forms allowed me to construct anything I wished to better suit my needs.

I learned perhaps one of the most important of all spiritual truths which remained with me; that even in the most horrifying conditions, meaning in living is still possible.

Suffering has value and we can choose to use suffering to gain knowledge.

Existentialism is where I discovered the concept of creation as the product of the outsider, the specially gifted who stand and live outside of the bounds of normal people and because of that stance, are able to see things more deeply and with greater clarity.

This was particularly attractive to me as a criminal, outlaw and outsider and I embraced this self-identity for many years.

Existentialism however, was ultimately too bleak for me, too redolent of stale coffee houses, the acrid smoke of cigarettes, and the aftermath of casual sex. I sought out sunnier visions and soon found the Eastern ways to spiritual truths for my somewhat worn-out spiritual palate.

For many years I studied the tangled thicket of Eastern belief that first appeared so bright and shiny, but ultimately also led into dark alleys and fatalistic dead ends. But even here, as in all the studies, there were great truths.

The East understands, appreciates and reverences nature like perhaps no other way and that stayed with me, deepening and enriching my emerging spirituality. I learned about sensuality, of the earth, of the flesh, of food, and the pleasure of the other senses in a way beyond that of hedonism; which now seemed the cruel play of children. I learned about quiet, contemplation, and letting go.

I became absorbed by the mystical ideas that revolved around the Gurdjieffian insight that man was a bundle of several selves; selves often hidden from one another. This was the human being's essential problem; he was a slave to the desires and drives of his hidden selves, whose appetites arose at the most inopportune times. He would be enjoying the peace and serenity of a contemplative sunset and coming closer to the link between matter and spirit so often found in those moments of natural change, and suddenly be hit by a sudden overpowering urge to have a steak dinner, and the moment is lost, the little self of appetite wins again.

This period and way of learning was very precious to me. The discipline and focus on self, caused me to continually remind myself of who I was while doing what I was doing and the various contexts within which it all was happening. This period merged into another which encompassed the study of paganism, the occult, nature poets, and Grail based mythology. There is a richness here that cuts across the larger, traditional religious traditions, deepening them. They are of a place, time and spirit that speak to us of the comfort of the old Goddess ways, and the power of ritual and symbols, which I ultimately found abundantly in Catholicism. What they all share, ever so subtly in some instances, is the knowledge that everything is alive, that everything has a certain accessible power, but only the wise human can become the high priest/priestess with the wisdom to release that power.

This was also the period, in which I wrote a lot of poetry, attempting to verbalize the spiritual. Writing poetry still gives me great enjoyment on those rare occasions when I feel moved to express myself and no other word format will do.

This amalgam of psycho-spiritual movements is the soup from which New Age belief has arisen and it is a strong blend, ancient in origin, tantalizing to the eye and mind; ultimately however, a diversion and distraction from the real task.

During my spiritual searching, there was one recurring concept that always seemed in front of me, "the harder you seek, the harder it is to find." So, several years ago I quit searching, settled into a roughly spiritual sort of life, finding among the debris and relics of spiritual paths I had left, enough fabric to fashion something that somewhat sustained me.

And, for a time, that satisfied me.

As I re-entered the world of criminal justice, I saw many changes in the field, particularly in the public organizational role and realized I needed to advance my education.

I enrolled at the University of San Francisco, a Jesuit University, as an undergraduate in organizational behavior and after earning my bachelor's degree, entered the master's program in public administration, graduating with both degrees five years later.

Though I had obviously heard about the Jesuits and the Catholic Church, I had never really studied either, as the message I had received from the religions I pursued, was that Catholics were bad and the Jesuits were the worst of them.

My Mormon parents succinctly described the Catholic Church as the Whore of Babylon.

However, during studies in prison I had been struck by the intellectual commitment of Jesuits like Fr. Teilhard de Chardin, and this seemed an appropriate time to look into their history while attending their college.

I began my study with the concept of social justice, which I had some familiarity with through my years of working in the nonprofit sector but I had never delved into the deeper discussion of its implications and historical development.

I learned that social justice is one of the central concepts in Catholic social teaching and eventually found my way to the source documents, the Universal Catechisms of Trent and Vatican II, and the papal encyclicals. The Catholic Church is a hierarchical structure, and when we have confusion or uncertainty about the interpretation of Christ's teaching, we ultimately need to rely on the Magisterium, that body of teaching composed of the catechisms, the papal encyclicals, church tradition and scriptural study.

The papal encyclicals are difficult but deeply rewarding reading. I developed a habit of studying only five pages at a time, after having downloaded the documents from the Vatican website to my computer as a Word document, so that I could make notes and highlight as I read.

One of the tenets of the faith I grew up in was that Christ would return once everyone had been exposed to the Christian—Mormon—doctrine, driving the Mormon's continual missionary work.

I felt at the time and more so later in life, that surely Christ would be returning soon, as who hadn't heard the Christian truth? The answer to that question shocked me—as I soon learned studying Catholicism— that many had not heard the Christian truth, including me, for the fullness of Christian truth is Catholic.

I had been studying all of the religions of the world when right in front of me was the true and only church Christ founded.

For me conversion was primarily an intellectual progression through the social teaching and by the time my wife and I entered the Rite of Christian Initiation for Adults—the year-long process of study that precedes baptism—I was certain I had found what I had been seeking for so long. A very powerful and precious moment was reading this, with entirely new eyes:

> **[Matthew 16: 18]** And I tell thee this in my turn, that thou art Peter, and it is upon this rock that I will build my church; and the gates of hell shall not prevail against it.

So, either Christ lied or the scripture was mistranslated, or Christ told the truth and the Catholic Church was the true church.

At the Easter Vigil, Saturday, April 10, 2004 in the Jesuit parish of St. Ignatius Loyola, my wife and I were baptized, confirmed, and received our first communion in the Roman Catholic Church.

It has been a long journey and is, as many Catholics are saying to us, "Welcome Home!" truly a return to a place we had given up on finding, our true spiritual home.

My earliest spiritual memories, tinged now with the warmth and golden hue imbuing memories of long ago, are of getting up at 5:00 AM, in the bitterly cold Nevada mornings, and being driven by my mom to the local seminary for scripture study before school.

As I sat in that wood paneled room, with a small group of other boys, focusing on the crinkly India paper pages of our bibles, shading with red pencils those scriptural verses most meaningful to us, I felt deeply at home.

Over the intervening years, seeking through the world's churches, religions, philosophies, and ways of being, I had found no such home again until now.

Part Two: A Criminal Transformation, Deep Knowledge

As my education proceeded I was struck by how necessary it is to embrace life-long learning, how much education informs experiential knowledge, and how being effective at transforming criminals was only possible with the combination of graduate education and criminal/carceral experience, all fully embraced and grounded in Catholic social teaching.

There is a rich past of experiential knowledge in self-help which lends itself to criminal transformation constructed on the building of a profession for transformed criminals working to transform others through the application of what I call deep knowledge.

Deep knowledge is the knowledge that comes from experience, is shaped through education, and informed by Catholic social teaching.

As I continued deepening my own knowledge around criminal justice issues, social teaching, higher education, and my consulting experience, it became clear the embrace of a dceper level of knowledge is required for effective work with criminal transformation, which ultimately requires dealing with the deepest part of a criminal's spiritual, emotional, and intellectual being.

Traditional books about working with people from life's margins often talk about how those comfortably situated in the center of the modern world can reach out to the marginal, but that is not far or deep enough and I would suggest that being from the marginal is crucial and as far as criminal transformation is concerned, from a Catholic perspective, even that is not deep enough. What is required here is the Catholic being created by the combination of criminal/carceral world experience, graduate academic success, and deep learning in Catholic social teaching; overlaid upon the daily life of creedal Catholicism.

Criminal Truth

Criminals, as all human beings, are hard-wired to seek God—to seek truth. For the criminal the search has ended at the truth of the will of the world.

Money and its fellow travelers, acquisition, exploitation, and power, is the truth of the world which the criminal believes and acts on and the visible world responds, validating his belief, while the spiritual world, still unknown to him, does not.

For criminals, the ultimate conquest of their fate is to learn how to be successful criminals—not be arrested or even known as a criminal while making plenty of money in crime. Criminal world heroes become mythic and through their exploits and holding to the professional criminal world ethos they continue to shape the criminal culture.

To the criminal, who already assumes—due to his living the truth of the world in its most direct way—a certain superiority to most of society, he *still knows* the search for truth is vital and this is the fulcrum upon which a conversion to Catholicism can move.

Criminals *know* almost everyone uses criminal methods to achieve great worldly success and continually see the wealth earned from that success forming a protective shield if those methods are ever discovered.

Criminals realize that though the occasional white-collar criminal is arrested and imprisoned, most are not. When the white-collar criminal is imprisoned, it is in what criminals call 'country clubs', those rural lock-ups that feature tennis courts and expansive visiting privileges.

Rarely do the white-collar criminals see the inside of Leavenworth, Marion, San Quentin, Pelican Bay, Sing Sing or Joliet.

This reality lies at the center of the truth for criminals, and the success of the organized criminal families, and the gangs who create and wait in the future.

Criminals understand the truth of prison, and the justifiable punishment their actions often bring and while not—among themselves—complaining too much about it, do see the unjustness of the white-collar criminals largely avoiding punishment.

The first criminal, Cain, was the father of the first city of the world, the city of man, while Abel, the second born, was the father of the city of God; and Cain—in this world—slew Abel.

The truth of the world is that crime pays. Cain lived and created the city of men and Abel died and who can see the city of God; and that is the essence of criminal truth.

Eternal Truth

Just punishment in prison is a spiritual act based on the penitential reaction to the criminal's action and from the suffering implicit in the penitential reality of imprisonment.

The criminal needs to become friends with eternal truth, Catholic truth, the only truth powerful enough to trump the truth of the world, and he will, if it is presented from an understanding of the essential dignity and honor of the criminal/carceral world—which he has embraced through years of living in it—from someone who has walked in his shoes.

A charge accepted by the transformed criminal and deep knowledge leader is to better the world we previously harmed, to be useful and to serve, to create more abundance for our fellow human beings, to care for and nourish the ground upon which we stand together by being gardeners of the soil of human fulfillment, to be just and loving in our dealings with others, and to always stand on truth, our final and greatest friend, guided by the loving hands of God.

Being friends with the truth embedded in Catholic social teaching is to walk *"with Peter, to Christ, through Mary"*, the guiding principle arching over the truth of the teaching, wedded to scripture through tradition and centuries of reflection.

Through this lens, and through this practice, the social teaching makes its way into our lives, embroidered and filled out through the Universal Catechisms from Trent and Vatican II, and papal encyclicals, a clear trajectory of correct practice informing us now.

Being friends with truth knows the absolute centrality of human beings within creation, in knowing innocent life absolutely must be protected, in knowing all things are possible through God, and even the darkest soul can discover the light.

This is our ultimate friend, this truth we seek, and for which in this complex and modern world where appearance shades reality, calls us to even deeper searching.

He awaits our call for guidance. He whose word has guided us through the millennia guides us still, as prevalent and fresh as when written on parchment in ancient times, but a breath in God's mystery for us.

He has died, He is risen, He shall come again.

He came for the criminals most of all, for did He not take with Him to heaven from Calvary one of us, the criminal Dismas, the first saint.

Criminals, deep inside, when we talked together within the cells of our prisons, believe what Dismas believed.

Christ came for us, He died with us, He created the Church for us and we are the prodigal sons of the Church, being called back to her embrace.

We are continuing to make decisions about transforming criminals by the study of marginal inhabitants of the criminal/carceral world—informants, sexual predators, serial killers—rather than from its professional core, the professional criminal whose drive is only to make money. The only authentic access to this professional core is the professional criminal himself, honorably bringing his former world into clarity—once having transformed from it—to help another.

A penitential criminal is helped best by a friend, a transformed criminal. The deep knowledge leader is from the community of the criminal. He knows—as being itself— the criminal/carceral world and now transformed stands ready to help as a friend. When he becomes educated and credentialed—the very formation of competence—he helps as a professional friend.

The solution is within the problem.

Subsidiarity asks that problems are best dealt with closest to their source. While social currents may affect the environment of social problems, it is the purely personal where we see most clearly their effect.

Helping the criminal brings us into work of great peril, moment, and consequence, where the guide capable of the deepest penetration is someone having already trod the criminal/carceral path.

Working within suffering redeemed is where spiritual power grows and where those who are called to work selflessly to help others are resolutely armored. They get tired, sometimes to their very bones, but they are working within a power which is inexhaustible.

The great transformational saints of the streets like Mother Teresa, St. John Bosco, St. Vincent de Paul, and the thousands of other street saints, known and unknown, say what keeps them strong in the face of the great suffering they see daily is Christ in every human face.

Each day's work is filled with the pain of others, each day of fatigue and silent weeping at the struggle to remain whole, each day grows the strength and endurance that is the stuff saints are made of.

The criminal/carceral world is otherworldly when compared to the world of the people largely charged by society to help the criminal transform and that is a central aspect of the failure of traditional rehabilitation. That otherworldly nature is perpetuated by the inability of criminal justice practitioners to often even understand what criminals are saying, as criminals have learned from long experience to deliver the message expected rather than the clarity of their interiority.

This can be seen in a simple way just in the response of the criminal to the prison versus the general perspective of its utility, for instance; where the prison has been seen through Catholic reflection as monastic, penitential, contemplative.

However, to the criminal, in a larger sense, the prison serves much more of a career building, network developing, and criminal character building role, driving one farther from reconciliation to the community rather than closer.

Deep Knowledge Leadership

[Psalms 41:7] Deep calls to deep at the thunder of thy cataracts; all thy waves and thy billows have gone over me.
Revised Standard Version Catholic Edition

A deep knowledge leader would be a triple-status professional, with deep experience in the criminal world, including several years of incarceration in a maximum security prison, graduate success in the academy, and advanced study in the social teaching of the Catholic Church.

The deep knowledge concept, in one form or another, has been expressed by many leaders in social capital building.

Liberation theology proposed that one had to *do,* or "faith in doing"

Deep knowledge leadership—rather than taking the perspective of the criminal, or serving them to gain a new spirit, as much of the work with the marginal within the Church has been done under this rubric—is a going beyond. It is *faith in being* rather than *faith in doing.*

The spiritual aspect of deep knowledge leadership implies a spiritual maturity earned through experience, education, and the punishment of prison, an important octave of the way of perfection.

The way of perfection is congruent with organizational upward growth and there is often an entrepreneurial vision—enhancing the process of organizational scaling up— fused with the motivation of those who have suffered, transformed their suffering, and now seek to heal others.

It was the pain of her suffering at losing her child to a drunk driver that inspired Candy Lightner to found MADD. It was the pain of his unresolved alcoholism that inspired Bill W. to found Alcoholics Anonymous. It was the pain of discrimination that inspired Martin Luther King to found the Southern Christian Leadership Conference. It was the pain of his suffering in the prisons and streets of America which propelled Malcolm X into mythic status as a leader in the black liberation movement. It was the deep pain of drug addiction, imprisonment, and the scorn of others that led John Maher to found Delancey Street.

Great leaders grow from great pain. They must act, they must change the circumstances which led to their suffering, and they embrace transformation.

This then is the nexus where the transformed criminal—the deep knowledge leader— can play a role; where those who have transformed their suffering into the power of teaching can help us all.

Deep knowledge leaders, fighting ignorance, lies and evil, are well-armored to fight a war they have already won within themselves.

Transformative Metaphors

Sending a thief to catch a thief is the metamorphic forerunner to sending a transformed criminal to transform criminals.

American intelligence professionals consider the human intelligence from in-country people sympathetic to the cause of America an asset of the highest value.

The informant, on the other hand, often gives information for personal gain rather than being mission driven.

The same holds true within the criminal/carceral world. Those criminals, who transform themselves through religion, will be driven to help others find their path, knowing the great joy that can replace the great suffering their criminal life often brings.

The informant, however, comes from the fringes of the criminal world, by definition not its heart, and even if well-positioned within the criminal organizational structure, still gives information about former friends from a motive of self-gain and is not to be trusted.

Like being cured by like—the core of homeopathic medicine—is an ancient principle used throughout history.

Uncovering and fixing the weakness in any system benefits from this concept.

Working with the criminal, trying to spark the bloom of self-transformation, or trying to keep the young among them from growing into what they are becoming, is tedious work and few relish it for any length of time. But those with the passion and skill that comes from having transformed themselves, gained the knowledge of possibility and change, and thrive on the challenge of bringing the lampstand into the darkest place, setting the lighted lamp of one soul upon it, and watching the darkness turn into light; can embrace it for a lifetime.

The criminal/carceral world is a world only known by those of and from it.
Most programs that work with criminals work around the edges, understanding neither their world, the necessity of honoring it, nor the only real path to transforming it being a love and understanding of the truth.

They try to bring the criminals to offices, schools, churches, businesses, or community centers, and there try to change them into productive citizens. But the criminal, heeding Omar Khayyam, will "take the cash and let the credit go".

Choosing to be Criminal

Criminals choose what they do, and the primary reason they choose crime as a way of life is because there is nothing else that equals the excitement, power, and money that committing crimes brings.

Many people are caught up in the relativism of our time, seeking an authentic life, genuine experience, and feeling the sacredness of the common event. Much of that search is unconscious and vicarious, lives lived through celebrity worship, media saturation, personal fantasy, various addictions, and following the many teachers selling their personal way to heaven to the unsuspecting and needy—and I've been there, haven't we all?

The successful criminal suffers none of this angst, for he has already found heaven, the bliss and ecstasy of the authentic life. That authenticity, that genuine reality of experience occurs when the entire being is focused on the singular moment, the eternal presence and the now; which is deeply realized by the criminal when committing a difficult, risky, and major crime promising great reward.

For the law-abiding, these moments are satisfied by yoga, meditation, group hugs of one sort or another, risky sports, extreme expeditions, adventurous sexuality, or the occasional intoxicating alcohol or drug binge. For the criminal it is virtually anything illegal, any moment when one's freedom and person is at risk, when the criminal steps out of that world inhabited by the law-abiding and acquires something of value for little effort. At that moment when they are entirely focused on crime, and most totally alive and vital, the criminal world is heaven. For them, there is very little in the law-abiding life which equals the adrenalin rush and the sense of complete centeredness of the successful completion of a major crime, and the more risk the better.

Understanding Crime

Crime has always been with us. The first human act was one of rebellion, Cain answering God when asked about his brother Abel who he had killed: "Am I my brother's keeper?" was not so much a question as a statement of position.

It is the evil hidden behind charm and intelligence, the ancient final frontier, and the great conundrum of human history.

Though the criminal world is a world resistant to change and seemingly perplexing the best minds of many generations, its essential nature has not changed since the beginning of time.

Most people also know that crime deeply hurts the criminal, eventually; yet this most tantalizing and poisonous of human activities still remains beyond any of our society's attempts to control it. Most of the declared "Wars on Crime" actually result in crime increasing and becoming more powerful. As will eventually happen with any flurry of prison building and tough sentencing legislation which, though it will clearly reduce crime rates, will also result in—as the millions of new prisoners created by this wave of reform return to the streets—better equipped and much more effective criminals.

The criminal justice studies of professionals are too often focused on techniques derived from theories and questionable statistical studies.

Crime is not, except in the most abstract sense, a result of social conditions, nor the sadness in one's life, nor a gallant rebellion against an unjust world, though the path to it may come from all three. Ultimately, crime is a breakdown spiritually. It is a distancing from God, the farther away, the deeper the crime. The criminal violates fundamental and core realities of human interaction when becoming criminal, yet very often feels spiritually fulfilled—or at least feels an interior filling—as a result of his crimes.

Criminal World Glamour

The law-abiding criminal/social justice practitioner who interviews the criminal after arrest or during treatment, in addition to bringing their law-abiding sense of moral judgment to the table, often brings a certain wonder at the criminal's ability to act with such freedom.

I cannot count the numerous times revealing my criminal/carceral past garnered admiration from people who should have known better.

This makes getting at the truth of criminal causation conflicted. What the criminals say, in their private and contemplative companionship mostly happening inside prisons or jails, is a story of having their way with the world and getting away with it.

For a time, during the turbulent 1960s and 1970s, a proponent of the criminal's victimization by the conditions of society has been the often Humanism-driven relativist and the Marxist-driven radical, to whom the criminal is an exotic creature whose acts are threatening to the foundations of order and stability—which they also wish to shake—and they would have had criminals in the vanguard of their army.
The relativist and radical has—and even still, sadly, does—proclaimed in literature, film, drama, and poetry that the criminal is special and privileged to know things that terrify the common man.

Crime and the attractiveness of it to youth are strong, and though the forces against crime grow stronger, the attraction has reached so deeply into the life of Americans that there is widespread agreement it is a major social problem and it is one of the bedrock issues that has propelled social conservatives into political power.

54

Many social reformers feel that a return to the values of an earlier time will change the criminal world's great attraction for youth. It won't. The imperative of social evolution will not let us. Crime is as old as time and ever since the acts of the first criminal it has adapted to accommodate new realities.

Many people are beginning to understand that the ancient way of Christians in reclaiming the prodigal son—love that flows from knowledge of liberation—is the only way of criminal transformation that works.

The criminal world is an immense and powerfully compelling world that has clearly shown it has the ability to drive the agenda and change individual behavior on a very large scale. It offers sensuality, excitement, danger, and the possibility of a mastery of mystery, a coming to terms with darkness and fear.

Within each criminal/carceral ethnic culture there are stories from their cultural pasts; Aztec stories, Viking stories, Arabian stories, African stories, which shape criminal/carceral reality; one, centered on the life of the legendary pimp, Iceberg Slim, has particular resonance within black urban culture with many of those cultural leaders adopting forms of his name into their own.

Many major movie actors—past and present—have at some point in their acting career felt it imperative to play a prisoner, thus facing, even if only in a make-believe way, the terrifying reality of prison life, which the non-criminal sees as the most horrific reality they could ever face, but which the criminal sees as merely a part of their life with little to fear and much to learn.

Government's Role

The beginning era of criminal reformation in the United States was correctly—though incorrectly structured on Protestant theology—built on the premise that criminal transformation was spiritual and so the first prisons were places of contemplation, single cells where the criminal could absorb his penitential punishment, commune with God, and purge the sin from his soul.

After many years and for many reasons including finances, politics, and religious diversity—as well as some criminals apparently being driven insane by the enforced solitude and the horror of confronting their crimes—this system was changed.

The modern method of treating criminals is still evolving around the poles of punishment and rehabilitation but there is precious little success to be found.

The major criminal justice success over the 1980s and 1990s was due to broken windows policing and three strikes sentencing, which dropped national crime rates as more prisons were built housing more criminals.

During the first two decades of the 21st century, liberals began to reassert control of criminal justice practice and consequently, by 2014 crimes rates began rising again.

For sixty years the major responsibility for helping transform criminals has been in the hands of government. That is beginning to change as practitioners realize the deep failure government programs have had, and with it the terrible sense of despair and helplessness that has surrounded professional work in the criminal justice field.

Recently there has been a tentative return towards faith-based efforts—with proselytizing prohibited—in criminal transformation, but as yet the research does not point to any great success being had there, nor will it with the prohibition against proselytizing.

Crime is undoubtedly our major unsolved social problem which government has addressed vigorously, and, though government funded criminal transformation programs do not yet work, it does not mean government should get out of the transformation business. They should consider becoming more of a facilitator and expediter rather than a program developer or manager.

Government should use its funding and technical support base to facilitate community programs developed and managed by deep knowledge leaders, reformed professional criminals—excluding informers, pedophiles, rapists, serial killers—with graduate degrees, practicing Catholics, part of a strong marriage and deeply learned in Catholic social teaching.

To meet government's need to acknowledge diversity, it should support similar programs informed by all of the major religions that wish to become involved and after a ten year period of evaluation, continue to support that which works best.

The struggle against evil—the evil of thc criminal world—has to be from the inside, and struggle from the inside is best accomplished by developing deep knowledge leadership and encouraging them to construct solutions.

Looking at it in military terms—also the terms describing spiritual warfare—we need transformed criminals acting as criminal/carceral world special operation forces armed with the most advanced spiritual and intellectual tools, suited up with the full armor of God, driven by love and knowledge, transformed and willing to reach out for the ready hands of others seeking the way.

Government can help build and fund this type of special operations criminal transformative force.

Spiritual World of the Criminal

The axis mundi of the criminal's spiritual world is that evil—the evil of the world's perceived reality—is good. The criminal has seen the reality of the world and it is a hard-earned knowledge from years in the criminal/carceral world; having the criminal will to choose evil is freedom, while being restrained by good is slavery.

The criminal is not an archetypical construct, but a real creature whose morality is based on the prince of this world to whom honor is due. The criminal world's attraction is the attraction *of* the world, *of* secret ways of power, *of* secret knowledge *and* unlimited access to forbidden fruit.

The criminal does not think of his world in spiritual terms, but in terms of the naturalness of the world. He sees the reality of the world as God immanent, pantheistic, and existential.

Embracing the will of the world creates the criminal holding to its truth and it is only the will of the criminal surrendering to a higher, deeper truth—as clearly seen and as powerfully willed to learn—through education, conversion, and the social teaching, (which was surely written for the prodigal sons and daughters) that he will find redemption and walking that path, bring others to it.

The demands honor makes, which is the animating force of much criminal/carceral world action, including killing, also turns evil into a good.

The good of evil is the power of the teaching that can flow from evil redeemed.

The leadership of the criminal/carceral world, the core group governing criminal organizations inside and outside prison, possesses a well-defined sense of honor, and lives by an ancient code of behavior based on the truth of this world.

It is the truth of acquisition and exploitation, vastly over-shadowing the eternal truths in a world where the Word of God is spoken with a still small voice one must seek to find.

Eternal truth, embodied in the Catholic Church, is deeper, stronger, and much more ancient that Eve's temptation and Cain's alienation.

The criminal, as much as any other, seeks truth, and in his criminal acts (and un-formed life) embraces the undeniable truth of the world. Willed criminality is rewarded (in many cases handsomely) and it will only be through the clear knowledge of the higher and well-formed truth, from the communal world of the Church, that will attract him with the necessary intensity to override his criminality and render him, truly, the prodigal son.

An apparent contradiction in the criminal/carceral world, except to those in it, is the eternal hope of the criminal to find the one true and just social institution that was, even if for one brief moment, presented to them during their life as the good of the world.

But alas, for most criminals the truth of the world negates that one true just institution, even the Church, and they grow in cynicism determined not to be tricked again.

Catholic Social Teaching

The ground of Catholic social teaching comes from scripture, tradition, and the papal encyclicals.
The key references deep knowledge leaders would use to further illuminate the encyclicals include the *Catechism of the Catholic Church,* the *Compendium of the Social Doctrine of the Church* by the Pontifical Council for Justice and Peace, and *Christian Social Witness and Teaching: The Catholic Tradition from Genesis to Centesimus Annus*: Volumes 1 & 2, by Rodger Charles S. J.

The Encyclical Letters they would draw from include: 1) *Rerum Novarum:* The Condition of Labor (1891) Leo XIII. 2) *Quadragesimo Anno*: After Forty Years (1931) Pius XI. 3) *Mystici Corporis Christi:* On the Mystical Body of Christ (1943) Pius XII. 4) *Mater Et Magistra*: Christianity and

Social Progress (1961) John XXIII. 5) *Pacem In Terris*: Peace on Earth (1963) John XXIII. 6) *Populorum Progressio*: On the Development of Peoples (1967) Paul VI. 7) *Dives in Misericordia*: On the Mercy of God (1980) John Paul II. 8) *Laborem Exercens*: On Human Work (1981) John Paul II. 9) *Sollicitudo Rei Socialis*: On Social Concern (1987) John Paul II. 10) *Redemptoris Mater*: On the Blessed Virgin Mary in the life of the Pilgrim Church (1987) John Paul II. 11) *Centesimus Annus*: On the Hundredth Anniversary of Rerun Novarum (1991) John Paul II. 12) *Evangelium Vitae*: The Gospel of Life (1995) John Paul II. 13) *Ecclesia De Eucharistia*: On the Eucharist (2003) John Paul II. 14) *Deus Caritas Est*: God is Love (2005) Benedict XVI, *Lumen Fidei*: The Light of Faith (2013) Francis.

Much of Lampstand's work is teaching about the acceptance and transformation of suffering, even that coming from punishment.

Embracing the redemptive power of suffering and that faith *is* works, resonates with criminal/carceral world values that actions must speak, the talk must be walked.

Though too often, the faith expressed in these luminous documents is not walked as strongly or as often as we would wish; yet the knowledge which emanates from these foundational documents will, once studied, reflected upon and absorbed, draw the transformed criminal into the apostolate of leadership within the work of criminal transformation.

Solidarity

My first memory of solidarity is political. It is the solidarity shared with the man standing against the tank in Tiananmen Square, but solidarity in its fullest sense would stand also with the tank driver, who stopped before running the man over.

And the preferential option for the poor would be the solidarity option embracing the rich, for solidarity stands *against* no one, but *for* all.

A root of solidarity is friendship among groups of strangers transcending strangeness, binding us all by the common ground of our existence as human beings and creatures of God.

Solidarity is friendship, friendship of the highest level, grounded in the ancient ritual of sacrifice of self to another.

The highest gift brings the greatest reward and laying down our earthly life is to have eternal life.

Our friends have created a home for us. Through countless ages human beings of good will, self-sacrifice and eternal vision, have laid down their lives, fortunes, and dreams on the floor of our existence. It is a floor of enduring stone, built with divine goodness and familial love.

Solidarity between human beings is best expressed by speaking truth to one another and the great tears in its fabric come through the conscious wounding of that truth.

I remember, as do you, those moments when the face of the *Other* became the face of a friend and in that moment solidarity breathes through us with its ancient, warm familial breath.

We have become so materialistic that we preclude spiritual authenticity to all immersed in it, yet should we not be in solidarity to those whose path to salvation is as passing through the eye of a needle, those who have become enemized by so many, and in solidarity with them fulfill our greatest commandment.

Criminals seeking the path of transformation are debtors and in solidarity with all criminals who have transformed their lives before, including the many saints among them,

St. Dismas, St. Augustine, and St. Callistus (d.223), the former Roman slave who served time in prison for theft and assault, but eventually was redeemed and became a Pope, many feeling he might have been among the greatest of all popes.

The first human fruit of the world was the first criminal, Cain was the first born after the fall and the first born in original sin.

The truth of the city of men is the truth the criminal embraces in his search for truth, for he does not see the city of God, whose face is only visible through the way of the saints.

With Peter, through the knowledge transmitted through the encyclicals and the papal teaching; **to Jesus** through Holy Communion, the gospels and the embrace of scriptural study; and **through Mary** by embracing the Church's Magisterium.

Criminal Reentry

Criminals go to prison, are eventually released and within three years, 60- 70 % of them return to prison

Most parts of the American criminal justice system work well. With the advent of broken windows policing and three strikes sentencing, crime rates have dropped as more criminals are arrested and imprisoned, though they are rising again ass big city liberal mayors halt broken windows policing and liberal courts abandon three strikes sentencing.

What still doesn't work is the process called prisoner reentry—post-prison criminal transformation—a social challenge.

The continual reliance on professionals unaware of the deep spiritual structure of the criminal world, who are unable to address reentry issues to help the criminal transform, and with a continued focus on the social process rather than the true root of crime—being far from God—doesn't work.

The leadership of the redeemed criminal, who has been toughened by his criminal/carceral world involvement and informed by graduate education and Catholic social teaching, while retaining his authentic voice within the criminal world, is to be treasured and, most importantly, used.

Relying on program development and management by transformed criminals is the only effective reentry strategy that will work over time and with large numbers of criminals. Until we are able to develop and integrate their deep knowledge leadership into the criminal justice reentry process, it will continue to fail.

We have in our hands many management tools and they include those from the nonprofit and organizational development world, both awash in advanced technologies and sound strategies for fund development, organizational management and sustainability, and issue advocacy.

Reentry—Helping the Stranger

It begins by helping the stranger, being the Good Samaritan, who saw not a member of an enemy tribe but a human being. Before Christ, among most tribal cultures, strangers were enemies. The teaching of praying for our enemy is a profound idea which you can only realize how well it works by actually doing it in the spirit in which it is meant to be done, charitably.

An indelible memory of the events during the early part of the war in Iraq happened soon after the dictator Saddam Hussein was captured and a picture was released of him disheveled and obviously in great distress. Many were happy to see this evidence of his downfall, but the Vatican reminded us of the ancient teaching with their plea that Saddam Hussein be treated with dignity and respect.

From the beginning, Christ and the Church have leaned towards the poor and unfortunate, calling for them to be treated with dignity and respect.

And for those criminals who do not know or embrace the Church, it will be the Catholic community organizations that can bring them into full communion, freely and from their own reaching out in response to the entreaty of a transformed criminal, a friend.

Reentry—Subsidiarity

Loving our neighbors and praying for our enemies can only be done freely. Love and prayer are free acts, the essence of charity. Grassroots Catholic nonprofits help freely and donors support them freely.

It is a good arrangement and congruent with the principle of subsidiarity. In this way the proper role of government is to act as a facilitator of technical and financial resources to help grassroots organizations with the embedded community expertise, do the work of criminal transformation.

This is where the Catholic reentry program must work, at this completely individual level, closest to the possibility of the transformation of individual criminals.

The social doctrine of the Catholic Church revolves about this interaction of one person with another, with preference for the poor, the marginal, the suffering, while embracing all. This essential human relationship with one another and with our Creator is where our work of transformation begins.

Reentry-Catholic Grassroots Organizations

The leaders of grassroots organizations are the social entrepreneurs of the nonprofit sector. They have seized hold of a truth and organized others around it for the good of the community. The community is best served by their being able to keep closely aligned with their core values, vision, and mission (their truth) as they evolve into a community institution.

While one of the goals of grassroots organizations is to become institutionalized to the point that community support becomes a stable given, it is too often precisely the point at which they become much less effective as a mission-driven organization.

The truth of their mission often gives way to the expediency of becoming stable and solvent.

Criminal transformation emerges from the small, grassroots organization through the work of a few committed individuals—ideally led by deep knowledge leaders—coming together for a great cause. It is from the grassroots that individual dignity is protected, hope encouraged and communities strengthened.

These grassroots transformative groups, linked by their common leadership of transformed criminals and common goal of transforming criminals, would provide a potent ingredient to the existing reentry landscape.

The leaders of these organizations are the true inheritors of the voluntary associations of virtue and service to the public good that Benjamin Franklin brought to fruition in colonial America.

This association of small community groups working on great national causes is very American and resonates particularly well with reentry whose animating force is community reintegration.

It is in community reintegration that the lack of parents—so many of whom are reentering criminals—to provide the moral guidance needed to avoid the criminal world's inducements can be mitigated.

Criminal Culture

Woven throughout the history of America is enjoyment of the pleasures surrounding the criminal way of life, however guiltily reveled in. Much of America's urban social life is the result of allowing the criminal world to become a viable alternative life, with its own symbols and cultural icons. One can now be born, grow up, live and die without ever knowing, but from a distance, any other way to live than the criminal way. This is how it now is in many neighborhoods of America.

The criminal world has grown very powerful in the past five decades in America. As a result of social trends that are long-rooted but accelerated in the 1950's; film, music, and fashion converged to enhance the attractiveness of rebellion and crime to youth. A corresponding inability of the traditional American socializing institutions to imbue youth with respect for the simple religious-based values that internally restrained so many generations of children has contributed to this situation.

The visual and audio world of film and music has great power to shape the interior lives of criminals.

Literacy and education play a crucial role here and are able to help reshape the interiority of criminals—who have found it easy to objectify the external world while reshaping it through violence and crime—particularly during the formative years when the values of the criminal world are most apt to take hold and be embraced.

Graduate education infused with Catholic social teaching is a powerful tool of liberation and for the criminal perhaps the most effective of all, as he begins to understand the how and why of larger social forces that help shape him and his world, but the ultimate role and power of individual choice.

It is a path of learning that can propel him into the same field of conversion from which so many leaders and saints have sown and reaped.

The intelligence of criminals which was once applied to crime, will, after having discovered a truth of greater moment, pursue it to the end.

Part Three: Transformative Teaching, Nonprofit Organizations

Nonprofit social service organizations in the United States, whose mission is the transformation of criminals, have historically been led primarily by religious communities.

Ever since their beginning in this country, the root of grassroots organizations was a root of faith—based largely on the ancient methods developed by the Catholic Church throughout history—adopted and utilized effectively by others.

From this Catholic past the great movements of individual liberation were born.

The abolition of slavery, women's emancipation, child labor laws, and the control of exploitive capitalism, were all begun in the religious voluntary associations characterizing our country's early history.

Today, the growth of nonprofit organizations embraces most of the world and they lead the way in opening many societies to the importance of respecting the essential dignity of human beings, as they did here.

This seminal religious role was reborn recently through the faith-based initiative developed by the federal government and federal funding sources were opened to religious groups.

The Catholic Church, with its well-developed social teaching centered upon the dignity and respect of the human being, provides the guiding principles upon which the intellectual and spiritual framework of successful grassroots programs is built; guidance which becomes evident once the teaching is examined.

Fortunately, over the past several years, the realization that the social teaching is a profound tool that needs to be more broadly exposed to the world, has prompted the Catholic Church to devote substantial resources to compiling the information needed to work within the framework of the social teaching.

Unfortunately, the primary use of it is by liberal (in the sense of laying blame for criminality on society rather than individuals) Catholic organizations who believe more in the unjust social structure influence on the development of criminals than the conservative (in the sense of conserving the past) Catholic doctrine of individual choice largely causing criminality.

Government Rehabilitation Programs

Most rehabilitation programs over the past several years are government developed, funded and managed, and are based on sociological principles rather than religious and are usually built on trying to convince criminals about the terrible consequences of their way of life; that drugs are bad, criminals always get caught, and prison is horrible.

This might be the truth for the law-abiding, but it is not the truth of the criminal.

To the criminal, drugs are generally terrific, and as you learn more about crime you get better at getting away with it, and prison is an occupational hazard with certain benefits like networking and providing some time to get back in shape from a too-riotous lifestyle.

The false foundation traditional rehabilitation practitioners operate from preclude success, while engendering disrespect from criminals who realize the professionals running the rehabilitation programs know very little about the fundamental reasons they have become criminals. Consequently, practitioner effectiveness at dissuading them from pursuing the criminal life is seriously compromised.

The essence of government run rehabilitation is transforming the evil of a criminal life into the good of a communal life and this—as the faith based programs understand—is a spiritual transformation; spirituality which the traditional practitioner ignores.

The truth provided by an effective transformative organization about how to live must be based on *truth that walks,* if it is to impact the inner life of criminals.

The criminal world meta-narrative is that everyone has a scam, so criminals understand they are just doing what everyone else does, except they—criminals—do it honestly.
If law-abiding people cannot be believed when they say they live a life of truth (according to the criminal meta-narrative) then why would criminals want to join their hypocrisy when they can continue to live the honest life of a criminal?

The historical evidence of research about the effectiveness of all current rehabilitation programs is one of failure, except for the 19th century—when estimates of 10% recidivism rates have been stated, versus 70% currently—when most criminals were considered sinners and most rehabilitation efforts were religious.

The current failure of rehabilitation could change with a relatively small public investment in training and educational loans for transformed criminals who commit to work helping transform other criminals for a certain period of time after graduation.

This service work would also pay off their school loans, similar to existing programs for doctors, teachers, and social workers.

Transformation in the Church

It is a simple thing for criminals whose personality is built on deception to lie about accepting Christ one day and getting baptized the next—so common within the Protestant criminal reformation world— if the benefits of flood, clothing, cash, and entrance into an embracing social group are proffered as a result.

The Catholic conversion process—Rite of Christian Initiation for Adults (RCIA)—takes almost a year and through the weekly series of meeting and education, the truth will usually come out, or be embraced.

The RCIA is a process—especially if led by laity and priests with deep knowledge of the criminal/carceral world—with potent transformative power. Its concluding ceremony is one of forgiveness of all sins and the cleansing of one's soul. It connects the redeemed sinner to the unbroken line of truth stretching back to Christ and beyond, to the founding of the central spiritual truths of the Church.

Divine and human, the person is the center of creation; everything revolves about the individual person and by moving in concert with Peter, breathing and thinking with the Church, the person is realizing his fullness; but by breathing with the world he is only tasting temporary sensation and losing eternity.

All of these blessings are embraced within the circle of a sacramental life in the Church, baptism, penance, communion, and marriage.

We respond to the criminal as this person, partly divine, yet having committed evil acts and needing deep reformation, reconciliation, and redemption, (do not all of us need such love?) though for the criminal—for me and my brothers and sisters—it is deeper, so much deeper.

It is very difficult for someone one not from a way of life like the criminal/carceral world to see into it and recognize the elemental dignity and respect within it; very difficult to help recover the lost souls of those who are there.

Transformation

Transformation is personal, based on love and surrender. For grassroots leaders it is the love of the other; surrendering to that love, and in their passion for seeing joy overwhelm suffering, they are transformed by the work.

The founding stone of the social teaching is the right to life for all human beings and all that entails; the right to the means to maintain life, to secure work and sustenance according to individual means, to educate ourselves to our potential, to associate with whom we wish, coming together to advocate for social change and the right to dignity and justice.

We know this exists but rarely upon earth, yet knowing it is inalienably due each of us as creatures of God, can irrevocably ground our work and give it strength of truth none can question.

We are called to learn the root of these rights, and this is a duty which inalienable rights demand we shoulder; to learn, to study, and to grasp the shaded meanings and clarity of purpose upon which our work with others stands.

Way of Perfection

The way of perfection is hidden under many names yet we know it is the path of seeking perfection as a human being and we know it embraces service to our highest nature.

We see people, as if from a distance, whose life seems to define this path, and that distance can shield us from the effort we can make, and sadly, hide us from the joy of living the great commandment; the happiness of others, the comforting of pain, the smooth support of unconditional love as it resonates within your heart, embracing you as you embrace it.

It is a way of humility, as we begin realizing that the highest things in life are found along the way of a pilgrim of old, head down, holding a staff in one hand and a lantern in the other, trudging onward, always towards the eternal city, one step at a time, building a life path of prayer and service, shaping a life, building a cathedral in time, an eternal home of charity and justice informed by knowledge of what is truly good.

The communion of saints within the Catholic Church are the eternal guides for each of us—we who should all want to become saints—in our way toward perfection, and we see from their examples that it is truly reachable; one can live a life of perfection.

Read the powerful book *Liturgy and Contemplation*, by Jacques & Raissa Maritain, in particular, Part Two: Chapter III: Contemplation and the call to perfection; and it is available in its entirety online.

Social Justice

Much of the work I have done over the past few years has revolved around trying to comprehend the concept of social justice in relation to working with grassroots organizations. The founding work leading to the creation of my apostolate partly consisted of a social justice discussion group I facilitated that came up with this definition of social justice:

> Social justice is an active state of human consciousness, based on the transcendent nature of human beings, in which respect for each person's human dignity governs all social action, where individual rights exist prior to society, and must be recognized by it, and where each of us are called by our Creator to defend the dignity of human beings, in every moment of our lives and at every moment in history.

Let's break this down:

"An active state of human consciousness" Social justice is not a static sensibility but is a way that you see the world and your place in it that must include justice work;

"Based on the transcendental nature of human beings" We are not animals that have evolved from amoebas but creatures created by God, whose nature is connected in a concrete way to God;

"In which respect for human dignity governs social action" This is the great law, love thy neighbor, it absolutely must govern, during each and every moment of our lives, all of our activity as human beings, to forget it is to sin, to remember it is to be saintly, which we are all called to be, clearly and unambiguously;

"Where individual rights exist prior to society" We are human beings whose rights were embedded within us before the foundation of the world;

"And must be recognized by it" We strive, in our calling to become saints, to inspire the world to acknowledge the

divine nature, the divinely protected and eternal rights of human beings.

And the restatement, the capstone;

"Where each of us are called by our Creator to defend the dignity of human beings, in every moment of our lives and at every moment in history."

And so, we have the very foundation upon which work within the social sector rests, human dignity, the fulfillment of the great commandment, and the sacred heart of every mission: "Do unto others as you would have them do unto you."

It is so simple, yet so difficult to live that we spend our lives trying, but with what noble reach, such gentle wish and soft harmony with our soul's greatest desire.

The Criminal's Search for God

The criminal is seeking objective truth, but feels he has found it in the truth of the world.

Showing him the truth embedded in Catholic social teaching, expressed through Peter and his encyclicals, which reveal Christ, grounded in Mary, embraced within the oldest institution in human history—showing him the forgiveness of all crimes, and the saving of souls for his life's work—can capture his passion to embrace a lifelong path toward the eternal truth

This conclusion, of the centrality of the Church's social teaching in criminal transformation, the building of deep knowledge leadership among transformed criminals, can form the backdrop for an increase in criminal transformation and a drop in criminal recidivism.

The institutional Catholic Church should consider embracing criminal transformation as a social mandate, and working through community Catholic grassroots organizations, find those who were once lost and are now found, and ask them to help transform the others still lost.

The Church, welcoming the prodigal son home, can also help work with government to develop legislation that will allow transformed criminals access to college and training loans, with debt forgiveness upon a promise to work in the field of criminal transformation for a specified period of time.

Government should consider reaching out to the transformed criminal and opening doors within the criminal justice system for his leadership and skill to help develop and manage criminal justice programs.

The academy, specifically those institutions connected with the Catholic Church, should consider embracing the folding of Catholic social teaching into their criminal justice curriculum and also reach out to transformed criminals to join their faculty.

The ancient scourge of crime can always be addressed with fresh strength and resolve, and we must never lose hope that it can always be struggled against successfully; particularly with the strength and dedication an educated and spiritually mature army of deep knowledge leaders can bring to it.

Chapter Two
Carceral World, Communal City
If we do not embrace our past, we have no future.

I open this chapter to those criminals for whom it is written, to those who commit crimes for money, for whom crime is a way of life, and to whom the criminal/carceral world is a world with a subtly defined code of behavior and strong cultural connection; excluding those who are informers, pedophiles, rapists, and serial killers.

For the criminal to transform himself, he must accept, as penance for his criminal life, to live the rest of his life following the path of the saints; for this is the call to the apostolate, this is the call to the spiritual life; this is the path to atonement and forgiveness.

This work is not about a theory of criminology, of which there are already many, nor a history of rehabilitation or of the prison, also many. My work looks at the terrain where crime, history, human and organizational behavior, and Catholicism, move on paths through the criminal/carceral city, paths we cannot readily perceive, but within which I see a deep rubric of transformation, redemption, the prodigal son, and urban contemplative spiritual warriors, enriched by Catholic teaching.

This is not work that will be embraced by many in the criminal justice field as it goes against the prevailing narrative, yet for those for whom it is written—penitential criminals—it may find a home.

For many years during its founding period, the study of criminology concerned itself with ultimate questions: What makes a criminal? Why do they do what they do? What kind of people are they? How do they change?
These questions occupied many of the founding criminologists, but for the past few decades, criminology,

with too few exceptions, seems to have turned its back on these seminal concerns and become preoccupied with technical questions very narrow in scope and of little relevance to the criminal's life of crime or his rehabilitation; which, in a world of progress, would seem to be the core rationale of criminology.

The full prisons resulting from broken windows policing and three strikes sentencing (disparaged by the left as the Marxist-themed term, "mass incarceration") clearly reduced crime significantly; but an unintended consequence is the growing influence of the criminal world—as it has become more deeply shaped by the carceral—and a deepening corrosiveness of already crimogenic neighborhoods by the huge increase of reentering criminals who, rather than being rehabilitated, have become more hardened criminals.

Those reentering society have not been rehabilitated while in prison, nor do they have access or inclination to effective rehabilitative programs on the outside. Current research shows very few even exist and many actually make the problem worse, but most all fail, something we chronicle on an ongoing basis on our website at www.catholiceye.wordpress.com/2011/11/07/evaluation-of-reentry-programs-3/

Consequently, they soon return to prison at a rate of around 70% nationally, of the 650,000 to 700,000 being released annually.

My work suggests a policy option of looking first to the 30% of reentering criminals who have succeeded, and from them seek out leaders who have gone on to higher education and have an inclination to become involved in developing and managing reentry programs; provide them with core funding, advanced Catholic social teaching training (which by definition includes ongoing catechetical education), and allow them to begin addressing this significant social problem from the deep knowledge of their own experience, education, and training.

The proper role of the state is to secure justice and the proper role of the Catholic Church is to encourage that just securing role of the state.

A cornerstone of justice, and the ultimate expression of the principle of subsidiarity, is to allow individuals to help themselves, to not impede their desire to do that.

For the state—primarily concerned with the increased level of public safety emanating from reformed criminals—it becomes a proper role of the Catholic Church to teach the state concerning the effective method of doing so. She does this through her teaching authority and through supporting apostolate work addressing criminal transformation.

To love those whom we fear and hate, those who have harmed us—as Pope John Paul II taught us so dramatically through his embracing and forgiving of his would-be assassin in his prison cell—is a great teaching and is the great law personified for us who would breathe with the Church.

Yes, we must continue to lock up the criminal, we must continue to protect the innocent by holding fast to the criminal, embracing him in the carceral world which can become for him a pathway to redemption, as the necessary suffering imbues his every cellular hour, as it surely does.

The criminal world in the United States, with the carceral shaping of it, has become a coherent entity and within that entity it is the criminal/carceral world leadership to whom we must look for transformative leadership who have already transformed the pain of their suffering into the power of teaching others.

The history of the reformed criminal's involvement in defining and shaping transformation in the United States over the past several decades has advanced from the retrograde glamorization of the revolutionary 1960's and 1970's.

During the 1980's and 1990's, through the power of the crime victim's movement and the utilitarian success of such strategies as broken windows policing and three strikes sentencing, the involvement of the reformed criminal in rehabilitation work dropped considerably.

The emergence of the faith-based paradigm in social service work has helped bring former criminals back into the work, as has the contributions of reformed criminal scholars.

It is this ground which I hope to further strengthen through this work, which is animated by the social teaching and my conversion to Catholicism.

We know from the very beginning of the Catholic Church what would be the reception of those who have fallen far and been redeemed.

Criminal justice throughout the history of the Kingdom of God, has been a balance between retribution and restoration, and though the pagans used death propitiatingly, the People of God valued human life of priceless coin, even the life of a criminal, as one, St. Dismas, the Good Thief, became the first canonized saint of the Church founded on Peter, and another, St. Callistus, becoming Peter.

Transformative Teaching, A Symbiotic Relationship

We need deep knowledge leaders with the endurance and strength of spirit surviving the prison yard and the death row cell.

The effectiveness of the criminal transformative teaching I am asserting is dependent upon the existence of a deep understanding of the principles of Catholic social teaching.

When I first began working with the social teaching and realized that the guiding principles animating it also formed the foundational ideas of the nonprofit sector, I assumed that the social teaching could be used effectively by anyone.

I now realize that—though that hope remains attainable—the most optimal use of the teaching can only come from being an active, well-catechized Catholic.

Through my work I hope to encourage the building of a new platform from which the social teaching can enter into congruence with the criminal justice system and the community organizations connected to it to become part of a more deeply Catholic influenced criminal transformative community.

Criminal transformation and Catholic social teaching form a symbiotic relationship, a natural law of criminal transformation, where the truth of the teaching is the only reality strong enough to trump the truth of the world—the city of men—which is the truth the criminal lives by.

Since the 18th Century Enlightenment—the true Dark Ages—when the spiritual basis of worldly living was largely stripped from human societies, the life values of the world have reverted to those of pagan times, seasoned with modern technology's ability to glamorize, beautify, endow with meaning, and globalize.

It is virtually impossible for agents of the world, though acting with the best of intentions and armed with sterling academic credentials and advanced professional certification, to transform criminals who live—in a clearer and more direct way than they—their values, rather than the ones they profess.

In the criminal world—particularly in prison—a central truth is that you have to walk the talk; you have to live your proclaimed truth for it to be accepted by others.

This is a profound concept deeply embedded in Catholic social teaching and the Church—certainly in her supernatural aspect through her saints, though hardly at all in her institutional aspect—has largely walked her talk for two thousand years.

The unbroken line of truth spoken by the popes, fathers, doctors, and saints of the Church, is striking in its congruence to the truths proclaimed by its founder, Jesus Christ, and written down in the Gospels to teach us still.

No organization's spiritual leaders walks the talk as does the Catholic Church. Social teaching is the talk of the Church and her saints are the walk.

The natural law is hard-wired into every human being by God—conscience and reason its guiding principles—and the social teaching is an expression of this law as it relates to how we are to live together.

Many seminal thinkers on criminal justice write about criminal transformation as a result of good counseling and effective vocational programs with attached support services.

Having personally experienced all of that, which were to no avail in changing my criminality—and knowing hundreds of other criminals with the same experience—it is true that neither counseling nor vocational education results in transformation.

What does result in transformation, and what has always been the strongest influence on human transformation (short of a powerful or intellectual spiritual transformative experience) is the wise counsel of a friend, a respected transformed criminal who has been where you have been and where you secretly want to go—the path of peace, harmony, and truth—man's ultimate dream and the search for which he is hard wired to continue to pursue once the dream of the city of men withers and dies under the onslaught of Catholic conversion.

This is a path discovered by untold millions throughout history within the embrace of the Church and through the vision embodied in the social teaching, delivered by a transformed criminal and a deep knowledge leader, criminals will discover it.

Catholic Criminal Justice, the Beginning

Crime is essentially a theological problem and it is only within theology that evil—the deepest dimension of crime—can be addressed. It is evil which must concern us in addressing crime, and we must recognize that evil rarely reforms, but most professional criminals can and will; given a reason and shown the way.

The first crime was Cain's slaying of Abel and the first murderer was punished by banishment—used as long as there were faraway places but with a planet digitally one world, prison is banishment—with a mark so no one would harm him and Cain became a builder of cities where crime grew even through the deluge its spirit clung to earth.

The entire Cain-Abel murderous sequence lays the ground for what has followed in the criminal world since.

We see the anger and envy that desires the others death, the acceptance doing well generates, the separation from God sin creates, and the curse sin lays upon man's life even to the ground upon which he walks, the mark of protection that Cain's life may not be taken for Abel's life, the criminal as eternal fugitive and wanderer, and the building of the city of men, the criminal city, home to the criminal world since.

Cain, in his greed would not share the first fruits of his work, and Abel, in his generosity shared the first fruits readily. Cain did not know that the spirit of the gift was more important than the flesh of it.

The first expression of the criminal law that became the fullness of the Church, embracing all Jews and Gentiles entering the Kingdom of God, is found in Exodus 20:22 to 23:33, the *Book of the Covenant*.

> **[Exodus 20:22]** And the Lord gave Moses this further message for the Israelites: You stood watching while I spoke to you out of heaven; **[23]** it is not for you to make yourselves gods of silver or of gold. **[24]** It is enough to build me an altar of turf, on which to present burnt sacrifices and welcome-offerings, of sheep or oxen, wherever my name is honoured; so I will come to thee, and give thee my blessing. **[25]** Even if thou shouldst make me an altar of stone, thou shalt not build it of hewn stones; to use any tool in the making of it is to profane it. **[26]** And when thou goest up to my altar, thou shalt not mount by steps, for fear of exposing thy body's nakedness.
>
> **[Exodus 21:1]** And these laws, he said, thou shalt promulgate to them. **[2]** If thou dost buy a slave that is a Hebrew by race, he shall do thee six years' service, and in the seventh year, without any ransom paid, he shall go free. **[3]** He shall leave thy service in the same guise in which he entered it; if he came to thee married, his wife shall go free with him. **[4]** But if his master has assigned a wife to him, and she has borne sons and daughters, this woman and her children shall belong to the master; the slave shall go free in the same guise as before. **[5]** It may be that the slave, for love of his master, and of his own wife and children, will refuse to take his leave; **[6]** if so, his master shall bring him before the judgement-seat, and then fasten his ear

with an auger to door or door-post, in token that the man is his slave in perpetuity. **[7]** If anyone sells his daughter into a man's service, she is not to go free on the same conditions as a slave. **[8]** The master to whom she has been made over may send her away, if he has no liking for her, but he may not sell her to foreign masters; he has done her despite enough already. **[9]** He may betroth her, if he will, to his son; but if he does that, he must treat her as his daughter; **[10]** and if he finds his son another wife instead, he must marry the girl off, and give her clothes, and make all amends for the loss of her virginity. **[11]** If he is not prepared to do these three things, then she must go free, with no ransom paid for her.

[12] Whoever kills a man with intent to kill, must pay for it with his life. **[13]** But where there was no malice aforethought, and God provides the occasion, he shall be allowed to find refuge in such place as I shall appoint for thee. **[14]** One who lies in wait on purpose to kill his neighbour shall be torn away even from my altar to die. **[15]** Death is the penalty for one who kills his father or his mother; **[16]** death is the penalty when a man is shewn to have carried off his fellow-man and sold him; **[17]** death is the penalty for one who curses father or mother.

[18] Two fall out, and one is struck with a stone, or with the fist, not fatally, but so that he must take to his bed; **[19]** must the man who struck the blow be held guilty? Only till the other is well enough to get up and walk abroad with a stick; but he must compensate him for his loss of work, and for the doctor's charges. **[20]** When a man beats his servant or his handmaid to death, if death follows at once, he must pay the full penalty; **[21]** but if they survive for a day or more, he shall go unpunished; the loss is his. **[22]** If men fall out, and one of them strikes a woman who is pregnant, so that the child is still-born, but she herself lives, he must pay whatever sum the woman's husband demands, and the judges agree to; [23] if her death follows, then life must pay for life. [24] So it is to be; an eye for an eye, a tooth for a tooth, a hand for a hand, a foot for a foot; [25] burning for burning, wound for wound, bruise for bruise. [26] If anyone gives servant or handmaid a blow on the eye, so that the sight of it is lost, he must set them free in return for the sight he robbed them of; [27] or if he knocks out a tooth, he must let servant or handmaid go free by the same title.

[28] If an ox gores a man or woman to death, it shall be stoned, and the flesh of it is not to be eaten. But the owner of the ox shall be held innocent, [29] unless the ox has been using its horns for some time past, and he has refused to shut it away when appeal was made to him. Then, if the ox gores man or woman, it shall be stoned, and he too shall be put to death, [30] unless a fine is imposed on him instead; if so, he shall pay whatever ransom is demanded for his life. [31] The parents shall have the same claim upon him, whether it be a son or daughter of theirs the ox has gored; [32] if it has attacked man-servant or woman-servant, the owner must pay thirty silver pieces, and the ox must be stoned. [33] If a man who has opened an old well, or is digging a new one, does not cover it up, and ox or ass falls into it, [34] the owner of the well shall pay the full value of the beasts; the carcase he may keep for himself. [35] If one man's ox is wounded by another's, and dies of it, they shall sell the live ox and share the price of it, dividing the carcase of the dead ox between them; [36] unless it has been known for some time past that the live ox was using its horns, and the owner has not kept it under control. If so, he shall restore ox for ox, and keep the whole carcase for himself.

[Exodus 22:1] The man who steals ox or sheep and slaughters or sells it, must make restitution at the rate of five oxen for one, and four sheep for one.

[2] When a thief is caught breaking into a house, or digging under the walls of it, the man who deals him a fatal wound is not guilty of murder, unless the deed was done after sun-rise. **[3]** If the sun be risen, there is murder done, and life must pay for life. The thief who has no money to make restitution with, must himself be sold as a slave.

[4] If something stolen, ox or ass or sheep, is found alive in the possession of the thief, he shall make restitution twofold.

[5] If anyone damages field or vineyard by letting some beast of his feed on another man's property, he must make good the estimated loss out of the best crop in his own field or vineyard. **[6]** If a fire breaks out and catches among thorn-bushes, setting light to heaps of grain or to corn standing in the fields, the man who lit the fire must make good the loss.

[7] Where money or goods entrusted to a friend's keeping have been stolen, the thief, if he is found, must make twofold restitution. **[8]** If he cannot be found, the owner of the house where they lay in keeping shall be brought before the judgement-seat. He must swear that he laid no hands on his neighbour's property with malicious intent. **[9]** Be there a loss of ox or ass or sheep or clothing or any other kind of property, the two parties shall come before the judgement-seat, and the defendant, if he is found guilty, shall make twofold restitution. **[10]** If a man entrusts his neighbour with ass or ox or sheep or any other beast for safe keeping, and it is killed or wounded or carried off by enemies, with no witness to the fact, **[11]** the matter shall be settled by an oath, which the owner shall accept, that the other did not lay hands on his property; there is no restitution to be made. **[12]** But where the loss is due to theft, the owner shall be compensated. **[13]** If it has been killed by a wild beast, the carcase must be brought before the owner, and no amends made. **[14]** Where a man has borrowed any such beast of his neighbour, and it is maimed or killed in the owner's absence, compensation must be made to him; **[15]** but not if the owner himself was present, and especially if hire was being paid for the work the beast did.

[16] One who seduces a virgin not yet betrothed, and beds with her, must give her a dowry and marry her, **[17]** unless the father will not give her in marriage; then amends must be made, equivalent to the dowry which a virgin customarily receives.

[18] Sorcerers must not be allowed to live. **[19]** The man who is guilty of bestiality must pay for it with his life. **[20]** Sacrifice is for the Lord alone; he who offers it to other gods must be put to death.

[21] There must be no harrying or oppression of the aliens that dwell among you; time was when you too dwelt as aliens in the land of Egypt. **[22]** You must not wrong the widow and the orphan; **[23]** wronged, they will cry out to me for redress, and their cry will be heard. **[24]** My anger will blaze out against you, and I will smite you with the sword, making widows of your own wives, orphans of your own children.

[25] If thou dost lend money to some poorer neighbour among my people, thou shalt not drive him hard as extortioners do, or burden him with usury. **[26]** If thou takest thy neighbour's garment for a pledge, thou shalt give it back to him by set of sun; **[27]** it is all he has to cover himself with, his body's protection, all he has to sleep under. He has but to cry for redress, and I, the ever merciful, will listen to him.

[28] Thou shalt not revile the powers above thee, or speak ill of him who rules thy people.

[29] There must be no delay in paying tithes and first-fruits. Thou shalt make me an offering of the first son that is born to thee, **[30]** and with thy oxen and sheep thou shalt do the like; for seven days the dam may keep her first-born, after that it must be offered to me.

[31] You are to be men marked out for my service. Meat that has once been tasted by wild beasts shall not be used for food; it must be thrown to the dogs.

[Exodus 23:1]Never must thou take up a false cry, or join hands with the guilty by giving false witness in their favour. **[2]** Never must thou follow with the crowd in doing wrong, or be swayed by many voices so as to give false judgement; **[3]** even pity for the poor must not sway thee when judgement is to be given.

[4] If thou hast an enemy, and findest his ox or his ass going astray, take it back to him. **[5]** Here is one that hates thee, and his ass has fallen under its burden; do not pass by, help him to lift it up.

[6] Do not give false judgement when the cause of the poor is tried. **[7]**Keep clear of untruth. Do not bring death on an innocent man that has justice on his side; I give no countenance to the wrong-doer. **[8]** Beware of accepting bribes; they blind even the prudent, and disturb the judgement even of just men. **[9]** Do not oppress the alien; you know what it is to be an alien, since you yourselves were exiles in the land of Egypt.

[10] For six years together thou mayst sow thy land, and gather the crop from it; [11] in the seventh year leave it alone, to lie fallow, and give thy poorer neighbours food; all that is left, the wild beasts may eat. And thou shalt do the like with thy vineyard and thy oliveyard. [12] For six days together thou shalt do the tasks thou hast to do, and on the seventh leave off working; so shall ox and ass of thine have rest, home-born slave and alien that works for thee revive their spirits.

[13] Observe all these commandments of mine, and never take an oath by the names of alien gods, or let such names be heard on your lips.

[14] Thrice a year keep holiday in my honour. [15] There is the feast of unleavened bread to be observed; for seven days, in the first month of spring, the month of thy rescue from Egypt, thou shalt eat unleavened bread in obedience to my command. Then thou shalt present thyself before me with gifts. [16] And there is the feast of harvest, when the fields thou hast sown reward thy labour with first-fruits; and another feast at the end of the year, when the last of thy crops has been gathered in. [17] Thrice, then, in the year all thy men folk must present themselves before the Lord thy God.

[18] When thou offerest living things in sacrifice to me, the bread that goes with them shall not be leavened, nor shalt thou leave the fat of my victims unconsumed till the morrow.

[19] The first-fruits of thy land must be brought to the house of the Lord thy God.

Seething a kid in its dam's milk is a rite forbidden thee.

[20] And now I am sending my angel to go before thee and guard thee on thy way, and lead thee to the place I have made ready for thee. **[21]** Give him good heed, and listen to his bidding; think not to treat him with neglect. He will not overlook thy faults, and in him dwells the power of my name. **[22]** If thou wilt listen to his warnings, and do all I bid thee, then thy enemies shall find an enemy in me, and those who shew thee no mercy shall find me merciless. **[23]** So this angel of mine will go on before thee, leading thee on into the land of Amorrhite and Hethite, Pherezite and Chanaanite, Hevite and Jebusite; and all these I will destroy. **[24]** Do not bow down to their gods and worship them, or follow their customs; sweep them away, and break down their monuments. **[25]** All your loyalty must be for the Lord your God. So I will enrich thee with the bread and the water thou needest, and keep sickness far away from thy company; **[26]** there shall be no unfruitfulness in thy land, no barrenness; and I will grant thee a full span of days.

[27] I mean to make the fear of me go in front of thee, bringing destruction upon the whole people thou goest to meet; all thy enemies shall turn their backs before thee. **[28]** I will send in hornets first, to make cowards of Hevite and Chanaanite and Hethite before ever thou goest in. **[29]**Only I will not drive them out before thee all in one year; that would make a wilderness of the land, and the wild beasts in it would multiply, to thy harm. **[30]** I will make them yield little by little before thy onset, so that thou wilt have time to increase, and populate the land. **[31]** The frontiers I give thee are the Red Sea and the sea of the Philistines, the desert and the river Euphrates. All the inhabitants of the land shall be at your mercy, and I will drive them out before you. **[32]** Thou shalt make no treaty with them, nor with their gods. **[33]** They must not share thy territory, or they would persuade thee to commit sin against me, by worshipping their gods; no doubt of it, they will ensnare thee.

Today, reading this, we can still see the divine wisdom guiding the Jewish people so soon after their freedom from Egypt.

The Great Commandment is the foundation of all of these:

> **[Matthew 22:34]** And now the Pharisees, hearing how he had put the Sadducees to silence, met together; **[35]** and one of them, a lawyer, put a question to try him: **[36]** Master, which commandment in the law is the greatest? **[37]** Jesus said to him, Thou shalt love the Lord thy God with thy whole heart and thy whole soul and thy whole mind. **[38]** This is the greatest of the commandments, and the first. **[39]** And the second, its like, is this, Thou shalt love thy neighbour as thyself. **[40]** On these two commandments, all the law and the prophets depend.

Every criminal act is personal, from a person it comes, from an idea shaping action, from desire and want, and as it moves from the person into the world, assaulting our neighbor—whom we have been instructed by the Great Commandment to love—it becomes crime against the justice balanced between individuals and the world, the justice we all have an inalienable right to expect, the God–infused dignity each of us deserves from each other.

The foundational ideas of Catholic criminal justice are punishment, penance and reform, return, and reinstatement.

The Decalogue defines the wrong requiring punishment, prison time is the penitential place and program, and reentry—though still being sought in its new manifestations of success, though one can see the Rite of Christian Initiation for Adults (RCIA) as a model—the ritual path to communal reentry.

Many criminal justice scholars, who are attempting to come to terms with their own fear and trepidation about prison, see it as a central animating concept to modern life; and prison's punishing reality, where the most intimate violation and the terror clouding men's minds is thus objectified, shaped, and placed within comfortable theories and explanatory ideologies; most remarkably of course by Michael Foucault's *Discipline & Punish: The Birth of the Prison*, where he finds elite power as the ultimate and underlying reality of the carceral and the larger world; indeed, the central animating factor.

From the traditional Catholic perspective on criminal justice, the animating factor is justice. Seeing prison as the shaper of criminal/carceral world values, the central animating factor of Catholic criminal justice is the human being, the *redeemable* human being, shorn of his terror-creating presence and humble in the sight of God, a quiet neighbor to men.

We see how the classic expressions of justice from Catholic social teaching and tradition inform different aspects of the criminal path—distributive (fair social distribution of resources, the criminal feels it is his right to steal)—commutative (to each his own)—with the prison as penitential (justice for crime, do the crime, do the time), yet the criminal will rarely consider transformation, and transformative justice (seeing distance from God, spiritual interiority, the relation with our creator as root cause, as the city of men defines the truth as he lives it) and he must learn or, more correctly, *be taught and embrace* the eternal truth which will lead him out of the criminal city.

In the history of the saints of the Church we see great transformative stories.

We know the first criminal to become a saint was Dismas, the Good Thief—crucified on the right hand of Christ—who Christ took with him from Calvary to heaven.

The first criminal to become a Pope and later saint, was Callistus I who died a martyr but was Pope for five years, from 217 to 222.

The first Catholic criminologist was surely St. Augustine, who in his developed reasoning around the city of men in his masterpiece, *The City of God*, essentially lays out the world whose truth criminals embrace in their descent into the criminal/carceral world.

It is fitting that the United States is a country where Catholic Criminal Justice might form strong roots—for though the term has possibly been used elsewhere, it is most congruent here, in America, where the prison world has grown in ways rarely imagined

The United States, even before it was the United States was a Catholic land, especially the vast southwestern region owned by Mexico.

In California, the locus of the American prison system and its most defining metaphor, the first civil governor was a devout convert to Catholicism, the lawyer Peter H. Burnett, who wrote the remarkable book: *The True Church: The Path Which Led a Protestant Lawyer to the Catholic Church; Christian Theory, Doctrine and Discipline* in 1860.

Again, the concepts animating Catholic Criminal Justice are original justice, communicative justice, legal justice, distributive justice and social justice.

This understanding of justice and its different aspects embraces the entire range of idea and polices that undergird Catholic Criminal Justice.

For most of the criminals who know what they are doing is wrong but do it anyway, they justify that crime had to be done as there was no other way to survive. Thus, the truth of the world—all that matters is survival—often dictates criminal actions.

Sin is ultimately a distance from God and the criminal suffers from his distance from God.

Sin is of the world and the criminal embraces the truth of the world.

The criminal/carceral world is ancient, built on cultural artifacts from the beginnings of civilization.

The criminal/carceral world is understood only by its members and understood most completely by its leaders.

Punishment for crime is appropriate and penitentially necessary.

Restorative justice, with its roots in Old Testament practice, encounters the problem of removing the penitential from justice, and, except in very minor crimes or civil violations, it has no provision for punishment in the ancient sense of removal and banishment which the prison serves as the modern equivalent.

All criminals are redeemable, but not all evil people are, for some who are too hopelessly lost to Satanic evil that only God can free them; not humans, not even humans acting for God.

Though there have always been Pharisaic movements in the Church to excommunicate most sinners—as during the second century by the purist Hippolytus—there have also always been Popes such as Callistus, the former criminal, to resist them and keep the Church always balanced on the fulcrum of love Christ set as the foundation stone.

Redeemed professional criminals who have served at least five years in maximum security prisons, and after release transformed their life through higher education, training in grassroots organizational management, reconciliation or conversion to Catholicism, and educated in Catholic social teaching—those I call deep knowledge leaders—are the only individuals with the experience, passion, dedication, and criminal/carceral world knowledge, able to develop and manage programs that transform other professional criminals (those who commit crimes for money representing the majority of criminals) effectively.

The Carceral & the Criminal World

One of the most significant developments in the criminal justice system over the past few decades is the impact of the carceral on the criminal world.

The American prison creates its own environment, its own world, which spreads outward, embracing the terrain where the released wander predatorily, continually reshaping and remaking the criminal world in its own evolving image.

As the number of criminals moving from the carceral to the outside world—becoming a critical mass in some neighborhoods—the influence of the carceral world spreads to that neighborhood, further criminalizing it.

In California the development of the criminal world related to the carceral is strongly congruent and the confused evolution of the California prison—from punishment to rehabilitation and back, and back once more—forlornly retains the uncertainty of the institutional world and the clarity of the criminal world within the carceral.

The carceral world looms underneath the criminal world—holding it up as it were—shaping the criminal world's leaders as they pass into and out its steel gates.

Mastering the carceral experience within the maximum security prison is a culturally defining experience determining criminal strength, tenacity, and boldness, much as similarly defined for the non-criminal through mastering the social, athletic, and intellectual rigor of the maximum prestige academy.

And yet the prison is also the most penitential of institutions—so correctly analyzed in its reverential and redeemable components—but rarely seen by Marxist oriented criminal justice academics (who have been shaping the narrative of the American academy since the 1970s) as that place of exclusion and penance which it is, but more often through the lens of theory critically finding dark motives and capitalistic strategies at work.

Transformation had once been considered a desirable aspect of the prison time given to the criminal, and the transformation was to be hoped for as a pure result of prison itself.

For the first century of America's experience with prisons, deeply influenced by religion, it is understood that this occurred more often than not, as we understand from the book, *Criminal Justice and the Catholic Church*, by Dr. Andrew Skotnicki, who notes a conjectured 10% recidivism rate.

Since the 20th century, with its corresponding complexity induced by the majority of humans living in the urban environments of the criminal city; prison induced transformation lost ground as a new meta-narrative extolling criminal exploits became part of the social fabric.

In the time we live in, with ethnic, religious, and national myths being folded and blended with the outlaw as hero, a much more convoluted terrain emerges, requiring guides to traverse.

The answer is in the problem. The answer is within the outlaw mind.

From a Catholic historic perspective the prison performs a necessary penitential and reformative function, an attribute still relied on yet rarely seen.

For the public, the need for the prison is more than the rational reaction of fear to that uncertainty arising from dangerous men and women, and how to be protected from them. It is also the shutting away of that which is feared, the *other*, which public criminal justice policy too often allows to grow without responsibility while assuming that the real cause of crime is something vague *out there*, rather than individual predatory thoughts shaping individual predatory actions; rather an individual moral decision than an unconscious reaction to social forces.

There are hundreds of thousands of people in prisons in the United States representing untold millions of crimes committed, many unaccounted and uncharged, for the criminal as supreme opportunist commits much more than he is ever arrested, charged, and committed for; a danger deep as the ocean.

In my work as a capacity building consultant to nonprofit organizations, when the strategic discussion concerns the continued utility of a specific course of action, I will bring the discussion back to the founding vision and mission of the organization and from that base, try to determine if indeed, the course of action under discussion is still appropriate.

The founding mission of prisons—punishment and redemption— has not lost its utility, nor the use of cellular confinement and separation of the criminal from the innocent as a protective and penitential response as well as a redemptive stimulation.

The growth of the carceral culture within the criminal world is a dangerous influence which is manifest, and increases as criminalization deepens through carceral influence on cultural reality.

Combat and the rules of strategy are important capabilities criminals share with the military—of being able to distance yourself from your emotions and what your body wants to do when confronted with prison or war—for then you have to will yourself to act, separating yourself from the urge to panic, if you are to survive, whether in prison or battle.

How one responds to the carceral is a crucial element in the development of criminal world leadership as is that of the soldier in battle crucial to military leadership development.

Criminals who have transformed their lives must speak and help shape the future formation of criminal justice so that it may reach its aspiration of protecting the public and reforming criminals—not currently happening with a 70% recidivism rate—which has little to do with tending to unconsciously generated symptoms, but much to do with transforming suffering into teaching.

The criminal world's leaders understanding is that the criminal is punished for being in congruence with the same reality accepted as true by the punishers.

Within the maximum security prison where criminal world leadership serves time, there exists a long-term solitude-generating contemplation, intimately woven through the Catholic pursuit of spiritual perfection.

For the criminal prior to transformation, this contemplation revolves around the purity of their attachment to the truth of the criminal world, their life in the city of men, most dreadfully realized in the prison itself.

The prison is the truth of the city of men writ hard, writ clearly in steel and stone that none can misunderstand its moment or its animating core reality.

This lays unconsciously under the day-thoughts of most whose work calls them to develop policy around the prison and criminal world—and the politics around prisons are strong—but in the continual struggle around their use and purpose.

Over the past 70 or 80 years in this country, since the depression of the 1930's, a criminal culture has developed which has become impenetrable, so that attempts by traditional criminal rehabilitation practitioners are—and statistics bear this out—a dismal failure.

Attempting to describe this world for those practitioners so that they can find success in it is probably not a fruitful avenue at this moment in rehabilitative history, but the development of reformed criminals, who are carceral cultural leaders, to advance their education and training in helping other criminals transform their lives, would be.

The Criminal City

I AM THE WAY INTO THE CITY OF WOE,
I AM THE WAY INTO ETERNAL PAIN.
I AM THE WAY TO GO AMONG THE LOST.

(Dante Alighieri's Inferno III: 1-3)

The criminal city is the city of men—first mentioned in Genesis—after killing Abel and being sent out by God as a vagabond:

> [16] So Cain was banished from God's presence, and lived as a fugitive, east of Eden. [17] And now Cain had knowledge of his wife, and she conceived. She called her child Henoch; and Cain built a city...
> [Genesis 4:16-17]

Jacques Ellul writes about this, how Cain substitutes God's Eden with his own city, in his wonderful 1970 book, *The Meaning of the City*.

Abel leaves no children as this is not to be a world of the righteous by blood, only by action; for it is only Cain's line that survives of the first sons and his line is that of the prince of this world, the true father of all cities.

The city is a metaphor of predatory human behavior—founded by the first predatory human— where, piling on top of one another with the alpha human in the pyramidal penthouse, it vividly portrays the materialism driving its life, where struggling for money is struggling for life, and struggle is marked by predation.

In some traditions, the city equals the underworld.

The first criminal founded the first city of men and it is from that beginning and within those precincts that the truth of the world has grown, forming the criminal city.

From the truths of the prince of the world, criminals see what is proclaimed and respond, acting boldly, appropriating the goods of men and relishing the corrupted life animating the criminal city.

The very heart of the city of men—the criminal city—is the prison and the criminal's carceral eyes sees the proclamations of greatness given to leaders in the world who violate their own precepts openly and whose fortune and fame have also been built upon deceit and crime, but whose wealth ensures greatness within the criminal city.

Would a criminal then become a fool and not steal and lie if the truth of the world is the only truth he knows? For he has not yet comprehended the great and certain truths of the Catholic Church resonating through the centuries since its birth on the shoulders of Peter from the blessing of Christ.

To move from the criminal city, the beginning of transformation and redemption, the Gospel teaches what lies in store for us:

> **[John 15:18]** If the world hates you, be sure that it hated me before it learned to hate you. **[19]** If you belonged to the world, the world would know you for its own and love you; it is because you do not belong to the world, because I have singled you out from the midst of the world, that the world hates you.

The criminal will not move from the comfortable confines of the criminal city he knows, to the unknown city hated by the world, except in the company of friends—reformed criminals—who've traveled the path before him.

The truth of the unknown city of human aspiration lies close to the hidden heart.

Many, like the poet Rimbaud and the Russian mystic Rasputin, venture in benighted search for enlightenment through degradation; a search glorified in the 1960's.

The sense that restraint causes repression—the founding idea of the 1960's—comes straight from the pagans.

And given the Puritan founding of American culture, a strong indictment of the foundational formative praxis of our culture has been, and continues to be, delivered by many.

For too much of our history and for too much of our criminal justice system, the prison has served as too much of a model of the nuclear bomb and mutually assured destruction has come with it.

Liberation Theology

This important movement in the Church, which began in Latin America, while focusing attention on the plight of the poor, deviated significantly from Church teaching and played a role in the revolutionizing of criminal leaders. It was corrected through the work of the Congregation of the Doctrine of the Faith (CDF) in its Instructions of 1984, 1986, and the 2006 Notification on doctrinal errors in two of the books by Father Jon Sobrino, SJ, one of the intellectual leaders of liberation theology. It has played an unfortunately large and very distractive role in the development of the social justice movement in the United States, in particular with its too strong reliance on the tenets of Marxism rather than of Christianity.

Liberation theology's focus on the poor has helped create a political slant too much of the work around social justice in the Church and, rather than helping the marginal as it is meant to do, it actually hurts them by allowing an idea that social conditions are responsible for their predicament rather than personal choices.

It also has tended to set up an adversarial relationship between poor and rich which is harmful to both, and directly contrary to the essential Catholic message of loving and praying for our neighbor.

Liberation theology replaces the spiritual core of the Church's teaching focused on changing the individual heart with material goods, focused on changing the structure of the state by taking the Church's care for the poor and conflating the Church's message of liberation from the oppression of sin with the Marxist message of liberation from oppressive social structure.

Liberation theology makes the same mistake as the Catholic monarchists—that the gospel is worldly—which breaks completely from the clear truth Christ gave us in the gospel:

[Matthew 22:15] After this the Pharisees withdrew, and plotted together, to make him betray himself in his talk. **[16]** And they sent their own disciples to him, with those who were of Herod's party, and said, Master, we know well that thou art sincere, and teachest in all sincerity the way of God; that thou holdest no one in awe, making no distinction between man and man; **[17]** tell us, then, is it right to pay tribute to Caesar, or not? **[18]** Jesus saw their malice; Hypocrites, he said, why do you thus put me to the test? **[19]** Shew me the coinage in which the tribute is paid. So they brought him a silver piece, **[20]** and he asked them, Whose is this likeness? Whose name is inscribed on it? **[21]** Caesar's, they said; whereupon he answered, Why then, give back to Caesar what is Caesar's, and to God what is God's.

The things of this world—most implicitly including the material realization of politics—are of Caesar, are of the prince of this world, while the spiritual force informing and animating them are of God, are of the King of Heaven.

For example: the Church will not correctly call for the state to obtain permission from it prior to passing a law outlawing abortion, but it will always call for the state to legislate the outlawing of abortion.

It is about free will, free choice. We are born with it, it is hard-wired into us, it is why the criminal always chooses to be a criminal or not.

While the internal criminal world is essentially congruent with capitalism and family values, most of the external actors who claim to speak for the criminal world are largely representatives of Marxist and statist values.

Recently, the emergence of external actors whose perspective is somewhat more congruent is seen in the faith-based organizations.

The development we hope to encourage is that of a transformation of criminal world leadership, who will speak for themselves,

However, here there awaits one important danger to avoid. We must ensure that our focus on the transformed criminal, as perhaps the most marginalized of the poor, does not fall into the error liberation theology did.

We must go beyond liberation theology by still fighting to change the system that brutalizes human beings, but as Peter guides us, by writing—praying—speaking—walking the talk.

Catholic Criminal Reentry, Formation & Transformation

Those who have suffered injustice are often best suited to advocate for justice.

In the process of criminal transformation, the social teaching of the Church and the relationship it creates with the Magisterium, can play the very important transformational role community often does.

The social teaching becomes the community wherein the contemplative leaders refresh themselves, as the liturgy build strength within, feeding the soul.

The difficulty with the evangelical approach to criminal transformation is that it is counter to the internal motivation of criminals which is bold rebelliousness; strongly self-centered to the point of pursuing criminal acts which, by their nature, involve those attributes of self-will precluding a bending to evangelical exhortation.

The social teaching approach introduces concepts which are actually very congruent to the criminal's view of himself, while critical of the very same worldly institutions he often sees allied against him; and most importantly, stresses a calm and still small voice approach rather than the salemanistic exhortation.

There is also around the exhortative approach a scent of the coercive, the Elmer Gantry like rock-ribbed persuasion built upon a vision of ever-lasting hell and damnation.

Coercive techniques may suppress crime, and in the case of imprisonment, certainly do; but they are virtually worthless for transformation.

Getting to the social teaching—in addition to calling for voluntary action—requires a clear, concise explanation of the truth of the Catholic Church, and what ultimately decided it for me was a series of facts beginning with the positions of the world's major religions founders.

Of the historically real founders of the great religions of the world, only one, Jesus Christ, proclaimed himself God—rather than a prophet as Moses and Muhammad, or an enlightened man, as Buddha—whose Godhood was extensively substantiated by contemporary witnesses.

The others are founded upon the life of a human, and I did not see how a religion, whose defined role is to direct us to knowledge of God, could proclaim truths from any other source than God.

I chose to believe that Jesus Christ, the founder of the Catholic Church, founded the religion whose primary purpose is the presentation of the knowledge of God.

In Christ's proclamation of himself as God, he established his Church upon the rock of Peter and the gates of hell would not prevail against it, and the Catholic Church stands still, buffeted yes, shook to its very core many times yes, but still stands, the pilgrim church.

So, this was my first step, accepting the truth of a man who said he was God and contemporaneous witnesses validated the miracles he performed which only God could do; and had founded a Church which still stands.

And now we come to the teaching, the social teaching of the Church—of the Kingdom of Heaven—that great body of work that has passed down to us from the beginning, through the old covenant into the new.

This justice, this solidarity, moves down through the history of the Church, speaking out for the respect of the dignity of all human beings under God, protecting the dignity even of the criminal, virtually from the beginning.

The development of the Magisterium through the expression of the papal encyclical is about as clear a development of how things should be in the world, as the chronicles of the world are about it as it is.

The City of God and the city of men; one clings to us and one calls to us, and in our striving toward transformation we need support.

We have the support of the Magisterium of the Church, which can become the community from which we draw our strength, where we can retreat to when suffering, seek advice when confused, and find solace when troubled.

In my work, I've learned that the path to transformation exists in and goes through the city of man, which scripture teaches is the city created by Cain, the first criminal, and whose ruler, even now, is Satan, the prince of this world.

Transformation through Christ is a narrow path, beset on all sides by the great temptations of the prince's world, which we see even our sacred priests struggling to resist.

It is a path through our interior life and emanating from our interior life, particularly if our interiority is strongly built on the sacraments, continual prayer and study.

Love illuminates the path, as we have been taught. It is the great commandment, the divine way, and the great light on the path.

Transformation is an interior process and this interior relationship with the Magisterium is now, on account of web-based technology and access to global resources, able to be reinforced and developed with the help of the entire universe of human knowledge.

I have found the deep interiority of the Latin Mass to be of great benefit, where the knee is bent and the head is bowed, and alone in my silence with the priest and the Latin, I am part of the sacrifice in a profound way and all of the works which go to make up the social teaching are presented to me weekly through the readings and the prayers from so long ago.

The larger body of Catholic thought that makes up the social teaching originated from before creation, was carved in stone at Sinai, was refined by the Sermon on the Mount, was preached throughout the ancient world by the Apostles and was recorded in the New Testament.

It is centered on the sacredness of the human being and the eternal nature of the associated rights, responsibilities, and duties of human beings created by God in their relations with one another and in the societies we create to live and act together in this world.

It tells us to be humble, kind, loving, and in a tremendous enrichment of the Sinai covenant, teaches us that even to harbor anger in our heart towards our enemy is to be judged:

[Matthew 5:21] You have heard that it was said to the men of old, Thou shalt do no murder; if a man commits murder, he must answer for it before the court of justice. **[22]** But I tell you that any man who is angry with his brother must answer for it before the court of justice, and any man who says Raca to his brother must answer for it before the Council; and any man who says to his brother, Thou fool, must answer for it in hell fire.

From this, and through the centuries of turmoil, of dissolving empires, of the barbaric hordes sweeping through Europe and North Africa, and of the Babel-like splitting from her, the Catholic Church held clear to the central themes of human dignity and respect due each individual person from before the foundations of the world were set.

The family, the crux of human development, was formed and created as the consensual norm it is through the influence of the Catholic Church through the ages.

St. Callistus, St. Augustine, and all of the fathers and doctors of the Church, formed and shaped the teaching through the centuries.

In the modern era, the work was collected in the papal encyclicals, beginning with that of 1891, Pope Leo XIII's *Rerum Novarum* (On the Rights and Duties of Capital and Labor).

This was an important intellectual shaping of the labor movement, which had seen Labor Day designated as a holiday in New York on September 5, 1882, and the national designation by act of Congress in June of 1894, making the first Monday in September their day.

Crime Belongs to Caesar, Criminals to God

While the response to the crimes criminals commit in the world belongs to Caesar and there is no choice in the matter; the response to the individual human being who is the criminal, his transformation and redemption—which is purely a matter of choice—belongs to God.

The social and legal structures the state creates around human beings are not as important as the human being. What is defined as crime and how it is to be responded to by the state is the concern of Caesar as the state, but the Church is called to inform those decisions of the state through the knowledge implicit within its social teaching.

The criminal world in the United States began to become a well-organized and coherent entity during the generation between World War I and World War II. By the period between the Korean War and the Vietnam War—wars being appropriate markers for its development—it had become a large, powerful, and virtually permanent aspect of American culture.

This is not a situation unique to this country or this time. During medieval times the underworld was well developed in Europe, as it was in Regency England. What is different is how the carceral world has become the prime cultural shaper of the criminal world, developing criminal world leadership unprecedented in our country.

What this means in terms of developing policies able to actually address criminal behavior with any hope of redemption and transformation, is that transformed criminal leadership—the only individuals with deep understanding of the criminal world—must become involved in the transformative process.

One of the most important reasons for that involvement is that the development and management of traditional rehabilitation efforts is—as some studies are clearly revealing—actually enhancing criminal behavior rather than reducing it.

Involving those who are part of the process in the leadership is similar to the business world's effective use of organizational development knowledge, ideas growing from, among others, Mary Parker Follett's concept of power-with rather than power-over.

What works in the business world facilitating the organizational aspects of transformation however, is not what works in the spiritual. In the spiritual we are called to revealed truth, absolute, clear, and final; truth which all human beings—including criminals—are hard-wired to seek.

That spiritual call is to the Catholic Church.

There is a great tradition among the popes to speak to prisoners, offering them hope and redemption through prayer and intervention.

Lighting the Path

The work of the Lampstand Foundation is specifically directed towards those transformed criminals, who are able, through inclination, redemption, education, and skill, to become a grassroots organizational leader who can generate the transformation of other criminals.

For optimal use, it is important to understand for whom the work of Lampstand is intended, from where those leaders would come, and what identifiers would reveal them to us.

Our work is directed to penitential criminals who are Catholic or potential converts who, because of their leadership in the criminal world, will have significant success and impact in the work of criminal transformation.

Those offenders, whose crimes are such that they would be included in this Gospel message of Christ, do not occupy those positions of leadership in the criminal or carceral world:

> **[Matthew 18:5]** He who gives welcome to such a child as this in my name, gives welcome to me. **[6]** And if anyone hurts the conscience of one of these little ones, that believe in me, he had better have been drowned in the depths of the sea, with a mill-stone hung about his neck. **[7]** Woe to the world, for the hurt done to consciences! It must needs be that such hurt should come, but woe to the man through whom it comes!

The path being lighted can only be traveled by reformed criminals who are Catholics, and this work is created for them. The effectiveness of criminal transformative teaching is dependent upon a deep understanding of the principles of Catholic social teaching, which is only possible by being devoutly Catholic.

From our perspective, we use the term professional criminal to refer to those individuals who committed crimes for money, to whom crime was a way of life and prison time an occupational hazard. We are also speaking of professional criminals who have spent at least five years in a maximum security prison—the benchmark of professional criminality after arrest and conviction.

It is from these criminals that the leadership in the carceral world comes and it is from them that effective reentry leadership will also come.

Each population has a certain percentage from which effective leadership usually emerges and it is no different within the criminal/carceral world.

There are certain characteristics and criminal/carceral experiences that serve as the foundation of criminal world leadership and others that preclude someone from being perceived as a leader.

Criminal/carceral world leaders are not informers, do not commit crimes against children and women, nor allow themselves to be victimized by others, particularly in prison.

There are many people who have served time in one type of prison or another—an honor farm, a medical facility, or a minimum or medium security prison—who have developed and manage prisoner rehabilitation efforts, but have not developed the leadership within the criminal/carceral world which give them either the stature or gravitas to become an effective rehabilitation practitioner.

Criminals become part of the communal community when they make the choice to transform themselves, to create from within a different person than what they were previously; a person whose motivation is based on eternal truth, only found in the Catholic Church, the City of God, than the truth of the world, the city of man. Rehabilitation is not a proper word for this process as it implies a return to something that previously existed—professional criminals are by and large born into the criminal world— and sets the entire criminal transformation process on the incorrect intellectual setting, which is partly the reason for its continued failure in the United States.

The community being reentered is the community of the Catholic Church—triumphant, suffering, and militant—and for transformed criminals involved with their apostolate of transforming others, it is the only community, beyond their family, needed.

Traditionally reentry is a three year period after release from prison when about 70% of criminals in the United States return to prison. Reentry is often used to designate those released from any type of criminal justice sanctioning, probation, parole, jail or prison release, but we use it specifically in reference to those professional criminals released from a maximum security prison (or a transitional prison after serving the bulk of their time in a maximum security facility).

We also use a ten year period of reentry as it allows for the fuller development of transformative behavior—and a more accurate reflection of return statistics— than the relatively short three year period does.

The reason Catholics need to be involved in transformation and reentry is because Catholicism is the only faith based on truth, a solid and robust enough truth—eternal truth, real truth, truthful truth—to provide a strong enough contrast to the truth of the world—sense truth, perceived truth, relative truth, truth-built-on-lies truth—to attract criminals, who whatever their faults, seeing things incorrectly based on what it is they know is not one of them.

While there are many small criminal transformative organizations and ministries developed and managed by individual religious, or orders, there is not, nor has there ever been that I am aware of, a criminal transformative effort developed and managed as part of the institutional, universal Catholic Church; and that is shameful.

Within the Catholic Magisterium, the social teaching, that body of documents primarily built upon papal encyclicals, tradition, and scripture, is the robust story that destroys the lie the world's truth is built on, the world truth criminals have built their lives on.

The knowledge about the city of men—the criminal city— and the City of God, so precisely presented to us in the Gospels, is amplified through the works of the early church fathers, and in the case of the criminal who builds his life on the truth of the city of men rather than the City of God.

The catechesis of the criminal brought through the social teaching—Catholic doctrine presented in universal terms—

works, because within the social teaching is found the unbroken line of truth that connects one to the beginning of the truth of creation and the institution housing it, still remaining true to those ancient roots; something that can be said of no other institution on earth.

The criminal will find that Christ specifically speaks to him and his entire sinning world, who has been deceived into believing the truth of the world, and living by the rules of men in the city of men, which the criminal does more boldly than the rest.

Being able to speak from brotherly love, the reformed criminal—who once deeply enjoyed many aspects of his criminal life—knows the failure of active love in the oft quoted "love the sinner, hate the sin" in a life where identification with the sin is often deep.

The process, for non-Catholic criminals, of coming into the Church, is not the instantaneous event Protestants proclaim.

Instead, it is a strenuous year-long process of catechesis that represents the true ritual of transformation every redemptive criminal (and every convert to Catholicism) need traverse, ending ultimately with the sacramental forgiveness of all sins.

The Church truly dwells in the human interior—in the communion with Christ—not in the human community, and through its interiority guides the walking of the talking.

For centuries the criminal, like Cain, could be banished, or voluntarily disappear, begin again as a new person, even during recent times and recent criminal lives that possibility existed, but no more.

Now all are connected and all crimes rest on the knowing electric conscience of the world and the only rebirth is through baptism.

Now, we all come in our ancient ways to fields love alone blooms.

Today, even outside of prison, the criminal is panopticized, backlit, fully visible, only requiring the eye of the examiner gazing upon the digital data summoned from the great maw and storehouse of the electric world.

Contemplating this, even if having begun an internal transformation, often renders change moot. Labeled and exposed the criminal too often accepts reality and returns to crime, or hopefully, turns to a friend.

Teaching from Suffering

The preeminent example of teaching from suffering is the cross.

Acknowledging the value inherent within the suffering from imprisonment that can deeply enrich the process of criminal transformation is one of the most important aspects of Lampstand's work.

Without prison suffering—gateway to the penitential process—corresponding to the suffering of the criminal's victims; the professional criminal has not built the foundation for the future work of transformation.

The movement towards the penitential is the movement of the natural law growing within us.

Within Catholic history the use of imprisonment, and the benefits of the suffering it has generated, have brought us precious flowers of knowledge.

Catholic criminal transformative work should be supported by Catholic institutional resources until its effectiveness is determined. The optimal sought would be government support of Catholic faith-based efforts for a specified trial period, determine which is most effective and direct more funding there.

One major benefit of working with criminals in determining the effectiveness of transformative programs is that criminal records are available through criminal justice data bases, unlike virtually any other segment of social work.

Using the reentry period of three years—or ten years as our marker—we can tell if involvement with our suggested Catholic faith-based program works by looking at arrest records over the three or ten year period.

The constitutional prescriptions allowing this can be built upon the same freedom of religion foundation currently allowing single-faith service and ritual within prisons.

The current legal issues surrounding the use of Catholic faith-based efforts will go on, but it is in the public interest to determine what is effective with reentering prisoners, as major public safety issues and large sums of public money are at stake.

We might have as much at stake in this effort and determining what works as we do in the military action embarked upon by our national government. We should consider if it is within national public priorities to be expending proportionately appropriate evaluative resources in determining program success with criminals at home, as we are with terrorists abroad.

Criminals who transform their lives can become intellectuals, philosophers, theologians and attain the highest honor on earth, sainthood; as witnessed by Dismas, Mary Magdalene, and Pope Callistus.

Many saints undergo a period of suffering that can help those of us who study the lives of the saints see the power of the light that comes from the deepest darkness.

The dark night of the soul is life without God, and for some of us, no internal sense that God exists, though happening rarely, even extremely rarely, would be horrible and few would survive it with faith intact, but those who do, are greater for it, as they have lived that of which Christ spoke, the knowing that you are a child of God, and that with the proper growth to the light, will return home to God for eternity, making this short abode on earth the reality it is.

The Grassroots

It is said that Satan, faced with the intrusion of eternal truth into the world, attempts to institutionalize it, thereby ensuring it is ignored by the public.

The leaders of individual transformational grassroots organizations are the social entrepreneurs of the nonprofit sector. They have discovered an aspect of eternal truth and organized others around it for the good of the community. The community, who needs their passion and commitment, is best served by their being able to keep closely aligned with their core values, vision, and their truth (mission) as they evolve into a community institution.

While one of the goals of all grassroots organizations is—or should be—to become institutionalized to the point that community support becomes a stable given, it is too often precisely the point at which they become much less effective as a mission-driven organization. The truth often gives way to the expediency of becoming stable and solvent.

Criminal transformation and so often, community transformation, emerges from the small, grassroots organization, through the work of a few committed

118

individuals coming together for a great cause. It is from the grassroots that individual dignity is protected, hope encouraged, and communities strengthened.

The leaders of these organizations are the true inheritors of the voluntary associations of virtue and service to the public good that Benjamin Franklin brought to fruition in colonial America, and Alexis de Tocqueville marveled at in the 19th century in his landmark book, *Democracy in America*.

When I think about what defines a grassroots organization generally, I think back to this initial formation: mission-driven, entrepreneurial, voluntary and community-based. The truly real grassroots organization begins in the heart of one person who has witnessed injustice and wants to remedy it, or been moved by beauty and wants to share it, or gained wisdom and wants to teach others, or transformed the pain of their suffering into the power of teaching and comforting others.

These leaders often begin without any money, but have an idea to help—in some way—the world they see in front of them. Through their passion and dedication they bring others along with them in their journey of healing and begin the process of transformation.

If they are wise, lucky, and committed, they and the organizations they create, will survive and grow strong, and we will be the richer for their struggles, as they bring their healing service to our troubled world. If they succumb to the lure of financial stability over the purity of their vision and mission, we will ultimately be the lesser as their promise of healing becomes the maintenance of the status quo.

Eric Hoffer, a longshoreman who worked in San Francisco for many years, wrote a book called *The True Believer*. His thesis was that the true believer, who strive for a belief to the exclusion of all else, are to be feared for they are the soil from which political and religious fanaticism springs. There is much truth in this, but at the same time, it is the true believer who drives the social mission onward. It is they whose passion and true beliefs drive a social agenda that enriches us all.

The role of the grassroots organization is to shake the establishment, it is to be true to a mission of truth, to venerate that truth and express it through love for those who need help, through justice in honor of their suffering, through sharing beauty and the joy of artistic discovery, and through community building in pursuit of the transformation of the great human heart of the commons, and a most proper place, perhaps the only place, for the transformation of criminals.

OD, the Natural Language of Nonprofits

One of the more important disciplines the deep knowledge leader can study to increase his capability to develop and manage an effective grassroots nonprofit criminal transformative organization, is Organization Development (OD).

OD and the mission-driven organizational imperatives of nonprofit Criminal Transformation Organizations (CTOs) share common values and complementary realities.

This congruence represents opportunities for the deep knowledge leadership of CTOs and OD practitioners.

Nonprofits serve the public good, they provide a public service, and they are humanistic by definition.

CTOs are generally grassroots nonprofit organizations who act as organizational change agents transforming criminals and their communities.

In the United States, there are over a hundred thousand human service nonprofit organizations.

Within that large group there are probably several hundred that could be classified as CTO's in some way—though I have not found any statistics to provide proof for that assertion—as many deal with some aspect of criminal transformation as part of their related mission work, for instance, an organization that deals with drug/alcohol addiction or homeless issues will often be dealing with former or current criminals who are addicted or homeless.

While the deep knowledge leaders of CTOs are driven by their mission, bringing passion and commitment to their cause, they are often lacking in the internal organizational capacity building tools needed for sustainability. The specific tools they are most deficient in are strategic planning, fund development, board & staff development, and communications & marketing, all of which can benefit from an OD perspective.

OD values include humanism, collaboration, cooperation, participation, knowledge of self and awareness of one's impact, empowerment of individuals, groups, and organizations, and social responsibility/sustainability.

CTOs can achieve individual and community transformation most effectively when embracing their own values as applied to their own organizational functioning.

This will affect the governance, strategy, and fund development capability of the board and staff, which directly impacts the mission fulfillment—the core reason for their existence—of the nonprofit organization.

An example where some of the basic techniques of OD can be helpful is in creating a learning community, using group work to help clients, sharing life experiences, mentor board and staff members, and board members, sharing educational/vocational and life experiences, mentor clients.

Co-creating an environment where the inherent corrosiveness of the criminal world can be mitigated through the inherent self-responsibility of the board and staff member's world—deepened by the shared experiences of clients—leading to an organizational culture of mutual learning and healing in a transformative setting.

I have worked with several small CTOs where this inability to connect the staff and board to the criminal world has dramatically affected the ability of the organization to help its criminal client base, particularly in growing to scale and organizational effectiveness.

Individuals with humanistic ideals self-select into both non-profit environments and OD careers, actively choosing settings they feel congruent with. This would indicate that nonprofit staff and board may be open to operating according to OD values, but do not have the exposure or tools. If they did so, they would be modeling and enhancing mission work, and becoming more congruent with the natural language of the nonprofit world.

Individual development, organization development, and development of the social environment cannot be truly separated; they are reciprocal. Many CTOs fail because they haven't transformed themselves.
OD has traditionally been marketed to for-profit organizations but CTOs are more able to realize the values aspirations of OD, and at a higher level of congruency.

The absence of a profit motive creates deeper ground for the enactment of OD and its values.

The CTO is a problem-solving entity which heals.

CTOs—animated by a mission of individual and community transformation—will benefit from discovering a mission of management imbued by values-driven transformation, consistent with the values and practice of OD.

The Grassroots & Criminal Transformation

Rehabilitating criminals is big business in America and there are ideas and programs continually being promoted that show some initial success which the federal government then attempts to scale up to national import.

This is a familiar pattern when dealing with criminal rehabilitation and appears doomed to the continual failure it has traditionally been, because of the tendency—most marked in those who develop new programs that do work—to move on from direct service success at the grassroots level to administrative positions at the corporate or governmental level, taking their energy, insight and dedication with them.

There is also a lack of effective succession planning among grassroots nonprofits.

Reformed criminals—particularly those who have gained deep knowledge—however, have a level of connection hard to break.

Regarding criminal reentry, we certainly have the social need, with hundreds of thousands of criminals being released annually to the community with virtually no record of successful reentry programs to help them. The triggering event could be the government and criminal justice professional practitioners asking for the reformed criminals help.

Those who have restored their life can help others restore theirs; the solution is often found within the mirrored image of the problem.

The reformed criminal could begin the process of preparedness by advancing into graduate level college work and organizational management training.

This could also begin to counter—during output—the deadening reality of the relative speechlessness of criminals in their interaction with the criminal justice system during input.

A current trend that will only continue to accelerate and which will require even deeper understanding of those who would help criminals transform is the increasing transparency of criminal records.

The *Home News Tribune*, a New Jersey newspaper was the first to allow criminal record searches for free from its website. These searches, which can normally cost from $10 to $50 through the private sector, put public record criminal information online.

This is a good public service, and while it is appropriate for the public to know about the background of criminals it has to deal with through hiring, renting, volunteering with, and attending church with; the public attitudes around being involved with people with criminal records creates another significant hurdle in the reentry process.

The only effective response to this is a public openness about one's past by the criminal transforming his life, and those transformed criminals working in the field will be modeling openness through their behavior as deep knowledge leaders.

Criminals & the Church

From the very beginning, criminals played a major role in the Church—the good thief Dismas being an early example—and another was the transformed criminal who became pope, St. Callistus (died 222). His experience-based decree selection caused a severe political break in the Church with those inflexible Christians who saw no chance for redemption for some sinners, but Callistus restored its heart of mercy and redemption when he decreed forgiveness for major sinners after confession and penance, against the wishes of many early Christians.

This inflexibility and strict adherence to the language of the Church's law rather than the spirit of it marks some brief moments in the history of the Church, as of all institutions, but none walks the talk as does the Church.

Hippolytus, the leader of those who attacked Callistus throughout his papacy was the anti-pope who came back to the Church, eventually becoming one of her fathers.

Hippolytus attacked Callistus with venom, and what struck me reading about his attacks and the ferocity with which they were raised, considering the great admiration most Catholics felt for Callistus, leads to the conclusion that perhaps what most troubled Hippolytus was that Callistus, a common criminal, was getting the honor he felt he, Hippolytus, deserved.

Callistus, as a redeemed criminal, understood better than most that redemption was always possible and Christ's message was, if it was anything, that all could be forgiven.

However, as Pope Callistus allowed many who had committed major sins to return, after proper penance, to the fold of the Church, Hippolytus and his supporters were enraged, feeling even the committing of one major sin precluded future involvement with the Church.

The powerful denouement to this wonderful story of two men—one pope and one anti-pope—in the early days of the Church; was that upon being imprisoned for claiming himself as pope in reaction to the acts of Pope Callistus, Hippolytus later redeemed himself, primarily as a result of the same sort of imprisonment once suffered by Callistus, and the knowledge gained from his suffering there.

Callistus spoke to the heart of the Pharisees of his time with his goodness and forgiveness of sinners they would not forgive.

Another early Church leader who spoke out against Pope Callistus' action in readmitting penitential sinners to the Church was Tertullian, a Father of the Church.

The consequences of Pope Callistus' policy, which also involved some struggle over the primacy of Rome in setting Church policy—in this case for those who had lapsed under persecution—reverberated through the early Church.

This continual history of forgiveness and acceptance forms the ground for a significant aspect of our work; developing a case for the use of Catholic social teaching in the transformation of criminals.

In the discussion I had with criminals who were cultural leaders in the criminal world over the twenty years I was involved in that world, one thing usually became clear once we got down to the real reasoning around the decision to become a criminal; "everyone's doing it".

Believing that the upperworld rewards criminal behavior just as much, if not more, than the underworld, the choice to become a criminal is not difficult. It is a matter of either accepting the way the world is or becoming good at dealing with it, or ignoring it and becoming a fool who is taken advantage of by it.

The institutions that would stand against this truth of the world and present eternal truth, too often show, upon examination, feet of clay.

However, with a presentation of the world of Catholic social teaching through the Magisterium and the Chair of Peter, this misconception can be addressed and the natural human tendency to move to what is true can be reinvigorated.

One of the clearest expressions from Peter through the recent centuries that stood against the truth of the world, is that regarding slavery.

There is no doubt that slavery is against God, the Law, and the Prophets, no doubt at all. But Christ, who did not speak out against slavery, was not a revolutionary come to overturn the social structure within which slavery was an accepted part of daily life. He rendered to Caesar that which was Caesars.

It is this type of institutional clarity, carried out through time that will resonate with other criminals as it has with me, let alone the multitude of recent converts to Catholicism who have found in the intellectual storehouse of the Church a great call home.

Grassroots Organizations & Subsidiarity

In the United States the founding of organizations helping prisoners began with churches, and were primarily managed by the wives of pastors or prominent businessmen who were members of the church.

They were very close to the individual prisoners and criminals they helped as they worked within their church community. Over time these organizations grew and became more professionalized as did the nonprofit sector.

By the middle of the 20th century, when the major source of funding for criminal helping organizations had shifted to government, management had largely become social service professionals from the ranks of college sociology departments.

Their influence had many disastrous effects within the work of criminal rehabilitation and all other social work with the marginal.

Whatever success had been accomplished before the tenure of the sociologists—through the government sponsored Great Society programs developed and funded by President's Kennedy and Johnson—turned to dust during their thirty years of leadership. By the 21st century any program working with criminals that could point to a well-documented, rigorously evaluated and significant success were essentially non-existent.

However, sociology breaks down—in its defining of reality—as surely as in defining of deviancy, as it is merely that, a *definition* based on an ideology rather than truth, solid revealed truth—from before the foundation of the world.

For most traditional rehabilitation programs, the concept revolved around adding insult to injury. The initial injury, from the criminal's perspective, is the arrest, jail and prison confinement. The insult is presenting rudimentary behavioral norms—not even believed by the culture—in a sophomoric way to street-savvy people who are a captive audience. The criminals respond to evaluative surveys with how much they like the program, they are rehabilitated, and can I go home now? Starkly put, this is the state of too many traditional rehabilitation programs.

Recently however, returning to its roots, the nonprofit human service sector began government funding of faith-based organizations under the rubric of compassionate conservatism.

This is essentially the concept of subsidiarity in action, that those closest to the problem could best develop solutions to it.

However, as yet there isn't any evidence of much success with faith-based programs, according to recent meta-analysis.

That is also the case with faith-based efforts in a more focused way, that of faith-based job programs.

I would contend this is more the result of faith-based efforts that are not sectarian, but are so generalized due to the legal barriers to conducting faith-based work, that they are essentially neutering their primary effectiveness benchmark, that of conversion.

The principle of subsidiarity, also notes the often negative consequences—as were evident from the Great Society programs—that can arise from excessive state intervention.

In seeking conversion from a criminal culture deeply valued by its members—particularly its leadership—it is imperative that this closeness govern action.

Within the mystery of the criminal culture, regardless of the vast amount of cultural material describing it allowing outsiders to believe they comprehend its internalities, the deepest markers for understanding are experiential, and it is only from that basis that cultural understanding can emerge.

Culture Only Criminals Understand

When the culture becomes criminalized, the only ones who understand it are the criminals.

Culture criminalized—as it largely is today—is a milieu criminals move confidently in.

A criminalized world is a world built upon traditional criminal phenomena of predatory acquisition, the untrammeled satisfying of sensual urge, and violence—real or threatened—as a major negotiating tool.

Some of the criminalization of culture in my time upon this earth, springs from those words and ideas flowing from the false sense of freedom and individuality surrounding the beat period—as shaped by Burroughs, Ginsburg and Kerouac, which laid the foundation for the 1960's— expressed primarily against the institution of the Catholic Church which, ironically, most strongly protects that freedom and individuality through its social teaching.

Great joy was felt when the poem—censored as obscene— *Howl* by Allen Ginsberg, was smuggled into the nation's prisons, as it was into Englewood Federal Correctional Institution when I was there, at the clear message that criminals were, after all, the "best minds of my generation".

In the dull and dreary cement encased confines of prison, this was a revolutionary document and under no conditions would it have been allowed to be read openly by the criminals imprisoned there as anyone reading it could see what it glorified and ultimately portended.

We have gone far beyond that attempt by society to censor material in today's world.

Deep Knowledge Leadership, Mapping the Terrain

"A desire to work for the common good is not enough. The way to make this desire effective is to form competent men and women who can transmit to others the maturity which they themselves have achieved." (St. Josemaria Escriva, Conversations with St. Josemaria Escriva. p. 115)

Before venturing into the wasteland heed the guides who have returned.

Deep knowledge is the knowledge that comes from experience, is shaped through education, and informed by Catholic social teaching.

Deep knowledge about criminal transformation is knowledge deeply embedded within the transformed criminal through three benchmarks I have established based on my analysis of the time and processes needed to acquire and embrace it.

1) The searing of experience:

- Having been involved for ten years in the criminal world committing crimes for money,
- Having served five years in a maximum security federal or state prison,
- Being ten years out of prison, off parole, crime free, and helping the community.

2) The sharpening of education:

- Possessing a Masters or Doctorate degree,
- Belonging to criminal justice and nonprofit management related professional associations.
- A commitment to lifelong learning.

3) The harmonizing of spiritual growth:

- Being a leader of a community criminal transformation program,
- Being married in a strong and committed Catholic partnership,
- Being involved in extended self-study of Catholic social teaching with a basic knowledge of the key concepts.

Some, though all too few, reentry practitioners realize that involving former criminals in traditional rehabilitation work is valuable.

Many criminals—and I base this on my personal experience and the experience of others—after being released from prison, spending time on the outside, maybe gaining some college, but with no management experience, and little spiritual grounding, are inclined and fortunate enough to acquire funding for a criminal transformation program.

However, due to their lack of management knowledge and spiritual grounding, are only able to manage it for a few years—even though perhaps very successfully—after which they become 'burnt-out' and leave the management of it to someone else who runs it into the ground.

This is a story replicated within the human service field in general, and with the depth of sorrow, anger, and pain accompanying working in the criminal transformative world specifically, you need tools of corresponding depth to survive the suffering and reach a level of sustainability to begin to realize the joy of this most rewarding work.

The most important tool needed is spiritual grounding and understanding the suffering you have brought upon others and yourself.

Time spent in prison and deep involvement in the criminal world, is time that ultimately causes deep suffering to the individual.

It does not matter that the pain of suffering arises from action you set into motion yourself or not, it is still pain.

It arises—the suffering prison causes—from action in the city of men, from action taken by the criminal in the city of men to survive, to survive in a city whose animating voice is to eat or be eaten.

It is your dignity that is scratched, clawed, and tore at, and it is this the criminal fights to protect, and it is the still, small voice of protection the Catholic Church has raised for centuries—to protect individual dignity no matter the action that individual has taken—which provides the only safe harbor, the only home, to the criminal transforming.

I believe that the criminal transforms—will only transform—to a higher truth than that of the criminal world and the Catholic Church is the truth that must be presented to the criminal for him to be able to make the transformation.

The truth from Jesus Christ was fought against from the beginning with the many heresies the early Church fathers had to address, through the split of the Eastern churches and that of the Protestants, continuing until the present now, when anyone who can find something in the bible they feel they can claim as their particular truth, forms another religious community around it.

It is truly the tower of Babel and the preying wolves spoken of, and the ongoing work of the prince of this world to destroy the truth throughout history, but the Church stands as Christ foretold and the gates of hell have not prevailed against her.

Without the balance of the criminal experiential knowledge with the criminal justice, organizational, academic, and social teaching knowledge, the ability to penetrate the often deceptive signals surrounding rehabilitative action in the carceral/criminal world will be virtually nil; explaining the failure of the traditional rehabilitative practitioner over these past several decades.

The criminal, having transformed the pain of his suffering into the power of teaching, and having transformed his love of the transitory truth of the world—the foundation stones of criminal world knowledge—into the virtuous ladder of communal living, with deep refreshment at the sacrificial table of the Mass, will embody the deep knowledge his experience, faith, and learning shapes, with a fierce conviction.

Guiding Criminal Justice Principles

The deep knowledge leader will need to adopt principles of criminal justice which he has learned from experience and education which resonate with reality.

The formal foundation of Judeo-Christian criminal justice principles was established in Exodus 20:22 to 23:20, the *Book of the Covenant*, included earlier (pp. 84-92).

For the deep knowledge leader working in the United States, these criminal justice principles will help guide our work.

1) Broken windows policing works.

Allowing even the minor violation of a broken window in an area helps create the impression of an environment where law and order does not prevail and where crime flourishes. Responding quickly and efficiently to all crimes, regardless of the perceived state of seriousness or other local community concerns, is the foundation of good police work.

2) The response to crime should be timely, balanced, and just.

When justice is for sale, either through wealth, influence, or ideology, a fertile soil is created from which crime grows. The training and education of professionals in the criminal justice system is built on a foundation of traditional and well-reasoned concepts of justice and it needs continual reinforcement to remain an effective response to crime:

> **[Leviticus 19:15]** Do not pervert justice by giving false awards, whether by taking a man's poverty into account, or by flattering the great; give every man his just due.

3) Prison is the most appropriate criminal sanction to protect society and punish the criminal, while allowing the opportunity for criminal reformation.

Prison is an effective sanction for crime which has been used by human beings since ancient times. It serves to protect the public from predatory crime, acts as a deterrence and as incapacitation, and allows the penitential criminal the opportunity—while removed from the community—to reflect upon and correct his criminal behavior.

From the U. S. Bishops (2006):

> **468.** A punishment imposed by legitimate public authority has the aim of redressing the disorder introduced by the offense, of defending public order and people's safety, and contributing to the correction of the guilty party. Compendium: Catechism of the Catholic Church (p. 137)

U.S. Bishops. (2006). *Compendium: Catechism of the Catholic Church*. Washington, D.C. United States Conference of Catholic Bishops.

4) Capital punishment is an appropriate response to the criminal evil of murder, rape and pedophilia.

Capital punishment is often the only effective social method available to protect the innocent and applied with dispatch after legal review of the crimes charged and determining the fitness of its application, should be considered an appropriate sentence for murderers, rapists and pedophiles; who, knowing the time of their death, are able, with certainty of their remaining time to do so, seek God's forgiveness.

Correctional professionals realize that if a pedophile is placed into a maximum security prison, where the population is primarily professional criminals, he will soon be killed, which poses an interesting question: "Why would the criminal respond more aggressively to the abuse of a child than the non-criminal?"

However, five states, as of May 2008, have approved the use of capital punishment in child rape cases; Louisiana, Montana, Oklahoma, South Carolina, and Texas.

5) Repentant criminals deserve a second chance.

Excepting those cases of serious predatory behavior deserving the death penalty or natural life in prison, repentant criminals, once they have clearly shown—over a ten year period after being released from criminal justice supervision—that they have transformed their life by becoming a productive member of their family, their church, their work, and their community, should be allowed to apply for a complete pardon in a simple straightforward process.

From Caesar forgiveness may be sought but is rarely given, but from God forgiveness is always given.

6) It takes a reformed criminal to reform criminals.

For generations the ability of non-criminals—even those with the highest professional and academic credentials—to effectively rehabilitate criminals has proven, based on sound evaluations, to be virtually non-existent. Recruiting reformed criminals who have, through education, training, and the development of a deep knowledge leadership approach to criminal transformation, may well succeed where others have failed. Considering the current recidivism rate of 70%, and with the consensus that peer-based help does, at the very least, attract those who want help to transformative programs, it is time to try this approach in a substantial enough way, over time and properly evaluated, to discover if we can rely on it as a valuable tool for large-scale implementation.

7) In the work of criminal reformation, it is vital to keep in mind that the criminal—not society, capitalism, or the criminal justice system—is the problem.

Some criminal justice advocates take the position that among the people connected with the carceral world, the good guys are the criminals; and the police, district attorneys, prison guards, and the legislators who support stringent criminal sanctions, are the bad guys.

This is the absolutely wrong position, for in virtually any carceral population in America it is the criminals who are the indisputable bad guys, while the good guys are the ones protecting the public from the depredations of criminals. Those who parlay the myths of Hollywood or Marxism into an intellectual stance that fails to understand this basic fact, does everyone a disservice—in particular the penitential criminal—who may find little reason for proper expiation within a culture defining criminality as somehow admirable.

Sherpas', Apostles & Forbidden Knowledge

Like many fields, criminal justice often benefits from or is hurt by ideas that take hold of an influential group able to create foundational ideology from which taboos against opposing ideas can be created; but in the midst of these philosophical and sociological meanderings, truth can emerge.

Climbing Mount Everest with its own climate, trails, geography, and general conditions unlike any other place, requires knowledgeable guides for even the most experienced climbers to find success and eventually stand at its peak.

The Sherpa guides live on the mountain and call the Himalayas home. They are the only people with the life experience so vital to really *knowing* the mountain, and it is only in *knowing it that one can traverse it.*

Without having been on Everest it's impossible to explain the conditions to an outsider, as they do not match anything experienced in any of earth's other regions.

It is a world unto itself, whose environment has been built over eons of weather shaping rocks, animals shaping trails, and the often futile efforts by humans, except for the Sherpas, of trying to conquer it.

The Sherpa's know that you really don't conquer Everest; you learn to live with it long enough to survive the climb up it.

This is analogous to the criminal/carceral world. This is what it is like to the outsider who attempts to traverse it and conquer it, to find among its ancient trails the secrets to sampling and mastering its wiles and treasures long enough to discover their meaninglessness against the greater treasure of a truth bringing peace and harmony instead of the violence and chaos the criminal/carceral city visits upon its sojourners.

The transformed criminal is the Sherpa guide, the only one who can lead the sojourning penitential criminal to the top of the mountain of reformation.

In many ways, deep knowledge would also fit within the category of forbidden knowledge.

And yes, in some ways, the deep knowledge of which I speak is knowledge we should not know, and in a better world Cain has not marked with his crime, perhaps it would not.

Criminals know that much of crime is enjoyable and rewarding, yet the traditional rehabilitative practitioner often focuses on only its negatives in an effort to make its pursuit less desirable, especially to youth.

This tendency creates great difficulty for those same practitioners as the criminals they are trying to rehabilitate don't have faith in their ability to distinguish between truth and lies so why would they be believed about anything?

The youth they are trying to keep from a life of crime, once discovering for themselves how rewarding and pleasurable many aspects of crime can be, come to the same conclusion and disregard their entreaties.

Criminals Working With Criminals

Former criminals who have redeemed themselves working with other criminals to help them find the same path of redemption, is not a new concept, but what is new is the understanding that it cannot be merely the experience of the criminal that is valuable, but the academic, organizational, and spiritual knowledge he can obtain that will create a sustainable transformative organization.

The story of criminal-run organizations working in the area of prisoner reentry is long and deep and almost all of the stories have ended in failure.

Those that appear to have succeeded are residential-based programs that accept relatively few new people, who they screen well, and have not really been replicable; but without rigorous evaluations conducted by an independent evaluator and using a control group, it is impossible to determine their real success.

If we can accept these first three steps then the fourth seems axiomatic:

1) that criminal and carceral involvement is a valuable experiential knowledge base; and

2) that personal transformation through education and spiritual development may prove valuable in developing criminal transformative programs; while

3) advanced education and training in organizational management and Catholic social teaching will enable one to manage and sustain effective programs; then

4) it would be of great value for government to fund pilot programs.

One of the great difficulties with those approaching criminal transformation from the traditional rehabilitative stance—usually either a sociological or psychological perspective—is that there is no absoluteness, no absolute good or bad; so why rehabilitate from criminal world success?

So we are back in the relativism of the city of men, when what is needed is the clarity of the absolute City of God.

In some sense, with the recent emphasis being shown in restoring rehabilitation into corrections—California even renamed its agency Department of Corrections and Rehabilitation—this has been modified.

However, the core carceral/criminal world population still encompasses this perpetual class which continually and more deeply, is reshaping the criminal world territory.

I am calling for leadership to be sought from among them, for they are the only resource able to reach other criminals in any substantive and transformative way.

Transformed criminals working with criminals will need to be contemplative and marital, using tools like the Spiritual Exercises of St. Ignatius, used for centuries to good effect by the Jesuits, once known as the shock troops of the Catholic empire.

They need to—not only think martially—but be valiant and fond of fighting verbally and not fearful of fighting physically, which usually comes with the experience of surviving in a maximum security prison.

They need to think of themselves, as did the early Jesuits, as those shock troops venturing into areas rarely entered in the way they will now be entering.

We have, from the Apostle Paul, an important message of the importance of shock troops who can go where others cannot.

Jacques Maritain and his wife Raissa, formed one of the most devout and influential contemplative and martial couples in Catholic history.

Their insistence on infusing their daily life with contemplation and prayer was the strength and clarity which led them to exert such tremendous influence on the Catholic and political world of the early 20th Century.

Before they discovered Catholicism, they had taken an oath to commit suicide if no true spiritual path could be found.

After being converted to Catholicism, they took an oath of chastity within their marriage and lived their life by that oath.

This contemplative and martial path—necessary to work effectively in our world where information and communications access us with astonishing speed—is vital to remain centered. In the work of criminal transformation the spiritual path is core, but along with it is the martial spirit resonating throughout the history of America and embraced by its most effective military leaders.

Also centrally important is to embrace the vision of the Church Triumphant and Militant; that great assemblage, stretching out through history and time, of the great saints, the archangels leading the heavenly hosts, the knights of times past, and the knights and saints of today, wielding swords of spirit, light shimmering from their blades; their banners of the Word carried as they advance against the eternal enemy, the prince of this world, who has been in a battling retreat since being banished from Heaven by St. Michael.

There are orders—such as that founded by St. Josemaria Escriva, Opus Dei—within the Church which incorporate this spirit; in many ways so like the ancient priests of the true faith, clothed in priestly garb always, resolute in their devotion and union to Holy Mother Church, and to the Rock of Peter, upon whom the gates of hell never have and never will prevail.

For most people, working in the field of the professional criminal is prohibitively dangerous work —perhaps why the professional criminal justice practitioner has largely retreated from direct contact with it.

For the transformed criminal it is still dangerous, though with a strong grounding in the virtually impenetrable armor of daily mass, daily rosary, morning and evening prayers, daily reflections, mortification, and regular spiritual direction from a priest; it will be the work of the highest spiritual order, work of great apostolate reward and deep personal joy, the work of a lifetime, work for an eternity of lifetimes.

Teaching Communal Reentry, The Papal Teaching

When the children of God act in their apostolate, they have to be like those great lighting systems which fill the world with light, but the lamp is not seen. (St. Josemaria Escriva, *The Forge #670*)

The Church, existing as a universal entity within the Kingdom of God, proclaims the essence of the apostolate to deep knowledge leaders.

In our Mother Church, formed before time, and existing as an earthly institution for over two thousand years and comprising today over one billion souls, it is vital that there be one teaching voice of clarity, strength, and vision from which the deep knowledge leader can continually refresh himself at the well of Catholic learning for the arduous task ahead.

That teaching voice is Peter. It is to Peter Christ entrusted the Church and it is from Peter that we seek the meaning of the work of the earthly Church, clarification of the eternal Gospel, education about the social teaching, and guidance for our apostolate.

The major sources for the teachings of Peter are the papal encyclicals and studying them is a necessary aspect of educating ourselves about the social teaching.

In this digital age, access to the Vatican is easily obtained 24/7 and when studying the words of Peter, it is crucial to read the Vatican translations directly from the Vatican website.

I first discovered the encyclicals during my studies on my way into the Church as it soon became clear that I needed to find a place, in addition to the *Catechism*, for authoritative teaching; and so I found the papal encyclicals, the great storehouse of the Church, where all of the crystallized knowledge of her great thinkers finds their home.

The papal encyclicals—drawing from scripture and the Church fathers—really form the interpretive bedrock of the social teaching.

Reading the encyclicals is difficult to begin with, but once you understand the Vatican's need to write universally for the Church whose audience is truly *universal,* the preciseness and deep beauty of the language starts to resonate within you.

My practice is to download the encyclical I am studying to my computer, read a few pages or less, highlight and make notes in brackets, and mark where I left off to begin when I come back to it.

For many months during RCIA I studied this way every morning and it was a wonderful entrance to the blessed knowledge of Peter, who truly is our pastor.

The Church, led by the office of Peter, the Bishop of Rome, which has been occupied by many men, some evil, some fallible, many saints, but all, in their own way—the evil and fallible used by God—kept the Barque of Peter intact as the vessel of the Church, always moving on its eternal voyage, always suffering through history and time.

Communal Reentry

The central concept animating successful communal reentry is the respect and maintenance of human dignity.

Traditional reentry programs fail to recognize this need for dignity, relying instead on a deviant model of criminality—creating hindrances—virtually guaranteeing non-acceptance by the criminal, even if he is seeking to build a different life.

Communal reentry for us is into the community of the Catholic Church, accepting and living its sacraments, growing in understanding of its social teaching, working through the personal apostolate of a transformed criminal—a deep knowledge leader and wise elder—and from this foundation, he is helping a friend, a fellow sojourner on the journey to Rome.

St. Paul, writing from prison in Rome in the winter of 63, to the Ephesians, teaches us:

> **[Ephesians 2:19]** You are no longer exiles, then, or aliens; the saints are your fellow citizens, you belong to God's household. **[20]** Apostles and prophets are the foundation on which you were built, and the chief corner-stone of it is Jesus Christ himself. **[21]** In him the whole fabric is bound together, as it grows into a temple, dedicated to the Lord; **[22]** in him you too are being built in with the rest, so that God may find in you a dwelling-place for his Spirit.

Along with the bonds of sacramental marriage and the children from that marriage, this is the first community and for most transformed criminals, perhaps the last.

This community, this primary community of the transformed criminal, is the communion of saints—the Church Triumphant—and his true pastor is Peter, and his local parish is any welcoming building where he attends Mass and receives Christ, all part of the true community we are blessed to be part of, the Kingdom of God.

The transformation from the criminal world to the Catholic communal world—the Kingdom of God—is a process of traversing through three spiritual stages.

The first stage is the spiritual understanding that the truths being followed to maintain status in the criminal world are inferior, in an objective sense, from those governing the communal world. This stage requires intense study—academic and theological—to reach an initial concluding step that God exists.

The second stage is a study of the communal world, learning about the culture and ways of living. This is primarily an experiential learning process of being involved with parish life as a sacramental Catholic.

The third stage is acceptance of an apostolate, which for a transformed criminal can be none other than that of helping other criminals who are lost find their way home to Rome.

Being a professional criminal is a committed life only fully exorcised through use of the goodness gifted by God's grace resulting from the transformation to good from the evil of its wrongful living.

In the Beatitudes opening the Sermon on the Mount, Christ begins by saying:

> **[Matthew 5:3]** Blessed are the poor in spirit, the kingdom of heaven is theirs.

It is here that the soul abandoned to God, knowing that all that comes, comes from God; completely trusting, as a little child, that God will do with him as he needs to be done with according to his highest nature, and that whatever happens, all will be well.

The potency of the confessional booth, alone with the priest, allows the flowering and deepening of guilt, even though forgiveness of sin is given with penance, the guilt in the sinner remains a strong spur to conscience acting on him in the future.

This single relationship, of one human to another is continued in the reentry program model Lampstand uses for the same purpose; for we know from the great work by Werner H. Kelber (1983) *The Oral and the Written Gospel*, that the gospel of transformation, the Gospel of Christ, is most powerfully passed on from teacher to student orally buttressed by text, not by text alone.

The difficulty with the group model, used in most of the work with criminals, is that it removes guilt rather than deepening it, thus also removing the spur to conscience needed for strength in the future.

As the wrongs committed are expressed within the group, with the promise to do better, the group forgives but without the professional and spiritual insight and expertise of the Catholic priest; and the message received is that it is okay to fall down, you are expected to fail, everyone does.

Though this therapeutic community approach appears to be the practice of much group oriented work with the alcoholic/addict/criminal population, and may even result in some benefit, the expectation of continual failure can be a fatal practice for criminals and their victims.

The transformative work occurs in the relationship of one to one, human to human, human to God.

The Kingdom of God

The Church, the repository of revealed truth, grows through the communion of each Catholic embracing that truth, taking in that Word of truth from Jesus Christ, learning from its shaping and exposition through the centuries by the saints of the Church, and from the work of each apostolate.

Working through the apostolate, helping birth the transformation of criminals, and they, having been reborn in the Church, add to the teaching of the word.

It is within the Kingdom of God that two of the ancient covenants with God are embraced, the Old Covenant with the Jews, to prepare the way to create the conditions among a people for the new, and the New Covenant with everyone.

The Kingdom of God is a universal kingdom of the spirit and its external organizational structure is the Catholic Church.

The Kingdom of God is the kingdom where all can live, finding eternal life, most importantly the penitential criminal, whose sin is greatest and whom Christ has called before all others, for did not He take the good thief Dismas with him to heaven from the Cross, thereby creating the first canonized saint of the Church.

The Kingdom of the Church

This chapter, this book, has been about the strategy of using reformed criminals to develop and manage criminal transformative efforts, but while I presuppose no absolute success in those efforts, I would anticipate a substantial increase in the current 30% success rate of reentry if the fullness of the ideas being expressed here are adopted and supported by government—through grants for programs and by including transformed criminals working in the nonprofit sector within the benefits of the College Cost Reduction and Access Act of 2007 which provides loan forgiveness after ten years of public service—and the Catholic Church who could be the first funder of demonstration programs in California, New York, and Florida.

The Catholic Church, in their involvement in the world, works from the foundation of their social teaching.

Beginning to implement the ideas in this book would touch on all aspects of Catholic Social Teaching, helping to reshape the current—almost purely punitive social handling of criminals—towards the traditional Catholic redemptive and forgiveness model (within which punishment is still necessary based on the crime) built on the ultimate power God has for forgiveness and transformation when the human heart reaches truly out for that grace.

It will take legislation to enact approval for rehabilitative programs developed and managed by transformed criminals, and the process of public education around the issues involved will be a steep and difficult one.

Prophetic-witness can come from the transformed criminals themselves, who once lost have been found, and return to the communal world as the prodigal son with an ability to reach other criminals at a deeper and more truthful level than anyone else has yet been able to do.

Criminal transformative efforts rely first of all on the truthfulness of the criminal to the transformative agent, and yet still, former criminals are almost as susceptible as being lied to, and accepting the lies, as most other transformative practitioners.

The success difference might be slight in the beginning, so instead of seven of every ten returning to prison under the current regime, maybe that could be lowered to four of ten and perhaps even three of ten, (turning the current statistics of a 70% recidivist rate around to one of 30%) bringing us closer to the 19th century reported recidivist rate—though evaluation of individual programs was rudimentary at best— when most American criminal justice work was in the hands of the religious, of 10%.

Criminals are neither born criminal, though often born into a criminal world, nor made so by society—though in following the innate urge to seek truth may happen upon the truth of the world and the criminal city—which often becomes in its embracing and living, a criminal life.

Criminals are like all of us, children of God, but they have become lost—are lost so much deeper than most. Some so far they should never again be allowed intercourse with other humans, remaining forever in solitary confinement or subject to the imposition of capital punishment. Some so far they should never again be allowed physical freedom and spend the rest of their natural life in prison. Some are lost only as far as still having a possibility of social intercourse and personal freedom, and for some who have been lost and are now found, even a hope of a lifetime of penitential contribution through the way of the apostolate.

Given what I know of the capabilities and passion former criminals would be bringing to the transformative work, that does not seem far-fetched at all. It is surely a restorative vision to work towards.

And perhaps Christ, in his original gesture of taking with him from Calvary, Dismas the criminal, is expressing his will in a way perhaps long hidden from us in its fullest meaning.

Christ's teaching call, reinforced by the Church for so many generations, is still what he said at the beginning of his ministry:

> [Mark 2:17] Jesus heard it, and said to them, It is not those who are in health that have need of the physician, it is those who are sick. I have come to call sinners, not the just.

Within the Kingdom of God gathered around Christ and the early Church, the formerly lost, the criminals first among them, marked our future.

St. Mary Magdalene, the former prostitute, was the first criminal to see Christ resurrected. St. Dismas, the former thief, was the first criminal to become a saint of the Church built on Peter. St. Callistus, the former thief, was the first criminal to become Peter.

Christ chose us, and we are perhaps the only ones—we transformed criminals who are Catholics—who can begin to empty the prisons and help the prodigal son return home.

The truth of Christ within the Church founded on the rock of Peter, prevailing over the gates of hell for these two thousand years, is the only truth trumping the truth of this world.

Only Christ defeats Satan, crushing his evil beneath his feet, casting him evermore into darkness; and only we are blessed and armed as spiritual warriors carrying the sword of the social teaching, refined in the blazing sensual fires of the criminal city whose glittering dust we have shaken from our feet, fashioned and blessed by the rites and sacraments of Mother Church, guided by Peter and Christ, able to venture into the deepest darkness here on earth to rescue the souls still lost there.

Only we few.

Chapter Three
The Criminal, the Cross & the Church

This chapter focuses on the interior journey of the penitential criminal working out his lifelong atonement within the Church, through the world, helping other criminals transform their lives.

It is virtually impossible to explain to the outside observer, regardless of their level of education or professional experience—even if that experience has been within the criminal justice system—the reality of living many years within the criminal world and the maximum security prison.

It is a reality that can only be approached by experiencing it (an experience, in terms of prison, no one chooses) and even for those working within the criminal justice system— with the freedom of being outside of either the criminal or carceral world—the guards, the prison workers, the administrators, and other law enforcement, legal, and correctional professionals, knowing the reality of it is just flat-out impossible, which is why my books are written for criminals, and will be best understood only by criminals; though I pray that value can be found by any with interest in the transformation of criminals through Catholicism.

However, in terms of *effective* criminal reformation, it is only the transformed professional criminal who will be able to transform other criminals. The professional criminal who commits crimes for money—not the rapist, the informer, the pedophile, the thrill killer, and the other variants of offenders generally bundled up in one group when outsiders speak of criminals—for these offenders are not safe within the maximum security prison where the ancient culture of the professional criminal that embodies the protection of the innocent and loyalty to partners, still endures and governs.

It is only those professional criminals who have served time in maximum security prisons who can become powerful rehabilitative professionals; for they and they alone, can speak to all criminals in an authentic voice, calling them to reformation and transformation.

Evil to Good

The criminal carries the cross of his secret past, revealed in his capture, and brought to the light in his penitential life of atonement in the Church; the interior journey of a lifetime and the only apostolate worthy of such a life.

The experience of evil being turned to good through the grace of God is a wonderful tool vitally needed by the world; a world within which criminals grow and deepen their commitment to the evil of the criminal world as it becomes more congruent with the world it seeks to fully embrace, an embrace where, in some places, it has already done so.

What eventually attracts criminals into a lifetime commitment to the criminal world is clarity, excitement, truth, and honor—all of which are only trumped by understanding the divine honor of Christ and the live of the Apostolate,while living the sacramental life with deep study of the social teaching of the Catholic Church—the deepest well of clarity, excitement, truth, and honor in the history of the world.

Within the Catholic Church the criminal discovers the truth that the only response to his many years of being a criminal is to live the rest of his life following the path of sainthood, atoning for the harm he caused during his criminal life.

Criminals are so because of their distance from God and the beginning path to erasing that distance is only found in the Catholic Church—the only repository of truth in the world.

Just as the Catholic Church exploded in growth under the protection of the Roman Emperor Constantine, so today the Church continues its mission to become accepted and protected as the universal and only Church by all governments—finally removing from Satan's hands the principalities, thrones, powers, states, and combines through which so much of his evil is enacted.

Since the early part of the 20th Century the criminal world in the United States has grown into a sophisticated enterprise closely linked to the worlds of business and politics; and since the middle decades of that century, the carceral world has grown to exert a substantial level of control over the criminal world culture.

Consequently, any attempt to develop and manage programs that are able to perform the task of reforming criminals, must be able to have authentic access to the criminal/carceral world to have any hope of success.

Criminals are not reformed by programs alone, or by specific services doled out by bureaucratic structures; but by a change of heart, an internal decision that transforming their life has more and longer sustainable value than their current life as a criminal; a criminal life possessing tremendous value from both their lived and imagined perspective.

There was a period in America—from its founding until the 20th Century—when people of good will were able to successfully intervene in the lives of criminals and bring many of them to the transformative path, and there are reports (especially through the works of Dr. Andrew Skotnicki, such as *Religion and the Development of the American Penal System* (2000), and *Criminal Justice and the Catholic Church* (2008) of a 10% recidivist rate throughout that period.

However, once the pinnacle of the criminal and carceral world culture became an admirable and sought after height to scale during the 20th Century—even within the public world—those relatively amateur attempts would no longer work and the results over the past decades reflect that.

The transformed professional criminal, who has come from the heights of the carceral/criminal world, has retained his personal honor, has accomplished his professional goals of higher education, has received training in the intricacies of managing a nonprofit grassroots organization, and received in-depth training in the social teaching of the Catholic Church; and consequently, is one of the very few people who will be able to effectively reach and reform the criminal.

The master story behind the ability of the transformed criminal to help other criminals begin to transform their lives, is the voice of the least having value in the world of the great, the great whose authorship of the stories of rehabilitation are and have been for some time, completely and utterly false.

The experiences of the lowly matter more to the Catholic faith and the rehabilitative profession than those of the mighty, and it is from the voice of the lowly that the transformed criminal speaks, while the traditional rehabilitation practitioner speaks from the voice of the mighty; and the way of the mighty, the way of riches, position and standing, is suspect, as it largely results from a too successful congruence with the way of the world while disowning eternal truths.

The Criminal, Three Criminal Saints

The path is narrow, we must not forget. It is not a wide road full of comfort and ease, but a narrow one of struggle and the cross, though blessed with a joy beyond understanding only saints are fortunate to know and it is sainthood we must have for our goal.

There are three major criminal saints—St. Mary Magdalene, (Feast Day July 22) St. Dismas (Feast Day March 25) & St. Callistus (Feast Day October 14)—whose lives dramatically furthered and marked the course of the early Church.

Christ speaks powerfully to us in the manner of his death and whom he chose to accompany him; and in his resurrection, whom he chose to first appear, both redeemed criminals; St. Dismas, the Good Thief and St. Mary Magdalene, the prostitute with pure heart.

For centuries Mary's conversion from prostitute to saint is continually being pulled away from her, and Dismas' feast day is not even celebrated, nor is Callistus often remembered; as a Church built on a mission to sinners often tries to remove sinners from its past and presents a thief of pears as a great story of criminal conversion, but as great as St. Augustine was, he never walked where the deep sinners did.

Jesus Christ, the criminal, and the Catholic Church form a triptych held together by love, informed by charity, and realized by suffering.

Christ's mission was to the sinners and one of his central teachings was to teach the truth to the Pharisees, yet they called for his death, plotting with Judas to deliver him to the Roman governor Pilate for execution.

And if Christ himself could not teach the Pharisees, whose prophecy he fulfilled the truth of, who are we to think we can. No, they are who we must always struggle with, and whose actions will cause suffering among the people as they struggle to impose pharisaic obedience.

The pharisaic conscience—which turns virtue into vice—is always among us, and the Pharisees who delivered Christ to crucifixion merely served as the paradigm setting in motion agents in Jerusalem who began a process of denial and oppression of the Church which continues today, and whose origin is the prince of the world.

Criminalized and executed himself, Christ's first act of canonization was making the penitential criminal Dismas a saint, and upon his resurrection the first person to whom he revealed himself was the penitential criminal Mary Magdalene, the apostle to the apostles.

Dismas is the only human being to accompany the Lord in death, from earth to heaven—his partner in act one of the eternal three act drama central to human history—Christ has died, Christ has risen, Christ will come again.

Christ could have merely said, for the kind comment of Dismas; "Your sins are forgiven you", or "You will receive your reward in heaven" or any number of promises he had previously made in his ministry on earth, but he chose instead the greatest gift he ever gave to one sinner "Truly, I say to you, today you will be with me in Paradise."

To the criminal, to the thief Dismas, that is what our Lord said. And we must ask why? But we already know why, he came for the criminals, the deepest sinners of all, and for those penitential and redeemed criminals, they will be with him in paradise.

This is part of the Great Story.

The joy of living God's law comes from choosing to live it and the deepest joy comes to those whose living of it has been a return and rebirth from the deepest sin.

Some biblical scholars have attempted to make a case that Mary Magdalene was not the prostitute legend says she was, but the stronger case is that she was; and it comes, not from critical biblical scholarship, but from an understanding of the transformed criminal, which she also certainly was.

The courage shown by Mary during the crucifixion and resurrection—and perhaps one of the reasons she is often called the apostle to the apostles—in the face of a threat great enough to send most of the other apostles into flight, is similar to that shown by Dismas the Good Thief, who even on the cross of crucifixion he shared next to Christ, had the courage to stand for truth and for Christ, rewarded by becoming the first canonized saint of the Church.

Great sinners who have become transformed into saints often bring with them a physical courage usually deeper than that of other saints (one cannot imagine Mary Magdalene denying Christ three times as did Peter); and it springs from a personal experiential knowledge of evil, from which they no longer feel fear, but transcendence.

What magnificent joy was birthed within the penitential Mary Magdalene as Christ drove the devils from her, saving her from her criminal life; and what greater joy became hers as she came alone to the tomb and saw the risen Christ.

What magnificent joy befell Dismas as he went from the criminal cross to Christ's heavenly home, the home which all seek and to which all spurs to sanctification and perfection lead.

St. Dismas and St. Mary Magdalene are the proto-criminal saints, canonical consorts—first to heaven with Christ, first to see Christ arisen.

St. Callistus, pope from 218-223, who was born a slave, became a thief, was sentenced to prison, escaped, transformed himself and became pope.

St. Callistus' greatest contribution to the Church was accomplished during the time when the strictest among its leaders, mainly Hippolytus, had succeeded in disallowing any return to the Church those members who sinned even only once. Callistus, having transformed himself so dramatically, would have none of this and allowed sinners, once having done penance, to return to the Church.

He established the practice of the absolution of all repented sins, against which much of the leadership of the Church at that time fought him, every step of the way, and gained him such strong enmity among the pharisaic members of the leadership that one of them, Hippolytus, set himself up—through an election of his supporters—as the anti-pope in response to Callistus and wrote scathingly against him for years.

Later, Hippolytus was also sent to prison and while there, discovered what Callistus had learned; that even with deep sin, redemption is offered. That is the essential message of the Lord, why Mary Magdalene was prophet to the prophets, Dismas the first canonized saint of the Church, and Callistus one of the greatest popes of the early Church.

For these three, it was their penitential criminality which canonized them.

Bended Knee

It has been said that the devil has very thin limbs with no knees, and not being able to kneel is the animating aspect of his evil.

Professional criminals resist bending to another's will, even God's, and this resistance is partly defiance and partly acknowledgement of the liberating power of freedom from influence.

Much of the drive to criminality is a drive for freedom, freedom from a world often seeking to oppress, seeking to deny, seeking to punish; yet it is this world the criminal seeks to avoid and thwart as he finds the criminal path—always leading into and through the great prison houses of history, the maximum security cells from which little light shines but that from internal liberty—and enters fully into the criminal world with its ancient rituals and laws; its crushing steel, stone, bone, and blood; and the loss of fear and the joy of power over crushing destiny.

This is the martyr's freedom, the martyr's path, which we see in the lives of the great sinner saints, the criminals, the prodigal children; St. Mary Magdalene, St. Dismas, St. Callistus, and all of the other deep sinners and criminals who, knowing evil became more deeply good.

We seek the blessings of those who found within the mysteries of the Church the simple truths of Christ and eternity, yet remained awhirl with the majesty of the accumulated knowledge of her saints—especially those of her criminal saints—whose deep knowledge led them to the Roman road.

It is a mistake to equate the theological position of obeisance (deferential respect) to God with obedience (doing what one is told), as the great call to perfection is not to do what one is told but to be what one truly is; a human being made in the image of God, whose earthly sin has been redeemed by Christ and whose promise is to fulfill perfection of life on this earth and bringing other souls to Christ through the daily work on that path of perfection.

The call is not to obey Christ; the call is to be like Christ.

And the most powerful attribute of man from God is his free will, which led him to eat of the fruit of the tree of knowledge—the tree of life; and this is perhaps where we see the sin of Satan, who wanted to force man to do well, where God gifted freedom of action.

This is perhaps most evident in the book of Job where God allows Satan to punish the good man with all manner of evils to forcefully influence Job's free will to decide to respond to evil with evil; yet Job does not and continues to praise the Lord

Children of Eve

Criminals are, like Eve, those who say no to God's plan and yes to the serpent promising knowledge, power, and freedom, but they must learn to become children of Mary and live her divine yes.

The children of Eve love the pleasures of the world, are drawn to the hope for secret knowledge and power that is assumed to come from a deeper tasting of them—often true, so true—yet in their relentless searching find that the way of delight is a path to sadness.

The criminal bears his cross with the Church; like St. Dismas, he deserves to be here, hanging on Golgotha; like St. Mary Magdalene, he deserves shame and a lifetime of penance; like St. Pope Callistus, he knows human redemption because he exemplifies it.

The bad is good. The bad, seeing itself as bad, becomes good. Only the sinner can become a saint. The merely good is a voice of no timbre, no octavel range or depth.

The good from the present evil in the Church of priests sexually abusing children and the bishops who countenanced it, is the reminder that, for as long as the Church has existed, the smoke and fire of Satan can enter into the hearts of its priests, bishops, and even its popes; but the Church will not fall, even unto the gates of Hell which the abuse of the innocent surely is.

Eve birthed a world through her succumbing to the great temptation to know, to become, and as we seek becoming through the exploration of the bad, let us find on the other side of it, the truly good.

Eve is the mother of us all as Mary is the Mother of the Church; one leads us to our free will and the great danger in exercising it, and the other leads us to eternal salvation through her Son.

The Great Story

Four men have stood on the ground of the world within history and each spoke his truth:

> I am a prophet, said Moses,
>
> I am an enlightened man, said Buddha,
>
> I am God, said Christ,
>
> I am a prophet, said Mohammed.

From each sprung a mighty religion, but only one is eternal and true and which door will we go through.

Only Christ said he was God, only He named his predecessor, by spiritual root and word, *and today* we are with him each day at the table of the mass in the world which he instituted as the mass of heaven.

The Great Story began at the beginning when God created us; but it was deepened when, to God's Chosen People, the Messiah came.

And from him grew the Catholic Church, and to be a member of the Catholic Church is to bear a cross as Christ bore the cross.

The cross we are to bear is fulfilling what we are here to do, when, at that point we realize that the most important thing to do is to take on our God given cross and shoulder the courage of Christ and the saints of the Church Triumphant, becoming a soldier here, in the great army of the Church Militant.

We cannot know the mind of God, but we can use the gifts from his word and image—our reason and our being—and embracing the reality of the deep knowledge we have acquired through our experience, our work in the academy, our professional training, our study of the social teaching of the Catholic Church, all animated by our sacramental Catholicism; connect with the substantive reality of the natural law, forming a union with our self as God's child, and come to comprehend, in a most elemental way, the pattern of his work.

In this way, let us look at the Great Story of our kind upon the earth, and beyond it, to see what has perhaps been revealed to us through the actions of God's work.

God created the first human being in his own image—he created us in his image—think of that, think of the heritage of that divine birth, reaching back from each of us to the first human, to the Adam/Eve core.

As he shaped the first humans from that primordial dust of earth, as into their faces God wove the divine features and as God is spirit able to become flesh, he imparted to us eternal spirit inhabiting our body, and as primarily spiritual beings, possessing a central spiritual asset, free will—thus God was giving up any control over human action save persuasion—and so, he established the first part of the Old Covenant with Adam.

There is only one concrete material way we can know of the truth of this creation; through the works of God can we know of the existence of God. Through the truths he has written on our heart; yet to discover these the criminal must search deep and long and return again to the halls of study and the bench of prayer; for, as criminals, we resist the imposition of any truth but that which we learn for ourselves, that which we see for ourselves, that which we experience for ourselves.

Exercising their free will, human beings embraced the evil—hidden in an appeal to their emerging vision of self—emanating from the persuasive words of Satan, the fallen angel whose free willed choice removed him from God forever with absolutely no chance for redemption.

Satan, and the angels who rejected God, with full knowledge of God, as created angelic beings of God, can never—on account of their irrevocable rejection of the Creator—find forgiveness; yet the greatest criminal can, even the most evil of criminals can; and though it may be with the bloody spur of approaching death from the execution by a state no longer able to protect the innocent against the criminal aggressor any other way than through his death; here still the salvation can come, the forgiveness can come.

This eternal forgiveness can only be found from God, and he has, through his divine authority, given the ability to his priests, working in concert with and from within the Church he founded upon earth, that those who sin can, by confession and penance, receive forgiveness and begin again with their life, renewed.

For thousands of years human beings practiced their evil upon the earth and most wickedly within its cities; cities founded by the darkest of the proto human evil-doers, Cain, where the city crowds acted and reached in their lives downward to the lure of Satan rather than upward to the call of God.

This pagan world became so intolerable and such an assault upon the face of God that he flooded the earth, removing all humans, animals, and cities; save those in the great ark, and with its helmsman Noah, God created the second part of the Old Covenant.

165

God established the third part of the Old Covenant with Abraham, the first man to have his name changed by God, as Abraham was to create the People of God, the Jews, and as the father of nations the prophecy of the creation of the Kingdom of God to be brought by Christ was foretold.

For the generations of Abraham, and then from the great exodus from Egypt, God worked through Moses to build up the People of God, wrote the commandments they were to live by with his own hand and the laws governing their behavior with his own voice, and with Moses and the Jews God created the third and final part of the Old Covenant, the Sinai Covenant.

For thousands of years the People of God struggled to live as God's People, fought against the admonishments of their prophets, and they failed him again. This brought him to earth as a human being, becoming that which was made in his father's image, becoming the Man God Jesus Christ, and walking among the People of God, he grew to manhood and for three years God taught his people directly, sealing his teaching with the universality of his Church under the New Covenant, and established his Church with Peter, upon whose rock of heart he expanded the People of God to include all who would hear the Word, the Word that became flesh.

Catholics are bound to the Jews—as the Jews are God's chosen people—and we are bound to the Jews as we are the people who chose God.

Christ built his church upon Peter, who had thrice denied him, and throughout the history of the Church would deny him again, but the marriage between God and Church would stand, through better or worse, as it had with his chosen people.

The beauty of the Great Story is that we already know the ending, we already know how it comes out, yet each day is still a test of our faith in that knowing, against the deadly and powerful allure of the temporal world and reaching to the still small voice of the eternal as we can hear it now.

God told the Great Story to humans many times, through prophets mostly, but it was ignored, then finally he came himself to tell it, to show it, to live it, and yet, it was still largely ignored, but for the Church he left behind, invested still with his life daily—though still largely ignored—even by his Church who counts angels upon needles and wonders if conception is really the beginning of human life.

The Great Story remains unfinished, yet God created us, in his image, for life in the eternal garden of the newly created earth, radiant with glorious life, beauty, and joy; but we failed him.

He called from among us, from among the dark pagan world, a people chosen to bring us all to eternal life, but they failed him.

He came among us himself, teaching with his divine power and living his human life and finally the truth came to earth and stayed, built upon the rock of Peter, restoring us still.

Evil in the World

The churning and turning of demographic trends due to some catastrophe or generational evil is as ancient as the earth and they will always continue as the prince of the world works his ways and we fall prey to them again and again.

Some scholars look at the demographics of prisons and conclude that the fact of a disproportionate number from one group or another defines the system as corrupt; while criminals know that the demographics only portray the increased opportunity to become a criminal in an environment where so many already have chosen the exciting and remunerative path to success criminality represents.

Our hope is always in the Lord and in his Church and in our own hearts yearning for freedom and eternal life, and we will endure till the end of time, for the war has already been won by Christ Jesus, though we still fight the battles of the cross every day.

Satan's involvement in evil has been clearly stated by the Church since the beginning and remains so.

Satan, after being thrown from heaven and falling to the world, was allowed to be the prince of this world, bringing evil into it, realized through the original temptation of Eve and the proto murder of Abel, but with the coming of Christ he was conquered.

It is in the Book of Job that we see the interaction between God and Satan around the human will, which Satan wants to destroy, and his sin that had him cast from heaven; which I think is that Satan wanted the humans to be forced to be good but God gave us free will, reflecting his nature and that of all heaven.

What is a wonder is not that evil runs rampant in the world, but that good still triumphs, not that criminals shape the culture of the world, but that saints subdue it, not that we are always tempted by it, but that we mostly resist it, not that we give in to it, but that we seek redemption when we do.

The perfect world for the predator is a world without protection for the innocent—states unwilling to declare war or use capital punishment—a world where there is literally no sin, all is relative; and if you do not know that the prince of the world is behind this way of thinking, you do not *know*.

There are those who have thought that the route to good, to saintliness, to enlightenment, is through the path of evil, coming to intimately know its shadow life and sensual reality to break through its tempting power to reach the Holy Grail.

There are those who have traveled this path and have learned, after deep sojourns into the criminal world of evil, that the suffering coming from the resulting soul-scarring and the depth of knowledge learned in those dark paths is certainly most valuable—though not necessarily in the pursuit of saintliness—but in the teaching of others discovering the eternal terror that lies in the future of one continuing down that path, and it is surely down, deeply down.

You cannot know evil by seeing it, by fighting it, by containing it, but only by doing it; for it is first being, then comes knowing.

If you don't know the power of evil, it is difficult to choose, with conviction, the greater power of good, which has to be known, not surmised.

The value of evil is the value of the good that can come from it, and the weapon those surviving evil unto redemption have to help those still caught by it—is a fiery sword wielded directly against Satan—and through the words of Catholic social teaching and the deep sharpening of daily suiting up in the armor of God, giving holy fire to its blade, creating the fiery sword through which souls can be saved.

Traditional rehabilitative programs for criminals rely on providing service to address specific needs the reentering criminal has, and it is in this very connection (service to need) that the larger truth of criminality is over-looked.

Criminality, in its professional sense of committing crime for money, is chosen, and the choice comes from an internal array of experience that sees no or little value—other than when sanctioned—to choose another way.

Somewhere around the middle of the 20ᵗʰ Century, Catholics quit talking about evil and Satan grew stronger.

Oh indeed, the scattered pieces of the great Church still murmured a bit about evil and Satan, but they had no weapons against it, so what did it matter?

And most of the Catholic priests were long ago silent with only Peter able to still see its markings clear.

Wars are as much a part of human history as crime and violence, and the attempts by the historically unwary to develop a pattern of thinking and behavior that they assume will result in world peace is not the best way to spend one's time, for the kingdom of heaven is not of this world.

A characteristic that appears to be present in the folks who spend their time resisting those social institutions in our country that are largely operating under the mantle of our society's responsibility to protect—whether their resistance involves working to shut down military installations, ban capital punishment, or release most criminals from prison—is a clear unawareness of the reality of evil, and for Catholics, who have at their fingertips, within the deep well of the magisterium, the most developed intellectual and spiritual resources concerning the work of the prince of this world available anywhere, that is inexcusable.

So often heresy occurs when dissenters try to create absolutes when contingency is needed, and create contingency when absolutes are needed; or they just go backwards.

Christ needed Dismas—who had protected him before as the *First Gospel of the Infancy of Jesus Christ* teaches—

and more than a few criminals had a good heart as did Dismas.

And I have dreamt that God, promising that the gates of hell would not prevail, created the Order of Dismas, knights from the gates to ensure they were closed about the Church, the Order of the Good Thief keeping the underworld from being an open door to the gates of hell.

After Christ's crucifixion, when he took Dismas with him to hell, but returned three days later in his resurrection, he left Dismas in hell, the criminal saint strong enough to save criminal souls.

The Order of Dismas is the final bulwark of redemption.

There is time enough to contemplate the vision from St. Dismas, of an underworld where resistance to the evil one was as strong as the submission, and it was only from us, penitential professional criminals—with transformed hearts and deeply armored with daily communion with God—yet familiar with the darkest joys of the criminal world and the deepest pits of the carceral, but with the strength of spirit to defy the will of the evil one in his natural home.

God allows evil to exist because we must have the choice to choose evil, otherwise what value is free will if the world is only good.

As we do this and as we reflect upon our doing, we see how important justice is to our work, how important that profit not drive our activity—harming the souls of transforming criminals and their potential and opportunities for life and happiness—but adding to that, growing it as the soundest profit of all.

Reflection and prayer, so necessary to the capitalist, to the professional, to the public servant, to the apostolate so that power so widely wielded may not harm another but always help.

In the economic arena where so much has gone wrong for so long and where the deception of liberation theology and its denying God as redemptive source and claiming Marxism as the way, led so many of the faithful astray— still so.

Sinai and Golgotha have forged the great link of solidarity between old and new, forged in those three days and blood seals.

Sinners become saints, and transformed criminals warring against evil, carry heavy armor into that war, deep scars of the internal battles waged in the steel and stone of prisons and the candelabra streets of the city nights.

Yet we wander in our helping ways often blindly, we follow where we do not know, we are called and we must go, each day, each enraged and evil soul to calm and transform. It is why we are here, it is what we are made to be, what we are made to do.

As the Sabbath is traditionally consecrated for good works, those whose work is an apostolate of transforming criminals, consecrate every day to it. How do we consecrate ourselves to continually receive the grace that underlies the power of good works, to continually struggle against the indifference of others, the suffering that deadens the will to grow, and the pain that stifles the spirit?

C.S. Lewis said that the greatest success of the devil was to have convinced people he didn't exist, but we have seen his works and we know that he exists.

Having once embraced evil but then awakening through the Church and God's grace, seeing and grasping the light, beginning the transformative process, walking again as a child in the sunlight, resolutely finding our way, until we know that our work has only just begun, that now it is the criminals still among us that we must help.

We are armed with the cruel hardness of our experience and the sharp edge of our salvation and the knowledge of walking in the light.

We were lost and now we are found, who but to us does the battle fall?

Life in the World

God is the fount of our perfection and provides the grace for the path but we are the instrument upon which the symphony of Christ's sacrifice is universalized.

Life is eternal life—which must be our only horizon in our daily life—and that of the world is the ground where we determine where our eternal life shall be lived, in heaven or hell.

The desert fathers felt their choice of life in the desert would put them on a ground of less temptation, thereby bringing them closer to an eternal heavenly life, and their prayers and powerful spiritual development did that, while blessing all others to whom their prayers were offered.

Our time on earth is choosing eternity—either of fire and pain or warmth and joy—it is as if we are preparing for the day, choosing what we will wear and from our closet, take the garments we'll wear forevermore—that brief moment at our closet door is an eternity compared to real eternal time and the life we choose therein from our work in the world.

Christ drove the moneychangers from the temple because they reversed the natural order of things; for it is the reality of the temple that should flow out into the world, not the reality of the world into the temple.

The priests had given away their calling and became part of the world, and it was this which called forth God's personal anger and its physical manifestations; as he would today if he was upon the earth in human form and entered the Church, and saw the great filth there from which Peter draws such shame, and from where he, Christ Jesus, would whip the pedophile priests and the bishops who moved them around like chess pieces, into the dark night and the deep ocean which they had called upon themselves, sinking with the great millstone about their necks, pulling them down into the hell they had created in the hearts of the little ones.

The world values the cold, calculating, bureaucratic precision that can dispatch life and treasure in pursuit of an organizational imperative with emotional and moral impunity and this calculus is woven into criminal world choices where death, maiming, or prison awaits failure.

How often we forget, in our fear of Satan as prince of this world, that our call to the apostolate is a call to always advance the world towards the Kingdom of Heaven the world is always, inexorably, becoming.

In this sense, the basic thread of liberation theology—faith without works is dead—is correct, merely writ large for our time in that place of tyrants.

There is no war between good and evil in the world, because God triumphed on the cross, but there is always one in the human soul struggling against the lies of Satan; which we effectively armor ourselves against by continual praying, the everyday practice of Mass, morning prayers, communion, midday prayers, praying the rosary, examination of conscience, resolutions, evening prayers, sacrifices and mortification—this daily practice renders the battle won when done with a humble heart, courageous will, and joyous soul.

As the solution for labor is the union, the solution to crime is the reformed criminal.

The great and constant call from the Church to serve God is not as much about service as it is about humility for us—a creature too often assuming we 'are as gods'—and while serving others as if they are God/Christ is a cross lightly borne.

Each of us is an instrument in the great symphony of the Kingdom of Heaven where the Trinity conducts, and our task is to learn to read the music, determining our places, our rhythm and rhyme; taking the Good News to whom God has called us to serve.

Learning about the great heresies, perhaps starting with the 1938 book, *The Great Heresies* by Hilaire Belloc, will define the enemies of the Church in this world and help us—along with our work helping one another—help the Church in her eternal struggle against them.

The greatest heresy, whose spread was and is still, by the sword, will only be defeated by the sword and it is not to the soft Catholics that chore falls, but to the hard, the men of steel and stone, the men whose transformation from evil to good has not removed their ability to fight with the blade.

Being involved in the politics of the time is crucial; to not only remain aware of the signs of the times, but to be able to support those political movements and leaders who best represent Catholic social teaching.

A great charge to us is to better our world, to be useful and to serve; to create more abundance for our fellow human beings, to care for and nourish the ground upon which we stand together by being gardeners of the soil of human fulfillment, to be just and loving in our dealings with others, and to always stand on truth, our final and greatest friend, guided by the loving hands of God.

Being friends with the truth embedded in Catholic social teaching is to *"Go with Peter, to Christ, through Mary"*, the guiding principle arching over the truth of the teaching, wedded to scripture through tradition, centuries of reflection and the Virgin Mother's appearances to us, such as the crowning one of Fatima.

Through this lens, and through this practice, the social teaching makes its way into our lives, embroidered and filled out through the papal encyclicals, a clear trajectory of correct practice informing us now.

Being friends with truth is in knowing the absolute centrality of human beings within creation, in knowing innocent life absolutely must be protected, in knowing all things are possible through God and even the darkest soul can discover the light.

Then, here is our ultimate friend, this truth we seek and for which, in this complex and modern world where appearance shades reality, calls us to even deeper searching.

He awaits our call for guidance; whose word has guided the millennia guides us still, as prevalent now and as fresh as when written on ancient parchment in ancient times, but a breath in God's mystery for us.

He has died, He is risen, He shall come again.

Life in the Church

Real time is eternal time, and real religion—the theology of the real—is built upon it. False time is human time and false religion is built upon it.

The architecture of the Church, from ancient times, reflects the embrace of God, who is represented in the Tridentine Mass by the People of God facing Him who embraces them as they embrace Him, while the new mass confuses still as the embrace often seems to be the people embracing the priest, the priest embracing the people, and God floats behind the priest, watching; and in front of the people, waiting.

The ancient material architecture reinforces the spiritual architecture, from a point above to the people below, the great hierarchy moves through space and time, creating a holy cathedral of our sacramental lives.

The ancient hierarchy is absolute as the truth is absolute and together they embody the material and spiritual architecture.

Christ made the covenant with Peter and the People of God:

> **[Matthew 16:18]** And I tell thee this in my turn, that thou art Peter, and it is upon this rock that I will build my church; and the gates of hell shall not prevail against it.

It is to Peter and the universal catechisms brought forth under his authority—*Catechism of the Council of Trent* under Pope Pius V and the *Catechism of the Catholic Church* under Pope John Paul II—that we need look for teaching authority as it is Peter who is the rock the Church is built upon.

The institutional church is a bureaucracy and that bureaucracy stretches from parish to the Vatican and by its nature—governance by the interiority of bureaucracies, so tragically seen during the sexual abuse crisis in the United States—is easily corrupted and seeking teaching authority from it can lead us astray, while Peter will not.

In this time of the internet we are fortunate to have at our fingertips access to the Vatican and Peter for it is a simple matter to refresh ourselves at the Rock as often as needed.

Today we can visit with Peter each day, and from his comings and goings draw solace and truth to armor us in our communion path.

Much of the life in the Church is dealing with the continual attacks by Satan on the Church, so often embedded in the frothy language of crowd appeal or directed toward human pride, the various ideologies that have attempted to destroy the Church over the past few centuries range from those of socialism, relativism, new age religions, ecological spirituality; but all come from the ancient revolt of Gnosticism, that the truth is held in secret, by initiates, by an elite who can share bits and pieces of it with the common folk, but the folk cannot reach the depth and breadth of it alone.

Revealed truth is housed openly in the Church and the more deeply we study its precepts, the more joyful we become, as it continues to unfold itself before our eyes, resonating within our heart and mind and spirit.

To the Buddhist, suffering cannot be stopped, all one can do it detach from it, indeed that is the best one can do.

To the Catholic, suffering can be transformed into exaltation.

The criminal, having rejected religion—civic, pagan, monotheistic—is essentially a nihilist, but can, through the carceral experience, find remorse and seek penance.

To the penitential criminal, the work that will be effective in the transformation of criminals will come from the grassroots community organizations developed and led by penitential and transformed criminals, who are deep knowledge leaders of efforts that have much in common with those that proved successful working with the poor through small groups in Latin America as part of the Liberation Theology movement.

To the institutional Catholic Church we would ask if the preferential option for the poor applies to penitential criminals.

Does this describe criminals? No and yes. No, while they are still active criminals because they wait for nothing, as do the poor, but take what they want, and rather than often being robbed by unjust laws, as are the poor, it is they who rob the innocent.

But yes, as penitential criminals, they become statistics, and stand before the halls of society waiting for admittance which never comes, and they are forevermore excluded.

The need for the Church within the criminal world is great now, as prisons—the universities and cathedrals of crime—have grown so massive that their underworld is shaping upperworld to a degree not seen since the darkest days of paganism, when Christ was compelled to come.

In the saying yes to the prince of this world, the criminal learns the ways of the predator, and becoming predators, have reason to be aware of the habits of their prey—who rarely know they are such—thus feeling no reason to become as they are, to rehabilitate.

In this sense, in most encounters between the two—particularly within the traditional rehabilitative field—the predator usually triumphs.

The Catholic Church in America is, as it pertains to coherent institutional support for the magisterium, in lax condition. As a result of many factors, but culminating in the sexual abuse tragedy, which itself is part of a larger loss of faith by the American bishops and priests, the points of interaction within the public square—almost all within the arena of the Church's social teaching—have almost all been dictated by the secular world.

Whether it involves the issues—abortion, euthanasia, capital punishment or war—the American institutional Church has virtually become the handmaid of the world rather than the bride of Christ, and the innocent faithful have paid the most horrific price as they, their families, and their parish communities have been corrosively degraded by corrupt priests and bishops.

Yet, among the ruins, the promise of our Lord that the gates of hell shall not prevail, must give us strength—the innocent faithful, the steadfast bishops and priests—to continue to speak out through the great apostolate work in protection of Christ's bride.

With Peter, to Christ, through Mary, for the Greater Glory of God

The Church existed before creation, the divine dream of a communion with God and human freely entered into from a world where the divine is rarely evident and evil is the rule of the world. Satan is its prince and humans are like Job scourged by devils at fever pitch, yet in that earthly fire and sensual passion, remains, after discovering it—a true holding to the still small voice of love—a true holding to God—a true holding to the eternal Church.

Honor has been largely lost in the world, largely lost in the priests of the Church, but it still reigns in the hearts of people of good will, with Peter and the teaching of the Church.

The clerical sexual abuse is incest as the celibate bound fathers who seduce the faithful are seducing their children, the children of the family of the Church.

The theologians are too often politicians and it takes the professional amateurs like Belloc or Chesterton to speak the truth clearly, again reinforcing the apostolate of the laity.

It is not about obedience, but love of our birthright of divinity, of our divine connection to our creator as his adopted sons and daughters.

Obedience is what Satan proposes, obedience to sin and it is for slaves; love is God's hope and it is for saints, angels, and human beings.

It begins by helping the stranger, being the Good Samaritan, who saw not a member of an enemy tribe but a human being. Before Christ, among tribal cultures, strangers were enemies. His teaching of praying for our enemy was a profound idea and still is. Witness Pope John Paul II visiting the man who attempted to assassinate him and forgiving him, witness the Vatican's plea that the tyrant of Iraq, Saddam Hussein, soon after being captured and photographed disheveled and dirty in the hospital where he was taken, be treated with dignity and respect.

Loving our neighbors and praying for our enemies can only be done freely. Grassroots nonprofits help freely and donors support them freely. It is the best arrangement and congruent with the principle of subsidiarity. In this way the role of government is to act as a facilitator of technical and financial resources to help grassroots organizations, who have the embedded community expertise, to do the work of personal transformation.

The social doctrine of the Catholic Church revolves about this interaction of one person with another, with preference for the poor, the marginal, the suffering. This essential human relationship with one another and with our Creator is where our work of transformation begins and ends; a transformational work largely oral, from mouth to heart, rather than textual, which supports but should not lead.

Capital Punishment

In the Great Commandment we have the whole of the Law, which cannot be changed; and love of neighbor means protecting the innocent against the aggressor; the divine justification of capital punishment and just war; neither of which can ever be changed within the Church—for they are doctrine expressed, verbally and through his actions, by Christ—though there is a current effort to do so.

Capital punishment is a central aspect of the social teaching of the Church in relation to the work of the Lampstand Foundation in the transformation of criminals, as it is the ultimate criminal sanction, and has been since ancient times a bulwark of the teaching of the Church regarding the protection of the innocent against the aggressor. One of the strongest statements from Christ concerning capital punishment is:

> **[Matthew 18:6]** And if anyone hurts the conscience of one of these little ones, that believe in me, he had better have been drowned in the depths of the sea, with a mill-stone hung about his neck.

Saint Augustine, St. Thomas Aquinas, the *Catechism of the Council of Trent* and the current *Catechism of the Catholic Church*, all continue that support.

The strength of the social teaching to transform criminals is in its eternal congruence—what was always true is true still—and God clearly mandated capital punishment as a just response to deep evil under the Old Covenant, which nothing in the New Covenant countermanded, regardless of the attempts to do so under some ill-defined spirit of the age argument which, even in its proffering, cuts at the rock of traditional truth.

Capital punishment is a rooted part of the Church's long advocated protection of the innocent against the aggressor,

182

whether through the abortion and euthanasia prohibition or the principles of just war.

It is a central element in the responsibility to protect—embraced by the prayer given to us, the *Our Father*—and carried forward into time by Peter.

The deep wonder is that Peter, though he may even be a sinful man, cannot destroy the Church, for Christ promised its survival, even unto the gates of hell.

Politics and public policy—and how they blend—has been difficult for the Catholic faithful for years, and the issues surrounding the political factions of the Catholic Church in the United States (generally divided by the level of congruence to the magisterium on the issue of abortion) are worth exploring.

The documents of the magisterium, because they have been written for the Church Universal are couched in intellectually subtle terms that are widely embracing, while still revealing to the attentive reader the narrow path.

Consequently, the documents can often lend support to those who find reason to conflate being against capital punishment (which the Church is not) to being against abortion (which the Church is).

There has always been a call for an end to the use of capital punishment—recently it is based primarily on statements by Popes John Paul II, Benedict and Francis—when other means, like the maximum security prison or super-max, can be used to protect the innocent from the aggressor, but this call has been built on a lack of understanding of the Catholic historic record regarding criminal justice issues and the understanding among criminal justice professionals that even within the confines of a maximum security prison or super-max, criminals are still able to influence aggression against the innocent.

Those calling for the end of capital punishment are often handicapped in presenting a proper analysis of criminal justice, as can be seen in their failure to properly understand the hard reality of the deep involvement of Satan in the criminal world, and could it be any more obvious that within the darkest bowels of our nation's prisons the animating visage is that of the devil.

Too many fail to face Satan and his works, but excuse away and become mere apologists for criminal behavior, rather than realizing it for what it often is, the work of the devil; and thus does he continue his greatest deception, of continuing the lie that he does not even exist.

Not knowing the lengths bad people will go to in pursuit of evil has long plagued the perspective of people of good will. However, it is a fundamental strength of the perspective of reformed criminals with a long sojourn in the criminal world and maximum security prisons to not be so plagued.

This great difficulty in experientially understanding the darkness of evil motivates the intentions of Catholics, whose traditional teaching has provided them the intellectual information and spiritual tools capable of countering it, who nevertheless, wish to abolish capital punishment.

In the struggle between good and evil the world only wins by its own values, but in eternal time the good triumphed long ago, and in the perspective we bring to the importance of retaining the option of capital punishment, we need to see the horizon of eternity and the knowledge of hell.

One of the portals Satan seeks to enter to weaken the Church is that of protecting the innocent life, and unfortunately, he often is helped by Catholics who do not understand the connection between the traditional support of the Church for capital punishment and its traditional censure of abortion.

By conflating life issues such as abortion, euthanasia, war, and capital punishment, they conflate the innocence of the pre-born, the elderly, and disabled, with the evil of the aggressor who has destroyed innocent life and has been justly condemned by lawful civil authorities, rendering unto Caesar which is his.

Banning capital punishment within the Catholic Church could very well be a stalking horse for approving abortion within the Catholic Church.

The weakening of the social prohibition of abortion also weakens that of murder to the point even the progressively self-defined members of the Catholic Church justify saying that nothing any longer calls for the ultimate punishment; a tradition that is as ancient as the church.

If the abolition of capital punishment succeeds, the responsibility of the evil doer to suffer punishment befitting the evil done, and the opportunity to be saved from the eternal torments of hell, has also been lost, and the further step of removing personal responsibility from those who commit the evil of abortion, euthanasia, and unjust war, begins to lose its moral standing.

Those Catholic professionals within the social science field, informed by Catholic teaching and with a professional knowledge of criminal justice issues and a deeper understanding of the hand of Satan within the criminal world, are clearer in their development of the doctrine.

The Church's traditional support for capital punishment— validated in Catholic teaching for millennia—is based on the assumption of the reality of evil (which the relativist thinking secular world, clearly influencing the Church in the West, struggles to accept) that some offenses are so terrible that the only just and charitable response is to consign the evil doer to hell, and hope that within that definite period of earthly life he now knows, after being sentenced to death, remains to him, he will be spurred to seek forgiveness.

The transition from traditional documents to new isn't one of languishing support for capital punishment but of language, and it is more sadly held as a regrettable aspect of human and Church history that none find joy or glory in its promotion.

The difference between the old *Roman Catechism*, the first edition of the current *Catechism* and the second edition of the current *Catechism of the Catholic Church* reflects modern language sensitivity—part of the modernist, relativist age we live in and not all bad—that treats difficult subjects with a subtle deference to compassion for the inevitability of our sin; but there has been no change in doctrine, nor the traditional support of the Church for capital punishment.

The proper response to evil is punishment—appropriately found in Hell—and capital punishment speeds that consequence while human mercy delays God's judgment, so clearly stated by Christ with the millstone statement in

> **[Matthew 18:6]** And if anyone hurts the conscience of one of these little ones, that believe in me, he had better have been drowned in the depths of the sea, with a mill-stone hung about his neck.

And this was a form of capital punishment used in that time by the Greeks, Syrians and Romans.

During the period of the 1960's through the 1980's, certain religious orders, cardinals, bishops, and priests of the Catholic Church—particularly in the Americas—became enamored of Marxist-inspired Liberation Theology and informed by its anti-capitalism, absorbed the corresponding attributes of restricting the power of capitalistic countries, including their legal and military power, resulting in strong anti-war and anti-capital punishment movements.

This perspective bled into the arguments incorporated in the formation of the current, *Second Edition of the Catechism*, watering down, particularly in those two areas, the historic clarity the Catholic Church had presented to the world regarding capital punishment.

As the Church now beats back the minor degradation of Church doctrine influenced by Liberation Theology—a battle still joined—the clarity should return, particularly around the issues of protecting the life of the innocent through the just use of war and capital punishment.

There are many reasons for concern in this 'language sensitivity', chief being the relative lack of knowledge of criminal justice issues, in the claim that the super-max prison can forever restrain the aggressor, yet those in the criminal justice field know how easily the imprisoned aggressor—even within super-max or death row—can act against those innocents outside of prison.

When we add to this language sensitivity, the terrible disruption of the sexual scandal the Church began experiencing during that period, though not becoming public until much later, the unraveling of even the settled language, and the rearrangement of the dogmatic expression emanating from the Second Vatican Council, it is a wonder that as much of the hard truths that sustained the Church for the millennia, survived as strongly expressed as they have.

And this confusion was only compounded by the lack of leadership, resulting from the corruption of the sexual scandal, of those most responsible for providing teaching to the Church around the social teaching issues.

Along with this degraded leadership, another weakness in the United States Catholic approach to capital punishment and other criminal justice issues is—as mentioned—a lack of professional knowledge from the field and an understanding of the Church's historic work around punishment and prisons.

Recently however, there are encouraging developments for a deeper understanding of criminal justice, social science, and Catholic historic contributions to it; one major contribution being the *Encyclopedia of Catholic Social Thought, Social Science, and Social Policy*, in a 2 volume set published in 2007 and with a supplement volume 3 published in 2012

It is from the examination of protecting society from convicted criminals that we consider the proper use of capital punishment as a legitimate sanction for serial pedophiles and serial rapists.

There is an aspect here that connects to the Just War doctrine, where it is the moral stance around the violence inherent in wars of many against many, where this addresses the violence within the war of the few against many and the many against the few.

Perhaps what is most marked about the position of the social teaching in the United States—and many others who study it—is the generally accepted assumption that the Church's work in this area began with the 1891 encyclical of Pope Leo XIII.

The difficulty with relying on this perception is that much of the foundational work of the social teaching—coming from the Old Testament and medieval sources—is not factored in, resulting in a skewed result.

This is particularly true with capital punishment, prisons, and punishment in general, which saw much of its most articulate principles developed during those periods, well documented by the work of Rodger Charles S.J. and Dr. Andrew Skotnicki.

We see a break with that tradition, for instance, in the publication of the United States Conference of Catholic Bishops *United States Catholic Catechism for Adults* in 2006, where the Bishops validated their earlier statements that capital punishment "cannot be justified".

The divergence here is a reminder that we should look to tradition, the Bishops of Rome and the universal *Catechisms*—Trent & Vatican II—for resolution when questions arise around interpretation.

For much of human history, the social value of human beings in the pagan world was barely above that of material objects, and this extreme devaluing of persons influenced the development of the practice around capital punishment.

With the moral development of the Judeo-Christian world the value of individual human beings increased and those of the innocent even more so, reflected by their protection in the law through the use of capital punishment.

In our reflections on the social teaching we want to use our historical perspective with a realization of the evolving nature of the teaching in relation to that of social development.

We see this played out in the teaching around capital punishment, as the Old Testament and the teachings of the medieval Fathers describe many occasions when it may be applied, yet it has developed such that today it is called for rarely.

The new language of the Church in the Vatican II *Catechism*—while perhaps a bit sensitive—has the right pitch, expressing great compassion for the executed, as is proper, while clearly retaining the authority to execute, and this is congruent with the Church's thinking around the development of doctrine.

God was very clear in what he revealed, both at Sinai and soon after his transfiguration when he taught his disciples about scandal, that the death of the evil doer is often justified when the physical or spiritual life of the innocent is involved.

The entire tradition of the Church has always and continues to support the use of capital punishment, and yet, we should always use it carefully, compassionately, justly, and treating even the evil doer with the dignity and respect his humanity has received from God.

The protection of the innocent grounds respect for human life on four pillars; 1) Protecting babies within the womb—as Christ was protected within Mary's blessed womb—and it requires all legal action to the point of passing a constitutional amendment banning abortion except through rape or to protect the life of the mother. 2) Protecting the individual from the criminal aggressor, requiring all legal restraint to the point of taking the life of the aggressor if it is the only way to protect the innocent. 3) Protecting the nation from the criminal nation, requiring going to war to protect the nation from a direct threat, even if that threat is only verbal but comes from a nation possessing weapons of mass destruction. 4) Protecting the aged, sick, and disabled from euthanasia, requiring all legal restraint to the point of passing a constitutional amendment banning euthanasia.

What greater love for the deeply evil than to specify, through a date certain to the minute—of the ending of a ruinous life—so that redemption can be sought for the eternal salvation God promises to the penitential sinner.

But the state, with endless delays, reaching to the final minutes over and over again removes this certainty and allows Satan the final say as the evil doer resists the penance in the realistic hope of yet another delay.

We are bound, as Catholics, from the very beginning, to protect the innocent from the aggressor, and when he comes for the children, we are all holy knights of the cross, ready to lay down our life fighting for the children. When he, the aggressor, came in America, he was a prince and a priest of the Church and he ravished the children for years and we did nothing, and he still sits in the bishop's chair, and the great millstone awaits his passing and it will drag him into the deepest depth of the fire seas of hell.

So, as we come to the end of our journey through the 5th commandment, the great *not* in the Great Commandment of neighborly love, we know that for sound guidance and the final word, we must look to tradition, to Scripture, to the Holy Fathers, to the Holy See throughout time, we must look to the center, for truly, the center holds.

The adversary is eternally patient, knowing man's fallen nature eventually turns his way, and the human creature, rather than standing clearly in the revealed truth of the ancient revelation animating the Church, bends to the spirit of the times, embraces the world and loses site of eternity; loses sight that from time immemorial justice has demanded the gravest punishment for the gravest sin; and in the spirit of the age lends his human agency in the remorseless pulling of a foundation stone from the eternal tabernacle; giving the tiniest—but just enough—entrance to the slithering serpent.

Beyond Liberation Theology

When I began, sometime after my final release from prison in 1969, to examine the world and my life from the eyes of freedom, I did not know that I was still using my criminal mind—with its perspective that evil is relative—and I embraced Marxism; which is profoundly evil and deeply criminal, as it represents a complete rejection of God, promoting the concept that man alone determines the ultimate reality and indeed, can create heaven on earth.

That concept entered the Church as liberation theology.

Liberation theology arose from the reflections of a Catholic priest in Peru—Fr. Gustavo Gutierrez—struggling with how he could comfort his parishioners who were oppressed by the predatory government common to Latin America during most of its history. His essential concept was the encouragement to parishioners that they form small church groups to support each other, develop their own solutions, become their own leaders, and work for change.

This concept was adopted and expanded by Marxist oriented Catholics—laity and priests, many of whom became involved in the various revolutionary movements in the region—to mean that the central work of the Church is the poor, leading to a major crisis of the Church in the last century which Pope Benedict as Cardinal Ratzinger spent much time on when Prefect of the Congregation for the Doctrine of the Faith.

Liberation theology has been used by many in the Church to address criminal behavior for several decades. However, in its Marxist orientation it has caused more harm than good, as it has focused attention on structural social deficiencies rather than individual responsibility—external causation rather than internal choice and defining the criminal as the oppressed—leading many people down dead-end streets seeking solutions while the problem deepens.

Going beyond liberation theology is in the development of criminal world leadership who will speak for, and create solutions for, themselves, freed from the self-contradictory Marxist core of liberation theology.

Going beyond liberation theology is realizing that there is no oppressor the criminal seeks relief from, for he is the oppressor.

Going beyond liberation theology is realizing that the only true liberation is from the greatest lie ever imagined to the greatest story ever told and while the great lie appears graspable and silkily real to touch, the Great Story only begins in a yearning hardly comprehended until the plot is unraveled, marked, and reformulated to fill the criminal's yearning soul.

The criminal seeking God—having already embraced the world and found promise in it—can only comprehend a God verifiable objectively, a God found in the prince of the world, seemingly concrete, solid and real as the sensuality of hedonism.

This path of liberation can only be *discovered* by the completely imprisoned criminal, for no criminal not so enmeshed can appreciate acceptance of eternity through the working of each day; but it can be only fully *practiced* by the completely free criminal, for no criminal having discovered true liberation can forever run from it.

Liberation theology began as a reflection on "faith without works is dead." Our Catholic faith, our baptism, our communion, is a reaffirmation that we are part of the People of God, working to bring others into the Kingdom of God, in the knowledge that Catholics with well-formed consciences will work for a better world and a singular aspect of a better world involves bringing our faith into the public square, voting it, expressing it, even to the point of personal danger, which in the cause of Christ—we are called to accept.

Going beyond liberation theology in the transformation of criminals is grasping the understanding that *true doing* can only follow *true being*.

Going beyond liberation theology is grasping the understanding that only one true theology exists and it is the theology of the real, the theology of the supernatural Catholic Church, ancient, wise, and eternal.

The eternal foundation upon which the Church rests is the sacredness of each real human life; not in the abstract, but in the specific sense of a real individual human being.

This foundation of the Church finds fulfillment in the summit of the Church during the daily Mass; where Christ enters again into each faithful human being during the real Eucharistic celebration.

This foundation also animates the international and traditional posture of the Church in the political arena through its eternal and very real responsibility to protect the innocent; whether through the call for the protection of the unborn, or through the violent exercise of a just war, or the legally proscribed use of capital punishment; and where the real political stance of the abortionists or the pacifistic stance of the war and capital punishment abolitionists is an assault upon the foundation and the summit.

Within the founding spirit of the United States, the overwhelming focus is on the protection of human dignity, human freedom, and religious freedom; powerful marks for a great power to assume and very congruent with those of the other great power in the world—and the only real power capable of truly defeating the prince of this world— the Church Christ founded upon the rock of Peter.

A stranger is helped best by a friend. The deep knowledge leader is from the community of the stranger, but has become transformed. He knows the secrets of the stranger and now transformed, stands ready to help as a friend. When he becomes educated and credentialed, the formation of competence, he helps as a professional friend.

The solution is within the problem.

Subsidiarity asks that problems are best dealt with closest to their source. While social currents may affect the environment of social problems, it is the purely personal where we see most clearly their effect.

Helping the stranger means helping their struggle against their inclination to harm themselves, and this brings us into work of great peril, moment, and consequence, where the best guide is often someone having already trod the path.

Working within suffering redeemed is where spiritual power grows, and those who are called to work selflessly to help others, often at dizzying hourly days, are resolute. They get tired, sometimes to their very bones, but they are working within a power which is inexhaustible.

The great transformational saints of the streets, all of those known and unknown, realize that what keeps them strong in the face of the great suffering they see daily is the Christ they see in every human face.

Each day of their work is filled with the pain of others, each day of fatigue and silent weeping at the struggle to remain whole, each day on the cross grows the strength and endurance that is the stuff saints are made of.

Transformation is personal, based on love and surrender. For grassroots leaders it is the love of the other; surrendering to that love, and in their passion for seeing joy overwhelm suffering, they are transformed by the work.

The founding stone of Catholic social teaching is the right to life for all human beings and all that entails; the right to the means to maintain life, to secure work and sustenance according to individual talent and need, to educate ourselves to our potential, to associate with whom we wish, coming together to advocate for social change, and the right to dignity and justice.

We know this exists but rarely upon earth—yet knowing it is inalienably due each of us as creatures of God—can irrevocably ground our work and give it the strength of divine truth none can question.

We are called to learn the root of these rights, and this is a duty which inalienable rights demand we shoulder; to learn, to study, and to grasp the shaded meanings and clarity of purpose upon which our work with others stands.

The Interior Journey, Deep Knowledge

It is a long and often dark way, but the promise of light and freedom sparkling bright beyond me, eternally present, pulls me forward.

Deep knowledge is the congruence of experiential knowledge, academic and professional learning; grounded and informed by extended study in the social teaching of the Catholic Church and participating in her sacramental life.

Deep knowledge is the knowledge arising from the informed thought that comes from *being—being* preceding *knowing.*

Being a child of God, being a child of the Church— breathing with the Church—within the apostolate God established for you before time began, and learning all that can be learned from the world about the work of your apostolate; so that it infuses your *being,* that is deep knowledge.

Why is the one who is lost, the prodigal son, so valuable to Christ?

Why is lost important?

Is it the supreme value placed on each person, or is it what the recovery of the lost returns to the whole, perhaps both?

The professional criminal, the battle-hardened soldier, the veteran street cop; each share an intimate knowledge of evil that even intellectual pyrotechnics cannot dislodge, and if they are Catholic and if they are coupling this experiential knowledge with that from the academy, professional training, a continual study of Catholic social teaching, and, applied to work for the common good connected to their life—this is deep knowledge and they can draw from this well, replenished with prayer, liturgy and contemplation, to bring many souls from Satan's grasp to Christ's Church.

The deepest knowledge of all is the practice of the Church—where the saints aborning walk—within the church, daily communion, daily rosary, daily examination and prayers unceasing.

Daily Practice

Our soul, like a tuning fork, becomes congruent with God through daily practice and a daily life informed by that practice. Christ comes daily; let us go to meet him.

The transformation of criminals is work of great spiritual peril, and the transformed criminal aspiring to a community leadership role has to accept certain minimal experiential requirements that will counteract the reality of his criminal/carceral world experience with that of communal world experience; by having lived ten years out of prison and already helping the community; having obtained a graduate college degree; and being married to another Catholic.

He also has to daily reach for the deepest knowledge of all, which is the knowledge gained from continuous communion with God; the continual prayer and daily practice set forth by the reach for perfection to which each are called through our baptism and communion within the Kingdom of God.

In olden times, the paths humans made to travel here and there were made by human feet, traveling the same way through the forest and over the plain as the day and year before, and as the years deepened the path, it became a hardened way that remained for guidance through the woods and mountains to the way home.

As it is with our own path, made daily through the rituals established by the Church to feed her saints and priests the food divine—morning prayer, communion, midday angelus, praying the rosary, evening prayer, examination of conscience, sacrifices to the Church, to God, to Peter, fighting against sin and building virtue; and through this daily practice, the armor of God is slowly crafted as the penitential, transformed criminal aspiring to community leadership—for whom this is a vital journey of lifetime penance from the years of harm caused to others through his criminality—enters into the hardened path of the priestly soul and saintly temperament on the long journey home.

I was baptized in 2004, so am still in the process of learning about this universal community stretching through eons of time and encompassing so much temporal and spiritual space.

For many months the glow from my baptism carried me happily along in the observance of the sacramental life of the Church so familiar to Cradle Catholics, attending Sunday Mass regularly, supporting the Church, blending many of the rituals around the liturgical seasons into our daily life; but then as the glow from the baptism wore somewhat off I encountered a period of spiritual dryness.

My spiritual dryness came largely from the increased reading and study of Catholic life in the United States and around the world. I began to see the human failures and satanic work in the priestly abuse of children; seemingly connected to the deep trough of relativism the Church in America and Europe had been wallowing in for several decades as she struggled to combat the enemies from within and without.

I began exploring membership in lay Catholic organizations which I felt would recapture the glow of baptism, but what I found was that what I thought I needed from other Catholic organizations was something I only needed to **do** myself; embrace the daily practice of communion, prayer, and devotion. The spiritual dryness I thought was calling me deeper back into the Church through lay organizational involvement was instead just a simple call back to the Church.

For three years I took each step of the daily path faithfully and have been blessed and surprised how satisfying it has become and how much peace I've received from it; and though now daily practice is more centered around study and writing I feel the same blessings flowing from the constant embrace of the works of the Church.

For penitential criminals, so long in the service of the prince of this world, daily enrichment is necessary so that the companionship with Christ becomes a daily walking with him and the Church he founded upon the rock of Peter two thousand years ago.

In my inherent pride of self—temptingly strengthened through faithful attendance at daily mass proving the supremacy of my will—I am also reminded, almost daily, by Old Testament prophets or New Testament apostles and Christ not to become as the scribes:

> **[Matthew 23:23]** Woe upon you, scribes and Pharisees, you hypocrites that will award to God his tithe, though it be of mint or dill or cummin, and have forgotten the weightier commandments of the law, justice, mercy, and honour; you did ill to forget

one duty while you performed the other; **[24]** you blind leaders, that have a strainer for the gnat, and then swallow the camel! **[25]** Woe upon you, scribes and Pharisees, you hypocrites that scour the outward part of cup and dish, while all within is running with avarice and incontinence.

I also found, in the daily homiletic teaching from the priests of my parish, refreshment and broadening of spiritual grace that was deeply enhancing my individual journey into Catholicism as well as the sacramental grace received through daily reception of the Holy Eucharist.

However, the most wonderful grace is that received from being in the company of saints—Mass with the saints—both those whose stories we acknowledge each day, and the many saints surrounding me in the parish pews whose stories I do not know but whose faith and devotion to Holy Mother Church is so evident through their daily practice.

The petition—"give us this day our daily bread"—in the *Our Father* began to acquire a different meaning for me after many months of daily mass and praying the rosary daily with its recitation of the prayer before each decade; becoming more eucharistic than earthly, and I discovered others had come to the same conclusion and beyond, then I understood that it was both; the saying of grace before partaking of the divine food, and the plea for today's earthly sustenance.

References to Christ as living water and bread of life are central to Catholic theology and the insertion of the petition about daily bread in the *Our Father*, said at every Mass, is congruent, leading to an injunction to daily Eucharistic celebration.

Women, who have been so marginalized throughout human history, yet retain the clarity of spirit—as did Mary, the mother of our Lord and Mary Magdalene—to see the truth; and it is they who are first in the daily mass, they who do almost all of the readings, they who mostly distribute the body and blood of our Lord; they the saints aborning, who I am privileged to be among each morning.

The thoughts of the lowly matter—but of course—for there are no least in the Kingdom of God—only children of God.

The greatest children and the least of children with only purity of thought congruent with action separating them.

It is not only the greatest who are able to solve problems— and as Henry VIII proclaimed as he tore the English Church asunder: *"I can become what I will"*; and as American Manifest Destiny grew from the Protestant definition of success filtered through Harvard, Catholics knew it is God's will behind becoming.

Lectio Divina

The practice of *lectio divina* (divine reading) is an ancient one, arising from the monasteries of the Church, and is a powerful form of contemplation carried out in daily life.

Reading a particular section of scripture and then contemplating it, praying about it, and discussing it, was the monastic way; but the way in which I use it can involve any reading from Church leaders—particularly the Holy Father—or Catholic scholars and working from the baseline of the magisterium and the work of the apostolate, dwell deeply on the idea for as much time as seems fruitful, often several days or weeks.

There are so many ways people choose to perceive the singular reality, that we quickly realize Babel is not only still central to the experience of life in the world; but remains Satan's most cherished tool and God's greatest gift—the freedom to choose how we see, how we hear, how we speak—and it is here in this quiet contemplation and decision making that the ancient practice of Lectio Divina plays such a major role.

Lectio Divina is a Catholic tool of spiritual contemplation that can bring one into such deep communion with God—if it is part of the daily practice of prayer and devotions incumbent upon those desiring priestly souls—that if enough criminals entered into its darkness leading to light; even those within super-max cells; eventually great and powerful blessings would flow upon the earth from their contemplative prayer.

Solidarity—a great teaching to contemplate—in its fullest sense would stand with all, rich and poor, criminal and saint, black and white.

And the preferential option for the poor would be the solidarity option embracing the rich, for solidarity stands *against* no one, but *for* all.

A root of solidarity is friendship among groups of strangers transcending strangeness, binding us all by the common ground of our existence as human beings and creatures of God.

Solidarity is friendship, friendship of the highest level, grounded in the ancient ritual of sacrifice of self to another.

The highest gift brings the greatest reward and laying down our earthly life is to have eternal life.

Our friends have created a home for us. Through countless ages, human beings of good will, self-sacrifice, and eternal visions, have laid down their lives, fortunes, and dreams on the floor of our existence. It is a floor of enduring stone, built with divine goodness and familial love.

Solidarity between human beings is best expressed by speaking truth to one another and the great tears in its fabric come through the conscious wounding of that truth.

I remember, as do you, those moments when the face of the *Other* became the face of a friend and in that moment solidarity breathes through us with its ancient, warm familial breath.

We have become so materialistic that we preclude spiritual authenticity to all immersed in it, yet should we not also be in solidarity to those whose path to salvation is as passing through the eye of a needle, those who have become enemized by so many, and in solidarity with them fulfill our greatest commandment

Now, as we go forth with God, let us look always to the boundaries of our lives for the call of truth laying there; and breaking through boundaries seek and acquire that deeper knowledge that—in its elemental form—is a continuation of the work Christ began, so powerfully even during his last moments when he canonized the first saint of the Catholic Church, the penitential criminal Dismas.

Chapter Four
Capital Punishment & Catholic Social Teaching: A Tradition of Support

This chapter is a defense of the scriptural and traditional Catholic position of support for capital punishment—as expressed in the two universal catechisms, the *Catechism of the Council of Trent,* published by Pope Pius V in 1566, and the *Catechism of the Catholic Church* published by Pope Saint John Paul II in 1994—in response to calls for its abolition.

Based on tradition, calls for abolition are premature, though the call has generated a renewed focus on not only the magisterial history of this most ancient of teachings, but also its theological resonance within the expression of that teaching by the Fathers of the Church—ancient and modern—who most deeply reflected on it.

Capital punishment as a way of protecting the innocent, is one of the central issues in the social teaching of the Church, but the ambiguity about it—particularly in the United States—over the past several decades, after two millennia of certainty, places the credibility of the teaching itself at risk; and that negatively impacts the Church's social teaching as an effective tool for criminal transformation, further risking the immortal souls of those who are lost and whose being found partially relies on the constancy of the teaching of the Catholic Church, on eternally walking the eternal talking.

My personal thinking on capital punishment has gone through three phases.

I was initially a supporter of capital punishment, especially for those heinous crimes we always associate with its use.

When I was becoming a Catholic, I moved in opposition to it, after being taught during the Rite of Christian Initiation for Adults (RCIA) process that brought me into the Catholic Church, that the Church was in opposition to it, as it was very important to me to think with the Church in all things.

After becoming Catholic and conducting my own study, I returned to a position of support when I learned that the Church's teaching did not oppose it, only the improper use of it; a position which has grown in certainty as I realized how deeply support for capital punishment is woven into Church doctrine as an important aspect of the protection of the innocent against the murderer, "for all time" as the *Catechism* notes:

> **2260** The covenant between God and mankind is interwoven with reminders of God's gift of human life and man's murderous violence:
>
>> For your lifeblood I will surely require a reckoning.... Whoever sheds the blood of man, by man shall his blood be shed; for God made man in his own image. (Genesis 9:5-6)
>
> The Old Testament always considered blood a sacred sign of life. (Leviticus 17:14) This teaching remains necessary for all time.

The most important reason however, for writing about it is not to share my position of support, but to reaffirm the constancy of the teaching of the Church in the context of the general perception among many Catholics that the Church does oppose its use, an incorrect perception which needs to be addressed in relation to the transformation of criminals—which is the mission of my apostolate work with the Lampstand Foundation—of which constancy of doctrine is a core element of success.

One of the most important aspects in ensuring capital punishment remains an option for protecting the innocent is that it is a clear response to evil, and it is vitally important that our Church remain committed to confronting and fighting evil directly; because ultimately, the constancy of the doctrine of the Church informs and animates its constancy in fighting evil, and a central aspect of fighting evil is saving the souls of those imprisoned in it.

It is constancy that teaches and holds; it is the constancy of God, the Creator of Covenants; for what can the father of lies and a murderer from the beginning teach about constancy to truth.

There is also a constancy of sorts among those who oppose the Church most fervently around capital punishment, such as some of the great heretical sects, like the Waldenses from the 12th century and the Albigenses.

And in modern times, the communist countries of the Soviet Bloc opposed capital punishment, though their relatively indiscriminate use of capital executions seems to belie this.

I do not know how the support for abolition of capital punishment by those who oppose the Church vehemently, and those who are leaders in the Church today, is related, or even if it is related, but it is an interesting point of departure for reflection especially due to the Marxist penetration of the Church through Liberation Theology and the machinations of Vatican II.

The protection of life is the central animating core of the Catholic Church and while that principle is clearly understood in relation to the prohibition against abortion and euthanasia, it has, in our time, become confused in relation to the Church's support for Just War and the juridical use of capital punishment.

Support for capital punishment has always existed within the Catholic Church, yet we still encounter within the Catholic community the damage done to the spiritual underpinning of the aspect of Catholic social teaching connected with the responsibility to protect the innocent by those opposing capital punishment. They conflate opposition to capital punishment with the traditional Catholic opposition to abortion—generally arising from the intellectually flawed consistent ethic of life approach—and unfortunately supported by many bishops.

Pope John Paul II and Benedict XVI (while still Cardinal Ratzinger) have stated that if recourse to capital punishment is no longer necessary to protect the innocent—a huge if that does not yet exist—it may be abolished.

That forms the foundation for the United States Conference of Catholic Bishops (USCCB) call to abolish capital punishment in the United States, and consequently, much of the intellectual and spiritual fuel for abolition comes from their work of many years, culminating in their 2005 Statement, *The Culture of Life and the Penalty of Death.*

The USCCB appear to have based their abolition policy on two intellectual threads.

One is the "consistent ethic or seamless garment of life" approach which many abolition advocates have used to conflate abortion, war, poverty, and euthanasia, with capital punishment.

A major problem with this argument—in addition to the fact that it is not congruent with the ancient teaching of the Church—is that it is innocent life that is protected by outlawing abortion and euthanasia, and innocent life that is also protected by supporting the juridical use of capital punishment and just war.

The other thread emanates from statements made by Pope John Paul II and supported by Pope Benedict XVI, who called upon all Catholics to approach capital punishment with extreme caution and care for the offender, reminding us that if there are any means other than taking life, in which we can protect the life of the innocent from the aggressor, we should use them; and, in fact, Pope John Paul II, Pope Benedict XVI & Pope Francis have even gone so far as to call for abolition, though not yet through the intellectual support of the papal magisterium.

The penal situation in the United States where our legal system guarantees right of visitation and communication in even the most secure confinement—as in a super-max prison or on death row, the aggressor still has the capacity to reach out and harm the innocent, whether through the possession of contraband cell phones, information transmitted through attorneys, guards, and visitors—and it is in this context that criminal justice professionals require the continued option of capital punishment; and it is from this perspective of still being able to threaten the innocent, that the magisterium of the Catholic Church, expressed through the centuries, continues to support capital punishment, as stated in the *Catechism*.

> **2267** The traditional teaching of the Church does not exclude, presupposing full ascertainment of the identity and responsibility of the offender, recourse to the death penalty, when this is the only practicable way to defend the lives of human beings effectively against the aggressor.
>
> If, instead, bloodless means are sufficient to defend against the aggressor and to protect the safety of persons, public authority should limit itself to such means, because they better correspond to the

concrete conditions of the common good and are more in conformity to the dignity of the human person.

Today, in fact, given the means at the State's disposal to effectively repress crime by rendering inoffensive the one who has committed it, without depriving him definitively of the possibility of redeeming himself, cases of absolute necessity for suppression of the offender 'today ... are very rare, if not practically non-existent.' 68: (John Paul II, Evangelium Vitae # 56)

If the system of confinement in the United States can advance to the point where the aggressor is confined so completely that communication is blocked by any means with the outside world, through outside contact by contraband cell phones, through guards, family, priests, or attorneys—all capable of being innocently manipulated or co-opted—and the possibility of a future legislative change of current lifetime sentences; then a truly bloodless means of protecting the innocent from the aggressor might have been reached and abolition can perhaps be then fruitfully discussed, though the issue of just retribution would need to be addressed simultaneously.

Crime is, underneath the genetic, sociological, psychological, economic and political arguments, essentially a theological problem and it is only within theology that evil—the deepest dimension of crime and an aspect rarely evidenced in the careers of professional criminals—can be addressed. It is evil which must concern Catholics in addressing crime, and we must recognize that evil rarely reforms, but most professional criminals can and will, given a reason and shown the way.

Capital Punishment & Matthew 18:6

Catholic social teaching helps us understand that capital punishment is the only sanction potent enough to create the redemptive environment most apt to influence the deeply evil sinner and that temporal death is much to be preferred over an eternal torment in hell.

Matthew 18:6 is perhaps the clearest expression of support for capital punishment spoken by Christ:

> **[Matthew 18:6]** And if anyone hurts the conscience of one of these little ones, that believe in me, he had better have been drowned in the depths of the sea, with a mill-stone hung about his neck.

Remember, this was used as a form of capital punishment in antiquity by the Greeks, Romans and Syrians.

The Catholic commentaries about this verse and the teaching of the entire chapter reveal the vigorous sanctions—capital punishment and banishment—Christ taught as applying to the members of the church community who violate its teachings. Matthew 18 has long been acknowledged as a *Discourse on the Church*, but not enough attention has been devoted to its support for capital punishment in relation to the historic support of the magisterium for capital punishment.

The necessary horizon and knowledge for understanding capital punishment as expressed in Matthew 18:6 is eternity and hell.

Christ teaches his disciples that the eternal torment of hell awaits the tempter who, through scandal, causes the converted believers in Him to sin, and the *Catechism* notes:

> **2284** Scandal is an attitude or behavior which leads another to do evil. the person who gives

scandal becomes his neighbor's tempter. He damages virtue and integrity; he may even draw his brother into spiritual death. Scandal is a grave offense if by deed or omission another is deliberately led into a grave offense.

For it is better for the tempter that he be put to death, in the hope that, facing temporal death, he will seek redemption and mercy from God and perhaps be saved from eternal torment.

The importance of examining Matthew 18:6 in relation to capital punishment is twofold; Matthew 18's status as a Discourse on the Church and its support for capital punishment in Christ's own words—a powerful affirmation of the responsibility of the community to protect the innocent and save the sinner.

The Old Testament spoke at length about capital punishment and many sinful activities were determined to justify bringing the sanction down upon the individual. The New Testament has not been as rich in instruction around this harshest of punishments, and modern Catholic commentaries connecting Matthew 18:6 to a supportive position for capital punishment are rare, so we must look to those from tradition for support.

The responsibility that the community has to protect the innocent has long been a core principle of the Catholic Church.

The responsibility to protect the innocent also animates the acceptance of Just War and the disapproval of abortion and euthanasia—foundational protection of life pillars of the Church—ancient and modern.

Jesus speaks clearly when condemning those who would scandalize those who believe in him—by tempting and leading them to sin—to suffer the ancient form of capital punishment, "drowned in the depths of the sea, with a mill-stone hung about his neck".

The *Catechism* notes:

> **2285** Scandal takes on a particular gravity by reason of the authority of those who cause it or the weakness of those who are scandalized. It prompted our Lord to utter this curse: "Whoever causes one of these little ones who believe in me to sin, it would be better for him to have a great millstone fastened round his neck and to be drowned in the depth of the sea." Scandal is grave when given by those who by nature or office are obliged to teach and educate others. Jesus reproaches the scribes and Pharisees on this account: he likens them to wolves in sheep's clothing.

With that method of capital punishment prescribed, attempting to proscribe it, as many in the Church are attempting to do—considering the relatively painless methods utilized today—appears deeply incongruent, in addition to forgetting the possibility of the spur of temporal death leading to redemptive liberation from eternal torment.

We cannot forget we have eternal life, and it is the spur of eternity that often brings redemption to an evil soul facing the certainty of temporal death. That is the good, the charity, that the Angelic Doctor of the Church St. Thomas Aquinas, and the ancient tradition of the Church, speaks of in relation to its strong and ancient support of capital punishment.

Catechism Change

There has been a change within the Catholic Church's Vatican II Catechisms around capital punishment.

From the first edition of 1992 to the second edition of 1997—five short years—the *Catechism*, the magisterial heart of the Church, moves from clear support by affirmation to muddy support by deprecation.

In the first edition of the *Catechism of the Catholic Church*, published by the Holy See in 1992 it was written:

Legitimate Defense

2266 Preserving the common good of society requires rendering the aggressor unable to inflict harm. For this reason, the traditional teaching of the Church has acknowledged as well-founded the right and duty of legitimate public authority to punish malefactors by means of penalties commensurate with the gravity of the crime not excluding, in cases of extreme gravity, the death penalty. For analogous reasons those holding authority have the right to repel by armed force aggressors against the community in their charge.

The primary effect of *punishment* is to redress the disorder caused by the offense. When his punishment is voluntarily accepted by the offender, it takes on the value of expiation. Moreover, punishment has the effect of preserving public order and the safety of persons. Finally punishment has a medicinal value; as far as possible it should contribute to the correction of the offender. (Luke 23:40-43)

2267 If bloodless means are sufficient to defend human lives against an aggressor and to protect public order and the safety of persons, public authority should limit itself to such means, because they better correspond to the concrete conditions of the common good and are more in conformity to the dignity of the human person. (p. 546)

In the second edition, published by the Holy See in 1997, it was written:

Capital Punishment

2266 The State's effort to contain the spread of behaviors injurious to human rights and the fundamental rules of civil coexistence corresponds to the requirement of watching over the common good. Legitimate public authority has the right and duty to inflict penalties commensurate with the gravity of the crime. The primary scope of the penalty is to redress the disorder caused by the offense. When his punishment is voluntarily accepted by the offender, it takes on the value of expiation. Moreover, punishment, in addition to preserving public order and the safety of persons, has a medicinal scope: as far as possible it should contribute to the correction of the offender. 67: (Luke 23:40-43)

2267 The traditional teaching of the Church does not exclude, presupposing full ascertainment of the identity and responsibility of the offender, recourse to the death penalty, when this is the only practicable way to defend the lives of human beings effectively against the aggressor.

If, instead, bloodless means are sufficient to defend against the aggressor and to protect the safety of persons, public authority should limit itself to such means, because they better correspond to the concrete conditions of the common good and are more in conformity to the dignity of the human person.

Today, in fact, given the means at the State's disposal to effectively repress crime by rendering inoffensive the one who has committed it, without

215

depriving him definitively of the possibility of redeeming himself, cases of absolute necessity for suppression of the offender 'today ... are very rare, if not practically non-existent.' 68: (John Paul II, Evangelium Vitae # 56.)

This is a significant movement, and one wonders what led to this change.

What happened?

We know that the new language in the second edition of the *CCC* originated from the encyclical of John Paul II, *Evangelium Vitae* of March 25, 1995.

While the change in language in the Catechism emanating from *Evangelium Vitae* may be beneficial for modern ears, it is not necessarily so for those reductionists assuming it signifies a true doctrinal change in the traditional support of capital punishment.

So, while what was changed was a more sensitive appreciation of the seriousness of capital punishment and an expression of a sincere hope that someday, in some way, under some conditions, it may not be necessary to resort to capital punishment, a future world we may all pray for, but it is not here yet, not yet.

John Paul II's expression of an appeal to reach a consensus on ending the use of the death penalty though not so strongly felt as to result in inclusion in the *Catechism*, was deeply felt, and possibly grew, in addition to his revulsion at the state's use of violence, from his long struggle against a central dissent of his papacy, liberation theology and the fatal violence often arising from it.

In battling liberation theology adherents—some of whom were priests—who felt justified in taking up arms to help liberate the poor from oppression in Latin America; John Paul struggled mightily.

It is a very short step from this struggle to feeling that the violence of capital punishment—in the supposedly secure imprisonment environment of the super-max prison in America—was no longer morally acceptable to protect innocent life.

The problem with this leap—if that did indeed play any role in the change John Paul expressed—beyond the violence it does to millennia of Church teaching, is that super-max confinement does not protect the innocent from the aggressor in an American context, and numerous instances of criminal enterprises, often involving the ordering of death for the innocent witnesses of crimes, are commonly known by correctional and prosecutorial professionals.

The second edition of the *Catechism*, however, due to this newer language, has proven to be more congruent with the USCCB call to change the ancient teaching than the first edition, as the clarity of capital punishment support—while still evident in the second edition—can be interpreted as not supportive, as many researchers and bishops have chosen to do.

It is clear that the second edition of the *Catechism*, while retaining the traditional support of capital punishment, embraces its current rarity, and anticipates a future level of carceral development—though super-max prisons in America were hoped to be that development, it has not yet proven to be so—where the evil aggressor can be restrained from harming the innocent, and that is a development devoutly to be wished and prayed for.

There may indeed come a time when the security of prison for life is so powerfully punitive and secluded from being able to harm the innocent, that expiation may occur and, within that deep solitude, the aggressor may seek redemption.

Christ Universalized the Torah

In Matthew 18, Christ is teaching the apostles about how to deal with the deep sinners in the new Church that will arise after he is gone and that they must be prepared to cut people off if they are not willing to repent, but he is clear in verse 6, that there are some sins, those of scandal, that are so serious that even the ultimate punishment may be required.

Christ universalized the Torah, and this universalization brought many of the Old Testament capital punishment prescriptions within the umbrella of the New Testament's law of scandal as much of the Decalogue was brought into the embrace of the Great Commandment.

Historic Catholic support for capital punishment—as part of the long tradition protecting the innocent—is vital to the social teaching of the Church, as that teaching needs to remain true to itself if it is to retain its potency in the conversion and transformation of criminals, and all other sinners.

To overturn a principle as ancient as the judicial use of capital punishment, as USCCB with their *Campaign to End the Use of the Death Penalty* would, could bring all of its enduring principles into question.

Today, the Church's social teaching protects the innocent from four major aggressors; the abortionist, the terrorist, the sexual predator, and the criminal, and against each its teaching must be steadfast and true, for it is a light unto the world.

Catholic Social Teaching & Capital Punishment

The Catechism of the Council of Trent states:

Execution of Criminals

Another kind of lawful slaying belongs to the civil authorities, to whom is entrusted power of life and death, by the legal and judicious exercise of which they punish the guilty and protect the innocent. The just use of this power, far from involving the crime of murder, is an act of paramount obedience to this Commandment which prohibits murder. The end of the Commandment is the preservation and security of human life. Now the punishments inflicted by the civil authority, which is the legitimate avenger of crime, naturally tend to this end, since they give security to life by repressing outrage and violence. Hence these words of David: In the morning I put to death all the wicked of the land, that I might cut off all the workers of iniquity from the city of the Lord. (p. 421)

Capital punishment is a rooted part of the Church's long advocated protection of the innocent against the aggressor, whether through the abortion and euthanasia prohibition or the Just War principles.

The recent call for an end to the use of capital punishment has been built on a underexplored reference to the Catholic historic record regarding criminal justice issues; and the current understanding among criminal justice professionals that even within the confines of a maximum security prison, criminals are still able to influence aggression against the innocent.

An even greater handicap in presenting a proper analysis of criminal justice is the modern liberal tendency to discount and properly understand the hard reality of the deep involvement of Satan in the criminal world, and could it be any more obvious, that within the darkest bowels of our nation's maximum security prisons, the animating visage is surely his; a fact known by all those living within the steel and stone.

All too many who study criminal justice issues fail to face Satan and his works, but too often excuse evil away as a result of structural sin, and become apologists for criminal behavior, rather than realizing it for what it often is, the work of the devil; and thus does he continue his greatest deception, of continuing the lie that he does not even exist.

As the *Catechism* teaches us:

> **2850** The last petition to our Father is also included in Jesus' prayer: "I am not asking you to take them out of the world, but I ask you to protect them from the evil one." It touches each of us personally, but it is always "we" who pray, in communion with the whole Church, for the deliverance of the whole human family. The Lord's Prayer continually opens us to the range of God's economy of salvation. Our interdependence in the drama of sin and death is turned into solidarity in the Body of Christ, the "communion of saints."

> **2851** In this petition, evil is not an abstraction, but refers to a person, Satan, the Evil One, the angel who opposes God. the devil (dia-bolos) is the one who "throws himself across" God's plan and his work of salvation accomplished in Christ.

> **2852** "A murderer from the beginning, . . . a liar and the father of lies," Satan is "the deceiver of the whole world. "Through him sin and death entered the world and by his definitive defeat all creation will be "freed from the corruption of sin and death." Now "we know that anyone born of God does not sin, but He who was born of God keeps him, and the evil one does not touch him.

We know that we are of God, and the whole world is in the power of the evil one."

The Lord who has taken away your sin and pardoned your faults also protects you and keeps you from the wiles of your adversary the devil, so that the enemy, who is accustomed to leading into sin, may not surprise you. One who entrusts himself to God does not dread the devil. "If God is for us, who is against us?"

The Church's traditional support for capital punishment—validated in Catholic teaching for millennia—is based on the assumption of the reality of evil (which the relativist thinking secular world, clearly influencing the Church in the West, struggles to accept), that some offenses are so terrible that the only just and charitable response is to consign the evildoer to hell, and hope that within that definite period of earthly life he now knows remains to him after sentenced to death, he will be spurred to seek forgiveness.

Support for it is sadly held as a regrettable aspect of human and Church history that none find joy or glory in its promotion, as so well-articulated — though confusing some because of the negative construct — in the current *Catechism*:

Capital Punishment

2266 The State's effort to contain the spread of behaviors injurious to human rights and the fundamental rules of civil coexistence corresponds to the requirement of watching over the common good. Legitimate public authority has the right and duty to inflict penalties commensurate with the gravity of the crime. The primary scope of the penalty is to redress the disorder caused by the offense. When his punishment is voluntarily

221

accepted by the offender, it takes on the value of expiation. Moreover, punishment, in addition to preserving public order and the safety of persons, has a medicinal scope: as far as possible it should contribute to the correction of the offender. 67: (Luke 23:4-43)

2267 The traditional teaching of the Church does not exclude, presupposing full ascertainment of the identity and responsibility of the offender, recourse to the death penalty, when this is the only practicable way to defend the lives of human beings effectively against the aggressor.

If, instead, bloodless means are sufficient to defend against the aggressor and to protect the safety of persons, public authority should limit itself to such means, because they better correspond to the concrete conditions of the common good and are more in conformity to the dignity of the human person.

Today, in fact, given the means at the State's disposal to effectively repress crime by rendering inoffensive the one who has committed it, without depriving him definitively of the possibility of redeeming himself, cases of absolute necessity for suppression of the offender 'today ... are very rare, if not practically non-existent.' 68: (John Paul II, Evangelium Vitae # 56.)

The difference between the two universal catechisms; the *Roman Catechism* (1566) from the Council of Trent, and the *Catechism of the Catholic Church* (1997) from the Second Vatican Council; partially reflects modern language sensitivity—part of the modernist, relativist age we live in and not all bad—that treats difficult subjects with a subtle deference to compassion for the inevitability of human sin, but still both hold to the traditional teaching of the Church that supports capital punishment.

The proper response to evil is punishment—appropriately found in Hell—and capital punishment speeds that consequence while human mercy delays God's judgment, so clearly stated by Christ with the millstone statement in Matthew 18:6.

During the period of the 1960's through the 1980's certain religious orders, cardinals, bishops, and parish priests of the Catholic Church—particularly in the Americas—became enamored of Marxist-inspired liberation theology and informed by its anti-capitalism, absorbed the corresponding attributes of restricting the religious, economic, legal, and military power of capitalistic countries and their primary target has been the United States, the largest and most powerful capitalistic country, resulting in strong anti-business, anti-war, pro-abortion, and anti-capital punishment movements.

This perspective unfortunately bled a bit into the arguments incorporated in the formation of the current catechism, watering down the historic clarity the Catholic Church had presented to the world regarding capital punishment.

As the Church now beats back the minor degradation of Church doctrine influenced by liberation theology—a battle still joined—the clarity will hopefully return, particularly around the issues of protecting the life of the innocent through the just use of war and capital punishment.

There are many reasons for concern regarding this 'language sensitivity', chief being the relative lack of knowledge of criminal justice issues, given the thought that "bloodless means are sufficient to defend against the aggressor and to protect the safety of persons, public authority should limit itself to such means," which, one assumes, refers to imprisonment in maximum security or

223

super-max prisons, yet, there are innumerable publically expressed examples revealing how easily the imprisoned aggressor can act towards those innocents outside of prison.

If nothing else can persuade the Catholic capital punishment abolition movement to reconsider their conclusion that other means exist to protect the innocent from the aggressor, surely the clearly exhibited porous nature of even the most secure American prisons may someday stimulate that needed reconsideration of their policy to abolish capital punishment.

When we add to this the terrible disruption of the sexual scandal the Church began experiencing during that period, though not becoming public until much later, the unraveling of even the settled language, and the rearrangement of the dogmatic expression emanating from the Second Vatican Council, it is a wonder that as much of the hard truths that sustained the Church for the millennia, survived as strongly expressed as they have.

And this confusion was only compounded by the lack of leadership, resulting from the corruption of the sexual scandal, of those most responsible for providing teaching to the Church around the social teaching issues.

Along with this degraded leadership, another weakness in the United States Conference of Catholic Bishop's (USCCB) approach to capital punishment and other criminal justice issues, is a lack of professional knowledge from the field and an understanding of the Church's historic work around punishment and prisons,

The support for abolishing capital punishment has long been part of the political left in the United States which the USCCB has moved in congruence with for a very long time.

Recently however, there are encouraging developments for a deeper understanding of criminal justice, social science, and Catholic historic contributions to it, in the work of the already mentioned Dr. Andrew Skotnicki, associate professor at Manhattan College, with his several related scholarly articles and two books: *Religion and the Development of the American Penal System* (2002) and *Criminal Justice and the Catholic Church* (2008); and the recent publication in 2007 of the two volume and one supplement in 2012 (as of 2015) *Encyclopedia of Catholic Social Thought, Social Science and Social Policy* edited by Michael L. Coulter, Stephen M. Krason, Richard S. Myers, and Joseph A. Varacalli.

It is from the examination of protecting society that we, the Lampstand Foundation, consider the proper use of capital punishment as a legitimate sanction for murderers, for serial pedophiles and serial rapists.

There is an aspect here that connects to the Just War doctrine, where it is the moral stance around the violence inherent in wars of many against many, where this addresses the violence within the war of the few against many and the many against the few.

The *Roman Catechism* says this about just war:

> In like manner, the soldier is guiltless who, actuated not by motives of ambition or cruelty, but by a pure desire of serving the interests of his country, takes away the life of an enemy in a just war. (p. 452)

The Policy of the Church

Perhaps what is most marked about the position of the social teaching in the United States—and many others who study it—is the generally accepted assumption that the Church's work in this area began with the 1891 encyclical of Pope Leo XIII.

The difficulty with relying on this perception is that much of the foundational work of the social teaching—coming from the Old Testament and medieval sources—is not factored in, resulting in a skewed result.

This is particularly true with capital punishment, prisons, and punishment in general, which saw much of its most articulate principles developed during those periods, well documented by the work of Fr. Rodger Charles and Fr. Andrew Skotnicki.

With the publication of the USCCB *United States Catholic Catechism for Adults* in 2006, the Bishops validated their position that capital punishment "cannot be justified".

What is not included here is the central aspect of Catholic anthropology concerning criminal acts, the agency of free individuals, and as we shall see in the next section regarding the approach of Pope Pius XII, the traditional teaching of the Church about capital punishment is based upon that anthropology.

Determining the evolution of this thinking by the USCCB from advocates of the Church's traditional support of capital punishment, to advocates for its abolition, is beyond the scope of this book, but we might discern some vestiges of roots in movement around the issue of abortion; the other major issue involving the protection of the innocent that has seen a substantial shift in political perception and action—at least by the Democratic party— in the United States.

And though the USCCB Statement in 2005 was clear that they were not formulating new doctrine, many of the faithful do now believe that it is the doctrine of the Church that capital punishment should be abolished, especially after the past three popes, John Paul II, Benedict XVI and now Francis, have specifically called for its abolition; though the papal call has been in a non-magisterial form that is not relevant to Catholic doctrine, since it is in direct conflict with the ancient tradition of the Church in support of capital punishment and the popes cannot teach that which is contrary to Church doctrine, though they may certainly have personal opinions, which these calls for abolition have to be construed as.

The cloudy thinking around the current position, the obvious lack of input from Catholic supporters of capital punishment, and the interpretive difficulty expressed in the translation of the *Catechism* underlying the USCCB position of abolition; is a reminder that, as deeply as we should respect our bishops and continually pray for them, there are times when we should also look to Catholic supporters of capital punishment, the Bishop of Rome, and the *Universal Catechisms*, for resolution when questions arise around interpretation.

Pope Pius XII

Pope Pius XII (1876-1958) was the last modern pope to have spoken extensively on capital punishment in two major speeches to jurists and doctors, and throughout his papacy he continued to comment on crime and punishment; and it is here we can look for modern papal validation of the ancient tradition of the Catholic Church's support for capital punishment.

Pius was a singularly talented pope and his effectiveness was reflected in the skill with which he kept the Nazi's at bay when they occupied Rome, saving thousands of Jews he had hidden away in the Vatican and other Church buildings; and in the post war attempt by the Communist government of the Soviet Union to destroy him, an attempt that was partially successful and it is only now, almost 50 years after his death, that the full story is coming out as he approaches canonization.

Pius became Pope in 1939, six months before the outbreak of World War II. He was very learned and came from a family—and developed a personal background—in the law.

227

What is marked through Pope Pius XII's teaching is its congruence with the Catholic anthropology of individual responsibility while the reason given for the abolitionist's position, is not.

While we are certainly bound by the magisterium of Pope John Paul II that capital punishment may only be used after the conditions expressed in the Catechism have been met, that is largely the existing situation already, and rather than calling for an abolition as the USCCB have, the retention of the traditional response of the Church, which Pope John Paul II also reaffirms, is rightly mandated within the *Catechism*.

The value of the magisterium of Pope Pius XII has been deepening as time allows further study of it, and that was remarked on by Pope Benedict XVI in a November 8, 2008 speech to the Congress on "The Heritage of the Magisterium of Pius XII and the Second Vatican Council":

> Everyone acknowledges Pius XII's uncommon intelligence, iron memory, singular familiarity with foreign languages and a noteworthy sensitivity. It is said that he was an accomplished diplomat, an outstanding jurist, an excellent theologian. All this is true but it does not explain everything; in him there was also the continuous effort and the firm will to give himself to God without regard for his delicate health. This was the true driving force of his behaviour: all was born from love for his Lord Jesus Christ and from love for the Church and for humanity. Indeed, before all else he was a priest in constant and intimate union with God, a priest who found the strength for his enormous work in long periods of prayer before the Blessed Sacrament, in silent colloquy with his Creator and Redeemer. From there sprang the origin and impulse of his Magisterium as, on the other hand, it was for his every other activity.

Therefore it must not be surprising that his teaching continues even today to shed light in the Church. Already 50 years have passed since his death, but his multifaceted and fruitful Magisterium remains even for Christians today one of priceless value. Certainly the Church, Mystical Body of Christ, is a living and vital organism, not steadfastly defending what was 50 years ago. But development occurs in coherency. This is why the heritage of the Magisterium of Pius XII has been gathered by the Second Vatican Council and reproposed to the later Christian generations. It is well known that of the oral interventions and writings presented by the Second Vatican Council Fathers, over 1,000 references cite the Magisterium of Pius XII. Not all the documents of the Council have an array of Notes, but in those documents that do have them, the name of Pius XII recurs more than 200 times. This means that, with the exception of Sacred Scripture, this Pope is the most authoritative and frequently cited source. It is also well known that the special notes of these documents are not, generally, simple explicative references, but often constitute true and proper integral parts of Conciliar texts. They do not furnish only justifications to support what the text affirms, but offer an interpretive key.

In a talk to the First International Congress of the Histopathology of the Nervous System in September 1952, Pope Pius XII said:

> Even when there is question of the execution of a condemned man, the state does not dispose of the individual's right to life. In this case, it is reserved to the public power to deprive the condemned person of the enjoyment of life in expiation of his crime when, by his crime, he has already disposed himself of his right to live. (pp. 232-233)

Pope Pius XII. (1961). *The major addresses of Pope Pius XII. Volume 1: Selected addresses.* Yzermans, V. A. (Ed.). St. Paul. North Central Publishing Company.

Catholic Position

For much of human history, the social value of human beings in the pagan world was barely above that of other objects, and this extreme devaluing of persons influenced the development of the practice around capital punishment.

This is revealed around the response by citizens of the Roman Empire to two issues, abortion and slavery, both of which were integral aspects of Roman society.

With the moral development of the Judeo-Christian world, the value of individual human beings increased and those of the innocent even more so, reflected by their protection in the law through the use of capital punishment.

In our reflections on the social teaching we want to use our historical perspective with a realization of the evolving nature of the teaching in relation to that of social development.

We see this played out in the teaching around capital punishment, as the Old Testament, and the teachings of the medieval Fathers describe many occasions when it may be applied, yet it has developed such that today it is called for rarely.

The new language of the Church has the right pitch, expressing compassion for the executed, as is proper, while clearly retaining the authority to execute, and this is congruent with the Church's thinking around the Development of Doctrine.

God was very clear in what He revealed, both at Sinai and soon after his transfiguration when he taught his disciples about scandal, that the death of the evil doer is often justified when the physical or spiritual life of the innocent is involved.

Let us see again what the *Catechism* has said to us regarding capital punishment:

Capital Punishment

2266 The State's effort to contain the spread of behaviors injurious to human rights and the fundamental rules of civil coexistence corresponds to the requirement of watching over the common good. Legitimate public authority has the right and duty to inflict penalties commensurate with the gravity of the crime. The primary scope of the penalty is to redress the disorder caused by the offense. When his punishment is voluntarily accepted by the offender, it takes on the value of expiation. Moreover, punishment, in addition to preserving public order and the safety of persons, has a medicinal scope: as far as possible it should contribute to the correction of the offender. 67: Luke 23:4-43)

2267 The traditional teaching of the Church does not exclude, presupposing full ascertainment of the identity and responsibility of the offender, recourse to the death penalty, when this is the only practicable way to defend the lives of human beings effectively against the aggressor.

"If, instead, bloodless means are sufficient to defend against the aggressor and to protect the safety of persons, public authority should limit itself to such means, because they better correspond to the concrete conditions of the common good and are more in conformity to the dignity of the human person.

"Today, in fact, given the means at the State's disposal to effectively repress crime by rendering inoffensive the one who has committed it, without depriving him definitively of the possibility of redeeming himself, cases of absolute necessity for suppression of the offender 'today ... are very rare, if not practically non-existent.' 68 (John Paul II, Evangelium vitae 56.)

In other words, the entire historical tradition of the Church has always and continues to support the use of capital punishment, and yet, we should always use it carefully, compassionately, justly, and treating even the evil doer with the dignity and respect human beings have received from God.

Obviously, not all Catholic leaders support capital punishment, and many of them calling for abolition do so based partly on arguments of cruelty, but it is not cruelty to execute the aggressor when that is the only option to protect the innocent; rather it is the power to say, *Stop, you shall no longer harm the innocent,* for if we are not willing to support the use of the power of the state to stop the aggressor from harming the innocent, we become complicit in that harm.

I do not feel the problems around the confusion on the formally clear teaching of the Church about capital punishment to necessarily be the fault of any particular priest or bishop, or their particular allegiance to their personal opinion or any political party; but rather the bending to the influence of the most ancient heresy all of us who are human struggle against; that we sometimes feel we don't need God, and we can make the decisions about primary things on our own, which always leads to sin, which always creates confusion, and which only the grace of a forgiving God, and the reaching out of a penitent soul can undo.

I believe that the gist of the current confusion arose from a reductionist view of the encyclical *Evangelium Vitae*, where while it appeared to be a development of the doctrine around capital punishment, it in fact was not.

Part of the work of the Lampstand Foundation was the creation of criminal justice principles and our fourth principle is: "Capital punishment is an appropriate response to the criminal evil of murder, rape, and pedophilia."

Capital punishment for pedophilia is not something unknown in the history of the Church, indeed Matthew 18:6 obviously addresses it as an especially evil aspect of scandal, but more specifically, St. Pope Pius V's *Catechism of the Council of Trent* felt it to be an appropriate deterrent.

The Church founded by Christ has stood alone against the world for millennia, speaking truth to power—always the same truth with different voices—and though as a humanly managed institution on earth has often stumbled—even as Peter stumbled, thrice denying Christ—the clarity of its truth remains triumphant.

Capital punishment, blood for blood, just retribution upon the aggressor who slays the innocent, has been a central part of that truth and though confusion about the traditional support for it has arisen over the past few decades, the repository of faith expressed in the *Catechism* still includes that support—though in the 1997 second edition has been expressed as a negative, rather than the positive of the first edition of 1992.

While the "oldest Roman catechism" (*Catechism* #196) is the apostles creed; the universal catechisms are the primary sources, and there have been two—which are truly only one—that of Pope Pius V, published in 1566 from the work of the Council of Trent (1545-1563), and that of Pope John Paul II, published in 1997 (2nd Ed.) from the work of the Second Vatican Council (1962-1965).

That is part of the cross we bear—that we live in the world—and though Christ called us to his path of being a sign of contradiction to the world—we are afraid and wish to live in peace with the world; so we choose peace in one battle while fighting others—an often wise strategy even sanctioned by the holy spirit and the apostles—for did not St. Paul instruct us in the craft of conversion.

Yet in learning and adopting the same lessons to become proficient in the craft of conversion, we also need to remain adept in the knowledge of truth and it is to know the nature of those for whom capital punishment has been proclaimed—for they are not of the faithful but outside, outlaws—as a response to criminal evil from the beginning of the Church, that we can learn from the first universal catechism, the *Catechism of the Council of Trent*, which states:

> From what has been said, it is easy to see how inclined man is to those sins which are prohibited by this Commandment, and how many are guilty of murder, if not in fact, at least in desire. As, then, the Sacred Scriptures prescribe remedies for so dangerous a disease, the pastor should spare no pains in making them known to the faithful.

> Of these remedies the most efficacious is to form a just conception of the wickedness of murder. The enormity of this sin is manifest from many and weighty passages of Holy Scripture. So much does God abominate homicide that He declares in Holy Writ that of the very beast of the field He will exact vengeance for the life of man, commanding the beast that injures man to be put to death. (*Gen.* 9:5, 6) And if (the Almighty) commanded man to have a

234

horror of blood, (*Gen.* 9:4), He did so for no other reason than to impress on his mind the obligation of entirely refraining, both in act and desire, from the enormity of homicide.

The murderer is the worst enemy of his species, and consequently of nature. To the utmost of his power he destroys the universal work of God by the destruction of man, since God declares that He created all things for man's sake. Nay, as it is forbidden in Genesis to take human life, because God created man to his own image and likeness, he who makes away with God's image offers great injury to God, and almost seems to lay violent hands on God Himself! (pp. 455-456)

As we come to the end of our journey through the 5th commandment, the great **not** in the Great Commandment of neighborly love, we know that for sound guidance and the final word, we must—in addition to maintaining our daily practice of prayer and communion—look to the Magisterium, we must look to the Holy Father, we must look to the Holy See, and we must look to the Universal Catechisms, we must look to the center, for truly, the center holds.

Speculating on how it has come to be that this seemingly most clear of the ancient sanctions of the Church that is—along with just war—a central part of the protection of the innocent from the aggressor, has come to be so hotly contested in the last days of the second millennium; leads us into deep waters and though we are in danger of drowning in the cesspool of the results of the attacks on the Church, from within and without, we must not avert our gaze; for it is often in the dark face of evil that the force of truth shines most brightly.

Remember the Albigensian Heresy and how they, along with other heretics, stood against war and capital punishment.

This is congruent with the cancerous growth of homosexuality and pederasty in the Catholic Church throughout history and its explosion into public consciousness in the 21st Century, especially in America so tragically and most completely documented by devout Catholic and investigative reporter, Randy Engels in the 2006 book all Catholics should read, *The Rite of Sodomy: Homosexuality and the Roman Catholic Church.*

This rejection of everything the Catholic Church stands on corresponds to the conclusion about the nature of the great heresies stemming from Manicheism.

And here is where we might discover the truth about the resistance to capital punishment that grew so fervently in America, as even our Lord had to deal with the evil within his Twelve Apostles for one of them was with the devil and is it any wonder that within the Church the devil should also have some reign, for is not Job the model for us rather than Judas.

Chapter Five
Invictus, The Way of the Apostolate

Pius XII once stated: "The Faithful, more precisely the lay faithful, find themselves on the front lines of the Church's life; for them the Church is the animating principle for human society. Therefore, they in particular, ought to have an ever-clearer consciousness *not only of belonging to the Church, but of being the Church,* that is to say, the community of the faithful on earth under the leadership of the Pope, the head of all, and of the Bishops in communion with him. These *are the Church...*"(Pope John Paul II. (1988). *Christifideles Laici* #9.)

This book, this chapter, is for penitential professional criminals whose involvement in the criminal/carceral world is of long duration and commitment.

Professional criminals commit crimes for money and live by the ancient criminal way that precludes betrayal of partners or hurting women and children.

To professional criminals, crime is their profession and way of life.

To those professional criminals who are very good—and lucky—at what they do and never get caught, my work will have little value.

It is for those professional criminals who do get caught and serve time in prison, comprising approximately 70 – 80% of the prison population; and who, at some point, may enter a penitential state.

This book is written for them so that through their penance and redemption they may ultimately enter into the apostolate work of reformation to help turn around the statistic that 70% of people released from prison return to prison.

I was born into the criminal world and grew up under its influence, learning that the world was a battleground in which I was on my own. I would have to fight to survive—I remember my father's words, "I've got mine, now you have to get yours"—and would have to do whatever was necessary to prosper, and these lessons were deepened and hammered into my soul through twelve years in the carceral world under three separate sentences; two in federal prison for car theft and one in state prison for assault with a deadly weapon.

Later, much later, I was reborn through the waters of baptism into the communal world of the Catholic Church and learned that not only was the world a battleground, the Church was also; but I was strengthened by the knowledge of the three houses of the Church—the Church Triumphant, the Church Militant and the Church Suffering—and that I was a soldier in the mightiest legion of all, the People of God.

And as is true in all of my books, I write for my fellow penitential criminals, seeking converts to join the army of the People of God, though if others who are not criminals should find value in my work, and perhaps a new or deeper journey to Rome, I will be very pleased.

Within the criminal/carceral world are many men whose way of life is built upon a strong code of honor which itself is constructed upon their view of the city of man where the rules of success are determined by the prince of the world where it seems evil triumphs; but they have not had the eternal truths of the Catholic magisterium countering the perceived success of evil in the world revealed to them in a context they can accept—a situation unfortunately also applicable to many Catholics who have been improperly catechized.

The criminal/carceral code of honor—if redirected towards crime-free living—is somewhat congruent with the most devoutly faithful within the communal world of the Catholic Church. I have no objective way of determining how many criminals fall into the group who actually live within this code of honor; but based on my 20 years within the criminal/carceral world I estimate that 10-15% would; and they very often include the top and middle leadership within that world.

It is from this pool of criminals that we would discover those who could become deep knowledge leaders of criminal transformative organizations reforming other criminals, once they are out of prison, or become prison monks if they should spend their entire earthly life in the carceral world.

Deep knowledge is the knowledge that comes from experience, is shaped through education, and informed by Catholic social teaching.

A deep knowledge leader is a transformed criminal with an advanced academic degree and Catholic social teaching knowledge, working through a grassroots community or prison apostolate, who can help reverse the long-term failure of the criminal rehabilitative effort, as they possess the elemental experiential knowledge of the criminal/carceral world allowing them, and them only, the authentic access to criminals long denied the social work professional.

The minimal eight benchmarks of deep knowledge leadership are:

- Ten years in the criminal world (includes prison) committing crimes for money

- Five years in a maximum security federal or state prison and not an informant, pedophile, serial killer, or rapist
- Ten years out of prison—unless serving a natural life sentence—off parole, crime free, and helping the community
- Educated about Catholic social teaching
- Master's degree
- Leader of a community or prison criminal transformation apostolate
- Married
- Catholic

We are describing a person probably in his mid-forties, with an opportunity to work in the development and management of a criminal reformation apostolate serving 70 clients annually for 25-30 years.

This particular work is for all those professional criminals with whom I served time—and those I do not know but by the life they lived—and from whom I have learned much, men of honor and character, who though criminals through and through, live their lives with fierce conviction and stood by those convictions, even in the deepest and darkest pit that prison can sometimes become.

And it is for those men who, whatever their way of life now, live it animated by love and good will, sharing their life experiences with family and friends, and even if not specifically working within the professional field of criminal transformation, still help others avoid the danger and harm they were fortunate to survive.

And it is especially for those men—within prison and without—who chose to enter the professional field of criminal transformation, and through their training, education, and apostolate vocation, bring others to the way of criminal transformation.

The work of criminal transformation is one of spirit and intellect, requiring great physical courage and the ability to work within the ring of the world's fire stoked to soul-searing heat by the prince of the world.

It is a work that requires love for the criminal and the good that can be drawn from the evil that he has brought into the world and a just and strong heart of love to fight the evil that marks his spirit and moves his action.

The way of the apostolate is marked clearly for us within the traditional teaching of the Catholic Church, enunciated through scripture, through the actions of the Triune God, deeply revealing the narrow gate to heaven and the wide road to hell.

The way is for those who understand, having seen the invisible threads driving the affairs of men, that faith is knowledge of the unseen, and the courage to act upon that faith, until the very end.

This chapter is for those men in prison serving natural life, those rare men who seek to realize a calling to deep spirituality, monastic spirituality, the powerful and consistent prayer life embroidering the lives of the consecrated serving in the Catholic monastery, itself the forerunner of the Western prison.

Natural life in a maximum security prison is the point of the spear and a path to an apostolate of greatest possibilities, greatest danger, greatest overcoming; and the spirituality of the prison cell, enfolding a life of prayer, contemplation, study, and teaching is a path to sainthood.

Out of the night that covers me

> Out of the night that covers me,
> Black as the Pit from pole to pole,
> I thank whatever gods may be
> For my unconquerable soul.
> (*Invictus*—William Ernest Henley—1849-1903)

God has taught us that we must be able to call forth our heart of justice against unrepentant evil and soften our hearts of mercy when penance is evident.

The masculine heart of the theology of the Church embraces the righteous rage that drove the moneychangers from the temple, drove the inhabitants from the land Israel would inherit, set Satan behind him as Peter bent to obstruct his mission, and drove the heel of the woman down crushing the head of the serpent.

The feminine heart of the theology of the Church is that mercy which forgives 7 times 70, bends the Samaritan knee to lift the stranger, stretches out Christ's hand to heal the beggar, and his great eternal heart to forgive those who crucified him.

The great heart of the Church is engraved with spiritual shock troops, able to go where no priest had gone before.

The great heart of the king of the citadel protects the souls of the innocent.

He rises in the morning, calling down the three great armies of the Church—triumphant, suffering and militant—into his vision as he touches his medal ever around his neck, of our patron saint, Dismas, the first canonized saint of the Church, canonized by Christ on Golgotha, and first among those saints leading the forces who make up the Church Triumphant.

242

He seals his left hand with the sacramental ring of marriage and parental vows taken for eternity, his right hand with the ring of the academy and the vow of a lifetime of learning, and on his wrist the timekeeper binding himself to the hours of the day within which his apostolate is performed, prayers and devotions are rendered, and communion with Christ consumed.

These are his weapons taken to battle, vows of meaning, protection, and spiritual warfare.

He makes the sign of the cross with holy water and then he prays:

Lord Jesus Christ, through the most pure Heart of Mary, I offer Thee all my prayers, works, joys and sufferings of this day, for all the intentions of Your Sacred Heart, in union with the Holy Sacrifice of the Mass throughout the world, in reparation for my sins, and in particular for the intentions of the Holy Father and please protect those being persecuted for our faith all around the world. Amen.

Holy Michael Archangel, defend us in the day of battle; be our safeguard against the wickedness and snares of the devil—May God rebuke him, we humbly pray: and do thou, Prince of the heavenly host, by the power of God thrust down to hell Satan and all wicked spirits, who wander through the world for the ruin of souls. Amen.

God our Father, in your living providence you sent your Holy Angel, to watch over me, to guard me from all evil in light and darkness, all the days of my life and at the hour of my death. Under his protection, and under the protection also of those guardian angels protecting my family, let us and the whole world shoulder our cross, gather our spiritual weapons, and standing with Christ and his Church, fight against evil so that we may live in peace and joy. Amen.

Hail Mary, full of grace, the Lord is with thee; blessed art thou among women and blessed is the fruit of thy womb, Jesus. Holy Mary, Mother of God, pray for us sinners, now and at the hour of our death. Amen.

Saint Callistus, penitential criminal who became Peter, bless all penitential criminals that they live in the light of God, as did you during your pontifical welcome to the redeemed sinner, and bring peace and guidance in their search for God. Amen

O Jesus, I want you for my sake, because I am nothing, because I am weak, because I am a sinner; for your sake, that I may know you, love you and grow to be like you; for the sake of others, that I may never do them harm, always do them good and give you to them. Since you want me, dear Jesus, take me: all that I have, all that I am and all that I can be. Amen.

With Peter, to Christ, through Mary, for the Greater Glory of God

If he is able, he goes to daily mass, arriving several minutes early to give him enough time for personal prayers and to read and reflect on the daily readings, prayers and devotions, and to follow the liturgy as it unfolds, reaching its climatic consuming of the body of Christ.

The Eucharist is the height of his reach and the rock upon which he stands; there is nothing more real, there is nothing more powerful, there is nothing more he needs for his apostolate.

Thus spiritually armored and fortified with the divinity of Almighty God, he enters into the daily battle.

The field of battle is outside his door and throughout the area within which those he has brought under his care live and attempt to slough off the bonds of sin and live as free men.

It is where he has erected his fortress within which the criminal world no longer rules; within which transformation and conversion is a daily struggle that he always wins, for Almighty God is his beacon, his guardian angel his protector, the deposit of faith his rock, and the magisterium his guide.

Each day has its moments and they are broken out into the responsibilities of managing his apostolate by educating the community of his work; sharpening and refining the tools within the apostolate and sustaining it as a learning organization; and building a learning community within which the mission of the apostolate is sharpened, distilled, and communicated to those within and without.

To counter our life of criminality and be sustained in our apostolate, and that other penitential criminals may know how our faith is lived—above and beyond our organizational work of preaching the faith and our personal daily practice of communion, scripture, prayer, and rosary—*we must witness our faith endlessly*; cross ourselves when appropriate, wear a crucifix or the medal of our patron saint, hang a rosary from the car mirror, share with others our daily practice, speak of the Holy Father and share the words from the great bishops, speak of the social teaching of the Church—*fly the colors*; for they are the bulwark against the demon and the rallying cry for the faint of heart to the banner of our Lord firmly planted in the field of battle, and the strengthening of our eternal soul and that of our apostolate.

In all discussions, let the magisterial Catholic perspective, which you have learned and continue to study each day, emerge as yours.

We sin at every moment—coveting, denying, carnality— and we counter this with daily practice, with knowledge of our weakness, our need for the Lord and his Church, the rest of our life is penance for our sins which are so deep and so all pervasive that only a lifetime of penance can restore the balance with the people and community we harmed and God who created us; for then we are strengthened and humbled, deflecting misplaced personal honor back to its source, for there is no honor in doing what we must.

Our oath of baptism governs our life, is sacred, and cannot be broken, ever:

We swore to reject sin so as to live in the freedom of Christ's children.

We swore to reject the glamour of evil and refused to be mastered by sin.

We swore to reject Satan, father of sin and prince of darkness.

We swore to reject Satan and all his works and all his empty promises.

We swore that we believe in God, the Father almighty, creator of heaven and earth.

We swore that we believe in Jesus Christ, his only Son, our Lord, who was born of the Virgin Mary, was crucified, died, and was buried, rose from the dead, and is now seated at the right hand of the Father.

We swore we believe in the Holy Spirit, the holy Catholic Church, the communion of saints, the forgiveness of sins, the resurrection of the body, and the life everlasting.

Catholic theologians and philosophers speak of the natural law as implanted upon the hearts and souls of all men, as if Cain and his descendants did not exist, upon whose heart surely the criminal law is what is implanted so much more securely than the "natural."

Rehabilitation efforts continue to fail because the criminal/carceral world blind are attempting to lead the criminal/carceral world sighted, though Christ, in his actions and words—though obscured—clearly pointed to the criminal as the most primary of those to be evangelized with the faith he clarified, and the redemption he brought, to us.

We cannot continue, as a Church, to ignore that the most important sinner our evangelical work must become successful with, is the criminal, for did not Christ confer upon the penitential criminal, Mary of Magdalene, the cloak of apostle to the apostles and the model for penance and did he not canonize as the first saint of the Church, the penitential criminal Dismas.

Who shall we call upon to help us in this work with the criminal if not the reformed criminal, who understands the inner workings of the life within the criminal/carceral world and who knows—from having lived it—that the law written upon his heart was the criminal world law, the ancient call of murder, theft, and the lie as the daily word.

Criminality is a state of being, as real within the world as sainthood is without and as difficult to transform once set through years of thought and action as its more substantial namesake. Street life, prison life, enriched by endless crimes uncaught for each caught, endless nights running free, fills out the interiority, which only a serendipitous series of events, which may occur, to begin an emptying of the darkness and a refilling with the light.

Our work, your work, is designed to introduce this cognitive disruption by connecting to a continuous relationship of the criminal mind encountering—after years in prison—the sensory and spiritual shock of the outside world in the company of a deep knowledge guide with bones earned inside and outside and a story, the Great Story, to tell that trumps his criminal narrative.

Artists have been writing and making films about the criminal/carceral world for generations, revealing its interiority, yet criminal justice and rehabilitative practitioners persist with the assumption that merely with a tweak here, a tweak there—a job, home, school, treatment—all will be right; an idea which ignores the years of revelation of the deepset culture of the criminal world which no transitory service can change.

It is simple to see why the good man accepts obedience to God as normative, but to the bad man, to the criminal, obedience to anyone is abnormal.

The criminal must go his own way and always resist authority, even when locked down at all points, he will resist, often to the death, and it is a way that is sophisticated and hardened; and to assume he can be redirected from a lifetime commitment to a way of life perceived as honorable and true, through jobs, education, counseling, etc., being thrown in his path, is insulting.

Identity politics is built upon the ancient principle, like to like, and, though in some cases it is not applicable—as for instance, the ability to analyze the criminal world may be deeper in those outside of it—but in the sense in which we speak of it, the transformation of criminals; that the reformed criminal, and only him, has authentic access to the penitential criminal.

Like to like in this case says that those who *are or have been* can teach what *is or has been,* and what can become.

This seems logical if we understand the truth that all perspectives come from somewhere, and though all are not equally valid, from my dogmatic Catholic perspective; what is valid is that *'being'* is foundational to *complete* teaching, teaching as a pouring out of oneself to one's students or clients.

The foundational human anthropology is but two ways: those who wish to serve, follow Christ and those who wish to be served, follow Satan.

One result of the wisdom that grows with age is a growing appreciation of the wisdom of the ages and reading Augustine, Aquinas, Newman, and Pius XII, is ageless wisdom indeed.

The attraction of evil being something inside of us, as Jung's shadow, or outside of us, as Marx's capitalist, but still responsible for the evil we do rather than our own actions, consciously chosen, is obvious; for how can we be faulted, shunned, negated, if it is not I who am evil, but I who am a victim of evil acting through me.

Catholic teaching resolves this.

Sin has always been defined by the Church as something *done* by an individual, as the *Catechism* notes:

> **1859** Mortal sin requires *full knowledge* and *complete consent*. It presupposes knowledge of the sinful character of the act, of its opposition to God's law. It also implies a consent sufficiently deliberate to be a personal choice. Feigned ignorance and hardness of heart do not diminish, but rather increase, the voluntary character of a sin.

Sin's deepest manifestation—moral evil—has also always been that which is *done* by individuals, again the *Catechism*:

> **311** Angels and men, as intelligent and free creatures, have to journey toward their ultimate destinies by their free choice and preferential love. They can therefore go astray. Indeed, they have sinned. Thus has *moral evil*, incommensurably more harmful than physical evil, entered the world.

God is in no way, directly or indirectly, the cause of moral evil. He permits it, however, because he respects the freedom of his creatures and, mysteriously, knows how to derive good from it:

For almighty God. . ., because he is supremely good, would never allow any evil whatsoever to exist in his works if he were not so all-powerful and good as to cause good to emerge from evil itself.

The first sin called forth from God this question to Eve:

[Genesis 3:13] "What made thee do this?"

And though Satan was punished—so was man and woman—for angels and humans have free choice and must accept consequences; as in the first crime, God said to Cain:

[Genesis 4:10] "What is this thou hast done?"

Why and *what* and after millennia of human sin, suffering and redemption, we know only too well the *how*.

The institutional Church is a human organization and even though founded by God, its human leaders can be corrupted by Satan. For us, the fortress of faith emanating from the institutional Church are when the leaders speak as one, Peter and the bishops, and they have spoken in this way in two universal catechisms, that of St. Pius V, the *Catechism of the Council of Trent* and that of John Paul II, the *Catechism of the Catholic Church*.

Individual priests, bishops, and popes, are to be considered as you consider all clerics, trust but verify. The history of the human beings in the Church, from the moment of Peter's triple denial, is marked by Satan's influence swirling around the sanctuary of the Church promised by Christ to withstand for eternity against the gates of hell, against the most evil attempts of Satan to capture it; and it will so stand, but people will stumble, even Peter, and in that respect, treat everyone with the skepticism well-earned in your deep journey through the criminal/carceral world.

Remember always to be guided, in this respect, not by the persons of the Church but the supernatural truth of the Church, the Apostle's Creed.

> I believe in God, the Father Almighty, Creator of heaven and earth; and in Jesus Christ, His only Son, our Lord; Who was conceived by the Holy Spirit, born of the Virgin Mary, suffered under Pontius Pilate, was crucified, died, and was buried. He descended into hell; the third day He arose again from the dead. He ascended into heaven, and sits at the right hand of God, the Father Almighty; from thence He shall come to judge the living and the dead. I believe in the Holy Spirit, the Holy Catholic Church, the communion of Saints, the forgiveness of sins, the resurrection of the body and life everlasting. Amen.

The Apostle's Creed is, as the *Catechism* teaches:

> **196** Our presentation of the faith will follow the Apostles' Creed, which constitutes, as it were, "the oldest Roman catechism".

Socialism is the child of communism and the mark of the truly misled, who see all events as beyond their control, all crimes as caused by others, all good flowing from the omnipresent state, all evil as the result of unbridled individuality; yet it is simply the historic continuation of the initial evil—that man is greater than God, that man is God.

251

In this eternal revolt against the father, emanating from Satan, the socialist of today marks the criminal justice system as a tool of the rich against the poor; and the uninformed criminal eager for a reason other than accepting the responsibility of his own choice governing his criminal life, perhaps in a plea for mercy or public favor among the academics, goes along to get along, violating his own hard fought source of honor in standing strong in his own actions, doing the time for the crime if need be, though always seeking an honorable way out.

Marxist ideology is not, in any way, philosophical grounds for reformation from criminal/carceral world ethics as its ideology is built on the concept that capitalism is theft—criminal in its being—and its reality has been a reign of tyrants stealing freedom, life, and vitality from the people they rule.

We see, in the books by many former criminals, language used that is based on Marxist assumptions alien to the criminal world, the largest alienation being that criminals want to leave the criminal world—an assumption continually negated by the narrative of the books these authors write, pleasing to the socialist, captivated by the stories of violence, lust, and intoxication, lives for which they secretly yearn—a narrative embracing the obvious remaining criminality.

The Catholic way is the only way out and it is a daily rhythm of prayer and battle with the deep bonds of the satanic life lived so long, which always clings to us, inviting us to return to the deep sleep.

In our daily practice we are upon the ancient path to that supernatural place, that mythical place of legend and dreams—but made of the hardest stone and steel of reality—where we pray unceasingly.

We are hard-wired towards God and it is not a wiring of control but of following our deepest desires, which are towards the call to sainthood foundational to human nature.

In the fell clutch of circumstance

> In the fell clutch of circumstance
> I have not winced nor cried aloud.
> Under the bludgeonings of chance
> My head is bloody, but unbowed.
> (*Invictus*—William Ernest Henley—1849-1903)

The suffering of the criminal is caused by the results of his own acts—he is never innocent—of predation upon the innocent which drive him further and further from God; and for the penitential criminal, the suffering he has caused will flow through him like an angry river for a very long time—perhaps forever.

The great knights, still suffering in purgatory for their sins, being purified for the triumphant entry into heaven, always knew that the central stone upon which the chivalry of their knightly oath, the protection of women and children, rested, was that they—as armed and trained men—had the overwhelming strength to protect women and children from evil men, and only they, the knights, possessed this power, for women and children rarely possessed such strength.

Like bonds to like, deep calls to deep. As children of God we are called to realize what we are, and in our realization, what we are to become.

Do not become a traitor, a Judas. Do not walk in partnership with a man and then betray his secrets, for did not our Lord teach:

[Matthew 26:24] The Son of Man goes on his way, as the scripture foretells of him; but woe upon that man by whom the Son of Man is to be betrayed; better for that man if he had never been born.

When you no longer are a criminal, at that point forward, then your cooperation with the policeman is right and just, but betrayal from looking back, other than in the confessional, is not.

Read the reports of the stumblings of the men and women—laity and religious, the humble and the mighty—of the Church, to remind you of Christ's promise that the gates of hell shall not prevail against her.

The battle is already won, but we, to be among the victorious forever, must continue the lifelong battle within ourselves.

In the constant calls from teaching to bow down to God is the truth that because of our original sin, we all physically die and become as the dust.

Being criminals, we will spend a very long time in Purgatory, unless we burn in the fire of suffering through the cross, refining our nature in service, and reaching to heaven through our evangelization.

Suffering, a unique thing we criminals bring upon ourselves, and deliver to others, often reveling in the transmission, can be reflected upon in the story of Job.

Though prison will rarely be the world where we walk the true path— except perhaps for those who are doing natural life and possess the wherewithal to become prison monks— it is the world where we can begin the process of learning around the issues connected to our life of crime, punishment, suffering, and will.

Great works abound for study.

The collection of timeless literature that has played a large role in the development of my thinking around criminal reformation is a transformative tool that can be used as a guide for those criminals seeking to restructure their lives.

While some of this literature, prevalent during the period (1940's – 1970's) when the carceral world was beginning to shape the criminal world—though still relevant today and tomorrow—will have perhaps been replaced by newer works, the essential message will have remained the same, if perhaps more graphic.

This brief bibliography is for transformed criminals, who are able, through inclination, redemption, education, and skill, to become a grassroots organizational leader who can generate the transformation of other criminals.

It is directed to penitential criminals who are Catholic or potential converts who, because of their leadership in the criminal/carceral world, will have significant success and impact in the work of criminal transformation.

It is directed to those individuals who committed crimes for money—professional criminals—to whom crime was a way of life and prison time an occupational hazard.

It is a small box or two of books that will open the doors of perception while in the cells of deception.

Benton, W. (1960) . *Never a Greater Need*. New York: Alfred A. Knopf.

Benton, W. (1968). *This is My Beloved*. New York: Alfred A. Knopf.

De Ropp, R. S. (1968). *The Master Game: Pathways to Higher Consciousness Beyond the Drug Experience*. New York: Dell Publishing.

Exupery, A. d. S. (1950). *The Wisdom of the Sands*. New York: Harcourt, Brace and Company.

Frankl, Viktor E. (1984). *Man's Search for Meaning*. New York: Simon & Schuster.

Frazer, J.G. (1959). *The New Golden Bough*. (Gaster, T. H. Ed.). New York: Criterion Books.

Ginsburg, A. (1956) *Howl & Other Poems*. City Lights Books; San Francisco.

Gurdjieff, G. I. (1973). *Beelzebub's Tales to his Grandson: An Objectively Impartial Criticism of the Life of Man: First, Second & Third Books*. New York: E. P. Dutton.

Hoffer, E. (1966) *The True Believer*. New York: Perennial Library.

Irwin, J. (1970). *The Felon*. New Jersey: Prentice-Hall.

Kennedy, Daniel B. & Kerber, August. (1973). *Resocialization: An American Experiment*. New York: Behavioral Publications.

Kerouac, J. (1999). *On the Road*. New York: Penguin Books.

Khayyam, Omar. (1970). Translated by Edward Fitzgerald (Fourth Version). *The Rubaiyat of Omar Khayyam*.

Le Bon, G. (1952). *The Crowd: A Study of the Popular Mind*. London: Ernest Benn Limited.

Maugham, W. S. (1954), *The Razor's Edge*.
Garden City, New Jersey: Garden City, New York.

Nietzsche, F. W. (1954). *The Portable Nietzsche*. (W. Kaufmann, Trans.). New York: Penguin Books.

Sartre, J. P. (1963). *Saint Genet: Actor & Martyr*. New York: Pantheon Books.

Watts, A. (1972). *The Book On the Taboo Against Knowing Who You Are*. New York: Vintage Books.

Watts, A. (1970). *Psychotherapy East & West*. New York: Ballantine Books.

Wilson, C. (1982). *The Outsider*. Los Angeles: Jeremy P. Tarcher, Inc.

One of the powerful realities of prison is that you are encouraged to bear what suffering you do, to accept that you have brought it upon yourself, and to respect suffering's voice, doom may seem imminent but that will pass; all that matters is how you stand under the sword of impending doom, unafraid and primed for battle, or cowering in the cold corner of fear-drenched marble.

The carceral world is a primer in the bearing of the cross of suffering upon which great Dismas hung, beside the Lord, who brought him to heaven, and made him the first canonized saint of the eternal Church now on earth, the criminal, the thief, the penitent.

And on that day of Golgotha, another penitential criminal, Mary of Magdalene, stood at the foot of the cross of wood, the tree of life, the arc of heaven, the two criminals embracing our Lord at the moment of his ascension.

Beyond this place of wrath and tears

> Beyond this place of wrath and tears
> Looms but the Horror of the shade,
> And yet the menace of the years
> Finds, and shall find, me unafraid.
> (*Invictus*—William Ernest Henley—1849-1903)

Of all those who stood upon the ground of earth and proclaimed a new faith only Christ called himself God and only Christ named his successor:

> **[Matthew 16:13]** Then Jesus came into the neighbourhood of Caesarea Philippi; and there he asked his disciples, What do men say of the Son of Man? Who do they think he is? **[14]** Some say John the Baptist, they told him, others Elias, others again, Jeremy or one of the prophets. **[15]** Jesus said to them, And what of you? Who do you say that I am? **[16]** Then Simon Peter answered, Thou art the Christ, the Son of the living God. **[17]** And Jesus answered him, Blessed art thou, Simon son of Jona; it is not flesh and blood, it is my Father in heaven that has revealed this to thee. **[18]** And I tell thee this in my turn, that thou art Peter, and it is upon this rock that I will build my church; and the gates of hell shall not prevail against it; **[19]** and I will give to thee the keys of the kingdom of heaven; and whatever thou shalt bind on earth shall be bound in heaven; and whatever thou shalt loose on earth shall be loosed in heaven.

And Peter is with us still, though being a different man called by God when it is time, though often stumbling as men do, yet remaining now for two thousand years, the Rock.

The shock troops of the Catholic Empire were many and some of the mightiest came from the soldier Ignatius Loyola, founder of the Jesuits.

From many martial saints, Loyola foremost among them, come the tools and sensibilities that govern our work, shape our days and nights, and guide our steps within the dark wars of the criminal and carceral world.

They have given us tools of remembrance and prayer, devotion and adoration, to hold us to the single truth, the single service, to Christ and his Church; with Peter, to Christ, through Mary, for the greater glory of God.

So much of the focused boldness personified by the Jesuits over the centuries is what is necessary for this work which others—for whatever reason—do not embrace with consistency, scale, and skill.

If we judge truth by the currently advancing power of secular institutions over the Catholic Church, we align ourselves with the gates of hell—with whom we shall always strive, but never succumb—as Christ promised.

We must always hold to the high road of Church history— the road of loving and protecting the innocent, retaining hope and guided by our faith in charity—the road occupied by the saints and under the standard of Our Lord Jesus Christ following the path to virtue.

The pacifist looks to the selected aspects of the words of Christ in the New Testament for affirmation that God is a God of *only* love, peace, and mercy and he is all that; but he is also the God of the Old Testament, the trinity with Christ and the Holy Spirit a God *also* of rage, war and vengeance; truly a God for all, truly a God able to defeat the enemy in spiritual and temporal combat.

As the great story settled into the souls of Catholics revealing ancient truths, various strategies of Satan attacked, from within and without the Church; the heresies, yet all have the one satanic root, that angels and humans know more than their creator.

The pacifists are those surrender-to-evil souls who also feel capital punishment is no longer justified because of advancements in prison technology—the super-max prison.

259

The way of the pacifist is the way of death. It is the way of all the great heresies, it is the way to the reign of evil in the world, for in the protection of innocent human life, and in respecting the dignity of all human beings, the primary protection is towards the dignity and life of yourself, and as you would give your life for that of your friend, you must fight to the death to protect your own.

The way of the pacifist removes action from the individual—within whom the eternal law, set into the human soul by God, informs the temporal actions human beings take in response to evil—and invests action within the state, whose human-made law bends and shapes itself around the whims and wisps of the politics and degraded morality of the criminal city, the city of humans.

Pacifism as national policy is utopian, perfection only attainable from the return of Christ, the divine king holding the sword of ultimate justice in his righteous hand.

Socialists, who always proclaim pacifism yet still see the strike against capital as just war; indeed to them, wars of labor against capital are just wars.

A cousin of pacifism—formed from the same socialistic roots—is the concept of restorative justice, where the essential Catholic truth of punishment for crime is replaced with the idea of restoration.

Punishment cannot be replaced for it lies at the center of Catholic anthropology, and without it there is no accountability.

Adam and Eve were punished by being driven from the garden, Satan was punished by being driven from heaven, and Cain was punished by being driven from his home and family.

The *Catechism* teaches:

2266 The efforts of the state to curb the spread of behavior harmful to people's rights and to the basic rules of civil society correspond to the requirement of safeguarding the common good. Legitimate public authority has the right and the duty to inflict punishment proportionate to the gravity of the offense. Punishment has the primary aim of redressing the disorder introduced by the offense. When it is willingly accepted by the guilty party, it assumes the value of expiation. Punishment then, in addition to defending public order and protecting people's safety, has a medicinal purpose: as far as possible, it must contribute to the correction of the guilty party.

Criminal justice, the discipline, is that of seeing justice rendered to criminals, the justice of their due; the justice of maintaining their dignity as human beings created in the image of God; the legal justice flowing from their criminal acts; and the redemptive justice emanating from their penance; all flowing from the spiritual foundation upon which the cardinal virtues—prudence, justice, fortitude, and temperance—stand.

We encounter in the Old Testament a martial perspective— but not, as some would proclaim, due to the higher level of barbarity of that time—but to the eternal need for man to fight evil, as the world remains, now as then, a battleground between good and evil.

Today it is even a more perilous battleground as the satanic truth envelops us in clouds—the greatest victory of the devil is to have convinced us he does not exist. This is why—though so many want only to look to the New Testament for guidance, somehow believing Jesus Christ was absent from the Trinity during the Old—as fighters in the eternal battle, raging always most fervently within the sanctuaries of the Church itself, Catholics must embrace both Testaments in the war against evil, for they are really only one, as the *Catechism* teaches:

102 Through all the words of Sacred Scripture, God speaks only one single Word, his one Utterance in whom he expresses himself completely.

You recall that one and the same Word of God extends throughout Scripture, that it is one and the same Utterance that resounds in the mouths of all the sacred writers, since he who was in the beginning God with God has no need of separate syllables; for he is not subject to time.

We cannot allow ourselves to become distracted from the ancient knowledge of the powerful connection reformed criminals have with the early roots of the Church because of Mary Magdalene and Dismas so deeply connected with the fullness of the ministry of Christ.

The way to triumph lies here, take it, surround yourself with the Word, it is not the book but the Word, from holy souls, who may not know they are holy, who know that only God can make that judgment, we can only follow the path before us, stumbling, haltingly, as the creatures we are, but always towards the Church triumphant.

Love, as Jesus taught us, is to follow the Great Commandment of loving God and our neighbor, but loving our neighbor does not include the criminal, for he has set himself outside the law, becoming an outlaw. To those who are aggressors against the person and property of the innocent, what applies is not the Great Commandment but the eternal teachings of the Church embodied in justice and mercy. To apply the Great Commandment to the aggressor is the way of death—the way of the pacifist who is merely raising up victims for the predatory aggressor.

For most of the years of the 2,000 years the Church has been on earth, she swam in martiality, with papal temporal leadership of armies but a few centuries behind us and spiritual leadership closer still, and holy war was embraced by Peter.

True knighthood has been, is now, and will be for all time, the sole act of defending Christ and those he loves.

True knighthood is being a knight of faith.

The theology of the body is the theology of husband and wife, knight and lady of the realm.

The Great Commandment to love God and our neighbor is practiced by loving that which is God, within ourselves and others and recognizing that which is of the devil, within ourselves and others, and fighting against that with righteous anger and destroying that; else we are like warm milk against the bitter cold of space, a momentary sop soon overtaken.

St. Thomas Aquinas revealed God to us as the prime mover—unmoved—and at each moment of essential decision it is so—pause—stop—death—battle—contemplation—meditation—here is the core of religion, the unmoved.

Isn't today, in the world, an approaching desert? Surely from the cold concrete and steel of the streets and the prison it surely is, and what do we pull from the desert, what great discipline and courage can it call forth from us.

Many years ago, while serving time in McNeil Island Federal Penitentiary, a group of us formed a study group to read writers whose works resonated with us, and one we chose was Antoine de Saint-Exupery's book *The Wisdom of the Sands*, the harsh and beautiful reflections of a desert king, whose narrative is almost scriptural; one of the greatest books of the desert mind and soul.

God does not know what is to happen, no more than we with our children. He must trust in what he has taught us—and that we learn to call upon him—as we trust in what we have taught our children once they are out in the world.

The real is not what we can see, feel, touch, or taste, only envision, imagine, dream, pray for, and ultimately it becomes the rock of granite, the mountain of stone we stand upon within the world as he once stood and stands still, the only one who says I am God, I am he. The others, the heretical prophets, seers, and enlightened men, those seekers after God who stand in their midst, are blinded to him by the ancient pride, that human pride that believes God is not—that only humans *are*—for we can see, feel, touch, and taste.

The responsibility we have in our apostolate was taught us by the Church.

The professional criminal is the strong man, unafraid to die for what he wants, with no fear of the darkness and silence; and once transformed through the blood of Christ, and forged through the combat theology of the carceral/criminal world, may join with one who is a stronger man yet, the truly faithful priest, the ascetic, unafraid to die for what he believes, who walks with Peter through Mary to Christ; and together—criminal and priest—they can recover those who are lost, together they can recover an essential aspect of the Christic mission, to the deep sinner, to Saint Mary Magdalene and Saint Dismas.

The Church on earth, the Church administered, represented, and continued by sinful human beings, is always being attacked and it is always being corrupted, so if it is to these stumblers you look to for validation of your faith, you shall always be disappointed, as the *Catechism* teaches:

> **567** The Kingdom of heaven was inaugurated on earth by Christ. "This kingdom shone out before men in the word, in the works, and in the presence of Christ." The Church is the seed and beginning of this kingdom. Her keys are entrusted to Peter.

One often hears from Catholics, who are defending their dissenting positions on a myriad of issues traditionally held by the Church, that if we but listened to what Christ was teaching us in the New Testament...all would be well. This is a refuge of the heretic who forgets Christ is a member of the Trinity, and from the Trinity came the complete covenants embodied in the Old *and* New. Testament, all of which still stand, as interpreted and taught by the Catholic Church

In the end, it is a spiritual war between those who believe in God and his teachings embodied within the Catholic Church and those who do not, those who live by the ways of the world, those who accepted the choice—rejected by Christ—from Satan to embrace the world.

The way of the Catholic is the way to eternal life in heaven. The way of the world is eternal life in hell.

It matters not how strait the gate

> It matters not how strait the gate,
> How charged with punishments the scroll.
> I am the master of my fate:
> I am the captain of my soul.
> (*Invictus*—William Ernest Henley—1849-1903)

In the end it is always back to each of us and the mastery we have over our life, which is only real when we *realize* that to which our life is most founded upon, the divinity and eternalness of God.

As the institutions defining and sustaining morality and honor break down, we are thrown back upon ourselves— and new honor groups—to maintain our blood connection to Holy Mother Church.

The ancient honor group of the Church, centered around the Church Militant, the Church Suffering, and the Church

Triumphant, bowing to the great table of the mass of the world, partaking of the divine flesh and blood of God, earthly knights eternal in the work only ending with the opening of eternity to all of the faithful with the coming of our Lord.

I have always known that the only path to personal transformation from the criminal/carceral world to the communal world, was an interior path, and if transformation was to occur, it must become the only path in life, and so it has been for me and so it must become for those who take on this charge: help your brothers.

Whether in prison or out, honor and truth is paramount and the ancient way of the Catholic Saint, to Christ through Mary, for the greater glory of God—in the great teaching of the Church that the strong protect the weak, thou shalt not harm the innocent nor betray thy brother, justice prevails eternally though not in this world, yet we are called to be just, prudent, courageous, and temperate, loving God and the way of the Saint.

It is never the living persons of the Church we follow, but the communion of saints—for there are only two perfect human beings, Mary and her son Jesus—for even Peter stumbles.

It is Peter the Pontiff, not Peter the man, and it is Christ who Peter follows, not himself, for Peter is captive to the teaching, to Christ, God the Father and the Holy Spirit, and through Mary—Human Mother of God—lies the eternal path.

The *Catechism* teaches:

> **150** Faith is first of all a personal adherence of man to God. At the same time, and inseparably, it is a *free assent to the whole truth that God has revealed*. As personal adherence to God and assent to his truth, Christian faith differs from our faith in

266

any human person. It is right and just to entrust oneself wholly to God and to believe absolutely what he says. It would be futile and false to place such faith in a creature.

It is dogma we can trust, the eternal truths of the Church and they are outlined for us in the two great universal catechisms, of Trent and Vatican II.

From the *Catechism*:

The dogmas of the faith

88 The Church's Magisterium exercises the authority it holds from Christ to the fullest extent when it defines dogmas, that is, when it proposes, in a form obliging the Christian people to an irrevocable adherence of faith, truths contained in divine Revelation or also when it proposes, in a definitive way, truths having a necessary connection with these.

89 There is an organic connection between our spiritual life and the dogmas. Dogmas are lights along the path of faith; they illuminate it and make it secure. Conversely, if our life is upright, our intellect and heart will be open to welcome the light shed by the dogmas of faith.

90 The mutual connections between dogmas, and their coherence, can be found in the whole of the Revelation of the mystery of Christ. "In Catholic doctrine there exists an order or hierarchy of truths, since they vary in their relation to the foundation of the Christian faith."

Through the revelatory movements of the Great Story we see the eternal cathedral in time, the True Church, founded by God, who came to earth as man that we might know.

The others, the heretical and paltry resemblances of truth which go under names of men and whim, they are nothing but shadows, angry ghosts in the mists of time.

The Catholic Church stands today as it stood over 2,000 years ago, and the Holy Mass today follows the same form as that of the apostles, as does the organization of the temporal church itself, arranged hierarchically under Peter.

Abolishing capital punishment is abolishing the fight against evil—surrendering to evil—for if evil is not worth fighting, nothing is.

The Church has become masterful at doing good but struggles fighting evil; and that is to be expected as a Church founded by God yet managed by humans, for whom even the recognition of evil often eludes them let alone the constancy of fighting it.

Evil did rule the ancient world before Christ and hangs on by its bloody talons yet today, but ever since he came, it has been in retreat and it lost its once mighty hold upon the world once the majority of human beings were no longer in real slavery.

In many ways my generation was a wasted generation, in its intoxicants, its overwhelming propensity to hate authority, its addiction to sensuality, its fear of Catholic truth and its corruption of institutions, yet from this waste grows good flowers and rich grasses.

Today, as we walk into the world, let us be within our armor.

Chapter Six
The Lampstand Prison Ministry: Constructed on Catholic Social Teaching & the History of the Catholic Church

The foundational ideas animating the Lampstand prison ministry—that it takes a reformed criminal to reform criminals and that the conversion approach must be intellectual—are ideas I have been working with since the beginning of my reformation from criminality at age thirty-five, as I began seeing the world from the perspective of a college education (leading to a successful criminal rehabilitative college-based educational program I developed and managed) and continuing to the final washing from my spirit the last remnants of a lifetime of criminal thinking twenty years later, in the waters of baptism.

The peer relationship is where the impact this apostolate may have on future criminal activity lies, and it will be seen most dramatically within the Lampstand prison ministry where the apostolate work will *only* be optimized by conversions of the criminal/carceral elite—the professional criminal—whose history within rehabilitative work is virtually nil, because for him, the rewards of deep immersion within the criminal/carceral culture are too great, and other than as a ruse, rehabilitation is considered a tragic fool's errand.

Prison ministries have traditionally been done as a corporal work of mercy, and the results—considering the recidivism rate of about 70% nationally—have not been very good.

The Lampstand prison ministry views prison ministry as a spiritual work of mercy, the *Catechism* describes the difference:

> **2447** The works of mercy are charitable actions by which we come to the aid of our neighbor in his spiritual and bodily necessities. Instructing, advising, consoling, comforting are spiritual works of mercy, as are forgiving and bearing wrongs patiently. The corporal works of mercy consist especially in feeding the hungry, sheltering the homeless, clothing the naked, visiting the sick and imprisoned, and burying the dead.

To the professional criminal being a fool is most certainly a form of suffering, for the worldview underlying his criminality is built on "knowing".

The corporal works of mercy with prisoners has individual application with little optimizational benefit, while the spiritual works of mercy—though also of individual application—have great benefit.

The difference is in who is ministered to. The traditional prison ministry works with any and all prisoners, while the Lampstand ministry, wanting to amplify its work, focuses exclusively on professional criminals—those who commit crimes for money, and who are not informants, serial killers, pedophiles, or rapists—as the professional criminals are those most apt to have success evangelizing other prisoners due to their criminal/carceral credibility.

The criminal/carceral world is a tightly closed culture in which personal character and reputation are known nationwide due to the prison cultural grapevine's effectiveness, and the ability of professional criminals who have been converted, to convert other criminals is amplified, due to their high status and reputation for constancy, which does not apply to informants, serial killers, pedophiles, or rapists.

In liberal Catholic narratives, the way of evil in the world is largely ignored, as if it did not exist. Liberal Catholics believe they can practice pacifism in the face of war and pacifism's criminal justice cousin, restorative justice, in the face of criminal evil. They believe they can abolish capital punishment and use psychotherapy to counsel rapists and pedophiles. They act as if love conquers all—the great misreading of Catholic tradition and scripture. The only love that does conquer all, is God's love for us and within the fire of that love resides the tempered steel of the sword of justice, the sword St. Michael the Archangel has wielded since time immemorial, driving Satan from Heaven and protecting the Church; reminding us of its efficacy in the hands of the Catholic Crusaders, the warrior monks who protected Christendom for centuries and whose need is ever more acute today; if not with steel swords—though those wielded by saints and angels should never be beaten into plowshares lest the innocent be plowed into dirt by evil men—with the fire tempered *Word*.

Principles of traditional martial Catholic thinking on criminal justice issues have rarely seen wide discussion throughout the Church and have largely lain fallow for some time, at least since the papacy of Pius XII.

Since then there has been little thinking around criminal justice.

Many Catholic thinkers reflecting on criminals begin with the assumption—wonderfully well-intentioned but woefully naïve to the way of evil in the world and how deeply evil has captured many human souls—that the criminal is Christ.

In the words and actions of Christ, this idea finds spare root, for what did he say about Judas, that

> **[Matthew 26:24]** ...it would have been better for that man if he had not been born"

271

And what did he say about those who harm children.

> **[Matthew-18:6]** ...but whoever causes one of these little ones who believe in me to sin, it would be better for him to have a great millstone fastened round his neck and to be drowned in the depth of the sea.

This tradition of seeing the face of Christ in the faces of criminals by many Catholics working in prison ministry can be troublesome, as the reality is more complex,

The Church teaches us—noted below—that we *are capable of entering into communion* with our neighbor and we *are called by grace* to a covenant with God, but Satan has a *certain dominion over us and our nature is wounded and inclined to evil.*

As a consequence, for the penitential criminal, our entire life will be on the battlefield and many will fall. To persevere and win the eternal, we must be armored of God and we must *struggle to do what is right*, as the *Catechism* teaches us:

> **357** Being in the image of God the human individual possesses the dignity of a person, who is not just something, but someone. He is capable of self-knowledge, of self-possession and of freely giving himself and entering into communion with other persons. And he is called by grace to a covenant with his Creator, to offer him a response of faith and love that no other creature can give in his stead.

> **407** The doctrine of original sin, closely connected with that of redemption by Christ, provides lucid discernment of man's situation and activity in the world. By our first parents' sin, the devil has acquired a certain domination over man, even

though man remains free. Original sin entails "captivity under the power of him who thenceforth had the power of death, that is, the devil". Ignorance of the fact that man has a wounded nature inclined to evil gives rise to serious errors in the areas of education, politics, social action and morals.

408 The consequences of original sin and of all men's personal sins put the world as a whole in the sinful condition aptly described in St. John's expression, "the sin of the world". This expression can also refer to the negative influence exerted on people by communal situations and social structures that are the fruit of men's sins.

409 This dramatic situation of "the whole world [which] is in the power of the evil one" makes man's life a battle:

> The whole of man's history has been the story of dour combat with the powers of evil, stretching, so our Lord tells us, from the very dawn of history until the last day. Finding himself in the midst of the battlefield man has to struggle to do what is right, and it is at great cost to himself, and aided by God's grace, that he succeeds in achieving his own inner integrity.

For the criminal, the beginning of that long and arduous battle is true penance and a transformation that will be remarked on by others, even the guards in his prison, and this penance will be carried in a struggling grasp for the rest of our lives.

Though we have received the forgiveness of baptism and our past has been cleansed, it will sometimes haunt us when the evil we have done surges up in our memory, drawn by a remembrance of the past triggered by an event in the present and this is how it should be, for the wages of our evil done, though cleansed, has marked our soul, and we can best continue to salve those scars through our apostolate helping evangelize other criminals.

Evil exists and it exists most potently within prisons, and that is an arena of the most dangerous apostolate work, which only the Catholic Church can effectively carry out, by virtue of her ancient truth and the promise embedded in her founding words:

> **[Matthew 16:18]** And I tell thee this in my turn, that thou art Peter, and it is upon this rock that I will build my church; and the gates of hell shall not prevail against it;

Each human being, including criminals, has within him an instinctual reaching for the supernatural—a divine invitation—but for those who do not encounter the truth of the Catholic Church in a form full enough and orthodox enough to call forth their response, there are an endless array of worldly lures promising a false supernatural aspect, and within the criminal world these lures are dark, deep, and powerfully alluring; reaching back into ancient pagan history and cult to call the criminal to the endless feast of power, money, intoxication, and sensuality.

But for the unbeliever, it is crucial that Catholic truth be revealed in a way and from a source from which he can open himself to the Divine invitation.

It is hoped that this work and all of the work of the Lampstand Foundation, will, along with the works of the other—though far too few—Catholics working in this field, add to a renewal of prison apostolate work, this vital ministry, for in the call from Christ to visit him in prison, it was also an individual call from the Cross, to help the Good Thief, for Christ extends to each of us the Divine Invitation, *Follow Me.*

Introducing the Prison Ministry

Professional criminals want, most of all, to not be taken as they take others, to not be robbed, thieved, burgled, conned or otherwise snookered about the truths of life, about which they are certain, in their choice of criminality, that they have mastered, along with its obviously congruent carceral world; and if they discover that there is another hidden world—for the truths of the criminal/carceral world are also deeply hidden—where a truth trumps his, as Christ's truth trumped Dismas' on Golgotha, he will grasp hold of it as surely as cash available to his quick hands.

The prison ministry in this chapter is designed for an individual Catholic parish working with a maximum security prison, through a ministry community of at least four parishioners, in conjunction with the prison's Catholic priest, and supported by prison officials.

In order for a Catholic parish to effectively provide a prison ministry that can lead to conversion, a new paradigm in thinking about the criminal world is required rather than the Hollywood dramas or Marxist fantasies too often animating many undertaking this most valuable of ministries called for by Christ in his final teaching to the apostles.

> **[Matthew 25: 31]** "When the Son of Man comes in his glory, and all the angels with him, he will sit upon his glorious throne, **32** and all the nations will be assembled before him. And he will separate them one from another, as a shepherd separates the sheep from the goats. **33** He will place the sheep on his right and the goats on his left. **34** Then the king will say to those on his right, 'Come, you who are blessed by my Father. Inherit the kingdom prepared for you from the foundation of the world. **35** For I was hungry and you gave me food, I was

thirsty and you gave me drink, a stranger and you welcomed me, **36** naked and you clothed me, ill and you cared for me, in prison and you visited me.' **37** Then the righteous will answer him and say, 'Lord, when did we see you hungry and feed you, or thirsty and give you drink? **38** When did we see you a stranger and welcome you, or naked and clothe you? **39** When did we see you ill or in prison, and visit you?' **40** And the king will say to them in reply, 'Amen, I say to you, whatever you did for one of these least brothers of mine, you did for me.' **41** Then he will say to those on his left, 'Depart from me, you accursed, into the eternal fire prepared for the devil and his angels. **42** For I was hungry and you gave me no food, I was thirsty and you gave me no drink, **43** a stranger and you gave me no welcome, naked and you gave me no clothing, ill and in prison, and you did not care for me.' **44** Then they will answer and say, 'Lord, when did we see you hungry or thirsty or a stranger or naked or ill or in prison, and not minister to your needs?' **45** He will answer them, 'Amen, I say to you, what you did not do for one of these least ones, you did not do for me.' **46** And these will go off to eternal punishment, but the righteous to eternal life." *New American Bible*

The greatest of these needs is the spiritual, for the prisoner, having willingly entered Satan's snare anticipating worldly rewards, has been captured by the prince of this world, and it is only through the weapons of spiritual warfare—learned from the social teaching of the Church—that he can free himself, weapons which the Catholic prison ministry can help bring to him.

Remember the spiritual works of mercy from the *Catechism*:

2447 Instructing, advising, consoling, comforting are spiritual works of mercy, as are forgiving and bearing wrongs patiently.

These are all works that can be accomplished effectively from a distance through letters and gifts.

Though the prince of this world is powerful and, in many cases can draw men into sin, he is not the cause of every sin.

The criminal world is a vast and ancient cultural entity—stretching back to the reign of the first criminal, Cain, and his building of the city of man wherein criminality rules—that traditionally was largely isolated within local or national boundaries, but which over the past several decades has become global.

Within this paradigm of a global criminal world connected through opportune action, prisons play a crucial role—especially in the United States—for it is in prison that the forging of criminal leadership is most dramatically developed, tested, and refined, and it is there that the greatest need for the work of the Church to minister to criminals enmeshed by the deepest evil, exists.

The same forces driving the paradigmatic clash of civilizations are driving criminal world cultural development, where internal ideology is the governor, and power and control of turf is the result and only the power of the social teaching of the Church can thwart it.

What is missing from the works on prison ministry I've studied is an understanding of the underlying criminal/carceral world narrative which animates professional criminality. Without addressing this and without daily sacramental practice—putting on the armor of God—by the prison minister, most professed prison conversions are as shallow as rain on the window pane.

The eternal reason criminals are criminals is because they are distant from God, and that is a result—as it is for all of us—of their individual choice.

The Lampstand prison ministry is partially animated by the axiomatic criminal and carceral world principle of *walking the talk*—so clearly tied to accepting individual responsibility for individual choices—by studying who the Church *says* she is through her social teaching, in relation to *who* she was throughout the high roads of her doctrinal history.

The ministry is also built upon the foundation of family that characterized our Lord's mission on earth—where his cousin John the Baptist and his good friend Lazarus, and Lazarus's sister Mary Magdalene, played such an important role—the family that presents the ministry is the parish and from the parish family will come the strength and love that will carry this ministry through the dark and dangerous days ahead to the great light upon Catholic truth it will shine.

Constructing the Prison Ministry

With Peter, to Christ, through Mary, shows us the path.

Peter stumbled (and as the prototype of all popes throughout history, stumbles still) denying Christ thrice and like the other apostles, save John, and Mary Magdalene—who tradition calls "Apostle to the Apostles" for her delivering the message of Christ's Resurrection to the other Apostles—ran away during the central event of the God-Man's ministry, the crucifixion, leaving only John and Magdalene with the Virgin Mother and the other Mary at the foot of the cross.

The ministry lesson here is not to base our faith on individuals whether laity, priests or popes, but on the sacred doctrine of the Church and the Church Triumphant which grows in eternity, and by using her social teaching which began in the beginning with Genesis, hand in hand with her history.

John was the most powerfully spiritual and intellectual of the apostles and Magdalene was a penitential and transformed criminal, while the other apostles and disciples were more representative of the people; fishermen, tax collector, doctor.

There were then two criminals, Dismas and Mary Magdalene, with Christ at his death and Dismas' given appellation, *The Good Thief*, resonates throughout the history of the Church.

What do we know about Dismas?

The good thief Dismas is the first human being Christ canonized as a saint of the Church he founded upon earth, sealing it by taking him to Paradise the day they both died.

This is a singular event in the history of Christ's ministry on earth, a singular event in human history, and a singular event in the conversion of criminals, for there is no more powerful intercessionary saint than Saint Dismas.

His story should play a major role in prison ministry.

What are we to make of these signature events in the death of Christ accompanied by the two proto criminal saints?

Dismas' life is a paradigm for the conversion of criminals; on the Egypt Road from the *Arabic Gospel of the Infancy*, how his essentially good heart recognized the Holy Family, and in his final moments, recognized God hanging beside him, God, the fount of the social teaching of the Church.

When we talk about the social teaching we are not talking about philosophical ramblings, new age meanderings, or occult ravings, but absolute truth revealed to us by the God-Man Christ, preserved for us by his Apostles, taught to us by the Fathers and Doctors of the Church, captured within the works of Peter and the universal *Catechisms* of Trent and Vatican II.

As we surely will, and often, encounter Modernism in our ministry, it is crucial to get our response right, as the Church has had it right since the beginning, as Modernism is nothing but the ancient heresy of Gnosticism—salvation by knowledge—in new language, but to know that you need to go to the source, you need to refresh yourself at the pool of clear water, the water of life.

Absolute truth resonates with your soul, and when you read the works of the greatest of all teachers, the Angelic Doctor St. Thomas Aquinas, the absolute truth rings out with stunning force.

Most teachers of the social teaching describe the 1891 encyclical *Rerum Novarum* (On Capital and Labor) by Pope Leo XIII as the beginning of the modern social teaching, but the teaching is all 'modern' because it is all eternal and the social teaching of Genesis is as crucial to our understanding of today as it was in the beginning.

One aspect of the modern interpretation of the social teaching—favored by liberation theologians and related liberal Catholics—is the preferential option for the materially poor.

This is a misreading of the teaching of the Church—as misread as the worldly tendency to think the materially rich are superior to the spiritually rich—for it is the spiritually poor who suffer most eternally. Christ revealed the truth of the spiritually rich and the materially rich to us in the parables of the widow's mite and the rich young man.

There have always been internal corruptions of the divine teaching and throughout the two thousand year history of the organized Catholic Church on earth, there have been, and will continue to be, many wayward, incompetent, misguided, and evil individuals among the laity and the priesthood, even stretching to the papacy.

In times within my memory the greatest disruption of the Church came around the time of Vatican II (1962-1965), when the entire Church seemed to wander ebulliently in the golden fields of temptation and dreams proffered by the world.

While also playing a role in Vatican II, Communism and Marxist analysis drove a great degradation of the Latin American Church through Liberation Theology, spearheaded by the Jesuits—see Jesuit Malachi Martin's book, *The Jesuits: The Society of Jesus and the Betrayal of the Roman Catholic Church*—which, through the choice of power over principle by the first Catholic president in America, led by the corruption of arguments protecting the life of the unborn and the virtual heresy of generations of Catholic politicians, see *The Politics of Abortion* by Alice Hendershott; all of which is undergirded by the changes emanating from the corrupted reading of the documents of Vatican II, see *Iota Unum: A Study of Changes in the Catholic Church in the XXth Century,* by Romano Amerio.

Upon this opening of the citadel to the serpent came the latest manifestation of the prince of this world's power to drive the Church to distraction, the sexual abuse crisis that engulfed the Church in earlier centuries (see *The Rite of Sodomy: Homosexuality and the Roman Catholic Church*, by Randy Engel)—and still engulfs—the Church.

All this is the corruption from within attempting to destroy the Church, but that from without was more, much more, for the world always attacks the Church and is all too often successful.

281

The Prison Ministry

The *Catechism of the Catholic Church* teaches us about the missionary path, which the prison ministry surely is, a hard, yet, potentially, rewarding path.

852 *Missionary paths.* The Holy Spirit is the protagonist, "the principal agent of the whole of the Church's mission." It is he who leads the Church on her missionary paths. "This mission continues and, in the course of history, unfolds the mission of Christ, who was sent to evangelize the poor; so the Church, urged on by the Spirit of Christ, must walk the road Christ himself walked, a way of poverty and obedience, of service and self-sacrifice even to death, a death from which he emerged victorious by his resurrection." So it is that "the blood of martyrs is the seed of Christians."

853 On her pilgrimage, the Church has also experienced the "discrepancy existing between the message she proclaims and the human weakness of those to whom the Gospel has been entrusted." Only by taking the "way of penance and renewal," the "narrow way of the cross," can the People of God extend Christ's reign. For "just as Christ carried out the work of redemption in poverty and oppression, so the Church is called to follow the same path if she is to communicate the fruits of salvation to men."

854 By her very mission, "the Church . . . travels the same journey as all humanity and shares the same earthly lot with the world: she is to be a leaven and, as it were, the soul of human society in its renewal by Christ and transformation into the family of God." Missionary endeavor requires patience. It begins with the proclamation of the Gospel to peoples and groups who do not yet believe in Christ, continues with the establishment of Christian communities that are "a sign of God's presence in the world," and leads to the foundation of local churches. It must involve a process of inculturation if the Gospel is to take flesh in each people's culture. There will be times of defeat. "With regard to individuals, groups, and peoples it is only by degrees that [the Church] touches and penetrates them and so receives them into a fullness which is Catholic."

The Lampstand prison ministry—for the protection of the ministers, the prisoners, and ultimately the objective furtherance of the ministry—is based upon community, distance, books, and time.

The ministry is built upon a community of parishioners, providing distance teaching to prisoners about the social teaching of the Church complimented by her history through the suggested books, and taking all of the time necessary to ensure conversion begins to take hold.

This ministry will provide a path to conversion for prisoners upon release, and for those prisoners who will never be released— who are serving life without the possibility of parole and who have the prison status to pursue the way of the prison monk or spiritual warrior—a transformative prison conversion that can occur through their study of the teaching and history of the Church.

This prison conversion is an optional outcome which can ultimately lead to the further conversion of other prisoners.

Some preparative and logistical elements of prison ministry should include:

- Four reference books which Lampstand suggests would be very important for the ministry group to read and discuss before beginning outreach are **(1)** *Inside the Criminal*

283

Mind: Revised and Updated Edition. Stanton E. Samenow. Ph.D. (2004) **(2)** *Criminal Justice and the Catholic Church*. Fr. Andrew Skotnicki, O. Carm. (2008) **(3)** The two volume work of Fr. Rodger Charles, SJ, *Christian Social Witness and Teaching: The Catholic Tradition from Genesis to Centesimus Annus,* (1998) **(4)** H. W. Crocker III, *Triumph: The Power and the Glory of the Catholic Church, A 2,000 Year History,* (2001).

- Set up a Post Office Box for distance teaching.
- A minimum of four parishioners are needed to start a ministry community.
- Seek a retired law enforcement parishioner to become part of the ministry.
- Group reading and response of all letters to and from prisoners.
- Work with a maximum of four prisoners at a time, with each weekly meeting focused on one of them, or with each monthly meeting focused on each of them sequentially, and one letter a month minimum to each, with money (for stamps, paper and envelopes, books, commitment).
- At the prison you choose to work with, ask for an interview with the Catholic Chaplain and the appropriate correctional officer to determine the details of prisoners you are dealing with, what are the details of their criminal history— and make sure you have access to the public court record involving their crime and subsequent sentencing.

In addition to a retired law enforcement professional, the parish prison ministry would be very fortunate to have a transformed criminal as a ministry member, one who meets the eight benchmarks of deep knowledge leadership:

- Ten years in the criminal world (includes prison) committing crimes for money
- Five years in a maximum security federal or state prison and not an informant, serial killer, pedophile, or rapist
- Ten years out of prison, off parole, crime free, and helping the community
- Educated about Catholic social teaching
- Master's degree
- Leader of a community transformation apostolate
- Married
- Catholic

Having someone who has actually been there, walking in the criminal's penitential, transformative shoes is preferred though not absolutely necessary.

Transformed criminals who meet these eight benchmarks will very likely feel a great compassion for criminals, and it is a compassion built upon a real understanding and sensitivity of the criminal/carceral world.

The depth of the criminal/carceral world's culture generally precludes the possibility of wide-spread conversion inside prison except for those certain prisoners with enough prison status able to transcend the prison culture without repercussions, and it is in the very process of conversion itself, in which the ministry seeks the resulting change repentance calls for, the metanoia, a real change of heart, a deep conversion.

The lack of Catholic conversion through time truth in most prison ministries are why many, particularly Protestant ministries, are able to claim evangelical success in prison, for an actual and deeply internal change of life is not required. A mere expression of salvation is enough to bring the prisoner to the rolls of the saved, though saved in this scenario rarely equates with transformation.

What we see—with the force and vigor characteristic of the prison ministry efforts of the evangelical sects most deeply associated with prison ministry currently, is an urgency, a coercive pleading to act, now, and within this is an implied (and sometimes actually supplied) connection to outside resources and influences—is not characteristic of the Catholic conversion process, with its built-in year or so of study prior to being allowed to become baptized.

Within this ministry cohort also, most efforts are primarily emotional.

When I was studying the social teaching and history of the Church during the months of my conversion process, it very often felt like prayer as I read the encyclicals of Peter and studied the documents of Vatican II, quiet thoughtful prayer, of seeking, pondering, and finding.

Effective Catholic prison ministry is a quiet, thoughtful walk between horror and hope; always remaining conscious of the horrible acts those being ministered to have done and can still do, while remaining hopeful for a redeemed future.

A thoughtful reliance on presenting the history and the social teaching of the Catholic Church is optimal.

What is so powerful about the evangelical power of the social teaching is, in addition to a depiction of "how society ought to work" is that—when studied in conjunction with the history of the Church—it reveals largely how the Church herself *has* worked over the 2,000 plus years of her existence on earth, an existence magnifying the divine power of love and an existence validating *walking the talk*, absolutely crucial to trump the criminal/carceral world narrative.

That love calls on us to respond to others in the same spirit and while seeing Christ in all people is often rightfully at the heart of virtually all of the ministries of the Church, it should not be so in the prison ministry.

Here in this evil-soaked carceral world, the actions of Christ we need remember are those of the exorcism of demons and remember that from the very model of penitential criminality proclaimed by Christ, Mary Magdalene, seven demons were cast out.

The ministry of teaching has exorcistic power and teaching the great social knowledge of the Church is the point of the sword for the prisoner, for it will be a field he enters willingly, as his search for hidden knowledge is eternally sated, calling him on to deeper exploration.

What is wonderful in one way, but can be deceptive in another, is the great value the American public places on a virtuous life. We need only examine the aftermath of a public figure—whether in the Church or not—whose life appears to exemplify the highest American standards, when it is revealed that their private life is diametrically opposed to their public.

Within the value the public places on virtue, lies another weapon in the dismantling of the criminal/carceral world narrative—that all worldly life is, in its essence, criminal.

Criminals believe this, that the animating energy of worldly life is greed and lust and if criminal methods are necessary to satisfy these, most individuals in the world will use those methods.

However, the value the world places on the virtuous life lived completely can be used to demonstrate, ultimately, the shallow hold criminality really has.

Lampstand's work began with a focus on penitential criminals after they leave prison because, we—as prisoners and former prisoners—understand that virtually all prison conversions are a ruse, for it is only through freedom, whether freedom conferred by a high status inside prison or after release, that conversion is true.

Everything in prison—except what occurs between prisoners—is infected with the coercive nature of the prison, rendering conversion stories without the validation of after-prison life or the freedom of a natural life sentence, virtually meaningless.

The only strategy effectively rehabilitating criminals is one involving an inner change and the only narrative capable of creating that inner change is one based on verifiable truth, and it is the verifiable truth of the internal social teaching of the Church, wrapped within the external history of the Church, which provides a pathway to change.

Into the deep we must go, to rescue souls cast into the path of hell by their grasping of the baubles thrown about by the prince of this world, and the saving words are within a 2,000 year history of teaching, of goodness and struggling pilgrims against the world. The only true city on the hill is the one built by the divinity of Christ—founder and father of the Catholic Church.

Guiding us is Christ's establishment of the way of the prison ministry with his clear call to minister to the criminal, in prison and out. We see it magnificently manifested in the closeness he felt to St. Mary Magdalene, and the Golgotha canonization of St. Dismas, and his statements in response to the Pharisees who were murmuring against him for eating with tax collectors and sinners:

> **[Luke 5:32]** I have not come to call the just; I have come to call sinners to repentance.

For who are the greatest sinners if not the criminals wherein devils, even seven, flourish and grow strong.

Criminals who make the journey from the criminal world to the communal world with their honor intact, must make the rest of their life meaningful by harvesting the fruit of turning evil into good for other penitential criminals and the communal world they are now part of.

Know that the prison may be the greatest apostolate of all.

The prison is an ancient institution and it first enters Western consciousness through Genesis and the story of Joseph sold by his brothers into slavery and ultimately becoming a prisoner.

> [19] Upon this Joseph's master, too easily convinced by what his wife told him, broke into a rage, [20] and committed him to the prison in which the king's prisoners were kept. There lay Joseph, then, a captive, [21] but the Lord was still with him, and by the Lord's mercy he became a favourite with the chief gaoler, [22] who put all the prisoners detained there in his charge, and would have nothing done save at his discretion. [23] Thus the chief gaoler, in his turn, knew nothing of what went forward, but left all to Joseph, well knowing that the Lord was with him, and prospered all he did.

The Western prison in America is modeled after the monastery and the monk's cells even give its name to the housing.

Visiting those in prison is given us as a work of corporal mercy by Christ, saving those in prison is given us as a spiritual work of mercy; both how we help one another and remember what the *Catechism* teaches us about the works of mercy.

> 2447 The *works of mercy* are charitable actions by which we come to the aid of our neighbor in his spiritual and bodily necessities. Instructing,

advising, consoling, comforting are spiritual works of mercy, as are forgiving and bearing wrongs patiently. The corporal works of mercy consist especially in feeding the hungry, sheltering the homeless, clothing the naked, visiting the sick and imprisoned, and burying the dead.

With these four elements in mind: the prison as an ancient institution, the prison in the modern West as Catholic inspired, prison visits as works of mercy, and works of mercy as how we aid one another; the Lampstand prison ministry is a spiritual work of mercy directed to prisoners in maximum security prisons, for the purpose of evangelization and the development of transformative criminal/carceral leadership who will then be able to help other prisoners.

Soon after I began Lampstand I had an opportunity to go into a local prison to work with a program that was generating some publicity for its work and I soon realized it was a protective custody wing of the prison, housing those prisoners—informants, pedophiles, serial rapists—who needed protection from the other prisoners.

As the work of the Lampstand Foundation is directed towards developing leaders among the criminal/carceral world whose status ensures the widest respect from other prisoners/criminals they could be bringing to the Church, work within protective custody prisons was not work providing that level of optimization.

The population in maximum security prisons is substantial, and the reason to focus on the prisoners in maximum security prisons is because they are able, if converted, to lead others to conversion that can hold, due to their influential status in the criminal/carceral world.

Christ calls us to extend our evangelical reach to the greatest sinners whose conversion creates the greatest joy in heaven, as revealed in the mystery of the prodigal son and the compassion he felt for the two proto criminal saints, Mary Magdalene and Dismas, the penitential criminals at the point and the root of the cross.

Maximum security prisoners are largely professional criminals—those who commit crimes for money and as a career—with a strong commitment to the carceral/criminal world, and it is in the roots of that commitment that the possibility of a commitment to conversion lays.

Professional criminals have the highest rearrest rates because they are committed to criminality and are willing to pay the inevitable price of capture and imprisonment, though three strikes sentencing has lessened that willingness.

Professional criminals are happy to see the rise of criminal justice liberalism again—encouraged by the false mass incarceration narrative—and the subsequent reduction of broken windows policing and three strikes sentencing

Maximum security prisoners in the general population are not informants or pedophiles—who will not long survive in prison except in protective custody. The evil of the acts of the pedophile and informant (informant being someone who, after being apprehended, betrays those he committed crimes with) is described in Christ's own words, respectively.

> [Matthew 18:6] And if anyone hurts the conscience of one of these little ones, that believe in me, he had better have been drowned in the depths of the sea, with a mill-stone hung about his neck. [7]Woe to the world, for the hurt done to consciences! It must needs be that such hurt should come, but woe to the man through whom it comes!

> [Matthew 26:24]The Son of Man goes on his way, as the scripture foretells of him; but woe upon that man by whom the Son of Man is to be

betrayed; better for that man if he had never been born.

The seminal betrayal by Judas was defined by Christ

> **[Luke 22:48]** Jesus said to him, "Judas, wouldst thou betray the Son of Man with a kiss?"

Why was the betrayal by Judas the epitome, the archetype of betrayal? Is it because it is only from one who is known and loved that a kiss is trustingly received and ultimately, betrayal can at times follow.

It is this turning away by the betrayer, from who they loved, toward their own self-interest of survival—away from sacrificing self on the altar of brotherhood and friendship—away from solidarity to selfishness.

Betrayers, pedophiles, and rapists are virtually never willing to change and it is this obstinacy wherein even God's mercy is conditional.

The professional criminal's immersion within the carceral/criminal world is spurred by his search for freedom, money, and power, which, from his perspective, is an honorable path—in itself and without accepting restrictions—as defined by the way of the world.

Professional criminals occupy the upper echelon within carceral/criminal culture and are most apt to respond to an intellectual ministry approach based on the social teaching of the Church and will, once converted, also share it with others—who will listen to them.

The ministry objective is to present the truths of the faith in the catechetical way to increase the potential for truth's reception, while deflecting the potential manipulative abuse of a personal relationship, because, it is Catholic truth which will free, not a relationship always being tested.

292

The only relationship which will break the hardness of the evil in prison is the personal one with Christ, and the intellectual one with the *words* of Peter and the saints.

The ideal prison ministry as a spiritual work of mercy, metaphorically, is like the Latin Mass where the ministers and the prisoners will both be facing Christ, not each other.

Traditional prison ministry practiced as a corporal work of mercy is from a simpler time, when many prisoners were first-time felons and often eagerly penitential. As the carceral/criminal world has deepened over the past several decades in America, only the most hardened go to prison. Within the maximum security prison the criminal culture is mandated—there are no bystanders—penance, except for the strongest among them, is weakness and weakness is surrender or death.

The greatest danger in prison ministry as a spiritual work of mercy—especially if you attempt it as an individual—is that you will very possibly be used for the prisoner's purpose rather than your purpose of helping bring him to conversion. Working in a group reduces the chance of this occurring.

A primal description of the prince of the criminal world— father of lies—is earned for an eternal method, not an occasional tool, for he lies always and eternally, it is a way of being and the professional criminal embraces the way of the world.

The imprisoned professional criminal is often an adept weaver of word magic schooled in the charm and glamour of criminal/carceral world darkness, and can usually induce the traditional evangelist—sometimes susceptible to that charm and glamour—to accept his claim of salvation. In the acceptance of a false salvation, the evangelist can become victim rather than witness.

In these dangerous fields, the evangelist once removed and armed with a deep understanding of the social teaching of the Church, will be engaging the prisoner intellectually and will reap a bounty of much deeper root.

The Lampstand apostolate focuses on professional criminals because this is the cohort I know and respect and for many years was part of, in prison and out.

Other prison ministries are apostolates who lump all criminals and prisoners into one cohort, not realizing how limiting this approach renders their work. It is impossible for professional criminals to respect an effort which does not understand the reality of the most basic criminal/carceral world typology and it will be very difficult for the criminal/prisoner to connect with an effort they do not respect.

Pacifism & Restorative Justice

A dilutive concept—in concert with the abolition of capital punishment currently enjoying some favor among many in the Church—impeding effective prison ministry in maximum security prisons, is restorative justice.

Abolishing capital punishment and replacing the traditionally straightforward Catholic teaching about crime and punishment with the restorative justice trend—strongly connected to the liberation theology trend—is seductive to many, but it is the constancy and clarity of Catholic teaching that has protected our faith from the gates of hell, not succumbing to trendy seductions.

Restorative justice grew out of the pacifistic perspective of some non-Catholic faith traditions—where no defense is mounted against evil as a signifier of Christian love—which is alien to a Catholic economy which historically confronts evil at every turn.

Many translate Jesus' surrender to crucifixion as evidence of his pacifism—*allowing* evil its way—but it was surrender to his earthly mission of redemption, the eternal victory *over* evil that guided him.

While we can appreciate the enhanced discussion the concept of restorative justice has brought to the criminal justice dialogue, its utility with professional criminals who have served time in maximum security prisons and are the dominant group defining and shaping criminal/carceral world culture, is much too limited, primarily because they understand—expressed often and clearly when among themselves—what is also at the heart of Catholic social teaching; that crime is primarily the result of individual choice, not social or familial circumstances.

With professional criminals, the salvific tool with the greatest potency is the classical Catholic teaching of punishment, penance, and redemption.

Congruent with liberation theology and the consistent ethic of life—primal positions of liberal Catholics—restorative justice tends to relativize Catholic social teaching away from the Church's traditional essence, so well thought out by St. Thomas Aquinas and other great Catholic thinkers, which sees the Church as a sign of contradiction to the normative vision of seeking worldly popularity and influence.

Restorative justice animates an idea shared by liberal Catholics, that Church practice should be decided democratically.

Traditional Catholic teaching concerning crime and justice is based upon revelation in scripture, traditional practice, and magisterial teaching from the great Catholic thinkers.

The professional criminal realizes this diversion by restorative justice into, essentially, the will of the moment, particularly as he studies Catholic social teaching and history and it will be the consistent linkage with the roots of that teaching to Church history that will call him to embrace Catholicism today.

Understanding the power of individual interior reflection provided by the prison is a compelling factor in effective prison ministry and it is why many compare time in prison to time in a monastery.

Unless prison ministers come to some understanding of the forging power—the deep strengthening of the will of those who, rather than being cowed, become more deeply unbowed and criminally resolute as a result of the prison experience—and the refining of the criminal world culture through the carceral experience, it will be impossible to appreciate the level of resistance to eternal truth by that of worldly truth animating the carceral/criminal world.

While true conversion is rare in prison, especially on the mainline among the general population of a maximum security facility, the introduction of the intellectual concepts and history of the social teaching of the Church in conjunction with its institutional history in the world, is a presentation of truth capable of trumping the criminal/carceral world truth the criminal relies on and it may remain with him long enough to develop enough traction to become of some direction upon his release.

The social teaching presented in conjunction with Church history can be found in many books but I would recommend the two volume work of Rodger Charles SJ, (1998) *Christian Social Witness and Teaching: The Catholic Tradition from Genesis to Centesimus Annus*; and by H. W. Crocker III, (2001) *Triumph: The Power and the Glory of the Catholic Church, A 2,000 Year History*, as works to place in the hands of prisoners after the first ministry contact.

There are simpler, introductory books to Charles' teaching: *An Introduction to Catholic Social Teaching* and *An*

Introduction to Catholic Social Teaching: Study Guide—as the two brief volumes of summary recommended are graduate level works—but please resist the temptation to use them and go for the fullest expression of Charles' work, remembering that the prisoner has huge blocks of time available to him in which to enter into the deepest study as well as a captive audience to discuss his studies with, and it will be the effort required, amplified by the ministry correspondence, which will open the prisoner's mind to the truths of the Church.

The 2,000+ year history of the Church on the earth, most brightly represented by its popes and saints, connected with the constancy of its social teaching through the worldly battlefields threatening it, is a true story of triumph, courage, honor, and truths held hard, that can resonate with the professional criminal, whose life is lived more than may be evident, by those same qualities, though clearly corrupted.

In the process of presenting the history of the Church, stories from the lives of the saints can be especially instructive, particularly from the great criminal saints.

The story of Mary Magdalene, Dismas and the history of Saint Callistus, the reformed criminal who became pope in the early church, are powerful stories of redemption and, in Callistus' case, centered on the impact that time in prison can have and the heights to which a penitential criminal may climb.

The Criminal is the Problem

It is crucial to remember that the criminal—not society, capitalism, or the criminal justice system—is the problem.

Some Catholics who are attracted to prison ministry believe, due to the myths of Hollywood or Marxism shrouded within Liberation Theology, that the good guys are the criminals, and the police, district attorneys, prison guards, and legislators who support stringent criminal sanctions, are the bad guys.

This stance, as well as being clearly incorrect, does everyone a disservice—in particular the penitential criminal—who may find little reason for proper expiation within a culture defining criminality as somehow admirable while at the same time attempting to induce him from its grip.

Most professional criminals understand that their criminality is only admirable in the context of the criminal/carceral world culture and if the ministry does not understand this, it will have little real resonance.

Also remember that regardless of the moral evil done by many Catholic bishops, priests, and laity—which will be thrown back at you during your ministry—the work of the Church on earth is magnificently good, strong, and true.

It will be your deep understanding of this history and the underlying social teaching, strengthened by your personal relationship with God that will eventually prove most valuable in your spiritual work of mercy with prisoners.

Sexual Abuse in the Church

The sexual abuse in the Catholic Church over the past several decades has deeply hurt the Church.

Regardless, the only possible response is an aggressive one, and with sexual abuse, bringing up the past struggles the Church has had with this issue—prior to the golden age of Christendom—can serve as a reminder of the eternal influence of evil upon the hearts of men and the power of reform.

The sexual abuse horrors of the past several years within the Church, well documented in many books, reports and news stories, is best compiled in these five books: *Goodbye*

Good Men: How Liberals Brought Corruption into the Catholic Church, by Michael S. Rose (2002), *The Rite of Sodomy: Homosexuality and the Roman Catholic Church*, by Randy Engel (2006), *The Faithful Departed: The Collapse of Boston's Catholic Culture*, by Philip F. Lawler (2008), *Sacrilege: Sexual Abuse in the Catholic Church*, by Leon J. Podles, and *After Asceticism: Sex, Prayer and Deviant Priests*, by the Linacre Institute (2006).

The Church has always been forced to deal with evil, indeed, that is one of her major missions, and her travails today are not new, nor shall they be the last, for on earth she is the Church Militant.

In this respect, the book by Saint Pete Damian and translated by Matthew Cullinan Hoffman : *The Book of Gomorrah and St. Peter Damian's Struggle Against Ecclesiastical Corruption*, an eleventh century saint who fought against the sexual corruption within the Church at that time, can be very instructive.

God-Talk & Thought-Talk

Priests, even as well armed as they are with the tools of spiritual warfare, if working alone and without special training, will generally have difficulty evangelizing criminals as they tend to use God-talk, when the most effective method will be thought-talk, the social thought of the Church, revealing the historical practice and ideals of the human institution herself, for it is through the world that the criminal, caught deeply in the ways of the world, can come to eternity.

God-talk is what the criminal will eventually come to, on his own and quietly, within the interiority of his soul.

The emptiness of so much God-talk—associated most glaringly with the Protestant sects—repels rather than attracts the worldly-wise criminal. Approaching the criminal from a historical, doctrinal, intellectual plane, showing the institutional Church *walking the talk*, however, will attract his attention.

Catholic prison chaplains rarely use the teachings of their religion for helping prisoners, yet that is the key.

An important part of converting criminals through the social teaching is showing how that teaching—used by the institutional Church—impacted history, and one of the clearest examples from recent history is the role Pope Saint John Paul II played in the defeat of communism.

God-talk, on the other hand, tends to be connected to the individual delivering it, while the social teaching, thought-talk, connects conversion to the institutional Church and Peter.

Individual God-talk sounds the same to the uber-worldly criminal, whether from Protestants or Catholics, while the history and social teaching of the Church—that reaches back to Genesis—can only come from the Catholic Church founded by Christ on the shoulders of Peter.

Prisoners in maximum security prisons are above all, pure realists—there are few things in life more real than a maximum security prison—and they *know* the nature of true justice, and it will only be from a full portrayal of the truth of the Catholic Church regarding justice, punishment, and reformation that true conversion will occur.

My memories of 12 years talking with my fellow prisoners, inclusive of my own familial history, is that we tend to view—with some pride—our personal history, even if it is horrific, as a necessary hardening for the world ahead.

Like another generation's story of trudging through five miles of waist high snow to school, proudly told, is the criminal/carceral cultural story of family violence, poverty, and personal suffering; though, if need be for social favor, we are always able to portray it according to the victim narrative many non-criminals hope to hear from us.

While speaking of God's love for us—God-talk—is *truly* speaking of the axis of the world and the divine ground upon which our lives on earth are lived, yet it can negate conversion; whereas the speaking of knightly power and chivalry and their greatest flowering in the Catholic warrior orders—thought-talk—*can* resonate the chord of conversion within the professional criminal's heart.

That history of seeking justice through war is still at the heart of the Church in her teaching around abortion, just war, and capital punishment—all connected to protecting the innocent—and learning of it will deepen the criminal's personal search through the teaching and history of the Church.

The history of the Church is full of stories that will truly excite the heart, mind, and spirit of the criminal, living a life within the daily threat of battle to the death in prison and needing strong internal resources to combat, survive, and for some, grow deeper spiritually.

The Catholic Chaplain

Being able to provide daily mass within the prison will sacramentally sharpen the saintly path that some criminals serving natural life will begin to choose, as the *Catechism* teaches:

> **1070** In the New Testament the word "liturgy" refers not only to the celebration of divine worship but also to the proclamation of the Gospel and to active charity. In all of these situations it is a question of the service of God and neighbor. In a liturgical celebration the Church is servant in the image of her Lord, the one "*leitourgos*"; she shares in Christ's priesthood (worship), which is both

301

prophetic (proclamation) and kingly (service of charity):

> The liturgy then is rightly seen as an exercise of the priestly office of Jesus Christ. It involves the presentation of man's sanctification under the guise of signs perceptible by the senses and its accomplishment in ways appropriate to each of these signs. In it full public worship is performed by the Mystical Body of Jesus Christ, that is, by the Head and his members. From this it follows that every liturgical celebration, because it is an action of Christ the priest and of his Body which is the Church, is a sacred action surpassing all others. No other action of the Church can equal its efficacy by the same title and to the same degree.

The importance of having a dedicated Catholic Chaplaincy—staffed by a priest rather than a lay person—in the prison cannot be overstated, and it is hoped that as the Church comes more to the realization of the great mission fields lying barren within the nation's maximum security prisons, and as the ranks of reformed Catholic prisoners reach out to the institutional Church for help in their prison apostolates, the Church will realize the paramount importance of developing specially trained priests to serve as prison chaplains.

During the crucifixion and resurrection of Our Lord, penitential criminals played central roles—St. Mary of Magdalene and St. Dismas—and it is because of these penitential criminal saints, in their names, and in the name of Our Lord who showed us the way, that we need to do all we can to ensure prisoners have full access to a Catholic priest.

Once the ministry team has been established, the prison has been selected, and work with the Catholic Chaplin at the prison has begun to develop relations with Catholic prisoners the chaplain feels may be most receptive to the intellectual work of learning about the social teaching and the history of the Church, the actual process can be developed.

Use the aforementioned works by Charles and Crocker in a structured process of mutual reading with the prisoners, amplified through letters, interaction through occasional visits—always going to prison as a group—with the prisoner, meetings with prison administrators and the Catholic priest, all buttressed by prayer.

Due to the differences in various regions of the country and within different prisons concerning visiting with and writing to prisoners, it is necessary to develop the specific logistics of contact and teaching based on those regional and specific prison factors, as well as the parish individuals involved in the ministry.

Though the heart of the ministry will remain the same, the particular methods of interaction will be different, depending on parish/prison differences and an understanding of the hierarchy of evil within the carceral/criminal world.

Hierarchy of Evil

We begin our exploration of evil as perceived within the criminal/carceral world—vital to understand as a prequel to an effective prison ministry—by examining the criminal/carceral world's perspective on the ground of evil's opposite, love.

Within the criminal/carceral world, love finds small consolation, for the harder edges of greed, lust, and power tend to cut it out.

The criminal/carceral world is intelligible once you discover the key, which is satanic thought, where the only human reality is self-interest and love does not exist, only selfish drives to satisfy selfish desire.

Beginning from that place where love cannot exist, where its expressions are merely means to an end, we can examine the hierarchy of evil within the criminal/carceral world.

Professional criminals occupy the upper echelons within prison; informants, rapists and pedophiles the lower. The hierarchy is inverted as those on the lower are considered most evil and those on the upper least evil. For pastoral work related to the rehabilitation or conversion of criminals, this hierarchy plays a crucial role.

The work of my apostolate to help reform professional criminals through exposure to the history and social teaching of the Catholic Church is only as effective as is my love for the professional criminal. That love is built on knowledge of the criminal/carceral world which I absorbed through twenty years as a criminal, with twelve years spent in maximum security state and federal prisons.

The love I have for criminals continues today, though it has been decades since I was in prison or living as a criminal among criminals, and it manifests itself in the pleasure and joyful anticipation I still feel when I have an opportunity to venture into a maximum security prison to speak with prisoners.

This love for the men and women professional criminals I came to know in the criminal/carceral world is built upon shared experiences and many shared perspectives of the world.

This love has grown as a result of my active immersion in Catholicism, begun during the months prior to entering the

Rite of Christian Initiation for Adults, and deepened since my baptism and the founding of the apostolate.

I am not the person I once was. I am not the criminal I once was, yet I retain a deep respect and quiet love for the cultural artifacts of the criminal/carceral world and the moral principles that have marked criminals since the criminal Dismas received canonization hanging at Christ's side on Golgotha.

Love based on knowledge of the criminal/carceral world is central to an effective prison ministry, as it is central to all Catholic evangelism.

This love informs my apostolate work—as love of neighbor should inform the ministry work with criminals undertaken by other Catholics—to try always to act in the spirit of charitable love.

The moral judgments implicit within the hierarchy of evil have come down to current practice in the criminal/carceral world through corruption of the popular devotion, contemplation, and practice of teaching emanating directly from Christ—particularly in his relationships with the two proto-criminal saints, Mary Magdalene and Dismas—what he did as much as what he said.

The historic popular devotion of St. Dismas contributed to a development of criminal/carceral world doctrine still largely prevalent—protecting the innocent—through reflection upon Dimas' actions on Golgotha and on the Road to Egypt, where legend reveals, he protected the Holy Family from robbery and violence at the hands of his band of thieves.

The Catholic hierarchy of evil—venal sins, sins of moral gravity, and sins that cry out to heaven, is, as the *Catechism* states:

1854 Sins are rightly evaluated according to their gravity. The distinction between mortal and venial sin, already evident in Scripture, became part of the tradition of the Church. It is corroborated by human experience....

1867 The catechetical tradition also recalls that there are *"sins that cry to heaven"*: the blood of Abel, the sin of the Sodomites, the cry of the people oppressed in Egypt, the cry of the foreigner, the widow, and the orphan, injustice to the wage earner.

1868 Sin is a personal act. Moreover, we have a responsibility for the sins committed by others when *we cooperate in them*:

- by participating directly and voluntarily in them;
- by ordering, advising, praising, or approving them;
- by not disclosing or not hindering them when we have an obligation to do so;
- by protecting evil-doers.

Within the criminal/carceral world it is only some of these that are considered evil, though the hierarchy of evil within the criminal/carceral world is an adaptation of that which has been set by the Judea-Christian world through the Old Law and deepened and clarified by the New.

Beyond the validation of the Old Law by Christ, it is also in his other words and actions, especially in his relationship with the betrayer Judas and the Good Thief Dismas, that the root of the criminal world adaptation appears, which, down through the centuries has reconstituted itself into the hard reality that governs the internal narrative of criminals—and as the criminal perceives it—much of the internal narrative of the world upon which that of criminals is structured.

The sanctioning created and imposed by professional criminal prisoners against criminal/carceral world evils that exists inside maximum security prisons—which for the past several decades has also determined that of the outside criminal world—is an element congruent with the nature of the prison.

The criminal/convict identity, built upon the necessity of survival in a brutal world where one mistake can mean death or horrible exploitation, is an identity that sticks.

Each act of Christ in his ministry, in its continuance as a deep influence on human behavior—consciously or unconsciously—is vital. He set an archetype in his condemnation of the betrayal by Judas.

> **[Matthew 26:24]** The Son of Man goes on his way, as the scripture foretells of him; but woe upon that man by whom the Son of Man is to be betrayed; better for that man if he had never been born.

Though the great condemnation was directed specifically at Judas, its use against any betrayal has become normative within the world of the professional criminal and even within much of the noncriminal world.

A condemnation was also set against those who harm children.

> **[Matthew 18:6]** And if anyone hurts the conscience of one of these little ones, that believe in me, he had better have been drowned in the depths of the sea, with a mill-stone hung about his neck.

The condemnation remains today against pedophiles, who are subject to being killed if placed within the mainline of maximum security prisons.

Professional criminals define those who inform on their crime partners (a relationship within the criminal/carceral world of great trust, honor, and respect) or prey on innocent women and children, as decidedly evil, beyond the pale and unworthy of respect, in prison or out.

The sanctions against the evil of rapists and pedophiles, partially stems from criminals who do not even perceive those acts as deserving of the honor of being defined as a crime.

Consequently, those acts are considered *outside* the morality of criminals and thus unable to expect protection within the normal bounds of respect within that world,

Some incidents legally defined as rape, such as statutory rape between two consenting individuals of similar age though one is legally under the age of consent, is not considered evil; though the violent serial rape of innocents is.

Pedophilia and informing are always deeply hated.

One type of outside criminal world informant situation, where a member of one criminal organization cooperates with law enforcement to effectively compete with a rival criminal organization by informing on them, is generally not considered a classical informant situation, but is generally defined as someone who corrupted law enforcement to satisfy personal criminal organizational goals, and can be seen as admirable.

The sanction within the criminal/carceral world visited upon sexual offenders and informers is marked by violence and goes much farther than that of the noncriminal community, which usually restricts its response, beyond the legal, to disgust and fear.

Professional criminals remember what the noncriminal world—including many rehabilitation practitioners—have forgotten (or perhaps criminals know what the practitioners do not know) that sexual predators and betrayers choose what they have done and are not acting because of corrosive familial or social influences and given the opportunity, will choose to repeat those acts.

Professional criminals understand the difference between the murder of one member of a gang by a member of another gang during a war for territory or profit (which is properly seen as an act of war soldiers are legitimately authorized to perform), and the murder of the child victim by a pedophiliac rapist, which is an act of the most predatory evil, which is more justly and severely sanctioned by professional criminals than most American criminal justice systems.

Capital punishment is the sentence professional criminals pronounce and execute upon child rapists, and this is where the misguided efforts by some Catholics to abolish capital punishment—a sanction which the historical tradition of the Church teaches as appropriate—conflicts with the conversion of criminals who would ask why a Church that does not understand the proper use of capital punishment for those predators who harm the innocent is a Church for the ages.

Murder committed under the well-known rubric: "It's just business" is considered by the criminal/carceral world as legitimate, while those committed on account of lust, thrill, or insanity, are not.

Doing organized rehabilitation work that mingles those who, by criminal/carceral world standards, should be executed, with those who would perform or support the execution, is almost certainly guaranteed to fail, for it has exhibited a lack of understanding of a fundamental aspect of criminal/carceral world culture.

Criminals differentiate between informing on a crime partner and reporting to the police after having seen a violent crime committed against innocents—once having left the criminal life and become, in all respects, a regular citizen of the world.

The former is always evil, the latter is always good.

I would be remiss in not again mentioning the theory of radical criminology built on Marxism, which has set a different hierarchy of evil, one many prisoners have adopted as their way of perceiving their crimes.

This Marxist and sociological perspective informs many in the academy and has exerted great influence upon several criminals who have earned graduate and post-graduate degrees and secured positions in the academy, rendering rehabilitative pastoral ministry somewhat difficult because the theories and arguments are of some depth and resonate among those criminals who cherish the idea that their crimes have made them into heroes.

It is however, in the actions of the true criminal hero, St. Dismas, that the honor of the professional criminal was set. Dismas, the Good Thief, is portrayed as finding repentance hanging beside Christ on Calvary, but nothing in the scriptural record of that central moment in human history, as I read it, indicates that it was repentance he was expressing, but that he *saw* the truth.

Dismas *recognized* that the man hanging next to him *was* God. We do not know how he came to see this while so many others witnessing the crucifixion did not. It began perhaps on the Road to Egypt, where, as legend reveals, Dismas *really saw* love and innocence in the prototype family that he had perhaps dreamt of, but had not known.

In the act of saving the Holy Family from the robbing and violence characterizing his band of thieves, he acted benevolently for the same reason professional criminals today will not harm children, but will punish harshly—even unto death—those who do.

It was perhaps on the Road to Calvary, as the two thieves and Christ carried their crosses, as Dismas *saw* how others responded to Christ and him to them.

On the day of crucifixion Dismas *saw* the truth and remembered the episode on the Road to Egypt, and his words to Christ were:

> **[Luke 23:42]** Then he said to Jesus, Lord, remember me when thou comest into thy kingdom.

Dismas might be saying: Remember that I have responded to you honorably, I have not pleaded for my life as Gestas— the other thief hanging on Golgotha—but have accepted my punishment honorably, for it is just. I have realized your innocence and know that while justice is being done with us, it is not being done to you, "Lord, remember me."

This is not an unusual response for a professional criminal even today, for among ourselves in the cells and on the streets, we will openly and proudly acknowledge who we are, without remorse, asking for no mercy, and though trying any and everything to escape the consequences, once captured by judge and jury, we will accept our punishment stoically if the opportunity to escape is finally closed.

One of the elements in the hierarchy of evil, something that if a professional criminal expresses he will do, will result in him losing the trust and respect of other criminals, is in claiming to desire to live a law-abiding life.

Criminals would react to this as would non-criminals react if a peer expressed becoming a criminal as a desired way of life—although in some circles the expression would only be seen as suspect if the criminal life being sought was one that had little chance of profit or success, so influenced has much of the public become to the blandishments of Hollywood and Marxism where criminals are as often seen as romantic figures than as evil predators.

Dismas *saw*—in the man hanging beside him—a Man/God who was truly walking the talk, and living the truth under the most horrific of circumstances, the Roman crucifixion of criminals.

The decision by Christ to take Dismas into Hell with him—
on the way to Paradise—is, from the human perspective
Christ still possessed, a good and sound idea, as to take a
criminal guide into the deepest lair of criminals, much as a
priest today, who had never been into a prison, might ask a
reformed criminal to accompany him to a prison ministry
visit, both for a sense-of-safety and credibility.

It is perhaps incongruous to think of Our Lord feeling the
need for a guide, but on the other hand, it is congruent
with his trepidation expressed in Gethsemane, and even on
Golgotha, for he was still a man, subject to the human
frailties which he would, however, soon leave behind him.

There are mysteries here I do not understand, but I know
each act and each word of the earthy ministry of Christ has
eternal meaning and all the books that could be written are
being written and they do fill the world, but we are still
mystified.

Part of the mystery is *why Dismas becomes* Christ's
companion on the Road from Calvary to Paradise and in
the process, becomes the first canonized saint of the
Catholic Church.

In converting criminals, we should seek to understand this
history and the related tradition of the Church regarding
the protection of the innocent through the use of capital
punishment and just war, so as not to fall into the
avoidance technique that these are issues people of good
will can disagree about; for it is through sharing your
understanding of the history and the tradition of protecting
the innocent (as Dismas did on the Road to Egypt) that
criminals will be able to see beyond the superficial
uncertainties expressed by many Catholics around these
traditional doctrines.

While the Church's current institutional approach to
criminal justice is a somewhat depleted vessel—at least
since the papacy of Pius XII—the grounding of the

Church's social teaching within the dogma of good and evil, still forms the axis around which the charitable and pastoral work of criminal rehabilitative ministry revolves.

In many ways, my life as a criminal and convict were some of the most important years of my life, for, as hard, as lonely, and as brutal as they so often were, surviving and thriving during those years gave me the experience that led to my apostolate work—as well as the foundation upon which I've found a peaceful, productive and fulfilling life— and it is in that work with professional criminals whose lives I've been part of during those many years past and those of the still unfolding future, that I have also found work that God has called me to do.

The Greatest Apostolate of All

While many Catholics have found great peace and happiness within the Church, the thought of evangelistically venturing into the terrifying world of the prison will often, especially in the beginning, somewhat hamper any resolve to do so, yet we can remember the great call to evangelization.

You enter the battlefield with the great and ancient sword of the social teaching of the Church, and whether your work is within or outside of prison, it is a sword that will protect you and can free the prisoner.

While the work of the Lampstand Foundation has focused primarily on community reentry outside of prison, most faith based organizations working with prisoners do not focus much on the life of the prisoner after release from prison.

During the 1970's and 1980's community based rehabilitation efforts were fairly substantial, with a lot of involvement from former criminals including myself, but after many years of substantial funding with virtually no success—though the program I developed and managed, as

were a few others such as Delancey Street, successful—
those slowly shut down.

Recently, through the Second Chance Act, funding for
outside reentry programming has begun to open up again.

While the coming and going, success and failure, of outside
prison reentry programs is common, it is my belief that the
non-Catholic faith-based inside prison ministries will
always fail, though individual stories of redemption will
occasionally occur. The force of the argumentation their
approaches take is key to their failure, while the slow and
thoughtful revealing of Catholic history and social teaching
principles allow for internal arguments, self-correcting
change, and eventual *true* conversion to emerge, even
given the deep sway the criminal/carceral culture exerts
over its cohort's lives.

This is especially true of prisoners, so self-directed by
nature, so rebellious by temperament, so resistant by
experience, and so tempered by the world that anything
driving change from outside is usually doomed in the long
term and probably used to manipulate reality in the short.

The failure of most prison ministry efforts has played a role
in the development of Lampstand's work to produce books
and papers that may have some value in helping former
prisoners become the type of leaders that can develop,
manage, and sustain reentry programs in the community.
A major aspect of our first ten books is to introduce the
readers to other books through extended quotes from great
writers who explain the eternal truths of Catholicism so
much better than your author.

Books are the pathway to friendships with the immortals
and through the many volumes of their works on earth, we
can come to a companionship informing and enlightening
our lives; and in this respect, perhaps the greatest of
companions is the Angelic Doctor, St. Thomas Aquinas,
whose works will enthrall you, challenge you and bring you

into congruence with the ancient teachings of the Church like no other.

The failure of most prison ministry has also played a role in Lampstand making the decision to become involved in prison ministry.

While outside prison reentry work is seen as dangerous by the traditional volunteer, it is not so for the reformed criminal, in fact just the opposite. The bonding between criminals, who have shared experience in committing crimes for the purpose of making money, and consequently serving time in maximum security prison, is often long-lasting, and once the initial parameters are established about criminal and carceral pasts, the relationship between the penitential criminal and transformed criminal helper builds rather quickly.

This will not be true in prison ministry between the prisoner and the volunteer, but it can become true between the prisoner and the intellectual and historical works of the social teaching, between the prisoner and the lives and works of the saints and luminous Catholic thinkers such as Jacques and Raissa Maritain and Hilaire Belloc.

The prison minister has to be prepared to respond to questions about other religions and here the seminal books by Belloc, *The Great Heresies* and *How the Reformation Happened*, will be invaluable, as will the magnificent 2003 work by the Vatican Pontifical Council for Culture & Pontifical Council for Interreligious Dialogue: *Jesus Christ, The Bearer of the Water of Life: A Christian Reflection on the "New Age"*.

This discussion needs to be done in an intellectual, historical doctrinal comparison sense, without a lot of God-talk. The corrupting concepts of pacifism and socialism, which infects liberal Catholicism and weakens the histories of otherwise saintly Catholics like Dorothy Day, also needs to be addressed with a clear historical understanding of the traditional teaching of the Church about just war and the evil of socialism.

Pacifism has been part of the liberal Catholic history since the beginning—laying open fences to evil's run through human fields.

The criminal/carceral world is a hard, clear world of steel and stone and it will only be the crystalline purity of the eternal teaching of the Church that can strongly trump it, not the misty wishes of liberalism.

When I was in McNeil Island Federal Penitentiary in the 1960's, several draft resisters were sentenced there, most of whom were pacifists from the academies of the Northwest.

Criminals *despise* pacifists as they are the perfect victims, so out of touch with reality as to deserve no respect and so they were victimized and disrespected.

Combat theology—the theology of St. Thomas Aquinas, the Catholic Knights and kings and popes who fought with steel to protect Holy Mother Church—is theology that understands the mandate to protect the innocent and the defense of ourselves first of all; and that is the only theology that will take root in the criminal soul.

Pacifism concedes the ground to evil and injustice, thus the favorite deception of the devil—that the heart of Christ's teaching is pacifistic.

Love is the heart, love of God and neighbor. Surrender is at the heart, surrender to that divine love.

Pacifism is surrender to earthly evil, and to the beasts that look like men.

Upon these bones, transformation can begin to occur and so can conversion.

316

Trust is at the root of faith; trust in what your mind and heart perceive beyond the obvious weight of the steel and stone prison world riven with evil, trust that the Kingdom of God exists even here, no less than in the open mountain meadows of our visions.

There are many people of good will in prison—this is something anyone who has worked with prisoners for any length of time already knows—but there are also many with the blackest of evil will.

Determining between them is a key element of prison ministry.

We will discover men of good will by their actions, not their words—as we do those of evil will—today and yesterday, particularly within the details of the crimes they committed that brought them to prison.

Penance encourages openness to evangelization, which can redeem the will and free it to act in its essential goodness, for the power of the *word* in that process is ultimate, as the *Catechism* teaches.

> **1122** Christ sent his apostles so that "repentance and forgiveness of sins should be preached in his name to all nations." "Go therefore and make disciples of all nations, baptizing them in the name of the Father and of the Son and of the Holy Spirit." The mission to baptize, and so the sacramental mission, is implied in the mission to evangelize, because the sacrament is prepared for by *the word of God and by the faith* which is assent to this word:
>
>> The People of God is formed into one in the first place by the Word of the living God. . . . The preaching of the Word is required for the sacramental ministry itself, since the sacraments are sacraments of faith, drawing

their origin and nourishment from the Word.

If your ministry is blessed by grace, and if, within the prison where you work, certain great souls emerge, there may be a time when you can direct them to the work of the spiritual director, Fr. Reginald Garrigou-Lagrange, O.P., who played a prominent role in the group around Jacques and Raissa Maritain, the influential evangelical Catholic couple who helped set in motion much of the reemergence of the modern devotion and study of St. Thomas Aquinas.
Fr. Lagrange's two volume work, *The Three Ages of the Interior Life* (1947) would be a sure guide for the advanced teaching of emerging prison monks and spiritual warriors.

The Lampstand prison ministry is evangelization using words, and when the words are from the sanctified teaching of the Church, enhanced through the Sacramental Word and congruent with the history of the Church, the seeds of transformation for prisoners due to be released and actual transformation of prisoners serving natural life into spiritual warriors or prison monks able to literally change prison life from the inside out, is possible, as all things are possible through Our Lord.

There are many stories in the world but the one we know of Christ is true, which we must help criminals discover and defend.

The Church is always right and when she is not, God corrects her through the agency of others, whether they are evil, as Martin Luther of the Reformation or good, as Queen Elizabeth I of Protestant England, or as today, the work of the laity.

Christ set the paradigm. Peter denied him and with the other apostles ran away at the climactic moment on Golgotha; save the apostle John, the Holy Virgin Mother, her sister Mary of Clopas, and Mary of Magdalene; but Peter is—as far as humanly possible—the Rock, and the contradiction is the truth we must always discern; for even as Peter stumbles how much more do we falter and fall. Forgive Peter, forgive our neighbor, forgive the criminal, yet serve justice as well.

Each detail, no matter how minor it might appear, in Christ's life, had meaning; and so it should be for our life of ministry; in each moment, in each act, in each thought we must attempt to create congruence with our apostolate for we cannot purpose an apostolate of love and truth to the world if we practice hate and lies at home and in our heart.

I have just finished watching the 1927, 155 minute version of the Cecil de Mille silent epic on the ministry of Christ, *King of Kings*, and it was the most beautiful presentation that I have ever seen; remarkable considering it was filmed over 80 years ago and is mostly black and white.

It opens in the courtesan Mary Magdalene's palace, filmed in brilliant color, and moves then to black and white, with several more bows to tradition, one being that the Holy Virgin Mother was the first to see the Risen Christ.

It is this combination of scripture and tradition from which we build the narrative of conversion and the building of this narrative comes from an immersion in Catholic teaching and history as portrayed in all of the venues the faithful have used throughout time.

Let us not forget the liturgy, which can play a central role in prisoner conversion and reformation.

As a convert—and still considering myself a novice Catholic though baptized in 2004—much of my study involves seeking the ancient roots of Catholic teaching and practice.

At many points during my Catholic journey I have been compelled to choose a particular path of further study.

The first was choosing conservative over liberal Catholicism, traditional teaching as expressed in the two universal Catechisms, Trent & Vatican II, as opposed to that preached by the liberal wing of Catholicism.

The second was to seek guidance from the writings Peter through the centuries, when uncertainties about Church teaching arose.

The liturgy is where we meet with God and seek to hear his quiet voice, but that took me years to truly understand, and our journey from our baptismal parish and liturgy to a Latin Mass parish has been an instructive one.

We were baptized into the Catholic Church at our home parish a few minutes' drive from our house in 2004. It is a lovely and relaxed suburban parish run by the Jesuits and we happily attended mass there for a couple of years until becoming dissatisfied with its too liberal leanings being presented much too often through homilies, announcements, and events.

We attended several other parishes but encountered much the same problem. We were just about ready to give up and stay with our home parish when we heard about the Latin Mass parish pastored by the Priestly Fraternity of Saint Peter.

Our first experience of the Solemn High Latin Mass was one of awestruck delight, much like that felt at our first mass after baptism, but deeper and more resonating as the choir chanted, the priest incensed, and the packed parish seemed to pulsate with sanctity.

We became regular members and attended Sunday Mass there for a year or so.

Then my wife's work situation changed and she had to work Sundays. About the same time—this was in June 2008—I was feeling the call to begin attending daily mass and began re-attending our home parish, but the level of activity of the new mass was disconcerting though the liberal leanings were not so evident in the daily mass as the Sunday.

After about a year and a half a friend told me about his son who was a very orthodox Catholic priest who pastored a parish only a few minutes farther away and would I attend.

I did and was completely won over, so for a year or so I attended daily mass there, though still uncomfortable with the externality of the new mass compared to the internality of the old.

In the end it is the Latin Mass I love, and I believe it is the Latin Mass that will have the greatest evangelical impact on criminals, in prison or out.

The Lampstand vision of the future of criminal transformation within the Catholic Church envisions a host of sanctified and transformed professional criminals, who, through their acquisition of deep knowledge, will become heavily armed spiritual warriors, triple crowned professionals helping their brothers and sisters move from the criminal/carceral world to the communal world.

The tri-crowning comes from criminal world experience outside and inside a maximum security prison, postgraduate degrees from the academy, and advanced study in Catholic Social Thought, all fortified by a regime of daily practice: Ordinary or Extraordinary Mass or Divine Office, 15 Decade Rosary, Prayer and Contemplation.

Deep knowledge leadership is a going beyond a daily life of worldly dictated movement and moving to the supernatural symphony. It is the true way of the apostolate, drawing from a deep well of interiority strengthened by a lifelong pursuit of knowledge from the Fathers and Saints of the Church, *literally walking with Peter, to Christ, through Mary.*

And here, let me share with you dear reader, three great books on the interior life:

The Soul of the Apostolate, by Fr. Jean-Baptist Chautard (1907)

The Three Ages of the Interior Life, by Fr. Réginald Marie Garrigou-Lagrange (1938)

The Way, by St. Josemaría Escrivá (1939)

Acquiring deep knowledge calls for a spiritual maturity earned through criminal experience, post-graduate education, and carceral suffering, a powerful octave in the way of perfection.

The way of perfection is congruent with entrepreneurial vision fused with spiritual knowledge, of those who have suffered, transformed their suffering, and can help others discover the path of transformation.

As criminals, we are people of the far edge, we must go to the maximum reach, for that is what draws us, and a rigorous daily practice built upon an ancient and formidable history and teaching, does and will draw us, it is the only foundation that will.

The 15 decade rosary will be among the primary tools in our arsenal—a powerful weapon.

For those who will remain in prison for the rest of their lives—and indeed, for the rest of us—the *Divine Office* is a great blessing.

Lampstand envisions a legion of spiritual shock troops manning the front lines in the ancient war against evil, their souls flying the logos of Christ, their minds embracing the social teaching of the Church, their intellects wielding the sword of St. Michael, and in their hands, the 15 decade Rosary, the *Divine Office* and the *Catechism of the Catholic*

Church, forming outposts in prison tiers, parish pews, neighborhood streets, and the halls of academia, united in seeking the reformation and transformation of their criminal brothers and sisters.

We will be penitential professional criminals—not informers, rapists, or pedophiles—men of honor retained in our world.

We will know that the only true path to freedom is internal—not mere provision of rehabilitative services—but growth from deep inside as knowledge and spirituality matures.

We will walk away from our criminal past, but not dishonor ourselves by revealing the who, when, and how of our past, throwing scraps of meat to the jailer from the table from which we once fed.

We will receive the forgiveness of baptism and our past will be cleansed.

We are called to be no less than saints and warriors within the great host in the eternal war against evil and the prince of this world, Special Forces shock troops in the legions of the mightiest angel in heaven, St. Michael the Archangel.

Chapter Seven
The Criminal's Search for God: Sources

Introduction

This chapter is a reflection on the collection of ideas within a group of books—sources—that played such a large role in the development of my thinking; initially to deepen my criminality, but eventually becoming the soil from which my transformation and conversion to Catholicism grew.

Most of my exploration of the ideas in these books occurred in prison or shortly after release and as such, they were works from which I drew ideas that largely supported and expanded the underlying narrative of the criminal/carceral world within which I lived, and are largely congruent with its driving ethos.

When I was in prison I read whatever books were available in the prison library or those I could get mailed in with my very limited budget.

Consequently, I was unable to exercise the great array of choices available outside prison and subsequently, a prisoner intellectually as well as physically.

Now having slowly discovered the wealth of the words in the world, and informed by Catholicism—through which I filter everything—I have discovered that it matters what you read and in the great work of criminal conversion and reformation, it helps to become familiar with their intellectual sources.

The common element of these source books is that they inspired a deep and critical reflection upon the ways of the world, with a particular focus on the social models and ideals criminals are told represent the world and to which they should aspire as part of their eventual rehabilitation. Professional criminals *know* that these models and ideals are misleading and that *they and their way of life* are closer to reality. Their perspective, which was once mine, is that criminals and the non-arrested (who are also criminals) who gain riches, fame, and power, share opposite faces of one self, but the criminal is true to self while the non-arrested is not.

I do not know the depth of sway these writings have in today's prisons, but suspect it is still considerable, for there are, living in the maximum security prisons of America—I met many such in the federal penitentiaries of Leavenworth and McNeil Island—men deep into their 70's and 80's still retaining the ferocity and physicality of men decades younger, and they remember and hold fast to the ideas that have long resonated within them and it is to them that younger criminals look to for benchmarks of criminal stature and worth.

This chapter can serve as a supplementary transformative tool by being used as a guide for other criminals seeking to restructure their lives, who are not yet prepared to enter into the study of Catholic works, because the ideas being fleshed out through them are ideas universal to many, in particular, criminals.

Much of this source literature comes from the 1940's to the 1970's, when the social adulation of the outsider, the outlaw, and the criminal came into full flower, and it was during the latter decade, that the carceral world was truly beginning to shape the criminal world.

The world of the maximum security prison, once you have adapted and found your place within its social structure, is possessed of many deep virtues highly prized by criminals;

first among them being that what one truly is, is known by all; and any attempts to present a personhood—interior or exterior—that is not truly yours is soon discovered, with consequences apt to be fatal.

This is a forging and refining quality also found in combat, and it is largely why the world of the prison has –over the past several decades—begun to play such a large and influential role in the world of the criminal.

What one is rather than what one presents himself to be is also at the heart of the Catholic Church and the congruence between what the Church has always presented herself to be with what she actually is—though one must examine closely and deeply the actual record—is strong and true.

This examination of the sources shaping one criminal's life and the review of the books playing the seminal role in the development of my intellectual life—their literary essence and transformative impact—is directed, as is all of my work, towards those men and women in prison or out, whose lives are shaped through their exposure to books and the ideas within which have the power to create transformed criminals, deep knowledge leaders, who not only have the academy to thank for their knowledge, but the city streets and the prison tiers, and who are able, through inclination, redemption, education, and skill, to become a grassroots organizational leader of an apostolate that can generate the transformation of other criminals, inside or outside of prison.

It is directed to penitential criminals who are Catholics or potential converts who, because of their stature and leadership in the criminal/carceral world, will have significant success and impact in the work of criminal transformation.

It is directed to those individuals who committed crimes for money—professional criminals—to whom crime was a way of life and prison time an occupational hazard.

It is directed to those professional criminals who have spent at least five years in a maximum security prison—the benchmark of professional criminality after arrest and conviction.

It is from these criminals that the leadership in the carceral world comes and it is from them that effective reentry leadership will also emerge.

Each distinct human population has a certain cohort from which effective leadership usually emerges and it is also so within the criminal world.

There are certain characteristics and criminal experiences that serve as the foundation of criminal world leadership and others that preclude someone from being perceived as a leader.

Criminal world leaders are not informers, do not commit crimes against children and women, nor allow themselves to be victimized by others in the maximum security prisons where they serve their time.

There are many people who have served time—in an honor farm, medical facility, or other minimum or medium security prison, who have developed and managed prisoner rehabilitation efforts—but their work has not sprung from their leadership within the carceral and criminal world, a leadership and status investing their work with the credibility and gravitas to provide effective rehabilitative work on a national scale.

Intellectual life is widespread among professional criminals in prison and it is a pursuit they have the time to pursue. The oft noted comparison of prisons with monasteries is partially true; though the Divine Office as practiced by monks and nuns is replaced by the Moloch game of acquiring and sustaining power and privilege from ever newly arriving contenders.

I could not have come to an appreciation of St. Thomas Aquinas without the early tutoring through the works examined in these pages, for it is through the critical search through the chaos of the thought of the world, that the brilliantly clear reasoning of the thought of the Angelic Doctor will later come to resonate as the true sign of contradiction, truth alone holds when stood up against the world.

This chapter is directed towards those criminals who become part of the long and winding path to the communal community of the Catholic Church—triumphant, suffering, militant—no matter at what place along that path they may be, for if they are on that path and if transformed criminals are close to them, then conversion is certain when they make the intellectual choice to transform themselves, to create from within a different person than what they were previously, a person whose motivation is based on the fullness of eternal truth, found only in the Catholic Church, the City of God, rather than on the transitory truth of the world, the city of man, the city of the prison.

Virtually everything of the world acts to validate the illusion that objective truth does not exist, but truth is so powerful that it always speaks to us. Even from the works of the illusionists—from whom many of the sources herein described come—the embedded ideas of truth call out to us, but we need the eye and mind of the Church to see the truth, for in it truth has been deposited since the beginning, first with the Jews and after Christ, with everyone willing to see.

I am speaking here of the Church through eternal time, the mighty ark of Christ guiding us, the pillar of fire leading through the desert to the land of milk and honey.

We must not become attached to the small and worldly Church, to the errant priests, nuns, and popes, for these shall always infect the People of God on earth, as they have throughout history and as is becoming increasingly evident, virtually conquering the institutional Church during the 20th Century, which the struggles of the 21st to reclaim her remain to be accomplished, but not in doubt.

Within the first universal catechism of the Catholic Church—that of Pope Pius V—first published in the Year of Our Lord 1566, it is written:

> We are, therefore, bound to believe that there is one Holy Catholic Church. With regard to the Three Persons of the Holy Trinity, the Father, the Son, and the Holy Ghost, we not only believe them, but also believe *in* them. But here we make use of a different form of expression, professing to believe the holy, not *in* the holy Catholic Church. By this difference of expression we distinguish God, the author of all things, from His works, and acknowledge that all the exalted benefits bestowed on the Church are due to God's bounty. (p. 113)

And men, even Peter, who lied thrice about our Lord and ran, rather than keeping watch over the crucifixion with the Apostle John, and the three Marys, often betray God; though Peter, after Pentecost, became the rock our Lord proclaimed and died a true martyr's death, refusing to be crucified upright as Our Lord, but died hanging upside down on his cross.

The Holy Catholic Church was deeply infiltrated by Communism through the Russian Orthodox leadership in league with the Kremlin, early in the 20th Century and communistically redirected during the mid-century council of Vatican II.

One of the clearest signs of her misdirection—along with removal of the Latin Mass—was the scandal of ignoring the charge from Our Lady of Fatima.

The appearance of the Holy Virgin Mother to the three children—Lúcia Santos and her cousins Jacinta and

Francisco Marto—delivering the instructions for the Pope, together with all of the bishops of the world, to consecrate Russia, was ignored.

Consequently Russia became the single largest sponsor of the evil of Communism in the world responsible for taking hundreds of millions of lives, and degrading billions more.

Even with that, the current time is the best of times—for it embodies all that has gone before—and it is the worst of times—as it embodies all that has gone before.

Laying blame, while a worthwhile intellectual exercise building a historic foundation upon which informed belief can rest, resolves little for it is as it is.

Peter is the embodiment of popes throughout history as dogma is embodiment of beliefs throughout history.

Everything that has happened in the Church is for the best.

The sexual abuse crisis revealed the true nature of the desanctification of the religious predators.

Vatican II's impact on liturgy led to Latin Mass redoubts where true Catholics live.

The legalization of abortion reveals the true nature of the world under its satanic prince.

We attach ourselves to the eternal truth of the Church—we love God, we love people, we protect the innocent, we fight evil—and every day, every minute, increase our knowledge of the truth, for it is the only path to eternal life.

We have the Lord to guide us and we have great teachers to teach us—St. Thomas Aquinas being supreme among them—and his work illuminates the great truth upon the narrow road to eternity, an eternity the Angelic Doctor entered just at that moment when he realized how little his words meant when compared to the beatific vision; but which mean so much to those of us reaching for that vision.

Finally, one of the most difficult chores in writing about the criminal/carceral world as a former criminal/prisoner is the misconceptions of many readers developed by the normative universe of criminal/carceral world books by former criminals/prisoners.

They tend to fall into two basic patterns: the penitential and the sociological and I have tried to keep each—as much as possible—from my books.

In order to help convince non-criminal/carceral world readers of the accuracy of my representation of my former world, I eagerly grab collaborating sources, for instance, the validating of one of our guiding criminal justice principles that precludes working with informants, pedophiles, or rapists because they do not have the criminal/carceral world status to become effective Catholic evangelizers—which is our essential mission.

Introducing the Terms

Rehabilitation and reentry are terms used by most rehabilitative practitioners to describe the process more accurately called criminal transformation. Rehabilitation or reentry are not proper concepts to use as they imply a return to something—a state of internality—that previously existed or in some community in which one previously resided, whereas professional criminals are generally born into the criminal world, and that is the only internality and community reality congruent with their perspective.

Working from a rehabilitative or reentry perspective, as does the normative rehabilitative practitioner, sets the criminal transformation process on the incorrect intellectual setting, partly the reason for its continued failure, widely evident when the rehabilitation programs used by the traditional rehabilitative practitioner, are evaluated rigorously.

Rehabilitative/reentry practitioners generally define success or failure after a three year period post-release from custody when about 70% of criminals in the United States recidivate, including those released from several criminal justice sanctions— probation, parole, jail, or prison—but in our work through the Lampstand Foundation, we use it in reference to professional criminals released from a maximum security prison or a transitional facility after serving the bulk of their time in maximum security.

We use a ten year period of reentry as a benchmark of transformation as it allows for the fuller development of transformative behavior—and a more accurate reflection of return statistics— than the relatively short three year period does.

We believe that only transformed married Catholic criminals should be involved in developing and managing criminal transformation programs because Catholicism is the only truth potent enough to trump the truth of the world—informing the truth of the criminal world—and professional criminals who've served at least five years in a maximum security prison, possess a graduate degree, and a deep knowledge of Catholic social teaching, are the only ones who understand the carceral and criminal world well enough to present that truth with enough vigor and standing to influence personal conversions that will ultimately reduce recidivism.

It is only within the Catholic Magisterium that the robust story of Christ exists in its fullness with the power to destroy the lie told by the prince of this world, the foundation the truth of the world and the truth of the criminal world is built upon.

While the response to the crimes criminals commit in the world belongs to Caesar's police, courts, and prisons, the response to the individual human being who is the criminal—his transformation and redemption—belongs to God and the teachings of His Church.

The catechesis of the criminal brought through study of the history of the Church and her social teaching—Catholic doctrine presented in universal terms—will work. For within the social teaching will be found the unbroken line of truth connecting the transforming criminal to the beginning of creation and the institution in which truth exists, which has held to it for over two thousand years; something that can be said of no other institution on earth.

Christ specifically speaks to the criminal world who has been deceived into believing the truth of the world and living by the rules of men in the city of men, which the criminal does more boldly than the rest.

Being able to speak from brotherly love and deep knowledge, the transformed criminal, who once relished many aspects of his former criminal life, knows the failure of active love in the oft quoted "love the sinner, hate the sin" in a life where identification with the sin is often deep.

The Church dwells in the interior of man—in the communion with Christ—not in the community of men, and through its interiority guides the walking of the talking.

For centuries the criminal, like Cain, could be banished, or voluntarily disappear and begin life again as a new person, but no more.

Now all are connected and all crimes rest on the all-knowing digital conscience of the world and the only rebirth, even since ancient times, is through baptism.

Reaching this point within that leads to the path of transformation, requires long and consistent study which will result in the creation of deep knowledge, and the classic works which are already alive within the carceral world's library are those works noted in this chapter will be of great help in the development and exercise of that love of knowledge which can eventually lead to love of the teaching and history of the Church, resulting in conversion and transformation.

The Criminal as Poet

Poetry is a powerfully attractive way for criminals in prison to express their inner life and its structured or free form, brevity, and spiritual roots, lend itself as an effective way to express suffering within a socially acceptable method with long history within the criminal/carceral world.

Outlaw poets share a certain aberrancy fully immersing them in convention bending reality reminiscent of criminal world values, but strangely apart from them also.

Three major poets—Ginsberg, Khayyam, Baudelaire—whose work illuminates the foundational ideas underlying the type of life often connected with criminality, infusing them with a sense of passion, destiny, and romantic foreboding within which criminals often sense a relationship and congruency that calls for a deeper exploration into many related works.

Many criminals, during the first reading of Ginsberg's poem *Howl*, begin such an exploration.

I remember when I first saw this poem, during my time in the Federal Correctional Institution at Inglewood, Colorado or as we affectionately called it "Little Alcatraz" due to its double barbed wire fence and multiple gun towers, making it somewhat impervious to escape.

335

This saddened me as I had escaped from my last three institutional confinements, Reno City Jail, Nevada State Foster Home, and Nevada State Reformatory and had planned to do the same here, but I was beginning to realize that I might be housed in a prison from which I could not easily escape.

Howl was smuggled into the prison as a handful of mimeographed sheets which was passed around to the group I hung out with, completely blowing our minds.

There are many words written in the cathedral of criminal veneration, but few as potent as those in *Howl* and *Footnote to Howl*.

We didn't really read it too close, being too young (15-17) to have the more adult literary ability we would later grow into, but we latched onto the sense of freedom and artistry that seemed to be describing the kind of lives we lived, at least before our imprisonment.

Having developed a sense of alienation from the daily life of normality through a love of the criminal life that led us to prison, many criminals eagerly feast on this work, which not only validates our sense of alienation, investing it with a mythical penetration of the invisible secrets underlying the visible, while reshaping the ongoing narrative of the truth of the world, while putting it into a context that elevates rather than denigrates the criminal life.

From Ginsberg's first lines of *Howl* many criminals are hooked—I still feel a thrill reading them—and see the possibility of not just a senseless battering against the unthinking stone and steel prison which has resulted from our acts, but an actual artistic and beautiful life being created from the *apparent* chaos others see, though perceived by the criminal as the way life is supposed to be.

We can see in the Moloch verses of *Howl,* a path to sacrificial understanding that illuminates a prison driven life.

In seeking out the real worship of the great god Moloch, which I later did, we find that he was a Carthaginian deity built of metal upon whose outstretched arms were cast the children of Carthage in a sacrifice.

Moloch was a powerful image to present as representative of the culture in which we lived and attributes fitting its dark visage were readily apparent to the drug illuminated minds of those who resonated with the images so skillfully woven by the Beat poets.

Howl overturned every convention of its time and did so gloriously, artistically, and poetically; claiming, as cultural revolutionaries always do, that theirs was a better—a higher—way.

Howl and the other works of the Beats paid homage to outlawry and social chaos, a deep and long-burning fuel for the emergent criminal mind, reshaping and deepening the truth of the world in its slow trajectory towards full embrace of criminal world truth, and I raced with it.

The story of Omar Khayyam, the author of the *Rubaiyat,* is intriguing and has deep connections to criminal world culture, involving the birth of the assassins (one of Omar's classmates with whom a life- long pact was formed among three of them to help one another if any of them became successful, was the man who began the cult of the assassins and became the *Old Man of the Mountain,* a legendary outlaw of the Middle East) and the joy of living a life of sensuality.

The *Rubaiyat* has such beauty and so well presents the life of ease, drink, and pleasure for self that one is hard pressed to resist it when in that peculiar place of seeking answers to what the reality of prison and life in the criminal world are revealing.

So many of the treatises proclaiming the truths of the world wind up to be empty shells of words and ring sad, forlorn, or angry in a boldly defying acceptance—music to criminal ears—such as *Howl* or the melancholic quietness of Eliot's *The Hollow Men.*

Khayyam however, is joyful, worldly and one would think a wonderful drinking companion, a wise voice in the prison cell reminding criminals of the transient nature of life, the treasures yet to be discovered and the readiness to bend to the fate of the world which claims us all.

The narrative companion to *Howl* is centered around a road trip the author of *On the Road*, Jack Kerouac, takes with Neal Cassady, the criminal and former prisoner who was the seminal lodestar to three of the founding Beats: Ginsberg, Kerouac, and Burroughs.

Cassady's reality may be more important to the formation of the spiritual and literary roots of the Beats and Hippies—he was also the bus driver of the bus *Further* which Ken Kesey and the Merry Pranksters moved into legend chronicled by Thomas Wolfe in the *Electric Kool-Aid Acid Test*—than any of the writers whose poems and prose captured and preserved the journey of convention rebellion and the spiritual seeking way of life over the hazy decades.

Cassady was Dean Moriarty in *On the Road* and the gravitas of his place in Kerouac's thinking is evident throughout.

In the middle of the book Kerouac hears from Cassady/Moriarty, the secret of Cassady's vision, a vision Kerouac desperately wishes to possess.

Being able to be dropped down into any place in the country, stone cold broke and without a friend—as one is usually released from prison—and survive, even prosper, within hours, is the mark of a professional criminal, a mark I had met many times, and it is the knowing Cassady/Moriarty possesses and Kerouac desperately desires.

Kerouac ends *On the Road* paying homage to Cassady, the one who knows.

Neal Cassady/Dean Moriarty was the man who knows, the criminal poet from the criminal world, the one who was not only not afraid, but absolutely relished the deep night of city streets and unknown highways and starless views; and he shared his knowing with those who needed to know and a way of life was formed, within which the poetry of the criminal world deepened still.

On the Road begins and ends idolizing the criminal who can live freely, who sees deeply the reality below the convention the Beats are so earnestly rebelling against, becoming in actuality their new father, even giving them expression as the style of Cassady's famous letter to Joan Anderson (which had been thought lost but was found in 2014) becomes Kerouac's writing style.

His own words, but Cassady's—the criminal world's—reality, and ultimately Kerouac realized he had failed in his search and that worldly fame obscured rather than illuminated the eternal he really sought, just as drugs, sex, convention warping, and the following of whim and passion wrapped Cassady, Ginsberg, Burroughs and the others so tightly as to make them scream with existential pain they passed to us, passing still, priests and priestesses of nothing eternal, nothing real, all wrapped in candy colored flakes blowing in the wind.

As the end approached and as death parted them from the reality they thought they had discovered the secret of—but really only an escape from—a narrative, poetic, and song writing escape which writhed in anguish and self-mortification based on no great vision of God, they finally realized the truth.

Kerouac was a cradle Catholic whose life and end was particularly and poetically tragic.

There are other poems exerting a powerful pull on the sensibilities of criminals in prison—during the period when the carceral world began reshaping that of the criminal world—whether exploring the mysteries of the love between a man and a woman, perhaps wrapped in a deep allegorical mist, as many feel the poems of Walter Benton to be.

Walter Benton graduated from Ohio University, worked as a social investigator in New York, and served in the army during the Second World War, becoming a captain.

Benton's *This My Beloved,* his first published book of poetry—in 1943—and his most well-known work, is a diary in verse.

The poetry embraced by the American carceral and criminal world, during whatever period of time, will relate those aspects of the criminal life emblematic of the reality seen by the criminal and the poetry of Benton does, in its foreboding and elegiac capturing of the emotional life between a couple or their loss.

Benton's *Never a Greater Need,* first published in 1948, was his selection of the best poems he wrote after the publication of *This My Beloved,* which had made him famous.

Hunched over in dark cells these words were often read metaphorically, seen to represent the addiction driven world—the heroin addicts I met in prison loved Benton's work and they said he was also a junkie—the surcease from a pain seeking world, the world of self-medication, the world wherein criminals so often travel, where many choose to dwell forever.

Two great poems from the criminal life are *The Blue Velvet Band* and *Stagger Lee*, both capturing in their own unique way a certain reality of the criminal world—the often ambiguous relationship between men and women and the honor-bound actions of the criminal often appearing incomprehensible to outsiders—and both poems loved by criminals and convict throughout the country for many generations.

There are many versions of *The Blue Velvet Band*, but the one that rings closest to that loved by most prisoners is the version sung by Porter Wagoner, which opens so hopefully romantic and closes in prison, sent there by the girl with the beautiful hair, wrapped in the blue velvet band

Stagger Lee also opens on a corner in the criminal city, at night, when the criminal world comes out and the lights shine so brightly, hiding the deep shadows looming, darkly inviting.

This work of poem and song, which has been so prominent in the criminal/carceral world, has been found to have originated from an actual event—which is surely also true, though as yet unsubstantiated, for *The Blue Velvet Band*—from the life of Lee Shelton, sometimes known as *Stagger Lee,* a criminal who murdered William Lyons on Christmas Eve in 1895 in St. Louis, and himself died in prison in 1912.

The traditional version of *Stagger Lee* which I first heard in prison is by Lloyd Price.

These poems, like many others which spoke to the life conditions of the criminal and carceral world, circulated, were refined and personalized by generations of criminals to express their feelings about what they were experiencing.

The long European tradition of singing praise of the corrupt and criminal life—Petronius' *Satryicon*, Marquis De Sade's *Justine*, Oscar Wilde's *The Picture of Dorian Gray*, Thomas De Quincey's *Confessions of an English Opium Eater*—seemed to be gathered together in a great chest and wrapped in a gaudy bow through the work of Charles Baudelaire and his aptly named major work, *Flowers of Evil* in which he captures the essence of his thought.

All the criminal positions are herein stated, the mental stance and guiding principle, the freedom from family and work-a-day entanglements, rightly fought against and enemized; the love of the true patron, and the always present playmates, from whose embrace time has no sting, nor are there any remembrances of things as they might have been.

This internal struggle also marked Kerouac's work and eventual dissolution, the great and eternal battle destined to play out in the fields of the Lord, shaping and marking the depths of the criminal world, mapping the streets of desire and loss in the criminal city.

At Play in the Fields of the Lord by Peter Matthiessen is another important book I read in McNeil Island Federal Penitentiary and the novel captures the on the road ethos loved by criminals in the character of Moon, the part American Indian man who is the protagonist.

A group of us in McNeil Island undertook to read and study it and the message for us was how to be a more internally integrated criminal, how to embrace our deepest and most vital self.

The book is built upon *discovering* and *accepting* who you are, internally, and living your life, externally, as that, and for the central character Moon, that involved a substantial level of risk he, as did we, deemed worthy for the resulting harmony of flesh and spirit.

We interpreted this to mean that the secret of the world was embodied in the criminal world and living as a professional criminal was what was secretly desired by all who were in the world.

The hidden history of the world, much of it revolving around private corruption of public paragons, is the history generally known within the criminal/carceral world and it is a major source—McCarthy, race, left-wing politics—which criminals, who tend to be very conservative, know the fallacy embedded in public pronouncements.

Prison was like this, riots, or at the very least, their potential, every day, when gangs mingled in the yards, getting too close to turf, either physical, financial, or psychological, the knifes could come out, the charge across the yard or down the tier, and the explosion as they met, dealing death out with ferocious abandon.

Poetry, with its freedom, impressionistic, symbolic and metamorphic way of attempting to frame the truth of something so difficult to explain—the criminal and carceral reality—is the one medium virtually all criminals appreciate and whether the poetry is turned to song, read in small groups, or silently contemplated and composed, it is a potent force in prison as without and often redemptive, as this poem I wrote in 2007 notes:

> I have brutalized the world and she now
> Stares back at me with grim bars
> Steel and stone for the color of my heart
> And the wickedness of my ways
>
> Washed clean in the fire of Christ's blood and the
> dark room of the confessional
> Father intoning the timeless words
> Go in peace my son
>
> I now walk another path embraced by
> Prayer and the sonorous rhythms of the Mass

Eyes following the finger
Scrolling the ancient scripture

The Criminal as Philosopher

Invariably, at some point during a long stretch in prison the thought occurs in the criminal's mind, as it did in mine, what is life about, what am I doing with my life?

Though it may be shunted aside temporarily in the daydreams of eventual release and restoration of the freedom criminal life brings when all is going well, it comes back if the right set of ideas, whether in a book or from other prison philosophers, enter into the criminal's field of vision.

The ideas have to be strong, presented with potency and clarity to even capture the attention of the criminal, and most often, initially based on a great injustice in the world that animates some of the sense of personal injustice, however unjustifiably felt, clouding the criminal's thinking.

Just such a book is *Man's Search for Meaning: An Introduction to Logotherapy,* by Viktor E. Frankl.

The original title of this book was *From Death-Camp to Existentialism,* and recounted the experiences of Dr. Frankl while imprisoned in the concentration camps at Auschwitz and Dachau established by the Nazi's during the reign of Adolf Hitler.

It is a powerful book, which continues to reach out to those finding themselves in the most horrible of circumstances, with its resonating message of the fierce will to retain one's humanity, even in the most barbaric and inhuman conditions.

Studying existentialism in prison is congruent with the prison culture and it serves the purpose of beginning to study books to facilitate studying one's self.

In the concentration camps, and in a maximum security prison, this message resonates with incredible depth and clarity of meaning, and if first encountered within the deepest cell in the dark prison—the great cell of solitude in the supermax facility where I first read it—it will resonate even the more deeply.

But even here, a choice can still be made, to continue with brutality and the entirely predictable response to it which always punishes the brutal, either spiritually or temporally; or to choose human kindness and allow the better angels of our nature to appear in our dealings with others and perhaps find the peace so often accompanying their exhibition.

The Crowd by Gustave Le Bon was printed in its first English edition in 1896, but its insight about the nature and behavior of crowds in different situations, and by supposition, that of individuals, is remarkable still.

Le Bon's primary reference point was the French Revolution and the barbarity it released among the French people towards the ancient monarchy, still singular in its expression, though replicated somewhat in the Russian Revolution occurring about 20 years after this book was published.

During the period in which Le Bon is writing, the vast majority of the public was illiterate, so he was writing, as much of the writing was before the 20th Century, particularly in Europe, to his fellow well-educated members of the social elite, the ruling class.

As such there was no need to shade what he was saying and his writing is sharp and clear.

The crowd is moved by emotion, which we see still and his description of what is used, should not be unfamiliar to those who have watched the speeches of politicians, exuberant preachers, or self-help gurus.

For the criminal this type of insight is rarely applied to his own actions, but to those of the herds of people populating the mass he feels he has bested, and who he feels are living lives largely constrained by rule and regulation they would willingly thwart had they the courage he has.

Consequently, much of what he reads concerning the motivation of others will be used for understanding motivation and shaping reality to more closely resemble that world he feels he has learned the truth of, the world of the criminal city, the world founded by men, not the world of the City of God.

This is not yet a place he has dared reach, nor even acknowledged exists in a potent enough way to be of concern to him and his life, but that moment is beginning to be felt.

A mention must be made here of another voice writing of crowds, mass movements; Eric Hoffer, whose masterpiece is *The True Believer: Thoughts on the Nature of Mass Movements*.

What is so remarkable about Hoffer's book, apart from its brilliance, is that he was a self-taught intellectual who spent his life working as a longshoreman in San Francisco.

A newer book about crowds, amplifying—while differing with—much of the work of the previous two mentioned, is *The Wisdom of Crowds: Why the Many Are Smarter that the Few and How Collective Wisdom Shapes Business, Economies, Societies, and Nations*, by James Surowiecki.

If the value of a life is determined by the proportion of it spent in service to others, as I believe it is, then the value of the lives of most of the avatars of the Sixties—marked by an intense self-preoccupation and virtually across the board endings more reminiscent of Gothic novels than American optimism—has been found to not be very great, except as object lessons in how not to live a life.

Alan Watts surely flows into this vein and his work to relativize religion—absolute truth—was very popular, and, at the time, I loved it.

This creating your own thing and "doing your own thing" shaped the Sixties—though it ultimately destroyed the lives of its prophets—while validating the criminal world ethos, giving it more cultural resonance than it had ever enjoyed in the 1920's or 1930's.

Jean Paul Sartre in his seminal work, *Saint Genet*, completed the picture of mystifying the boundaries between right and wrong, creating a reality in which a child *becoming* a criminal—rather than *becoming* a being centered on divinity—is centered on a theology of criminality.

This work is the most detailed and interesting of the works created studying the criminal. Jean Genet, criminal, poet, writer, and actor, who was also, because of Sartre's work, a well-known literary figure whose criminality was the mark of otherness that marked him for fame.

For several months in McNeil Island Federal Penitentiary, the same group of us also read and discussed this work and the broader implications of existentialism on our lives.

From that group grew a longer discussion around ideas that continued for the almost four years I was there.

Genet had embraced his being defined by the world—when caught as a child stealing—as the thief, and he became the thief, discovering in the process the delicious freedom of death of the self by embracing his defining from others.

There is, within the intensity of the point of that tipping moment during a criminal act when one's very life is at stake, when all falls on that one razor-edged moment, when one can feel that one is entering the sacred, and this moment often defines, as Sartre captured, the sublimity of the criminal life.

Genet wrote the introduction to the seminal book by George Jackson, a prisoner in San Quentin whose life and political philosophy still plays a major role in the criminal/carceral culture.

George Jackson was in Deuel Vocational Institution (DVI) from May to December of 1962, a time when I was also in DVI though I do not remember him, but the truths he was forming, are remembered.

DVI was in a particularly historic moment as the prison gangs were just beginning to take their most lethal form, and politics had seeped in.

This was an extraordinary moment in the history of the criminal/carceral world, when criminals were considered to be the vanguard of a revolution, and this moment's impact continues to strengthen criminal/carceral world culture today.

Though the search for truth from Catholicism is one of individual salvation rather than collective, its attraction to the seeker of collective liberation is powerful.

Somewhere at the root of the political truth seeker is a desire for power and there is no power greater in the world than the Catholic faith whose source is not even of this world, not even susceptible to any movements of empire or legislature, as Imperial Rome discovered.

I've always perceived liberation as a result of spiritual work rather than political, so the attractions of Karl Marx, though alluring, didn't influence me as much as those of Teilhard de Chardin.

Having entered into my intellectual studies through the door of history, I had some awareness of the failures of the collective search for freedom while the individual search proffered many stories of success.

Consequently, my reaction to the writings of Franz Fanon, Angela Davis, George Jackson, and others, was lacking in any sustained desire to become part of a collective effort, though many of their intellectual arguments had an impact on my thinking.

The idea that criminals were to be the vanguard of the revolution, so central to the writing of the California prisoners in the 1960's and 1970's, (explored in depth in *The Rise and Fall of California's Radical Prison Movement,* (1994) by Eric Cummins) made sense to me in the context of the deep lack of any propensity for violence—clearly central to the normative Communistic theory around revolution— for most of the college-based revolutionaries I met in prison and out.

This joining of the criminal/carceral world to the world of the insiders leads inexorably to the world of *The Outsider.*

The Outsider is one of a series of books by Colin Wilson that reflects on the nexus between creativity, alienation, and society, by examining the works of various artists, like Nietzsche, Shaw, Blake, Van Gogh, Hesse, Hemingway, Camus, Nijinsky, and Gurdjieff.

Wilson proposes that it is through the work of the Outsider, those artists who have seen, who are compelled to see, reality more deeply than the common man, and by bringing their vision back to the world, help propel it upward.

The Outsiders' vision is one of a wholeness they struggle to capture in a world of broken systems and valueless cultures, and it is in the results of their search, even when failing, that the rest of us are provided glimpses of the path ahead.

Most of them fail and go mad in the failing, but the few who succeed, bring back something for us of great value, but whether it is a positive or negative value—depending on one's perspective—can be often difficult to determine.

The result of his study embraces the sensuality and self-ratifying seeking of the light at the center of the criminal city—occupying an ever more prominent place in its burning towers, even to the penthouse—and for criminals fabricating their perspective for deeper penetration into the criminal world, it is a dark light indeed.

Wilson's book and the foundational ideas seemingly so congruent with those of many other writers and thinkers who loved the notion of being considered an Outsider, vaulted him into the rarefied atmosphere of the other avatars of the Sixties, from which the same reviewers of his work that placed him there, tried, after becoming disenchanted with his writing and behavior, to remove him.

The mystical way so many thought was a deep penetration of the profoundest level of truth, emerged then from the drug culture—as it had so many times before in so many different guises—resonating with the Sixties seeker and taking its deepest root in the theory of the game.

One of the most seductive presentations of the game theory map of life was *The Master Game,* by Robert De Ropp which defined the scripts and traps of the many ways the seeker could lose, and then ultimately find, his truest and highest self.

Tied in to the existential praxis and Esalenistic therapeutic theories, it took the position that what we really needed to make our lives complete and fulfilling was a game worth playing and several were presented, high and low.

Game theory is so congruent with the criminal world that many times the street/prison query, "What is your game?"

is asked; contrasting to "What do you do?" heard in the suburban lounges where the non-criminal world congregates, though both are driven by the still unconscious values of acquisition and success at any cost, foundational to the criminal city.

Many of the paradigms of thought endemic to various forms of human interaction are based on the dog-eat-dog reality of the perceived world, often labeled *real* politics; get *real,* and so on.

And this is what game theory is based on, the *real* versus the illusion, and should you subscribe to it, you then become *real,* an illusion no longer.

Part of becoming *real* is discovering the truth about humanity that lie behind the illusion, and for that one needs the key.

The greatest expression of the spiritual potency of life as game is *Magister Ludi*—which I'll mention later—by Herman Hesse, the author who captivated so many of us during the Sixties, and rereading his autobiographical novel, *Steppenwolf*—which I first read in prison while still in my twenties, passing over the injunction that it was written by Hesse at fifty and meant for readers in their fifties—know that I became that man in some fashion as I absorbed the animating cores of so many of the books I read deeply, as all books are read in prison, deeply.

For all of us, the dark and dour men who struggle with their own interpretations of how life has caused them to suffer and how it is so unworthy of our ideals, yet, with our own Maria/Hermine safely at our side, showing us through her lived life, the indescribable joys of the daily comings and goings, the sun and flowers and bees dancing through red roses.

Magister Ludi attracted me because its common name, *The Bead Game* was congruent with my thinking at the time—mid 1960's in McNeil Island Federal Penitentiary—I read it, that life was a game.

In rereading the book today, I realize that the bead game has been and is played, though for real, by our greatest Catholic philosophers and theologians—in harmony with the Church, by St. Thomas Aquinas and disharmoniously by Teilhard de Chardin and Leonardo Boff—because they have access to the thought of the world, through the history and teaching of the Church; and of these the greatest is surely St. Thomas Aquinas, so I was somewhat floored when the first historical personage mentioned by name and context, by Hesse in the book is the Angelic Doctor.

The Bead Game fascinated me for its reduction of all and everything to one system, which I finally discovered existed only, completely and fully, in the Sacred Doctrine of the Catholic Church.

Another synthesizer was Antoine De Saint-Exupery, the great French author and pilot who died while on a military flight during World War II, gained fame as the author of *The Little Prince*, a fable about a little boy containing profound truths for adults, but his real claim to fame among the wisdom seekers in the criminal world is his magnum opus *The Wisdom of the Sands,* which is a powerful and magnificent statement about the essential nobility and grandeur of man.

His clarity and insight resonates today, and its deep footsteps tracking across the endless desert sands of our modern world where the forlorn are mourned beyond recompense and their cries reach eternity, as endless as the sands their lives sleep upon, reminding us of what is solid, built on rock, built upon Peter.

Saint-Exupery was a devout Catholic, who refined his spiritual perspective from his experiences in the Sahara Desert, revealing to us another and deeper vision of the great City of God — paradoxically and imaginatively built upon the shifting desert sands— which stands forever against the willow world of the city of men.

Life's meaning is shaped by the interior mansions richly adorned, the empty deserts resolutely traversed, and the beckoning sunlit skies our open hands grasp; embraced deeply and eternally.

Exupery's work, of such fierce beauty, resonates with the criminal bound within the prison of stone and steel, for it carves velvet soft and wondrous love from such bleakness.

Saint-Exupery bridges philosophy and religion with his soaring speculations on the paradoxes of life which he contemplated most often during his flights, particularly across the deserts of Africa, where he disappeared on July 31, 1944 while flying reconnaissance for the Allies to determine if there were any German troop movements in the region.

In 1998 a bracelet with his name and that of his wife was found in the sea south of Marseille and in 2000 his plane was found, scattered over the sea bed out of Marseille, and verified by the French Government in 2004 as his plane.

The fervent philosophy of the desert prince, who was his protagonist in *The Wisdom of the Sands,* resonates deeply with men involved in life or death situations on a daily basis, whether it is from combat duty in the military or the normal razor-edge of life within the criminal/carceral world.

It is a stark philosophy, hard, clear, and resolute; where each act is reflected in the glare of impending death from any mistaken movement, or uncertainty when certainty is the only option.

It is a philosophy of absolutes. Things are. You act accordingly. Hesitation is weakness and ultimate disaster, which may come immediately or years later.

Saint-Exupery's gift was to have tried to live this way—the book, *Saint Exupery: A Biography*, by Stacy Schiff is excellent—to have contemplated his life deeply, and to have written about it, inspiring others with his thoughts.

In a world of relativity, the attraction of this type of clarity is enormous to those who live the harrowing lives its profundity is built upon.

Another writer whose works perhaps most led me directly to Catholicism, were those by Taylor Caldwell, and most of all, her greatest work, in my opinion; *A Pillar of Iron*, about Cicero of Rome, but who many assumed it was also about the United States.

In reading about Taylor Caldwell on Wikipedia, it is clear her final days were not so good, and her infatuation with strident conservatism—she wrote articles for the John Birch Society (whose blandishments I also succumbed to temporarily after being invited to join by a cousin who was an officer of the organization)—and reincarnation did not mesh to her benefit.

The dynamic duo of Laing & Szasz turned it all upside down with their consensus that mental illness was a sane response to an insane culture; which to criminals became: "becoming a criminal in a criminal culture is a smart move."

I read the book by R.D. Laing, *The Politics of Experience*, after I had been released from prison and it corroborated the ideas—from a psychotherapeutic position—which I had been reading and thinking about for years, and really blew the lid off with its contention (putting a bow around the other ideas promoting disorder and chaos loose in the culture) that the people labeled insane were really sane.

It takes absolutely no imagination at all to see how this can be folded into a justification and experience of the criminal through his experience in the criminal/carceral world.

I carried and spread this ideology around for years and it wasn't until I entered into the deepest discussion with the Catholic Church as the sign of contradiction, that the argument finally became obsolete.

The last book I read before being released from McNeil Island Federal Penitentiary in 1969 was *The Temptation to Exist* by E. M. Cioran.

Of all the writers who expressed a philosophic position, whether within a fiction or nonfiction vehicle, the one who had one of the most powerful impacts on me was the fellow Russian Jew, Alissa Zinovievna Rosenbaum, born in St. Petersburg February 2, 1905, who later, in one of the most triumphal accounts of personal transformation in the 20th Century, became Ayn Rand.

My grandmother, Lillian Oren, was a Ukrainian Jew, who, in adapting to America, was a non-practicing Jew, and married my grandfather, Wesley Hewitt, an English, Scot, salesman and real estate investor; but it was not until many years later, during our exploration of Judaism prior to becoming Catholic, that I discovered my Jewish heritage.

My first reading of Ayn Rand was *The Fountainhead*, in a dark, dingy, dirty, cell in Ogden City Jail while being transferred from Salt Lake City Jail—where I was imprisoned for escaping from the Nevada State Reformatory in Elko, Nevada—to the Federal Correctional Institution in Englewood, Colorado.

I read the fat, scruffy paperback in one great gulp, and embraced it, as the complete self-centered, individualistic philosophy that is—at its axial core—deeply criminal, and my thief's heart reveled at the harmonious congruence, though I could only relate in dreams with Rand's protagonist's lives of high drama and high finance.

It was in her thought, especially as expressed in *The Virtue of Selfishness: A New Concept of Egoism* that I first found elevated ideas central to the American experience which corresponded to my very limited knowledge and experience of that America; which from my prison cell looked like the interior world she described.

She was, and remains, a major American philosopher, who was clearly an atheist, but as I just learned recently, felt a certain collegial kinship with the greatest Catholic theologian, St. Thomas Aquinas.

Rand's work shares the sense of clear absolutes that I have always found so attractive in Exupery's *Wisdom of the Sands*, but while his is universal and deeply mystical, hers is only in America and deeply practical, while built upon ideas that are as sweepingly mystical as his.

I have come to believe that if Rand could have come into contact with comparable Catholic thinkers early in her life, she would have become one of the great Catholic philosophers because so many of her ideas radiate traditional Catholicism and that is why so many current Catholics are reading her.

When I read now, two of the thinkers who have had a great influence on my thinking, Rand and Abraham Maslow, it is clear to me that all good thinkers who discover truth and see it reflected through their eyes and through the lens of their knowledge and experience, have discovered some aspect of Catholic truth and we know this because the Lord came to earth and told us:

> **[John 14:6]** Jesus said to him, I am the way; I am truth and life; nobody can come to the Father, except through me.

In so many ways Ayn Rand makes a clear distinction between man and animals, in which she reveals her unspoken underlying acknowledgment of the absolute eternal, which in any form shaped, points towards God; which if, again, exposed to the subtle thought of a John Courtenay Murray, or even more appropriate, Father John McCloskey, the influential Opus Dei priest, might have made a Catholic out of her.

However, anyone reading Rand's blistering denunciation of the 1967 Encyclical from Pope Paul VI, *Populorum Progressio* (On the Development of Peoples) would conclude that becoming Catholic would be impossible for her, regardless of the brilliance of the evangelists.

Rand's aversion to Catholicism might stem, in my opinion, to the experience she had growing up in Russia and seeing the much-too-close relationship between the Communists and Russian Orthodoxy.

But, surely people living in Russia would have known that the Orthodox was under the control of the government, and if anything would have added fuel to the anti-religious fire burning within the breast of young Ayn Rand, this surely would have.

And yet, reading her book, *Anthem*, we find an expression of the eternal truth of the individual that is at its core, Catholic.

I first encountered Abraham Maslow in a psychology class at Sacramento City College in 1973, and once studying his theory of self-actualization, realized that here was an intellect that saw the beauty of life and love of work rather than horror or drudgery as the over-arching narrative.

I bought his book on management, *Eupsychian Management: A Journal*, in 1974 when I was receiving funding for a federal grant to reform criminals through exposure to college education and peer-counseling and would be managing 13 people, something I had never done before.

From the very first paragraphs, I saw personal reference points in my upcoming work.

Central to the idea of the self-actualizing human being is the peak experience, that moment when all that is seems appropriate and we stand central to and a part of it.

This justified my drug taking and sexual proclivities for many years until I realized that the *truth* of peak experiences was inner congruence with the truth of my life, which was built upon God and his Church, all else was a mirage of the world and its prince.

The Criminal as Religious

The Transcendentalist, an essay given by Ralph Waldo Emerson in the Masonic Temple in 1842 resonates deeply with Americans, particularly those in the criminal world familiar with its eloquent expression of reliance on self as the final arbiter of individual destiny and creation.

This stance is deeply religious in its definition of the individual soul as divine, and in no need of divinity beyond it, but whose only pursuit should be to understand and grasp its essential nature.

The essence of the criminal city is self, all revolves around the satisfying of the desires of self, however attained, and what has once been virtue may now be vice, crime, and so the opposite.

The completely self-focused spirituality often appeals to those enamored of the more global holistically focused spiritualities, as did Emerson with his Unitarian background and his strong attraction to Buddhism.

They see nature as alive in a conscious way, reducing humanity and themselves to a simple part of creation, rather than the crown of creation, reducing God to a nymph in the woods or a satyr on a tree stump playing pipes, and all the old pagan personages roll back into view, swamping us once again in their shallow relativity and endless bickering.

Born in the protestations of the Reformation and the break with the Catholic Church, the Babel of faiths and creeds that sprung forth, building on already primal roots; and Emerson, ever the seeker of his own myth, constructed an entire career and scholarly life upon their wobbly foundations, wherein many criminals find spiritual succor and weighty rationalizations for creating a way of life that perceives no absolutes, only self and the endless games self plays.

The New Golden Bough, which orders and blends new research material into the 1890 classic of Sir James Frazer, explores the ground upon which, to the still learning eye, the reality of later religious and organizational truths have been constructed; and its opening tale of the King of the Wood—a tale I shared many times with my fellow prisoners—whose sovereignty was passed through the execution of the reigning king by a usurper, approximates that of how the leadership of criminal and carceral world gangs often passes to a new generation.

And in its deeper explorations of the passages of gods, whose births, deaths and resurrections, congruent with the passage of the seasons from fertile to barren and back again; the myths of the prince of this world attempt to destroy the truths of its Lord.

The New Golden Bough is a magnificent collection of the early stories of men and cultures, broadening and deepening the foundations upon which we live our lives, and it resonates with the criminal through the great richness of mythic freedoms and the strengths of men faced with the supernatural, which is the position without the strength weapons bestow, of the criminal confronting the communal world.

The rich textures, sensual framings, and personal attraction of the individual ability to shape reality presented by the truths of the pagan world is a large reason for its primal attraction within the criminal world, particularly in major carceral concentrations where mystical physicality is of premium value in the struggle for survival and dominance.

This field has been deeply penetrated and cultivated by artists since before Homer and Virgil, and its more modern fields elaborated and given even more credibility through Jungian analysis, which itself is built upon the foundations of myth and dreams which drove so much of the pagan world view and its governing policy.

Being grounded (whether in reality or literally) may mean many things, but among the ancient pagan nobility, it may have meant spiritual death.

From the primitive we inherited the defining of the sacred as the realm of the secret and branching from the ancient Gnostic root—Gnosticism being the first heresy, which proclaimed that the truth was reserved for the elect, remaining secret to the unworthy—came the Babel of spiritualities confusing and clouding the simple and transparent truths of Christ.

One of the most secretive of these spiritualities from the great cathedral of time is the system developed by G. I. Gurdjieff and outlined in his books, the first of which resonates under the title of *Beelzebub's Tales to His Grandson*, which begins most portentously, and I remember still the wonder I experienced reading it for the first time in McNeil Island Federal Penitentiary, deeply enjoying the long elaborate sentences I have found once again in so many papal encyclicals.

Thus begins an intellectual venture of profound and humorous delight that can occupy one for a very long time, even for a full lifetime, but which is built upon one principle congruent with many spiritual traditions, that of the process of self-remembering.

It is here that we call to ourselves the will to realize what it is we are doing, at all moments, for whatever purpose, and in whatever circumstances; what are we doing now?

What those who have grown to love the various messages that are embedded in the Gurdjieffian system of thinking have done is to continue what it is that Gurdjieff left them with.

And so, the second and third series have been completed since this was written in 1950 and the system so beloved by many—including those in the criminal world attracted to the mixture of absoluteness, complete rejection of all existing and created knowledge, and the opportunity to be part of creating something entirely new—have moved on, building a better world evident best to themselves; self-involvement being the real cornerstone of the various perambulations of the New Age and the outgrowths of the first and still present heresy, Gnosticism.

Alan Watts' books continued and deepened the development of the Gnostic inspired story line elaborated into social policy driving the youth culture of the 60's, through continued explanation of why life was a game, how one could obtain the secrets about reality which were only available to the elect—thereby becoming one of the elect—and the crowning jewel of thought freeing one from the chains of the past, and, God was a myth.

In several books Alan Watts worked through these ideas.

Within the criminal world, the truth of its most secret stories revolves around these set of concepts, amplified and charged with the glowing urbanities emanating from the criminal city—particularly the city at night—as the field of heroic endeavor; and breaking Watt's ideas free of their rather flowery presentation revealed a perspective resonating with its intellectual leadership.

We, all of us human beings, seek meaning in our lives—we are hard-wired to do this—and the plethora of ideas, intellectual systems, philosophies, religions and spiritual formulations that continue to be created within which we may discover it, provide something for every taste.

And long ago, at the very foundation of the world, that taste for power, darkness and the glowing embers of desire awaiting the traveler in the city at night—the criminal city first founded by Cain—was what attracted the criminal and what fulfilled the empty spaces within his world.

There may be chaos and confusion surrounding the ideas and spiritualities and that may be much of their attraction, for confusion seeks meaning as much as one who provides it controls that seeking, and Watts reminds us of that.

In a world where it often seems there is nothing that can be referenced to charity, faith or hope, the concept that God does not exist can be a seductive one, which has wrapped many deeply spiritual people who have suffered more deeply than their faith could bear, into its web.

In this bleak place, the bleakest of the prophets finds a ready home, hearth fires lit, forlornly eager faces turned to his wisdom and Friedrich Nietzsche does not disappoint.

As the pronouncement of the Overman rang from the mountains, the endlessly opened Pandora's Box released the symphony of ills, which flew out and settled in the fertile plains of man's indecision and lack of faith in the message of his heart. Now, he believed, all was possible, through him alone, again. The ancient heresy once more claimed his allegiance and no better field than the dark streets of the criminal world city could be found for its bittersweet fruit.

Nietzsche's work—as does so often the work congruent with the belief that man is god rather than a child of God—informed and enhanced social developments as varied as fascism, gangsterism, socialism, uber-capitalism, atheism, relativism, and the super-individualism of the 1960's.

The ideas shaping the motivation that any individual, powerful or influential enough to do so, could reshape moral and political reality into his own image, held a seductive attraction to those unhinged from the eternal truth embedded in Catholicism and enmeshes them in a web of action leading inexorably towards spiritual destruction.

For many, the very chaos thus brought on holds an equal attraction, validating the rightness of their path as a creative and deeply inspired artist, so sadly described (in their frenzied seeking of truth in all the wrong places, leading to their eventual self-destruction) by Colin Wilson in his *Outsider* series of books.

Nietzsche, son of a Lutheran pastor who died mad, and driven by a lifelong hate of Christianity, dying himself in 1900 after years of mental illness many feel was brought on by untreated syphilis—believed to have contributed to his ideas as the advanced stages of syphilis often cause megalomania—later resented the adoption of his work by the German Reich.

The Varieties of Religious Experience by William James, was the epitome of the well-evidenced good will and soundness of thinking that infuses James work, so unlike the strained neurosis characterizing so much of my reading in those years and because of that, it took some time to adjust myself to this most wondrous of thinkers.

James looks at the authors of the seminal works of Christianity, as his psychological training compels him, from a perspective that, while common now, was not so when he wrote (1901-1902).

For the criminal struggling—though few did—with the teaching of their youth that the actions of their life were clearly wrong and would bring down upon them the severest spiritual punishment much beyond that which they now were suffering in prison; the idea that religious writing could be looked at in this relative manner, was a huge and dismissive opening for shedding that belief.

The Criminal as Catholic

The ultimate source is the Catholic Church, her sacred doctrine, her social teaching and the guiding mantra I have used to access this body of holy teaching since I read it in a book by Saint Josemaria Escriva, the founder of Opus Dei, is:

With Peter, Through Mary, To Christ.

Peter is the Holy Father. Peter is all the Holy Fathers. Peter who asked to be crucified upside down so as not to imitate Christ, not the Peter who denied and ran, but the Peter who stays, Peter the rock; the Holy Father throughout the eternal history of the Church, the saintly popes whose thought and lives guide us still; and for those popes who have had their hand on the tiller of the Barque of Peter over the past several hundred years, an embracing of the works of the Angelic Doctor, the greatest theologian of the Church, Saint Thomas Aquinas.

Through Mary, whose intercessory power is unparalleled, as the Mother of God and our Mother, as the *Catechism* teaches us:

> **968** Her role in relation to the Church and to all humanity goes still further. "In a wholly singular way she cooperated by her obedience, faith, hope, and burning charity in the Savior's work of restoring supernatural

life to souls. For this reason she is a mother to us in the order of grace."

969 "This motherhood of Mary in the order of grace continues uninterruptedly from the consent which she loyally gave at the Annunciation and which she sustained without wavering beneath the cross, until the eternal fulfillment of all the elect. Taken up to heaven she did not lay aside this saving office but by her manifold intercession continues to bring us the gifts of eternal salvation . ... Therefore the Blessed Virgin is invoked in the Church under the titles of Advocate, Helper, Benefactress, and Mediatrix."

The statement that we are what we become, rather than who we say we are, is so evidently self-explanatory and self-defining, that it bears no more study, but its very obviousness renders it subject to once again being explained.

To Christ, Our Lord, who we take into our very being during Mass, whose Word will illuminate and guide our path in this life towards life eternal, and the relationship with Christ is one that must be entwined with an active interior life.

The great ideas of great men and women, to have any eternal merit, must be shown to have such through their living of them and if one ends failing in virtually all aspects of greatness, then what were their ideas truly worth, except to harm those who partook of them as sustenance.

On the other hand, those great ones I later discovered, such as Thomas Aquinas, Jacques and Raissa Maritain, Mother Teresa, William F. Buckley, Alexander

Solzhenitsyn, G. K. Chesterton and Hilaire Belloc, whose old age was burnished and glowing with the wisdom they had gained and shared and ratifies and concretizes their truth.

In this respect, the greatest of Catholic thinkers is surely St. Thomas Aquinas, the great Dominican, and once his work is encountered, one of the final places to look for confirmation of Catholic sacred doctrine, has been found, it is within his work.

I have been searching for a good biography of St. Thomas for some time, having exhausted the online versions of his life, and wanting a little more context. I finally found it in this book, *St. Thomas Aquinas* by the Jesuit priest, Martin Cyril D'Arcy, published in 1954, and as I read the first pages which are about the period in which St. Thomas lived and his contemporaries, two of whom St. Albertus Magnus (Albert the Great) and Duns Scotus were names familiar to me from my long-ago studies in the occult, and a reminder that much of the occult is merely a perversion of authentic Catholic thought and practice; a fact really evident to me during my first experience with Latin Mass, which is the root—much perverted and demonized—of the calling down ritual used by witches.

For the first five or so years after my final release from prison, while I was attending college—majoring in criminal justice—and formulating the proposal for a rehabilitative program centered around college education I eventually received funding for, the reading I was doing was still connected to that which I had been reading in prison, with the very enlightening addition of criminal justice literature, which allowed me, for the first time, to begin seeing myself as others saw me.

Though the critical sociological academic perspective that treated criminals as revolutionary forerunners was very appealing to me, I knew it was largely balderdash; but it wasn't until I encountered the writings of James Q. Wilson in his book, *Thinking About Crime,* that I found writing that actually paralleled the reality about the criminal world that I had lived, criminals are criminals by choice, not because of social circumstance or psychological deficits.

The sociologists have not improved their approach much since then, though the latest effort to brand prisons—and thereby prisoners—as a disease or the creation of the narrative of mass incarceration as a continued attempt to keep slavery alive, has breathed new life into the academy's meanderings.

While many academics consider mass incarceration as a problem—and are swooning over this new narrative—criminal justice practitioners whose perspective is more balanced (like James Q. Wilson) understand that the increase in prison populations is what has largely contributed, through incapacitation, the current crime rate reduction.

Rereading these books calls up my interiority from that time—an interiority I shared with so many others in prison—an interiority of diamond hardness, of dark clarity, I *knew,* and in that *knowing,* no one could reach me, surely not the soft pleas of correction—regardless of the vigor of their presentation—coming from those who did not *know.*

Knowing the truth of the Catholic Church is all you need, and though the blandishments of Marxism—or the earthly paradise—also known as liberation theology by dissenting Catholics, are very seductive, for who is not seduced by work that can change the world one sees, touches, tastes, smells, and hears; it is a mighty seduction one even those *knowing* God are prey to.

Concluding Thoughts

So much of the make-up of the sources comes from writers and thinkers who saw themselves as outlaws, but they were not, only outlaws are outlaws; those truly living outside of the law, the criminals; not the wispy souls raging against the machines of their lives—which for so many were lives of wealth and privilege—they were only sad shadows sulking at the feet of real outlaws who they dreamt they could become by merely writing that they were; however, and this must be remembered, many of them wrote beautiful stuff which pleasured the minds and hearts of many real outlaws, including me.

Virtually all of the writing on criminal justice coming from the academy, even the Catholic academy in general is promoting the incorrect argument that crime is a result of social failing rather than the truth of Catholic teaching that it is a result of an individual decision, as the *Catechism* teaches us:

> **1868** Sin is a personal act. Moreover, we have a responsibility for the sins committed by others when *we cooperate in them*:
>
> > - by participating directly and voluntarily in them;
> > - by ordering, advising, praising, or approving them;
> > - by not disclosing or not hindering them when we have an obligation to do so;
> > - by protecting evil-doers.
>
> **1869** Thus sin makes men accomplices of one another and causes concupiscence, violence, and injustice to reign among them. Sins give rise to social situations and institutions that are contrary to the divine goodness. "Structures of sin" are the expression and effect of personal sins. They lead their victims to do evil in their turn. In an analogous sense, they constitute a "social sin."

Correspondingly, virtually all of the traditional attempts to rehabilitate criminals operate from this same incorrect premise, adding to the reasons for their continuous failure.

Even the American Catholic Church, though often forgetting this primary teaching in her pursuit of political expediency and acceptance, still remains the repository of ancient truth.

Scripture teaches us, in the complete word of revelation, that the Old Covenant remains, now part of the New Covenant, and though many of the practices naturally evolve according to the signs of the times—the core dialogue remains as given—as do the immediate results of it, such as capital punishment being the just response to crimes calling out from the ground for justice.

The *Catechism* notes:

> **1867** The catechetical tradition also recalls that there are *"sins that cry to heaven"*: the blood of Abel, (Genesis 4:10) the sin of the Sodomites, Genesis 18:20 & 19:13) the cry of the people oppressed in Egypt, (Exodus 3:7-10) the cry of the foreigner, the widow, and the orphan, (Exodus 20:20-22) injustice to the wage earner (Deuteronomy 24:14-15 & James 5:4)

The Catholic academy is a great flower in the garden of the Church, though often it produces thorns and thickets calling for radical pruning, as was the case with liberation theology, still a central praxis in the crime-as-social-failing argument and still being carried aloft as a banner of battle by many wayward elements of the Church.

The Church, as the only global institution possessing the truth of crime's source, is the only global institution able to effectively respond to the false doctrine about its cause and correspondingly, the personal rehabilitation of the criminal, the individual animating the social reality called crime.

The leadership has to come from Peter, to guide the bishops, who, on their own, tend to become fellow travelers with the secular prophet; whose current fascination with restorative justice is only the latest manifestation—parallel with liberation theology—using the language of scripture and tradition to create a new magisterium.

The last pope who spoke and wrote at a substantial level about crime was Pius XII, which, given his biography, was to be expected.

The work of past American theologians, Murray, Dulles, and one present, George Weigel—whose work on just war folds nicely into what is needed for deeper work on protecting the innocent—form a foundation for hope.

It is so important the Church become deeply involved in the criminal rehabilitation field—there is very good work being done by the Society of Catholic Social Scientists and their two volumes & a supplement: *Encyclopedia of Catholic Social Thought, Social Science, and Social Policy* is a required reference for any Catholics working in the field—to help keep the policy and sociological conversation anchored in truth.

As it is now, the criminal justice/sociological academy is too often veering into areas of discussion so far removed from what is actually happening as a result of criminality— to the criminal and to society—that it often borders on the absurd and the recent effort to create a medical definition of prisons as the 2011 book by Professor Ernest Drucker, *A Plague of Prisons: The Epidemiology of Mass Incarceration in America* attempts.

The only faith-based people currently involved in criminal rehabilitation at any level are the Protestants and their method of providing conversion based on emotion, never works for very long for an overwhelming majority of criminals because the rewards of the criminal life generate emotions more powerful; but the conversion by intellect— the core of the Lampstand Prison Ministry—holds, for few men will leave a hard-won truth.

While in prison, I could not appreciate the intensity with which my generational cohorts outside of prison were reshaping reality; primarily through the ancient gnostic lens—though I only believed, at the time, after I was released from prison and became part of the psychedelic hippie community, that supernatural power did indeed exists—far above philosophical speculation—and it could only be accessed and wielded by adepts, which we felt we were becoming as we penetrated deeper into ourselves through the psychedelic portal.

This essential belief stayed with me in some form or another for many years, but finally began to dissipate as more evidence of the emptiness of so many of the 60's gurus became more evident. Whether reading about their foibles and follies or seeing in person their ambition addled faces radiating their lust for power and money and sex—so contrary to the proclaimed truths of 60's mysticism and enlightenment.

Becoming Catholic saved my life.

Chapter 8
Catholicism, Communism, &
Criminal Reformation

Introduction

What is important—in the context of our apostolate work through The Lampstand Foundation—is not the theory of Communism, "to each according to need", which many may support; but the influence on criminals from the system of government and its practice under Lenin and Stalin in Russia, Mao in China, and the lessor monsters of our world; practice continuing largely unchanged today except as modified within the constrictions created by the ability of global communications about governmental atrocities making it much more difficult to keep such atrocities hidden now than during the last century; and a governing practice diametrically opposed to the sacred doctrine of the Catholic Church, the Church Communism sees as its most dangerous enemy, though now; because of Vatican II and Liberation Theology, somewhat neutered.

Communism—in addition to the countries under its capture—is experiencing a resurgence among young leftists.

Encouraging this revival is a new venture by radical publishers—such as Verso's, *Pocket Communism*—offering several new books on the emergence of the new interest in Communism.

Getting our mind wrapped around this historical atheistic evil requires a journey through the virtual hurricane of words used to describe it and another point: Communism is rarely believed in by the leaders of Communist countries as they are totalitarians and their hidden operating narrative is power; but Communism is used as the public operating narrative—virtually a faith system, though atheistic—for the people to believe in; important to keep in mind as we wind our way through the intersection of the Church and Communism since the appearance of Our Holy Mother at Fatima.

Communism is one of the most malevolent manifestations of Modernism, that philosophical emanation that rejects the traditional including religious tradition.

The leaders of Communist countries, as we now well know from the research and revelations over the past several decades, did not and do not, always personally believe in Communist principles, and we see this in the great wealth they take for themselves while leaving little for the people, and here is a great contrast with the Church, whose leaders still remain largely poor, committed to their oath of poverty and chastity.

During the Ecumenical Council of Vatican II, once an agreement was reached between the Vatican and Russia not to mention Communism, the Church used the term "Modern atheism", as proclaimed in the *Pastoral Constitution on the Modern World: Gaudium et Specs.*

In the *Catechism* which emanated from Vatican II, it was also addressed as Atheism:

Atheism

2123 "Many . . . of our contemporaries either do not at all perceive, or explicitly reject, this intimate and vital bond of man to God. Atheism must therefore be regarded as one of the most serious problems of our time."

2124 The name "atheism" covers many very different phenomena. One common form is the practical materialism which restricts its needs and aspirations to space and time. Atheistic humanism falsely considers man to be "an end to himself, and the sole maker, with supreme control, of his own history." Another form of contemporary atheism looks for the liberation of man through economic and social liberation. "It holds that religion, of its very nature, thwarts such emancipation by raising man's hopes in a future life, thus both deceiving him and discouraging him from working for a better form of life on earth."

2125 Since it rejects or denies the existence of God, atheism is a sin against the virtue of religion. The imputability of this offense can be significantly diminished in virtue of the intentions and the circumstances. "Believers can have more than a little to do with the rise of atheism. To the extent that they are careless about their instruction in the faith, or present its teaching falsely, or even fail in their religious, moral, or social life, they must be said to conceal rather than to reveal the true nature of God and of religion."

2126 Atheism is often based on a false conception of human autonomy, exaggerated to the point of refusing any dependence on God. Yet, "to acknowledge God is in no way to oppose the dignity of man, since such dignity is grounded and brought to perfection in God. . . . " "For the Church knows full well that her message is in harmony with the most secret desires of the human heart."

Communist practice over the last century and continuing today, of using violence and the threat of violence as the primary tool of control, while suppressing freedom of speech and religion, and having its agents infiltrating within those institutions, are the evil markers of totalitarian states everywhere; markers most adeptly developed by Russian Communism; markers representing the tyrannical reality becoming widespread, which is why Our Lady of Fatima warned us about Russia in 1917.

The worldly effectiveness of the practice of using violence and the threat of violence is something professional criminals understand and accept as a central aspect of the criminal/carceral world and any evangelization directed towards professional criminals—defined as those who commit crimes for money excluding pedophiles, rapists, informants, and the insane—that is not congruent with the traditional, pre-conciliar history of Catholicism's response to the evil of Communist totalitarianism will not gain deep and long-lasting traction.

A Church that speaks loudly against evil but does little or nothing in its daily practice to confront it will be seen as a religion that does not walk the talk, a fatal characteristic within the criminal/carceral world.

An example: Bishops who proclaim abortion the great evil it is but allow public leaders and politicians in their diocese, to continually proclaim support for abortion and enlist the public in that support, to escape the sanction of ex-communication for scandal, are those bishops spoken of by the ancients, "The floor of hell is paved with the skulls of bishops."

We desperately need Church shepherds who understand the ongoing threat of the ideas spawned by Communism.

The Communist misconception is that nothing is about transcendence; everything is about the earthly world. There is no God, there is only man. And the most effective promulgator of this atheistic ideology over the past century has been Communism.

This helps explain the deep Communist anger—still evident today in anti-capitalist demonstrations here and abroad—emanating from Marxist labor theory as it is based on the perceived thievery of a particularly insidious nature, that of the rich and powerful stealing from the poor and weak.

In this chapter, we will focus—as we always have—on the internal development of professional criminals moving toward reformation, whether consciously or unconsciously, with a specific focus on the influence Communism (in its hard and soft forms) has had on religion—especially prison ministry—the academy, and criminal justice professionals, and by extension, many criminals; all in relation to Fatima where our Holy Mother warned us about Russia, asking it to be consecrated to her Immaculate Heart , for she saw what was developing from Russia Communism without divine intervention called for through the joint prayers of Peter and all the bishops in concert.

Lenin returned to Russia April 8, 1917 and the first appearance of Our Lady of Fatima was May 13, 1917.

Our Lady saw that what was emanating from Russia was satanically powerful, and the influential power of Communism—though known by many other names, virtually a legion of names—is still alive in the prisons, woven into the doctrinal narrative of some powerful prison gangs.

An unusual cultural aspect of criminal/carceral world culture is the power and influence the elder exerts—almost tribal like in its potency—due to the simple fact that no criminal/prisoner, hardly, ever retires due to age.

I have seen men well into their seventies and eighties (like many private corporate leaders today) who retain the physicality and intellectual heft of men decades younger.

Prison, like corporate success at the highest level, often preserves body and mind.

In the maximum security prisons, the ruling narrative of the criminal/carceral world is still exemplified and maintained by these elders, many of whom still possess the physical and mental wherewithal and most of all, the historical and cultural networks, required to exert leadership.

For many of these elders, their intellectual formation was birthed in the 1960s and 1970s and the writings that emanated from that period, many of whom were written by or influenced by Communist and Communist-inspired intellectuals who saw the world in terms of class struggle and violence.

A major Communist voice during this time—and several decades prior—was Jean-Paul Sartre.

For decades Sartre's voice inspired the revolutionary soul of many criminals, as in his famous preface—describing the souls of the colonized who become revolutionaries—to the seminal book by Fanon, *The Wretched of the Earth*.

I have heard variations of this central theme voiced by many professional criminals—and strongly alive within the deepest cells of super-max—as the art of being a successful criminal, a romantic fatalism in which violence is a necessary tool.

No one more deeply connects existentialism to Communism and to criminals/prisoners than Sartre, most effectively in one of his magisterial works, also very popular in prison: *St. Genet: Actor and Martyr*—one of the finest studies of a certain type of criminal, which a group of us studied while I was imprisoned in McNeil Island Federal Penitentiary in the 1960s—a deeply analytical study of the criminal/artist Jean Genet.

It helps explain how criminals can reach a psychological place where—except within the manipulative visions they tell needed for one reason or another—nothing can destroy them, certainly not prison.

Perhaps the most important existential work read by American prisoners is *Man's Search for Meaning*, originally entitled *From Death Camp to Existentialism*, by Viktor E. Frankl and its central theme that no matter what type of environment one is mired in, no matter what type of oppressive control is exerted, one still has the power of deciding how to respond.

You cannot imagine how powerful this thought is to prisoners.

One of the great classics about the path of converts to Communism who then woke up is *The God That Failed* by Arthur Koestler.

Communism, as a way of developing power and shaping history, remains among the most insidious of Soviet habits.

Communism is the ruling mantra that China—under Stalin's tutelage—the most populous nation on earth; wakes up to each morning after being whipped and beaten into accepting it in 1949, thirty-two years after Russia brought her people under its evil yoke in 1917, the year of the apparition of our Holy Mother at Fatima.

Russia's continued involvement in Communist strategy—though it may now be more properly termed, criminal strategy—is underscored by the recent exposure of one of their spies in the United States, Anna Chapman who was arrested in June 2010.

The strategies developed and released into the world through the Communist International—known as the Comintern—over the many decades that dramatically shaped Russia under Lenin and Stalin, are strategies that continue; though the dividends may not be classified as revolutionary, as under the International, they are effective economically, politically and powerfully influential.

Communism and its Socialistic method of government, its Marxist method of historical criticism, its violent form of revolution when called for—as today in the third world—its state control of religion, and its deep atheism, is still a very powerful enemy of the Church.

It is not just that Communism is a godless ideology, but that it is—since its introduction into the world—the most influential advocate of materialistic atheism intent on destroying the Catholic Church; and whatever name Communism works under, and they are legion, it seeks a final solution.

Though, as Reagan described it, the evil empire (the U.S.S.R.) was broken up under the leadership of Pope John Paul II, President Ronald Reagan, and Prime Minister Margaret Thatcher, the evil idea underlying it— total government control, including over religion—remains active in the world, exercising direct control over more than one billion people and indirectly hundreds of millions more.

One of its most potent weapons being used today, emanating from its Stalinist past, is the practice of disinformation, which produces incorrect information to cast aspersions on the enemies of Communism, primarily the Catholic Church and America.

Russian disinformation was also at the root of the largely successful campaign, until recently, convincing many that Pope Pius XII was an anti-Semite when he personally saved many Jewish lives and worked vigorously against Nazism.

This idea of the essential evil of Catholic leadership and American leadership also retains influence within the cultural heights of American—and even more deeply in

European and Asian—public life, in the academy, government, media, religion, and to a surprising depth within Catholicism itself.

The primary tools used in the political propaganda wars that pit right against left and the Catholic Church against atheists and secular governments—where demonization is the normative argument of left against right in the Catholic Church in America—are tools of disinformation developed most effectively in the last century by Communism.

In this chapter, we are specifically focusing on Russian Communism, as that is what the Holy Mother of God warned us about at Fatima, and that is the Communism that is the intellectual father of all of the others, deeply engaged since its founding on spreading its revolution worldwide; a revolution that has led, in Russia itself, to the criminal corruption endemic to atheistic governments

The Church has gone from a clear denunciation of Russian Communism by Peter during the 19th and the early 20th century to an accommodation with it immediately prior to and since Vatican II.

The language the Church uses today is congruent with that used in the Garden where God spoke clearly, but where Satan, using flattery, deception, and persuasion, seduced Adam and Eve to disregard that clarity and seek the hidden meaning behind the Word.

To more effectively combat Satan for souls, the Church has learned to use the arts of persuasion.

History will tell if this is a wise change of direction by the Church and it may very well be; but because of the failure to follow the warnings of the Holy Mother at Fatima of what would happen if the Holy Father and all the bishops did not consecrate Russia to her Immaculate Heart, warnings which history has shown to be true, we have to wonder what future history will reveal.

It has been my experience, through personal interaction with many Catholics, and academic study, that Communist-inspired Liberation Theology, working through the social justice mantra as developed by Communist-inspired Catholics in America, Asia, and Europe, and further elaborated by many religious throughout the Church, with particular depth in Latin America, that Communism is alive and well within the Church.

Professional criminals catechized with this form of Catholicism—with its restorative justice, prison and capital punishment abolition, and social causation rather than individual choice, approach to crime—which, though they may respond to initially, does not possess the clarity, depth, or truth, that will hold for the long term.

The reason for that is connected to the focus of this apostolate on the professional criminal, excluding pedophiles, rapists, and informers; for professional criminals who have served time in maximum security prisons, whose abhorrence for sexual predators and those who betray their brothers in crime, extends to the death, would not become part of an apostolate who welcomed those who they so strongly reject.

The Lampstand Foundation's work focuses on professional criminals who commit crimes for money as professional criminals constitute the majority of criminals (approximately 70%) housed in state and federal prisons, and professional criminals have the credibility, in prison or out, to authentically communicate with other criminals about personal reformation and conversion through the Catholic Church, or as we like to say, "It takes a reformed criminal to reform criminals."

Much of the lure of Communism to the poor and oppressed people of the world is their yearning for freedom and peace in this world—a yearning exploited by many prison ministries—and though the Communist government that so often assumes control of a country's revolution, becomes as great a tyrant as the oppressor they revolted against; this yearning for peace and freedom is deeply real and not to be discounted.

Some historians lay the cause of the successful penetration of Communism into American government and society at the feet of the presidential administration of Franklin Delano Roosevelt because FDR was captivated by 'Uncle Joe' Stalin and many of FDR's top advisors were Communists themselves (Alger Hiss for one) but even with the presidential aid, scarcely a few decades later Russia Communism morphed into open gangsterism—Communisms essential and long hidden heart—and the looming threat of a Communist Russia annihilating Western civilization seems to be well over as the intent of criminals is merely to be allowed to manage and expand their criminal turf with little interference.

Feeding the beast satiates him and though he gets hungry again, it is as much from habit, than from the old 'lean and hungry look' that motivated him to feed again.

As God allows Satan to prey on us, earthly empires often allow enemies to prey on the weak and this is where the promise of justice in eternity rings as true, for the rewards for Satan of evil souls to extend his turf are also rewards for God as saints arise from the ancient war between good and evil.

Russia also reads the words of its severest critics and, in the spirit of accommodation and with its reliable tools of deception and misdirection, continues in fine form.

Finally, the contemporary influence of Communism among some of the most organized of former criminals is revealed through the Marxian analysis describing how criminals are constructed socially.

In Marxian analysis individuals at the bottom of the social ladder—and in America, it is most surely and most thankfully, still a ladder—are helpless players in the movement of social forces controlled by the rich capitalists and the officialdom they control; while the reality is that crime is a result of individual choice, and rehabilitation, true transformation from being a member of the criminal/carceral world to joining the communal world, is always solely within the power of the individual, as it has always been, as it always will be.

Communism in Russia

Russia and the Communist system of governance which Our Lady warned us about at Fatima while calling for Russia to be consecrated to her Immaculate Heart, evolved within a history of autocracy; unfortunately the history of all too many people.

Russian Communism has had particular success reshaping the worldly ground upon which the Church stands.

The vision of Jesus as a revolutionary embroiled in a Marxist struggle to free the people from the powers of the rich and powerful, including the priests of Israel and the Roman Empire, is a powerful motif and attracts many to its ranks, a message continuing today as promulgated through books, film, and theatre.

The continuing influence emanating from the atheistic intellectual and artistic community is part of the reason Our Lady of Fatima told us to consecrate Russia, as Russian Communism is the most dangerous manifestation of the ancient heresy, primarily attractive to the intellectually elite, of Gnosticism.

Communism's religiosity, its modern spiritual root, birthed from Gnosticism, but woven throughout another influence, is Nietzschean, the atheistic, materialist spirituality of the Overman, the man who knows.

A historical infection endemic to the Russian Communist state—as of all Communist states—in congruence with its militant atheistic core beliefs, is corruption and criminality, and Russia has morphed into the most potent criminal state in history, dominating the global criminal world.

This shift has ramifications of enormous consequence, and the role of the Catholic Church, because of the knowledge bequeathed to it by Our Lady at Fatima, is crucial.

Fatima is a miracle believed by faith, but investigating it with the intellect reveals proofs of its existence impossible to escape; just as an intellectual exploration of Communism reveals an evil emptiness impossible to escape.

As the primary process of reformation used by Lampstand is through the intellectual portal to the soul, based on a study of the history and social teaching of the Church, graduate academic degrees, and training in criminal reform organizational administration; the intellectual attraction of Communism and its many portals—socialism, Marxism, and Liberation Theology among them—needs to be addressed.

I note the importance of the intellect in approaching Catholic truth from the perspective of the father of Western intellectuals, Aristotle, and the seminal Catholic intellectual, Saint Thomas Aquinas, the Angelic Doctor.

An interesting side note is that for a brief period of time in the 1960s/1970s, especially in California, criminals were seen as *the vanguard* of the revolution.

What this makes clear is that the common usage of the term Socialism or Marxism rather than Communism can be deceptive—to either soften or intellectualize the reality—so we'll use them as intended by Marx and Engels, as synonymous, while keeping in mind modern usage.

Russian Communism was identified by Our Lady of Fatima as a most pernicious threat to the Church, a position ratified by several popes, but later, during Vatican II softened and virtually disappearing as a papal warning.

Communism in America

Many Catholics—especially those from the prime era of Soviet influence, the 1930s-1970s—who were caught up in the Nietzschean drama of Communism and later in its newest incarnation, Liberation Theology, liked to say that the horrors of Leninism/Stalinism were vestiges of the past and necessary to reform a tsarist dominated peoples into a modern industrialized society, an argument only to be believed by those who want to believe.

Catholic teaching knows that the truths of the Church trump those of Communism.

Communist influence on most criminals—though some prison/criminal gangs have Communism woven throughout their gang narrative—is surreptitious because by temperament, criminals are conservative, so its influence is hidden under the guise of Liberation Theology, Socialism, or Social Justice, the softer generic terms used by liberal Catholics and non-Catholics.

A counter-intuitive perspective is that much of the intellectual impact of Communism was—and remains—in the West, rather than in Russia (perhaps explaining its recent descent into state criminality).

What is fairly common among many Communist-inspired groups is the now well-established pattern of propaganda promoting peace and natural political evolution while working for civil war and political revolution; and the great hidden agenda, destruction of the Catholic Church.

In the West it has been a long-term strategy to reduce the attention paid to Communism by refocusing the attention on the evils of capitalism and, in large part, it has been a successful strategy.

Newly released Communist files are a powerful reminder of the very deep restructuring of the individual psychology of the secret police which Communist governments in Eastern Europe used to control the captured country's population.

This deep training and enforcement throughout the Communist dominated countries of Eastern Europe and within Russia itself, is not something that would dissipate over a few years out from under the Soviet yoke, but, as we have learned since, has been usefully brought into service of the criminal state Russia has become.

In the context of the apparition of the Holy Virgin Mother at Fatima (six consecutive monthly apparitions beginning in May, 1917) calling for the consecration of Russia to save the world from the horrors of Communism, what has happened since has given truth to Fatima.

Communist training has proven to be very prophetic as the ideal of the revolutionary captured many intellectuals in the decades during and shortly after Fatima, as it sadly—though under different names—still does today.

Communism, in this context, is the further extension of Nietzsche's Overman, from insane fantasy to insane action.

And is it not so always with the young—it certainly was with me—that the allures of idealism, great adventure, and the creation of a heaven on earth, a heaven one can see, touch, really feel, far outweigh the wispy promises about heaven after life; and more, this eternal yearning of the young provides the underpinning of the importance of Catholic evangelism, especially among the young, so well exemplified by World Youth Day.

One of the books which made a huge impression upon Communist idealists was *Ten Days That Shook the World*, by John Reed; and its romantic, while still technical, approach fired the spirits of many who would become American Communists.

This book and the author's deep influence over the intelligentsia of the early Twentieth Century—captured brilliantly in the insightful docudrama *Reds* in which Warren Beatty plays John Reed, which, by the way, is a very powerful, romantic, and idealistic film—played a substantial role in the Russian Communist penetration into American life.

The importance reached into heaven and the Holy Virgin Mother Mary appeared at Fatima to warn of the results of this event, should the Church—acting through the Holy Father and all of the world's bishops—*not consecrate* Russia to her Immaculate Heart, which the Church *did not and has not*, as of this date, done.

There have been many consecrations proclaiming to be in response to Fatima, but virtually none of them mention Russia by name, which were her precise instructions, virtually all are presented as consecrations of the world.

Communism in America—as represented by American Communists and a complicit liberal/progressive political community, helped largely through the representation of former U.S. Senator Joseph McCarthy as an out-of-control, foaming-at-the-mouth political extremist pursuing imaginary enemies—has accomplished the same result as Satan, convincing everyone that he doesn't exist.

What decades of research and new books on Senator McCarthy's accusations that the American government was penetrated by Communists have proven is that he was absolutely right.

He was certainly a flawed messenger, but his central message was correct.

The central fact in the ability of Catholicism to defeat Communism in the conversion of criminals is that the former has walked the talk and the latter has not.

Communism's narrative core is that humanity is composed of economic beings struggling against one another to gain power over others.

Catholicism's narrative core is that humanity is composed of spiritual beings struggling against sin to gain heaven.

At the center of the Communist system is terror and government coercion.

At the center of Catholicism is love and individual choice.

It is easy to see the attraction Communism represents for some criminals to whom money in the hand is far more valuable than a check in the mail, a stolen wallet more joy than a paycheck.

But, ironically, it is easier to prove the truth of Catholicism through its worldly history's congruence with its social teaching, than that of Communism through its worldly history's incongruence with its social teaching.

The Church and its doctrine of each life being precious to God, has always been attacked by the world from the day its founder was crucified, and far too often, it has become corrupted in its worldly institutional form, but the corruption by Communism, which the 19th and early 20th century popes had warned about so clearly, seems to have begun in earnest by the failure of the Holy Father to fulfill the command of the Holy Virgin at Fatima in 1917, to consecrate Russia to her Immaculate Heart.

Much of the horrors she foretold which would happen if Russia was not consecrated, have happened.

It is within the diplomacy-influenced reasons partially responsible for that failure—the Russian Orthodox Metropolitan who lobbied to ensure the consecration would not happen, was a KGB directed operative—that we see the Vatican corruption that infected the clear support of Catholic teaching about Communism, rendering it virtually mute.

Also occurring during the 1960's was the notorious meeting—related to Russian Orthodox lobbying in refusing to condemn evil—at the Kennedy compound where American Catholic religious leaders developed the strategy for Democratic Catholic politicians to support abortion against the clear teaching of the Church.

Communism's work with Catholics appears to have focused to some extent on two major orders of the Church, the Society of Jesus and the Maryknoll Society, as well as the lay Catholic Worker Movement founded by Dorothy Day and Peter Maurin.

Communist influence on the two orders has been written about by others, but as Dorothy Day is being proposed for sainthood, her movement will be noted here.

The Catholic Worker Movement remained aligned with Communism in its most central strategy, public control of property.

Dorothy Day, having been a Communist, could have become, after her baptism, a powerful advocate warning of the dangers of Communism, as Whittaker Chambers became; the traditional route taken by former Communists who became Catholic, as part of becoming Catholic is realizing the revealed truth *is* true, rendering all other proclaimed truths false, suspect, wrong; as I have discovered.

Not to act on this and reveal the wrongness of Communism and the rightness of Catholicism, is, almost in itself, proof that Dorothy Day did not find Communism wrong; and in fact, her work throughout her life, remained supportive of Communist positions, leaders, and countries.

Dorothy Day was surely the major Communist-inspired voice in progressive American Catholic circles (often working under the social justice banner) and the Catholic Worker Movement she founded virtually parallels the anti-war, anti-prison, anti-capital punishment mantras which Communist governments working in America advocate.

Working under the social justice mantra is an idea evolving from the Russian Communist and pre-Communist intelligentsia.

I think that in Dorothy Day's case, she had conflated Communism with Catholicism so deeply in her own mind and spirit that they were virtually one and the same thing to her—a classic case of being duped—a form of thinking still very prevalent within the Catholic left, especially those still, and they are many, enamored with Liberation Theology.

Now that her cause for sainthood has been approved by the American bishops to move her from the current designation as Servant of God, to the next step in the canonization process, the history of the Vatican's connection to Russian Communism through the period when the Fatima call from the Holy Virgin to consecrate Russia to her Immaculate Heart was not responded to, due, in large part, to the Vatican influence of Orthodox Russian Metropolitans now known to have been KGB directed, will perhaps be examined.

These positions can also be considered to have formed through manipulation by Communist propaganda—especially as in the case of Day's pre-Catholic Worker history of involvement with Communist newspapers and

American Communists, representing an extensive background of Communist cooperation.

Catholic social justice is a very good thing, Catholic Communism is not, and the difference is important.

One of the methods used by the early Catholic Worker Movement to spread Communist-inspired ideas were their Round Table Discussions, usually led by Peter Maurin.

It doesn't really matter what labels Communist-inspired Catholic social advocates like Dorothy Day use to describe themselves, as the actions they take and the people they chose to be associated with are what determines their character and mission; and by these standards Dorothy Day was a Communist-inspired Catholic working within the Catholic Church promoting people and policies the Catholic Church had declared anathema, just as so many other Communist-inspired Catholics working under the guise of Liberation Theology are doing today.

The most comprehensive book to read which explores all of this is *The Catholic Worker Movement (1933-1980): A Critical Analysis*, by Dr. Carol Byrne, published in 2010.

Pope Leo XIII in his 1878 encyclical warning about Socialism was clear on the primacy of private property, and the Communist's desire to seize it.

As stated, one of the vehicles used for Communist penetration of the Church is Liberation Theology and the preferential option for the poor.

Many Catholics labeling themselves liberal or progressive who define their work as class struggle and the often needed use of violence to change history, have been caught, and are caught still, by the imagined dreams of Communism—completely blocking the effective reformation of criminals by placing the problem outside instead of inside—so clearly warned against in the 1878 encyclical on socialism by Pope Leo XIII, *Quod Apostolici Muneris.*

With the Vatican being surrounded by Italian culture and history, it is not surprising that this perspective infiltrated the Church in Rome and eventually, the Church throughout the world.

Being a Communist in a capitalist country gives one a rather glamorous position—especially in glamour-addicted America—of revolutionary; and they are not generally perceived as being connected to the violent and brutal governments led by Communists who use the state power they control to oppress people under the guise of caring for them.

The great enemy of the Church—the prince of this world—has found Communism a worthy tool for many years, and Communism's predilection for violence is congruent with his satanic hate of free human beings.

The romantic description of the revolutionary—calculating, hard, immune to human compassion—is very congruent with that expressed by many professional criminals as a necessary mental and spiritual state to occupy in order to be a successful criminal.

Intellectuals of the early 20th Century were enamored by the courage and relentlessness of the revolutionary men and women of the early labor union movement of the late 19th century and early 20th, which brought dignity and justice to the workers, power in their labor, and much good to America; but in the latter decades of the 20th century unions became a corrupt force virtually eating its young, degrading the ability of public leadership—once public unions became their major campaign funding source—to provide for the public good without policies being filtered through the demands of public employee unions.

Once the public began to realize that the average pay for public employees demanded by public employee unions was greater than that of the average employee in the private sector, the tide began to turn in the early 21st century, and we are now witnessing, slowly but steadily, the returning of the ability of public leadership to actually work for the public's good rather than the good of the unions.

The strong efforts of the Communist-inspired Catholics—like Dorothy Day and Peter Maurin—and the many sisters and priests who worked with them, to change the social structures of the United States as they have changed the internal structure of the American Catholic Church, continue, and it is strategy their fans have found to be most effectively practiced at the local level under the social justice rubric.

All of this stems from the ancient sin, that humans know better than God, and for Catholics, who live in the faith whose teachings come from God, and are clearly presented within the two universal Catechisms of the Church, Trent & Vatican II, there is always this authority to seek out when confusion arises, a confusion which the advocates of change driving the social justice movement are deeply enmeshed in.

Holiness for some may be through the Church but for Communist-inspired Catholics who have been trying to redirect the Catholic Church into their very own Kingdom of Heaven on earth for decades; it is through Communism.

Whether it is the Catholic Worker Movement, Liberation Theology, or the environmental movement, virtually all now linked under the social justice banner, which is a misinterpretation of the true social justice work of the Church as outlined in the *Catechism*:

> **1928.** Society ensures social justice when it provides the conditions that allow associations or

394

individuals to obtain what is their due, according to their nature and their vocation. Social justice is linked to the common good and the exercise of authority.

1929. Social justice can be obtained only in respecting the transcendent dignity of man. The person represents the ultimate end of society, which is ordered to him:

What is at stake is the dignity of the human person, whose defense and promotion have been entrusted to us by the Creator, and to whom the men and women at every moment of history are strictly and responsibly in debt.

1930. Respect for the human person entails respect for the rights that flow from his dignity as a creature. These rights are prior to society and must be recognized by it. They are the basis of the moral legitimacy of every authority: by flouting them, or refusing to recognize them in its positive legislation, a society undermines its own moral legitimacy. If it does not respect them, authority can rely only on force or violence to obtain obedience from its subjects. It is the Church's role to remind men of good will of these rights and to distinguish them from unwarranted or false claims."

The Communist-inspired movements want to *mandate* social justice through legislative fiat enforced by governmental power, while Catholic social justice is *proposed* to men and women of good will as the preferred way, the way Christ taught us to live and to treat each other.

The social justice mantra, while particularly attractive for its focus on helping the poor, may be incorrectly presented.

The 1920s and 1930s were the periods when the Russian Revolution spread its wings, certain of world revolution, and in that expansion the use of the great lie was advocated—speak to others in their language, hide your true intentions, speak of peace and love while excusing violence and advocating class hatred.

Propaganda became an art form and the Russian Communists and German Fascists became its greatest artists in those horrific decades.

A classic example—and a central plank in Catholic social justice—is the political utility of advocating pacifism.

The intellectual basis of American Catholic pacifism has never been developed appropriately—primarily because it cannot stand up to a rigorous examination through the lens of Aquinas-inspired Catholic teaching—and remains primarily a political stance embraced by the Catholic left.

Moral blindness formed the foundation upon which the revolutionary violence of Liberation Theology—shaped by Communist theory and practice—grew within the Church and, which still exerts substantial control over the strategies of many religious orders and members of the laity, as well as Catholic organizations.

Another plank in the Catholic Left's vision of social justice is the prison abolition movement, whose roots are based in Communist ideology of state control of production and the mass distribution of wealth to ensure all are well-fed, housed and otherwise taken care of; social goals devoutly to be wished by all Catholics but properly to be manifested through capitalism and the generosity of the charitable impulse.

Undergirding virtually all of the Liberation Theology work emanating from Catholics influenced by Dorothy Day and the Catholic Worker Movement, is the idea of helping others freely, requiring nothing from them save their need, the no-means-test approach to charitable action.

This approach, while having a Catholic history, is not congruent with America's founding principles.

During the colonial period, when America's methods of charitable help to the unfortunate were being set into the American character, building or rebuilding the character of the unfortunate not considered worthy of freely given help was essential.

Fortunately, this directing of charitable help to those who would help themselves still resonates among many in the private philanthropic class, though government unwisely still administers aid recklessly and often to the detriment of the people it claims to be helping.

There is a virtual library of books written on the corrosiveness of the billions of dollars spent by government in pure welfare with little regard for stimulating self-help.

One of the best is *The Dream & the Nightmare: The Sixties' Legacy to the Underclass* by Myron Magnet, written in 2000.

Communism & Fatima

Fatima was the most important event of the 20th Century and beyond.

However, if the apparition really happened and I believe it did, then the shepherds of the Church failed Our Lady and our Church then and continue that failure today.

They not only failed to protect our Church from the Communist wolves, but in all too many cases, became Communist wolves themselves.

The speculation surrounding why the appearance of the Holy Mother and her plea to consecrate Russia to her Immaculate Heart, has not been followed; continues to this day.

The request for the Collegial Consecration was first promised before the Bolsheviks overcame Russia and her Catholic monarchy, eventually killing the entire family of Czar Romanov, and specifically called for later, and it is still unfulfilled.

Part of the reason—the influential power of human relationships—has been uncovered by several historians.

Russian Communism's penetration and attempt to control Catholic strategy continued through the papacy of John Paul II.

The Russian Communist presence within the Vatican appears to have been the mortar that kept the Vatican from ever—to this day—fulfilling the wishes of the Holy Mother at Fatima.

No matter how many times I read about this, I am still shocked that it happened and has been so completely documented from so many sources, yet so completely absent within the perspective of the Catholic public.

One book that covers this is *The End and the Beginning: Pope John Paul II—The Victory of Freedom, the Last Years, the Legacy* by George Weigel, published in 2010.

Communism, being able to accomplish this powerful strategy against critiques from the one force on earth with the spiritual authority to be heard and to combat it, thus proved itself a very powerful and effective adversary.

Communism is a religion, its bible is *The Communist Manifesto*, its theologians are Lenin, Stalin, Mao, Debray, Fanon; its priests are legion, and its shock troops are too often criminals, harking to the first name of the organization Communism's founders, Marx and Engels, joined, the *League of the Outlaws*.

The Holy Mother at Fatima also knew about the real criminal danger of an unconsecrated Russia, due to the crimes—though of a much less magnitude of national violence and brutality than the horror of the Nazi holocaust and the Stalinist terror—which have resulted via a world-wide explosion of organized crime emanating from Russia.

The Marxist infiltration of Catholicism began in Europe after years of occupation by the Nazis and the Communists, solidifying their atheistic ideology over oppressed European peoples, where the ambitious and unscrupulous assumed positions of cultural superiority because of their lack of religious commitment.

Some in the traditional wing of Catholicism—of which I am somewhat partial to, and I will explain the 'somewhat'—believes the solution to Modernism, of which Communism can be considered an aspect, is a reassertion of Christendom; the time when European governments, all of which were monarchial, accepted the kingship of God and his vicar, Peter.

The problem here, the 'somewhat', is that a central element of God's plan—until he comes again—is the reign over earth (but not human souls) by Satan, the prince of this world; whose blandishments the Christian way of life is protection against.

Understanding all of this, coming to terms with history and the various blandishments offered by all sides in the Catholic versus Communism debate requires a process of spiritual maturation too few of us reach for.

Maturing in God, is a process each of us has to go through if we are to become mature Catholics, leaving the primitive and childish things like Liberation Theology and

Communism behind, and part of this maturation is growing in wisdom and knowledge through the studying of human life on earth through the lens of Catholic doctrine.

Is this not the wonderful way of divine parentage, which we as humans so often strive to attain in our childraising?

Rebellion and questioning authority are congruent with youth, then as now, and for those of us whose youth was influenced by the siren calls of the rebellion prevalent in our youth, the critical examination of the avatars of our youth is always both difficult and exciting; difficult as it shreds a passion of youth, exciting because it presages the wisdom of age.

And so it is for me, writing about Communism, whose Marxist roots briefly influenced my work in prison and for a time after being released.

Concluding Thoughts

The great movement after World War II which began to address the huge impact Communism had made within the academy, government, and media, so exemplified by the investigations of Senator Joseph McCarthy; was initially and very successfully represented as a national aberration that had no basis in truth, but which, after the slow release of files from the fall of Soviet Communism, was seen to be, not an aberration, but a valiant effort by heroic people, like Senator McCarthy, to save their country from Communism.

In essence then, the later domination of the Russian Orthodox Church by the Communist Party's security force, the KGB, was congruent with some central streams of the history of Russian philosophy and socio-political thought.

The power of Communism to attract and hold the allegiance of the Russian people for as long as it did is also connected to its masquerading as religion.

In relation to all that we have examined in this chapter, the traditional position of the Church regarding Communism, Fatima and the call for the consecration of Russia and the failure to answer that call, what does all of it mean in relation to criminal reformation?

The answer may be a response to the signs of the times, when through the emancipation of class, slaves, women and youth, so painfully and vividly represented by the French Revolution, the American Civil War, the women's suffragette movement, and the 1960's movement of youth, the denouncement of things carried little weight coming from authority—Question Authority being a clarion call of all emancipation movements—and softer appeals to reason and self-interest were seen as the path to conversion.

Criminals will respond to truth weightier than the criminal/carceral truth they live by when it is lived by its proponents. Talk is cheap, but when men and women walk their talk, it is priceless.

Though it is difficult to find within the modern Catholic Church in America those men and women, they do exist, and the golden rod of faith they represent and carry forth, whether it is through their membership and leadership of Church organizations and orders, they are men and women who live by the ancient faith, the faith of our fathers as represented within the Universal Catechisms of Trent and Vatican II, and the papal magisterium, and through them and through all of the faithful, the Holy Catholic Church Christ promised would not fall under the gates of hell, still and will always, stand.

For it is a Church outliving bad popes, bad bishops, bad priests, bad nuns, and keeping within the heart of faith, those innocent faithful who the great apparitions of Our Lady reveal as truly the heart of the Church, as her son proclaimed through Mary Magdalene and Dismas, those who the world does not see, are so often those Christ sees most clearly and holds most closely.

An ambiguous Vatican II, the machinations of Freemasons, Communists—Catholic or non-Catholic— and other secular enemies are but wind in the willows to the infinite roar of Almighty God, creator and king of the world the prince of the world may not influence; and it is the heel of the Virgin Woman who crushes the serpent head of all worldly troubles whose only effect on the Holy Catholic Church who cannot fall though the Gates of Hell be opened upon her, as they have been since the beginning.

I read laments outlining the end of civilization because the Church has lost her way, misguided by confused popes, corrupt priests, bishops, and nuns, yet I do not tremble for the Church and I pray the writers of laments seek greater understanding.

The Church is not a single pope, bishop, priest or nun. The Church is Christ, Mary and the Communion of Saints; and those pilgrims fulfilling their earthly mission will stumble but Christianity will not.

Indeed, the true Church is the Church beneath the church, not the institutional church but the supernatural church, not the result of the actions of men, but resulting from the actions of God and his apostles on earth.

The Vatican II Ecumenical Council of the Church from October 11, 1962 to December 8, 1965 was a significant event in the life of the Church, where all the bishops of the world gathered and under the leadership of the Pope—Pope John XXIII who opened it and Pope Paul VI who closed it—created magisterial documents that still cause controversy through misinterpretation and misrepresentation.

What happened during Vatican II was a struggle between liberal Catholics and conservative Catholics—though inaccurate terms as all Catholics, by their oath of baptism, have to conserve the deposit of faith—but still descriptive and useful. It was a struggle between those who wanted to liberalize her practice and language—often with very good reason—and those who wanted to conserve her practice and language, also, with very good reason.

The liberals largely won, so well documented in two magisterial works: *The Rhine Flows into the Tiber: A History of Vatican II,* by Fr. Ralph M. Wiltgen, S.V.D. (1985) Tan Books, and *Iota Unum: A Study of Changes in the Catholic Church in the XXth Century,* by Romano Amerio (1996) Sarto House.

Reading the Vatican II documents again, confirms to me that while we may find what we wish in the often dense prose, we can lose ourselves in the interpretations by others, though seeking out the relatively balanced work commenting on Vatican II, such as the aforementioned works by Wiltgen and Amerio, will pay dividends.

The decades-long discussion, or perhaps more accurately described, war, between the liberal wing of the Catholic Church and the conservatives over the interpretation, and in some cases, validity, of its doctrinal and pastoral documents (a war that since the beginning of the Church) is an issue that anyone involved in ministry to criminals—inside prison or out—has to come to terms with.

I first became aware of this during the Rite of Christian Initiation for Adults (RCIA) process I was going through in preparation for baptism, but it was not an issue I deeply engaged with until about eight years later.

From the liberal perspective, Vatican II and the Pope who opened it, Pope John XXIII—who many liberals refer to as "Good Pope John", also opened the Church to the modern world with love, compassion, and good humor from the oft perceived closed, rigid, and overly medieval and intellectual Catholic world represented by the Pius Popes, most notably Pope Saint Pius X and Pope Pius XII, though it was also a Church of clarity and one whose writings I return to often, with those of Pope Pius XII remaining a favorite.

From a conservative perspective—one I largely share—the Pius popes were the last great and strongly traditional leaders of the Catholic world in relation to Communism.

For instance, the Pastoral Constitution on the Church in the Modern World, *Gaudium et Spes,* does not have a section on Communism, but it examined economic theory.

With all of the good things that occurred at Vatican II and also with many of the other unfortunate events that occurred during the Council, the conclusion I have reached—in harmony with the Church—is that Vatican II was a legitimate Ecumenical Council, as traditionally defined by the Church.

It is true many of the documents greatly favored the positions taken by liberals and some even protected Communism, but that was because liberals were much better organized during the Council to ensure their perspective took precedence; but, in many cases—Mass in the vernacular being one, though I love and prefer the Latin Mass—were appropriate decisions.

In the Western world, including Latin America, where Catholicism was well established, opening up the Mass to the vernacular was seen by many as a loss. In the mission fields, such as Africa, it was seen as a blessing.

The Dogmatic Constitution, *Lumen Gentium,* Section 8, saying: "...although many elements of sanctification and of truth are found outside of its visible structure. These elements, as gifts belonging to the Church of Christ, are forces impelling toward catholic unity", implied to many that the Church was not the sole path to salvation as stated by Catholic tradition.

But, while the first sentence seems to say that, the second reaffirms that the full truth is only generated from within the Catholic Church, though it may find its way to other places, as through—for instance—the Protestants via their founder, the Catholic priest, Martin Luther.

This quality of the writings coming from Vatican II, stating one thing but perhaps implying another, is, I have come to realize, one of the methods the Church has decided upon for confronting modernity—maintaining the clarity of tradition while allowing the ambiguity of the times.

This method softens the clarity of the Church's one truth and allows those who would run from that sort of 'golden rod clarity' to stick around.

It is not a method I particularly like, but I certainly see the wisdom of it, and it may lay at the heart of the Church's softening of its relations with Communism, especially through the long papacy of John Paul II, the first pope from a Communist Country, who had several decades of dealing with the Communists while priest, bishop, and cardinal in Poland; and may have decided that, once pope, that there could be a more effective way of converting Communists than the historical method developed by previous popes.

And the results may very well be seen in the recent speculation that the Orthodox Church is very close to rejoining the Roman Catholic fold.

This being said, it is still troubling that the Church promised to not speak of Communism during Vatican II, especially considering the perspective on that silence mentioned by Romano Amerio in his book *Iota Unum*.

This is troubling and little seems resolved about the trouble by characterizing thinking and speaking about totalitarianism without reference to the very model of totalitarianism since 1917, Communism.

We see in the writings of many superb thinkers, even some who wrote against the Church, such as Ayn Rand, the essentials of truth, once we have gotten hold of the whole truth from which to view them; but sadly, many of these thinkers ended their lives in bitterness, sadness, acrimony, and ultimately failure as deep as the chasm between their discovered truth and the full truth they never accepted.

One aspect of Fatima that I've not seen mentioned much is its timeliness. Our Holy Mother promised in 1917 she would call for the consecration of Russia, warning of great suffering if that consecration was not carried out.

The Church says it was carried out within the consecration of the entire world by Pope John Paul II, and Sister Lucia, one of the Fatima children, agreed.

However, it would seem to me, and I certainly have no special knowledge other than my study of the issue for the past couple of years, that when she promised on July 13, 1917 to call for the consecration of Russia and following it up with the specific call within a vision to Sister Lucia on June 13, 1929, she meant it to take place then and when we consider the sufferings of the world since—Communist takeover of Russia and the approximately 100 million estimated that were killed by its edicts, world-wide depression, WWII and the genocide against the Jewish people taking the lives of six million, Communist takeover of China, Korea, and Southeast Asia and the millions of lives lost in the process, and the hundreds of millions lost to abortion, the sexual abuse crisis in the Church—it is hard to see how any one century could have been much worse.

The still active effort to have the pope consecrate Russia, while certainly not really harmful as Russia is a criminal state and can certainly benefit from consecration, the time it should have been done was the time our Holy Mother called for it to be done, and since it was not done then, much of the damage surely has already been done.

Our walking the talk of Catholicism, our prayers for the world, for our faith, for the Holy Father, priests and nuns, all religious and all the faithful are still the one certain way we can help Our Lord help our world.

The ambiguity of the Catechism produced by Vatican II cuts both ways; solidifying tradition or disrupting it, depending on who is reading it.

The faithful will hew to the traditional doctrine woven through it, the dissident will see innovation and disruption to traditional doctrine and will hew to that, and so it has always been, even since the Garden.

Vatican II was a true council, congruent with the tradition of many ecumenical councils of the Church in the world, but it also continued the eternal war the Church in the world has been engaged, with more ammunition perhaps given to Satan than to Christ; but regardless of the quantity of ammunition, the ultimate end has already been decided by God and, as written since the Garden, Satan loses.

Ammunition is only as sound as the gun from which it is fired.

Though the ambiguity of Vatican II and the Catechism later promulgated by Pope John Paul II, gave many bullets to Satan in his penetration of the Church, it also identified his minions through their use of those bullets; as did the interpretations of Vatican II and the Catechism as supporting Catholic dogma identify those who stood with Peter, Christ and Mary.

Scientific theology is clearly that from St. Thomas Aquinas and pastoral theology would describe that which has been coming from the Vatican since Pope John XXIII, but both are a reflection of the traditional theology of the Catholic Church, but expressed in different ways, for different times; a strategy straight from St. Paul.

For John Paul II, knowing from personal experience that Communism does not work and ultimately degrades into corruption and criminality; he knew that salvation would then be possible, conversion would then be possible, for he knew that the 2,000 years of Catholic history enduring truth and practice would attract the ideological riven Communist who had seen his bright vision become a dark nightmare.

Our Church is a pilgrim Church.

Our Church is divinely founded and divinely protected though worldly stained, even to the point of housing satanic evil.

Our Church—and here we must clearly include Jerusalem of the Old Covenant and stretching back to Genesis—has, yes, sometimes whored herself and the ancient condemnations as the Whore of Babylon passed on to the children of heretics as it was to me by my Mormon parents, is therefore accurate, as is the acclamation by the faithful as Holy Mother Church.

Both Marys—the mother of Jesus and the Magdalene—were present at the close of the Old Covenant and the opening of the New, and both Marys are with us still, especially the Magdalene whose penitential life is a mark of criminal transformation unequaled.

Now then, with the Miracle of Fatima in our mind, when the narrative within the minds of most Americans, is that Communism is dead, what is the point mulling it over once again.

The point is, dear reader, that the very same forgetfulness of incarnate evil represented by Communism is a forgetfulness clouding the mind for time immemorial when it comes to the works of those principalities and powers allied with Satan against God and the Church; which is exactly why Our Lady came to Fatima.

It is happening again, now, today, always, regarding the historical implacable enemy of the Church, rampant evil and the tendency of people to ignore it, deny it, hope it leaves them, us, alone.

Communism, perhaps in new forms—while retaining its historical nature in Russia—is certainly not dead.

The more the financial systems of the world struggle to provide fairness and opportunity to their citizens, the more Communism wends its way in through the weakened defenses.

Do we not all fall prey to this and do we not all know the surest defense is a strong relationship with God through prayer and living a life of as much sanctity as we can, remembering that betrayal is written into our very bones and blood, beginning with Adam and Eve.

After studying the issue, the conclusion I reached regarding the failure of the Council to vigorously condemn Communism as had so many previous popes, was that, at best, Vatican II was a council whose decisions on this issue were confused.

My research into the subject has continued (as does my research on all the subjects of which I have written) as I have worked on this book covering the same ground, and now I am reaching the conclusion that what I saw in the beginning as confusion may very well have been wisdom.

One of the great benefits of the ambiguity expressed in the interpretations of the Council's work, was how it has drawn out the venom that had lain festering in the Church as those religious and laity who had simmered in dissent now flamed into a raging fire of opposition and all now know who they are and of whom they speak, as they cast off their religious garb and way of life.

Remembering the world-wide atmosphere of the 1960s in which Vatican II evolved, where we largely moved from the historical age of the tyrants, kings, and dictators to the age of committees and dialogue; is it any wonder that the Vatican, accustomed more than any other institution in the world, to think in terms of centuries rather than years, would play a leading role in this shift, an idea with deepened resonance watching the evolving papacy of our new Holy Father Francis as a congruent link in the Holy Fathers since Vatican II.

When I last got out of prison in August of 1969, and returned to California, I immediately was swept up in the revolutionary movement wherein criminals, paradoxically, were seen as leaders.

Though my deepest involvement was with the counterculture themes, the mantra that most of us shared during that period was "Question Authority"; and coming out of the 1950s, where the most authoritative institutions of the culture wrapped obedience to authority in steel webs, it was an incredibly liberating—but as we eventually learned, corrosive—mantra, as those of us who lived through that time remember.

At that time, my bibles were *The Wisdom of the Sands* by Antoine de Saint Exupery, which I embraced during my last stretch in prison at McNeil Island Federal Penitentiary, and *The Whole Earth Catalog*, which someone thrust into my hands shortly after I had gotten out and said "Here, catch up." My drug of choice was mescaline, and in that befuddled state, I believed we—the smiley long-haired bearded ones and our earth mother women—were creating a new world, which seemed to be validated in the other beaming faces (who were also peaked out on psychedelics) I encountered as I walked the streets of Lake Tahoe, Berkeley, San Francisco, Vancouver, British Columbia, and all points in between, with my small entourage.

We believed psychedelics opened the doors of perception—as Aldous Huxley so aptly phrased—allowing us to discover our latent powers, and when *The Aquarian Conspiracy* by Marilyn Ferguson was published, we knew that what we had thought we were doing was in fact what we had been about.

Later, much later, I would discover that the *real*, powerful conspiracy was founded by Christ and led by Peter which had existed for millennia, radically changing the meaning of life on earth.

This was the Catholic Church, the foundation of Western thought; and the saints of the Church had been accessing latent human powers through the grace of God ever since.

Within this environment of change, the decision by Vatican II to focus on change or as the elements were called then: *aggiornamento*, *development*, and *ressourcement*, or, modernizing, evolving, and returning to sources, respectively, was a wise response to the spirit of the Aquarian times.

One of the ideas, once obscured but now leaping out, is that rather than continuing the strong pronouncements against Communism characterizing the first five decades of the 20th Century, the Church now decided *to embrace in order to convert* Communism.

And one wonders how much this approach opened the door for Pope John Paul II to play one of the leading roles in vanquishing the Soviet empire a few decades later, and to the emerging potential coming together of the Russian Orthodox with Rome.

On the other hand, this may well be the making a bad situation a little better by acknowledging the reality on the ground; the bad situation being the failure of Peter and the bishops to consecrate Russia to the Immaculate Heart of the Holy Mother of God, and the acknowledgement that the Church was not able to defeat Communism during its formative stage through the intersession of the Holy Mother; the best policy now might be to dialogue with them, seeking men and women of good will with whom conversion might be possible; and that might very well be a wise strategy.

The decision to engage rather than condemn Communism might prove to be a wise decision or it might prove to be, as the current pope and the two previously have done by calling for the abolition of capital punishment, indicate a lack of understanding of evil.

While this may seem fanciful for men—the Vicars of Christ on earth—whose life is focused on helping sinners, but an examination of the life of most priests can reveal little opportunity to fully appreciate the hardness and clarity of evil intent, of an evil life lived consciously.

Though the three Holy Fathers—one who dealt with the Communists, one with Nazis and one with a military dictatorship—have seen evil, one would think their knowledge would be deep but here is where the within and the without of the human soul crucially determines soul knowledge and why many traditions advocate salvation coming through self-degradation; but not sought as by Rimbaud, Rasputin and Huysmans, but having happened in life, like Pope Saint Callistus, the former criminal who became pope, perhaps one of the greatest popes.

Again, though I am still researching and praying about all of this, it does add to the wonder that this convert feels as I come to learn more and more about my adopted faith, and am validated in my knowledge—especially for those of us approaching the Church intellectually, which is the way most penitential professional criminals will actually convert—that lifelong study is crucial to truly understand and appreciate the Church and her social teaching.

Our faith requires us to live in the present, not in an imagined past or dreamt future.

Our Catholic faith requires us to honor her tenets, and to live, supernaturally, in the present, and always remember, our Church is a Church of the Word, not a Church of the human, the Eternal Church underneath and above the brick church.

Chapter Nine

Women in the Church, St. Catherine of Siena, Fr. Teilhard de Chardin, & Criminal Reformation

Introduction

The Church stands in the world as a sign of contradiction and as the world since time immemorial excluded women from full personhood; the Church must now ensure that within her embrace, woman's full personhood is deeply rooted and complete; which can only be accomplished by priestly ordination and full equality with men in the leadership of the Church on earth as that equality is certainly so in Heaven.

I have come to believe, fully and completely, that the institutional Church has been wrong in not ordaining women to be priests; just as the Church was wrong for centuries in seeing the earth as the center of the solar system, slavery as acceptable and usury not; and this wrongness, in the treatment of women, will become obvious to criminals being evangelized, for they know, better than most, the pain and sorrow of being marginalized, even though their marginalization is self-imposed while that of the women in the Church comes from Vatican politics and the twisting of history.

Underneath and alongside the institutional church, the deeper reality of the supernatural church has always existed, the Church founded and shaped by Christ, the Church the people in their hearts have always seen—for the institutional church has too much that has been claimed as doctrine, then changed—but the supernatural church, the mystical church, has always known the true and equal power of the women of the Church; a power manifested most powerfully through the lives contemporaneous with Christ, of Holy Mother Mary and Mary Magdalene.

My Catholic belief is centered on the Great Story; that throughout human history the idea of God has been prevalent within the human heart and mind; and of the four major religions: Christianity, Islam, Hinduism, Buddhism, only three, Christianity, Islam, and Buddhism can claim an individual as founder, and of them only one, Christianity, can claim a founder who was God; the other two merely claiming to be a prophet and an enlightened human respectively.

Christ's Godhood is certified by eye witness accounts of miracles he performed unexplainable by any human ability; in particular, his resurrection.

Christ formed his church on the rock of Peter, and the gates of hell have not prevailed against it, and as the Roman Catholic Church survives still, I know that, as a Catholic, I am of the People of God, and I am as certain that God is in the soul of each human being on earth.

"Question Authority"; that was the foundational mantra of the 1960s; choosing to question the authority that was instructing us to do something we felt was wrong and incorrect teaching is, unfortunately, an aspect of Catholic institutional life; but it is corrected by the Catholic teaching mandating listening to our conscience.

This comes from the point made in Romans:

> **[Romans 2: 14]:** As for the Gentiles, though they have no law to guide them, there are times when they carry out the precepts of the law unbidden, finding in their own natures a rule to guide them, in default of any other rule; **[15]** and this shews that the obligations of the law are written in their hearts; their conscience utters its own testimony, and when they dispute with one another they find themselves condemning this, approving that. **[16]** And there will be a day when God (according to the gospel I preach) will pass judgement, through Jesus Christ, on the hidden thoughts of men.

All human beings have the eternal written on their hearts and even within those who do not believe in God, even some who call themselves Humanists, as is evident when the father of Humanism, Abraham Maslow teaches, us that the first step to the supreme heights a human being can reach, is that of self-actualization, a concept surely emanating from the divine nature of human conscience.

Our conscience, the ability to determine right from wrong, of listening, in that quietness, the still small voice, which, when heeded, serves us well.

Catholic teaching is absolutely correct, one's conscience, one's connection with God, is surely what one must align with, which calls for the attitude, "trust but verify" and verify through our own study, our own conscience, our own listening to that still small voice from God, our own entering into the silence.

I was born in 1942, to a German/Russian father and Jewish/English mother. My father soon was sentenced to prison for crimes committed as a member of an organized crime family and after a time, my mother remarried.
My stepfather was a Danish Mormon and I was raised— from 5 years old to 13—as a Mormon.

At 13 I committed my first theft and it was glorious. I became a criminal—thief and robber—and for the next 20 years plied my trade, not always successfully as I spent 12 of those years in jails, youth homes, reformatories (all of which I escaped from) and maximum security state and federal prisons, (from which I could not escape).

Later, after release in the waning days of the 1960s, I became a New Ager, and wandered drug-soaked, sensually gorged and joyful, among the glittering trappings of Gnosticism.

Many years later, when I married and we had a child, we decided to explore religions to find a faith home for our family life and slowly rewound our way through Protestantism, Judaism, and Mormonism, until finally settling on Catholicism; being baptized in 2004.

At each step in my journey to the Catholic Church, I studied deeply the theology and praxis of the chosen faith and in each case, the theology came up short; except for Catholicism, whose richness kept rewarding—rewards me still—me the deeper I studied.

Even when I began a deep study of the dissenting theologians of the Church—as I have always believed in the role of the devil's advocate—I found much to confirm my Catholic faith; but less to confirm the institutional church.

Here is where I found myself, some years ago, when I began to realize that the true church was the Mystical Church; but the greatest gate to the Mystical Church was the Apostolic Gate, the gate of the apostles and the fathers and mothers of the Catholic Church.

The Mystical Church, Supernatural Church, is the Church God created when he created us; it is the way of life we know, in our God infused souls, that we should live by.

Human souls have directly communicated with God since the beginning and though they have often misunderstood God, or chosen to ignore or go against God, they have known what God wants them to do, how God wants then to live their lives on earth.

This is the Mystical Church

The Mystical Church is the church Christ—God become man—enhanced upon the earth two thousand years ago in Israel.

He was born on earth as a member of the Chosen People of God, from a Jewish woman, impregnated by God.

He was the Messiah foretold in Jewish history and the Mystical Church created by him embraced and enhanced Judaism, opening the Apostolic Gate to the Catholic Church.

Today, the Mystical Church is the Church found scattered—as is the way of humans since Babel—throughout the thousands of humanly corrupted gates of divine light

It is not the humanly corrupted churches of Catholicism, Buddhism, Islam, Protestantism, Hinduism, or Judaism; but through the Apostolic Gate is the truest path to the Mystical Church, and through the Apostolic Gate the greatest light shines on God's words to humans.

The universe is the creation of God and it is within the human mind's power—through our linkage to God—to envision the universe and traverse it and the divine image to be found.

We are warmed by the abyss of the night sky because human eyes gaze back at us and it is our destiny, as we traverse space and time, to someday meet our created brothers and sisters and we will find creedal and familial congruence with others who will also pray the Apostle's Creed as found in the *Catechism* of Vatican II:

> I believe in God, the Father Almighty, Creator of heaven and earth.
>
> I believe in in Jesus Christ, his only Son, our Lord.
>
> He was conceived by the Holy Spirit and born of the Virgin Mary.
>
> He suffered under Pontius Pilate, was crucified, died and was buried. He descended into hell.
>
> On the third day He rose again.
>
> He ascended into heaven and is seated at the right hand of the Father. He will come again to judge the living and the dead.
>
> I believe in the Holy Spirit,
> the holy catholic Church,
> the communion of saints,
> the forgiveness of sins,
> the resurrection of the body,
> and the life everlasting.
> Amen. (pp. 49-50)

We stand now at the Apostolic Gate and the Holy Catholic Church is the Mystical Church beyond. It is the Church that is Holy, uncorrupted by human sin, and it is here for us, has always been here for us, it cannot fall, nor can the evil of Satan tarnish it as he can tarnish the human institutional church.

It is here in the Apostle's Creed, in the writings of the Holy Fathers and the Holy Mothers of the Church; the Angelic Doctor, the Universal Catechisms of Trent and Vatican II, and yes, the documents of Vatican II, perhaps the most sublime set of documents ever to come from the modern Church.

Truth is rationale, beautiful and harmonious. Faith is built on reason, logic and order. The rational mind of human beings can comprehend the ways of God, even if it is only the current Doctors of the Church like Saint Catherine of Siena and St. Thomas Aquinas, or a future Doctor of the Church—I am sure of it—Fr. Teilhard de Chardin, who can so comprehend at the deepest level and then, teach us.

Catherine reasoned with worldly powers through her mystical faith; Aquinas taught us that reason and faith are congruent; and Fr. Teilhard de Chardin taught us that the practice emanating from their congruence is evolutionary, though not always as it witnessed by women's ordination, which as I write, Pope Francis has said he will think about establishing a commission to examine women as deacons, as was so in the early church.

With this richness of past doctrinal study at their command, I am saddened by the lack of reasonable discourse being used by the Church to combat women's ordination, and the seminal argument of the Church is found in the *Catechism* of Vatican II:

> **1577** "Only a baptized man (vir) validly receives sacred ordination." The Lord Jesus chose men (viri) to form the college of the twelve apostles, and the apostles did the same when they chose collaborators to succeed them in their ministry. The college of bishops, with whom the priests are united in the priesthood, makes the college of the twelve an ever-present and ever-active reality until Christ's return. The Church recognizes herself to be bound by this choice made by the Lord himself. For this reason the ordination of women is not possible.

Of course, Jesus Christ also only chose Jews to be apostles, but that is not now, nor has it ever been, considered as

another scripturally-based requirement ; and even more
cogent in Scripture:

> **[Galatians 3:27]:** All you who have been baptized
> in Christ's name have put on the person of Christ;
> **[28]** no more Jew or Gentile, no more slave and
> freeman, no more male and female; you are all one
> person in Jesus Christ. **[29]** And if you belong to
> Christ, then you are indeed Abraham's children; the
> promised inheritance is yours.

What to do, what to do?

Our questions lead us to the Kingdom of Conscience, the
house of self-knowledge infused with knowledge of God,
but always study, study, life-long learning, and prayer,
daily prayer, hourly prayer, continuous prayer, seek the
truth of doctrine.

Yes, prostitutes and criminals are the farthest from God,
yet, as we see with the prostitute Saint Mary of Magdalene
and the thief Saint Dismas, they were among those closest
to him.

Yes, the search for truth is endless and we know that what
once seemed reasonable and true can become false,
perhaps not any better exhibited than through the case of
the great scientist Galileo, imprisoned for life by the
Catholic Church for expressing a truth which the Church,
at that time, reasonably denied.

It was reasonable, during the time of Galileo, to believe
that the earth was the center of the universe because that is
what our senses told us was true, and certain scriptures
seemed to support that.

This was Church doctrine at the time—as was the perfidy of
the Jews, the rightness of slavery, the chattelism of women,
and the evil of usury—and as fervently subscribed to then,
as the denial of the priesthood to women is now.

Personal Aside #1

Being a man and writing about women in the Church is suspect and though I also have been marginalized due to my criminal/carceral status, my marginalization is self-inflicted, while that of women is a fact of birth and historic teaching in the Church that women are the source of sin in the world.

The reason I never fully connected with the various religions I studied prior to becoming Catholic (Mormonism, New Age, Protestantism, and Judaism) is that, upon study—their theology, their morality, their practice—broke down into contradiction and irrationality.

What attracted and held me within the Catholic Church was that the deeper I dug, the deeper I studied, the sounder, more beautiful, and more logical her theology, morality, and practice became.

My path to the Catholic Church was an intellectual one; everything had to eventually align with reason, and this will be true within the ministries to the criminal/carceral world of the professional criminal: those who commit crimes for money and have made a conscious decision to live as a criminal based on the belief that the world is built upon criminality and one is either prey or predator.

As I begin this study I realize that, in many ways, this is the most significant study I've authored because it deals with the oldest oppression of human upon human, that of the man upon the woman.

St. Mary Magdalene

One of the cornerstones of the argument that only men can be priests comes from the documentation of the facts on the ground during Christ's ministry on earth, where the Church has consistently maintained that the leader of the apostles was Peter and it was upon him that the Church was built by Christ and because only men were chosen as apostles, only men can be ordained as priests.

I cannot see how God approves the unequal status of women which the world has proclaimed since time immemorial.

And though it is generally agreed by practicing theologians, that the conflating of the three Marys is what led to the tradition that Mary Magdalene was a prostitute, theologians today separate them.

I still believe in the tradition of the Magdalene as a prostitute, as it resonates with me, and more fully resonates with the scriptures as now canonized; and even the long attempt to separate her from prostitution seems an attempt to take away the power of penance in flowering the power of apostleship or Church leadership and the model of penance Christ conferred upon Magdalene seems unearned if she was merely a sinner, as all are, rather than a great sinner, a criminal sinner, a predatory sinner, a whore.

Many women theologians want her to have not been a prostitute as they see that as disempowering her, but Magdalene, having been a prostitute, or more accurately, a grand courtesan whose lovers were men of power and privilege who were deeply captured by her exotic appearance and erotic potency; possessed dual powers from her sinful life which gave her, in her penitential life, apostolic authority.

Mary Magdalene was the magnificently penitential woman who was the apostle to the apostles, called so by Christ, so clearly endorsed by his appearing to her first after his resurrection and by commissioning her to go tell the apostles that he had arisen; assuming the status of first among the apostles.

St. Catherine of Siena

St. Catherine, one of two women Doctors of the Church, was a powerful mystic, member of the third order of the Dominicans, who only lived for 33 years (March 25, 1347 – April 29, 1380) but who, in her short life, exerted profound political influence during a time of turmoil in the Church where the popes reigned from Avignon, France; but she was able to influence Pope Gregory XI to return to Rome, cultivated by the revelations of St. Bridget of Sweden.

In St. Catherine of Siena we have an example of a woman who was arguably more of a pope in spirit than Pope Gregory XI, who she essentially told to man up and get thee back to Rome from France; and he did.

Yes, St. Catherine of Siena is a Doctor of the Church and one of the most powerful and influential Catholic religious leaders during the chaotic 14th century.

During the Middle Ages, religion was the only sector of society in which a woman, other than royalty, could exert a powerful influence on world affairs and Catherine was part of that.

St. Catherine was a woman who was clearly able to be a priest, bishop, cardinal, or pope; and when a child, she dreamed of running away, putting on boys clothes and becoming a priest

Slavery

Women as chattels, as property of men and without virtually any rights at all, was accepted doctrine within the Church and throughout society until relatively a short time ago and is, even now, accepted religious dogma inscribed into law within much of the Islamic world.

In the Western world, women as co-equal with men has become the norm, and though still too often aligned with more in theory than practice, it has been intellectually established, solidly, that women can do virtually anything involved with being a priest as can men.

One of the central aspects of Catholic tradition which attracted me to the Church was its openness to anyone and walking the talk—acting on its words—especially around slavery and abortion, both of which the Church has condemned throughout its history, at least, as the orthodox histories I had read at that time, stated.

Further study uncovered the *Bull Romanus Pontifex* of Pope Nicholas V (1455, January 8), which changed my mind and left no doubt about papal support for slavery.

We see in this the split of knowledge, between the average Catholic and between those who study or live the issues, and in the ministry to criminals, the ministry will have to come down on the side of those who study, for the criminals will study to see why they should forgo a narrative that matches their vision of the world enabling them to, in good conscience, be criminals.

Unfortunately, as with all human institutions, even within the Catholic Church founded by God, confusion and contradiction will reign more often than not, though in the balance, the Church stands strong as walking the talk more than any other earthly institution throughout her more than 2,000 years of history.

Fr. Pierre Teilhard de Chardin

About a hundred years ago a French Jesuit, Fr. Pierre Teilhard de Chardin, began thinking and writing about a grand vision he had regarding Christ and Evolution; a vision so advanced that the Vatican theologians of the time could scarcely understand nor begin to embrace it—though some prominent theologians such as Henri de Lubac, S.J., whose books about Teilhard are an excellent introduction to his work, certainly did—and forbade him from publishing his writing during his lifetime; he died in 1955.

Slowly however, after his death, as his work began to see the light of day, the Catholic theologians caught up, led by de Lubac, and eventually even the popes realized how profound his work was and how much it would change the mind of the Church.

For a time, his actual faith was questioned through the complexity and speculative nature of his work, something which even happened to St. Thomas Aquinas for a time.

One root he helped plant, the clerical reevaluation of women from repository of sin and a dangerous being to be feared to a sister devoutly to be embraced, will someday lead to the creation of women priests, I am sure of it, I pray for it.

And so it is with the chastity of the Church, true chastity lies on the other side of women becoming priests-bishops-cardinals-popes, beyond fearing them.

It is so clear that women have been acting functionally as priests in the Catholic Church in the past and should be now, that the circular arguments the institutional Church makes to justify not allowing women into the priesthood are an intellectual and moral embarrassment, virtually rendering Vatican pronouncements on any issue more suspect than they should be.

Evolution of matter and spirit—the work of humans co-creates future reality with God—marks a defining aspect of women in the Church, and where once it did signify virgin and mother, now, in an industrial and technological world reality co-created by God and humans, it no longer suffices; and as the Church ultimately accepted the sun's centrality in the solar system rather than the earths, it is past time to move away from the centrality of men to the

Church, to a mutual and collaborative centrality of men and women, where each can become, priest, bishop, pope.

Ah, the evolution of all, of which human consciousness plays such an important role—imagine the human experience being synthesized from the super-rich in sixty million dollar penthouses in Hong Kong and Manhattan to busted-out homeless in Bowery corners and Brazilian favelas.

Every truth is His truth, the great convergence which draws all to Christ, as Fr. Teilhard taught us, and a truth still needing to be drawn to Christ's Vicar on earth is the truth of women's equality in all things, now and forever more; a great truth calling for women in the priesthood, women in the Curia, women on the papal throne; for as the Mother of God looks over us, and as Magdalene, Apostle to the Apostles and the closest companion of God on earth, has revealed to us, women are truly created in the image of God.

This is the connection between women in the Church and Fr. Teilhard de Chardin, that he, of all the male Catholic theologians I have read, best explains the optimal relationship between the Church and women.

The feminist movement in the West is over a hundred years old. Embracing the feminine as Teilhard envisioned within the Church is not yet realized, but today, May 18, 2016 as I write, there are signs that Pope Francis will establish a commission to examine women becoming deacons.

The work from two doctors of the Church—one future, Teilhard, one present, Catherine of Sienna—are a cornerstone of evolution and faith upon which the future of Church practice will be built; embracing the theology of Teilhard, who has understood and explained the Cosmic Christ, and Catherine who was—in practice—priest and pope during her fullest moments on earth.

Teilhard explains the evolution of matter, spirit and Catholic teaching; Catherine lived it.

We pray the Church will soon embrace her wisest daughters and sons.

Descent of Aquinas, Ascent of Teilhard

During the early half of the 20th Century there was a deep renewal of Thomism—the foundational and intellectual floor of Catholicism for centuries now—within the Church, led by the papal magisterium and lay Catholic thinkers like the stunningly devout and talented couple, Jacques & Raissa Maritain, whose work had a great impact on my conversion and Catholic becoming; and during the same period, a great wave of deep—though foundational shaking—and mystical theology emanated from the Jesuit Father Teilhard de Chardin which so confused the Vatican that the Church restricted his writings.

Then the bottom dropped out for Thomism.

The ascent of Teilhardism has actually been going on for some time, sometimes even when the Catholic theologian is unaware of it.

The encyclical of Pope Francis, *Laudato Si*, is the first papal encyclical I am aware of that mentions the work of Teilhard, as the Holy Father does in n. 53.

The central element in Teilhard's thought, in my understanding of it, is the evolutionary growth, of the entire universe—spiritual and material—towards the ultimate end, the Universal Christ, when the love that defines God, infuses all, and all are conscious of it, all are conscious of being part of everything, yet still singular, still individual.

Within the Church, this spiritual evolution is recorded within the magisterium, primarily that of Peter and the saints, where we see the halting—sometimes two steps backwards for each forward—progress of the Pilgrim Church as she struggles through time and space, struggles with the world and the kingdom of heaven, each joined to one another, each evolving and adding to the consciousness of humans and God, within which we grow to convergence.

This vision first entranced me in prison over 50 years ago, and Teilhard's Catholicism was immaterial against the solidity of his vision; then when I became Catholic, it all came together; and when I studied Aquinas, it came together at an even deeper level, for Aquinas, in his synthesizing of the science of Aristotle with second millennium Catholicism was a necessary prelude to Teilhard and his synthesizing of third millennium Catholicism and evolutionary science.

Aquinas and Teilhard both synthesize faith and science, and in that respect, what appears to be a descent of the former and ascent of the latter is just a continuation, an evolution, an expansion, and a convergence of Catholic consciousness.

Personal Aside #2

I am a Catholic convert baptized into the Church in 2004, am decidedly conservative, preferring the Latin Mass and the Church as seen by St. Thomas Aquinas, Pope John Paul II, Pope Benedict XVI, and Pope Francis; I came into the Church after studying the works of and attending meetings with, Opus Dei; but have a life background that created many of my ideas in the 1960s American ferment.

All this being said, I find myself going against that Catholic tradition in the matter of women as priests and now fully believe they should be.

I have been following the Church pronouncements on this for some time but haven't really thought about it till now and as I read and think and write I am changing.

My heart tells me that women are equal to men in all things that priests do.

The Jesuits

Nowhere does the break between conservative and liberal Catholicism appear more disastrous than when reflecting upon this seminal issue of women in the Church.

Where the conservative popes proclaim women becoming priests an issue not even worth any more discussion, the Jesuits, in their 34th General Congregation, devoted special attention to women as equal partners in collaboration within Jesuit Ministry.

The Jesuit Pope Francis followed the lead of other popes in proclaiming his position regarding women as priests, as not being open to discussion.

And one wonders, how is something that is "not open to discussion" resonating within the world of women who are Catholics and women perhaps thinking of becoming Catholic?

There is no denying that the humble Pope Francis has changed some people's opinions of the Catholic Church for the better, but for many in the Western world, there's still the question of female equality in the Vatican. Namely, why can't women be priests, too, and how is it resonating within the minds of everyone who is Catholic and has thought through the issue—reading the pros and cons—on their own?

Beginning

There are many convoluted theories accounting for woman's oppression throughout history and each of them that I have read have some element of truth to them; but regardless, it is obvious that women, virtually one half of the human family, have been—virtually across the global and historical board—treated as second-class citizens at best and as virtual slaves at worst; even too often, all too often, within first-class societies and including within the two major religions, Catholicism and Islam.

Personal Aside #3

I had largely forgotten the women's movement, what I had learned about it and believed during the Sixties—other than noting the horrors of the oppression of women internationally within the third world; as the status of women in America seemed approaching parity on a steady upward trajectory—it was generally assumed we would soon have a women president.

It is now obvious to me that it is time—it is past time—that the Catholic Church once again open the process of study, prayer and reflection that will surely lead to a dramatic increase of women in Catholic leadership at the highest levels, including ordination as priests.

This is what should have happened—much evidence says did happen—from the beginning days of the Church, and one can only dream of the difference this would have made in the world where the most organized institution in the Western world gave full equality to women; and how would this have impacted the deep historical subjugation of women that even now inflicts too much of the Eastern world.

I reached this conclusion after several months of study and as I continued my studies of women religious in the

Church, the time came to begin examining the opposing views as I have always found it imperative to research the thought leaders on each side of an argument—the devil's advocate—important to me. Since I have already been doing so on the hierarchical Church position for some time—at least in terms of general Church teaching—I ventured to do so on the position of the women religious and accessed several crucial works about the issue

One of the most important organizing events for women's ordination was the Women's Ordination Conference of 1975 in Detroit.

It was there that the current movement towards women's ordination truly took on an organized and focused nature.

Personal Aside #4

As I began reading the Catholic feminist material I realized again, that of all the liberation movements, that of women was the mother of them all; and as I read about the seminal liberation movement in relation to the Catholic Church, from the perspective of women religious, I realized how right they are, more, how right both positions are.

Women have been oppressed within the Church since Genesis and they are right to struggle against it, and the Church is right to struggle to protect Church tradition, but the Church must ultimately bow to reason, the benchmark of truth.

Two seminal women of the West whose secular writing captured my attention in this regard were Mary Parker Follett and Simone de Beauvoir, whose magisterial work, *The Second Sex*, must be read in its unabridged edition, translated by Constance Borde and Sheila Malovany-Chevallier, published by Alfred A, Knopf in 2012.

More about Follett later.

Fr. Teilhard & Joseph Campbell

The connection Teilhard de Chardin made between Catholicism and evolution is obvious almost a century later; that spirit and matter evolve, that they converge, that we are our body and soul.

Free will is the determinative factor. Free will explains the oft appearing herky jerky movement that is actually ascension, and it is so with the women in the Church, who will someday, as Dr. Clarissa Pinkola Estes so eloquently puts it in the title of her book: *Untie the Strong Woman*, become true partners on earth, physically and spiritually.

We are part of the convergence of Joseph Campbell's mythicness and Teilhard's mysticism.

We can see a convergence of the Wise Woman and the Holy Father and when we do see that convergence, our children will rejoice.

What Campbell called myth, is, for us, religious truth, the highest truth; but in his search for meaning and the journey to truth, he sparked deep conversations among non-religious about the truth of myth, for in the great stories from the mythical traditions of the world, lay clear truths, universal truths, that have been gathered and embroidered into a wondrous tapestry under the rubrics Christ gave us.

Before Christ, the Jews were the Church and after Christ the Catholics were the Church; yet both are and will forever remain, the People of God.

Personal Aside #5

What is becoming clear to me after all the research is that the patterns of thought and action within the Leadership Conference of Women Religious (LCWR) reflects decades of practice within many of the communities of women religious that is based on a feminism that is itself based on years of feminist scholar's research that leads to conclusions which will probably not be changed at a personal level, conclusions which are deeply embedded.

In every paradigm change I have experienced, there has often been an intellectual hinge, an idea that answers the chaos of the past, creating a future unity.

In my conversion to Catholicism it was the scripture from Matthew:

> **[Matthew 16:18]:** And I tell thee this in my turn, that thou art Peter, and it is upon this rock that I will build my church; and the gates of hell shall not prevail against it;

In my coming to believe in the rightness of women priests, it was the response to: "Christ only selected men as apostles", yes, but he also only selected Jews.

Papal Perspectives

The discussion around women's ordination has been intense and even more so in the year of the 20th annual anniversary of one of the seminal papal documents, the Apostolic Letter, *Ordinatio Sacerdotalis*, On Reserving Priestly Ordination to Men Alone, by Pope John Paul II (1994).

With all due respect to John Paul II whose writings and papacy played a major role in my conversion, the reason exhibited in this Apostolic Letter is very weak: that Christ only chose men and the Church has maintained that tradition and the consistency of that teaching authority.

This is actually only one reason, Christ chose only men, with the other two merely practice of the first.

Yes, Christ only selected men to be apostles; and the response from women religious, yes, but he also only selected Jews, and no one is saying that only Jews can become priests.

Sometimes the most elaborate edifice falls from the weakness of one rock; and sometimes an eternal cathedral is built upon the strength of one rock.

Patriarchy in the Catholic Church is so accepted that Pope Francis recently accused Eve of dialoguing with the devil rather than choosing to follow the word of God, but, when we read the Bible about this episode:

> **[Genesis 3:1]**: Of all the beasts which the Lord God had made, there was none that could match the serpent in cunning. It was he who said to the woman, What is this command God has given you, not to eat the fruit of any tree in the garden? **[2]** To which the woman answered, We can eat the fruit of any tree in the garden **[3]** except the tree in the middle of it; it is this God has forbidden us to eat or even to touch, on pain of death. **[4]** And the serpent said to her, What is this talk of death? **[5]** God knows well that as soon as you eat this fruit your eyes will be opened, and you yourselves will be like gods, knowing good and evil.

We see that Eve did not dialogue with the devil but repeated the instruction the Lord gave her; but Satan lied to her and told her she would not die, and she believed him, which caused her moment of weakness, leading to the Original Sin, humans acting from their free will.

The concept that Eve—women—are weak and more subject to sin than men is so normative within the Church, even simple daily comments reinforce it, incorrectly as in this case.

Spiritual Evolution

Some of the foundational ideas of the women religious seem to be connected to the work of Teilhard de Chardin S. J. (work which stresses the evolutionary nature of matter and spirit) and with his ideas being more accepted by the Church in recent years—he was prohibited from publishing while he was alive—it gives some concreteness, especially in the minds of women religious, to their own ideas.

While examining the ideas and strategies of the dissenting women religious—and we use the word dissenting advisedly as there can be found scriptural validation of their position, especially in:

> **[Galatians 3:27]** All you who have been baptized in Christ's name have put on the person of Christ; **[28]** no more Jew or Gentile, no more slave and freeman, no more male and female; you are all one person in Jesus Christ.

We definitely have to take into account the absolutely vile history of humankind in its treatment of women, still being practiced in all too many countries; and in the development of feminist theology within the Catholic Church and without, we have to give it the same level of personhood's determinative final value (very little) as we do to the corrupted social/familial structures within which many criminals grew up, blaming that on why they became criminals.

That structural brutality and oppression of women was, and is, still true, is horrific and tragic; but once adulthood is reached and it becomes time to put away childish things, even the bad ones, we all, through dedicated prayer and studying of the essential earthly goodness and divine birth of our Church, can learn that our true human nature is to know and love God and that knowing and that loving is most completely discovered through the sacramental life of the Roman Catholic Church.

Everything sound the Church teaches stands on reason which even the laity understand, but when they no longer understand, it is no longer believed, and for decades now, many Catholics have accepted women as having the standing to become priests; and had women been priests, there would very possibly not have been a world-wide scandal of sexually abused children.

This issue is one sapping the passion of the Church; the unwillingness to acknowledge the reasonableness and rightness of women priests as the kind of change that will rekindle the eternal fire of the pilgrim Church and restrengthen the barque of Peter.

Mea culpas are demanded, yes, but penance is healthy, as healthy for the Church as for its members.

As the Holy Father has sought forgiveness from the Jews so should he seek it from women and it will be given in a mighty wave washing though Holy Mother Church with Pentecostal power.

More Papal Perspectives

The mantra of the three popes, John Paul, Benedict and Francis, has been that the issue is one not even open to discussion anymore; though from *Women in Canon Law* in 1975 by the Canon Law Society of America, through *Decree on the Attempted Priestly Ordination of Some Catholic Women* in 2002 by the Congregation for the Doctrine of the Faith, and the 26 other documents from either the Vatican, the U.S. Bishop's Conference, Catholic Orders like the Jesuits, or Catholic Theological Societies, it has been discussed continuously; summaries of which are included in the magisterial book by Halter (2004), *The Papal No: A Comprehensive Guide to the Vatican's Rejection of Women's Ordination*.

One gets the distinct impression that what the popes are really saying is that they *do not wish* to discuss this issue any longer, as the longer it is discussed the more feeble the reasoning for denying women the priesthood becomes:

- Christ called only men, but he also called only Jews
- Christ incarnated as a man, but how else would he incarnate as in first century Israel women barely existed in any legal sense and surely even less in a religious sense.
- Women are inferior, an idiocy made even more idiotic in the 20th century and beyond.
- Christ as groom of the Church as bride, a theological argument hardly relevant, ever, in the context that Christ is Almighty God, creator of all things, neither man nor woman, both man and woman.
- It is tradition, but supporting slavery was also a Church tradition for millennia, but as social conditions changed, it changed.

Sexual Abuse in the Church

We have to wonder how much the news of the purported homosexual lobby within the Vatican plays in the lack of willingness to continue the discussion of women as priests.

To obtain more depth on this subject, accessing two magisterial works on it: *The Rite of Sodomy: Homosexuality and the Roman Catholic Church* by Randy Engel, and *Sacrilege: Sexual Abuse in the Catholic Church* by Leon J. Podles, both devout Catholics, provides that.

Reading these books is a horrifying walk in the sewer—especially painful for Catholics—but a vital walk to understand what has happened in the Church, not only in the present, but for centuries, which Engels book covers, while Podles book focuses on the modern scandal in the United States.

Mary Parker Follett

Isn't the noosphere—the concept Teilhard de Chardin learned from Russian scientist Vladimir Ivanovich Vernadsky and Christianized—the global vision of Mary Parker Follett's dream of group evolution, where every blogger, internet commenter and twitter tweeter contributes to the electronic internet group shaping our new reality.

One of the characteristics of the recent struggle between the women religious of the Leadership Conference of Women Religious (LCWR) and the Vatican, is that it is a classic case of group negotiating as studied by Mary Parker Follett who felt human definitions, human's highest selfhood, came from working within a group, not alone as individuals.

Both groups—the LCWR and the Vatican—operate from a group formed psychology, but only that of the women moves and grows as Follett had hoped, while the Vatican, the papacy and attendant cardinals/bishops move in lockstep according to a matrix established—as it claims—at the beginnings of the Church, yet words, ideas and events also established at the beginnings of the Church counteract the locksteps, taking the ground from beneath their feet, the most powerful being:

> **[Galatians 3:25]**: When faith comes, then we are no longer under the rule of a tutor; **[26]** through faith in Christ Jesus you are all now God's sons. **[27]**All you who have been baptized in Christ's name have put on the person of Christ; **[28]** no more Jew or Gentile, no more slave and freeman, no more male and female; you are all one person in Jesus Christ. **[29]** And if you belong to Christ, then you are indeed Abraham's children; the promised inheritance is yours.

This is such a clarion call.

The saddest result of Follett's exclusion because she was a women, from the canon of management thinkers during her life and after was the loss of her vision added to the body of work—virtually all by men—taught in the academy.

What she specialized in was retaining the emotional content of individual lives in the rather dry and objectified writings of male management theorists; but it was not to be until decades later, when men—most of who were influenced by her writings—began introducing the personalist perspective.

Follett also pioneered the concept of power-with rather than power-over.

This is the model of the archetypical loss of women's collaborative leadership the Catholic Church has been suffering from for 2,000 years, but over the past few decades Catholic feminist theologians have been challenging and changing it.

Fr. Teilhard

In my opinion, because of the depth and breadth of Fr. Teilhard's theological speculations, it will be some time before the Church properly understands him and gives him his earned position in her universe of Doctors of the Church; but as much as St. Thomas Aquinas' thought determined the medieval Church, and guides her still; Fr. Teilhard's thought will shape and guide her in the future; but it could be a century or so before he is finally and deeply appreciated.

Pope Emeritus Benedict XVI understood Teilhard's immense value to Catholic theological thinking today, commenting on Johannine theology about Christ drawing all things to himself:

> **[John 12:30]** Jesus answered, It was for your sake, not for mine, that this utterance was made.

441

[31] Sentence is now being passed on this world; now is the time when the prince of this world is to be cast out. **[32]** Yes, if only I am lifted up from the earth, I will attract all men to myself. **[33]** (In saying this, he prophesied the death he was to die.)

Fr. Pierre Teilhard de Chardin, S.J. was one of the most extraordinary Catholic thinkers of the modern age; but, he was also a man of action as indicated by the list of citations from his war service as a medical orderly in World War I, one of which was the highest medal awarded by France, the National Order of the Legion of Honour in May of 1921.

In addition to the luminosity of his theological writings and his war record, he was also an eminent scientist.

If the Catholic Church is the Universal Church—though how can it be while subjugating women—how can unbelievers ever believe and believers continue to believe.

As the Church embraced the Mother Goddess of Mesoamerica, so the Church embraced pagan gods and their modern expressions: Freud/Jungian psychoanalysis, but all too often the Church has lost the passion of those they embraced.

The Catholic Church, so long the center of education, has become the center of rules; so long the center of scientific creativity, has become stale; so long a center of ministry, has become the home of clericalism.

All of these are natural human tendencies, to regulate, to stagnate, to negate.

Fr. Teilhard shows us a different vision of evolutive learning on a Thomist foundation, embracing science and reason through the synthesis of spirit and matter.

God created all, but God's crowning creation is human beings—men and women—who, through their growth and evolution grow and evolve God.

The idea that God is within all, all matter and all spirit, is not a new idea.

Criminal Reformation

I for one, have reached the conclusion that women should be priests and the continued closed-to-discussion stance of the popes seems to render much of what they are saying about other issues of Catholicism, much less important; and here is where we must come to a realization that, as important as it is to follow Peter, we must differentiate between Peter as he often acts in concert with the world's wishes and those of the club of priests, and Peter as he should act as the Vicar of Christ—welcoming all, causing no discrimination, except that based on sin, and even the priests cannot, in intellectual fairness, claim that women, by their very nature, are in sin, but that is what the current status of women in relation to not being allowed to become priests does in fact seem to proclaim.

How important is this to criminal reformation among ministry to Catholics who are criminals in prison or outside of prison?

Very important, because in the outside world, in the United States, women are generally acknowledged as equal to men in all things, even now it is being easily considered that a woman will soon become president.

With this reality in the world and with the reality that in the professional criminal world, women have held roughly equal stature for many years, seeing how women in the Catholic Church are not permitted to do what the men can, and seeing that the reasons given are logically weak, well, that will just not do, that will create a problem, with other professional criminals as it has with me; and whether it is ten or so years after baptism, as it has been with me, the impact will be the same; a weakening of faith in the authority of the institutional Church.

An important point concerns the times and social circumstances in which certain practices originated versus the times and social circumstances in which they are challenged.

With the criminal/carceral world there are many who are quite conscious of the meaning of sociobiological conditions determining theological principles.

I've mentioned it before, but it can't be said enough; the theologians who support women's ordination have been making excellent arguments—better than those of the Vatican—for decades now.

Concerning the current sociological conditions, Pew Research Center (2013, March 13-17) recently polled Catholics and 59% want women to become priests.

Criminal reformation includes understanding the personhood of women in opposition to the lust-drunk siren song of male fantasy, magnified within the criminal/carceral world to dangerous and outlandish levels; though tempered by the normative association within the criminal life with entrepreneurial women in the thievery, sex work, drug sales, and other activities of the professional criminal.

The woman saint that professional criminals most relate to is certainly St. Mary Magdalene, for, according to the ancient tradition in the Church, she too was a professional criminal, and she too was loved by Christ, who chose her to witness his resurrection before all others and, as 'apostle to the apostles' then take that history shattering—nothing would ever again be the same—news to the twelve.

Within Teilhard's expansion of Johannine theology of the drawing "of all men to myself" **[John 12:32]** lies the root of why only the reformed criminal can reform criminals; and, of course, even better, those few and so rare Catholics who possess a deep and saintly Christological interiority.

St. Catherine of Siena

St. Catherine lived a youthful life opposite that of Magdalene—whose youth was one of debauchery—rather Catherine spent hers in prayer and service.

It is difficult to imagine a life like hers today, when the distractions of our technological age, especially for the young, fill our days, generally excluding such rarefied spiritual events as Catherine experienced.

It is so appropriate that Catherine grew within the embrace of the Dominicans (another Doctor of the Church, St. Thomas Aquinas, was a Dominican) becoming a member of the Third Order of the Dominicans, the Sisters of Penance of St. Dominic, through her own exhortation.

Aquinas, the Angelic Doctor, and also an Italian Dominican, died March 7, 1274, seventy three years before she was born, March 25, 1347, and twenty four years before she was born, in 1323, Thomas was declared a saint.

These were very important times for the Church and few women, nor men for that matter, played a role as important as Catherine.

Concluding Thoughts

For many years after baptism I was scornful of cafeteria Catholics who picked the doctrines they chose to believe and ignored the rest; however, beginning with my study of the Church's dealing with capital punishment—where 2,000 years of teaching support its use, but recent popes and virtually all bishops now support calls for its abolition—I realized that a properly formed conscience, based on an in-depth study of Church history and teaching, can justify the cafeteria approach.

This became validated once I began studying the issue of women's ordination where the reasons given for it not being allowed were theologically weak and rationally unsound—so much so that the Holy Father now claimed it was not even open to discussion anymore; this after preceding popes and Curia organizations had discussed it at length.

And here is where the concept of the People of God comes into play. Before Christ there was Judaism, the religion of God's Chosen People. After Christ came Catholicism and just as the Pharisees corrupted Judaism, so has the Vatican corrupted Catholicism; yet one appellation remains constant—the People of God, Jews and Catholics.

The tabernacle, the sanctuary, the synagogue, is in the humble heart of the people, who do not say, follow me for I know the truth; but they pray to God to help them live a life of truth, a life they know is governed by the Great Law: 'Love God and Neighbor'.

There are two covenants within Judaism/Catholicism; the Old and the New. The Old is Judaism, the new is Catholicism, but they are two sides of the same coin, we are brothers and sisters in faith. We are God's Chosen People, we are the People of God.

Israel is the home of our faith; Rome is the center of governance.

Liberal/Conservative, Traditional/Cafeteria, these are handy labels, but they only have meaning in relation to our stand on issues. If we follow our conscience regarding Catholic practice, our conscience must be informed, we must study, pray, reflect and reach conclusions only after we have done the work; accepting that in the future, we may learn more and change our conclusions.

I think it was Walt Whitman who said regarding this, "I embrace my contradictions", or something to that effect, but whatever, so true.

Underlying any discussion about women in the priesthood or the broad acceptance of spiritual/material evolutionary theory as put forward by Teilhard de Chardin, is the resistance of large institutions, like the Roman Catholic Church, to change.

This is the quandary the institutional Church finds itself in regarding women's ordination, feeling the institutional Church must be protected is proving much more disastrous to the Church than admitting mistakes; and not only with this issue, but also, as we have seen, with the issue of sexual abuse of children by priests and bishops.

There are now women—including religious—in the Church whose major reason for staying in the Church is to struggle against the Church as a machine, to change it from within; and their number will change dramatically once women are priests and join the true ordained leadership of Holy Mother Church.

There are a group of liberal Catholic theologians and writers who have connected themselves to the work of Fr. Teilhard, claiming to be his inheritors, but it is an inherited connection only having validity with folks unfamiliar with Teilhard or willfully misreading him; for this group of theologians and writers are essentially writing about a New Age vision of the future with specific warnings about protecting the ecology from the evil capitalists, a political reading Teilhard did not appear to even consider.

These liberal theologians and writers speak from the perspective that human beings are merely a part of creation while Teilhard, reflecting his Catholic beliefs, knows humans are the pinnacle of creation, the virtual, evolving mind of Christ as he draws all to him, the human mind and experiences—co-creating with God—form the primary ingredient of the future of humans.

These liberal theologian and writers, tend to see human beings as a cancer upon the earth; they are deep ecologists, generally Gaia adherents, intellectual primitives, who believe that all of the technological work humans do to use earth's resources to make human life safer, longer, more productive, and more comfortable, is a rape of the earth, rather than what it truly is, the right use of the gifts of creation.

To Teilhard, God was the Cosmic Christ who, having risen draws everything to him, rooted in the Apostle Paul's theology. To those for whom God is Gaia—rooted in primitive earth/animal worship, coming from pre-Christian, pagan visions; their thought, whether they know it or not, is ultimately Satanic.

While it is easy to see how this New Age perspective can be conflated with the work of Fr. Teilhard, the conflation is a result of laziness and a lack of deep study of Teilhard.

However, a call from some Catholic women theologians to develop a "Magdalene function" within ecclesiology is crucial if the Church is to move further.

We desperately need more work on this and fortunately, now, there are a great many Catholic women theologians working on issues related to women in the Church and as they mature and deepen in the theological studies men have been toiling in for hundreds of years, we, and the Church, will benefit from their work.

We all need—in partnership with these theologians—to ask the Catholic Church to release women from 2,000 years of clerical bondage, seek forgiveness from them 70 times 7 times, and welcome them, finally, into the work God intends for them, as priests, bishops, and popes, in partnership with men in the saving of souls and building the eternal cathedral of the Church in the world and in heaven.

The Church must embrace its full moral power by ordaining women—power-with the Russian Orthodox as it struggles to emerge from domination by Communism—as the great re-unification becomes possible, for Russia is crucial, as Fatima taught us.

Perhaps, as Catherine of Siena so long ago brought the pope back from France to Rome, it will be a woman priest, bishop, or pope, who will lead the joining of the two great lungs of the Church, Russia and Rome, together again.

And now, after the fall of the USSR, Russia rises again—grasping Ukraine once more to its bosom, and we see the formation of the first Orthodox Council in over a thousand years being discussed.

Should, could, this Council lead to unity? What a glorious day that would be.

What we are now part of, through the noosphere, the power of the Mystical Church, and the opening wide the anciently narrow Catholic Gate, is conscious evolution, which because God began it has always been conscious, but now human beings are part of it.

Here again, the Apostles' Creed (each of the 12 apostles was believed to have contributed a line):

1. I believe in God the Father almighty, creator of heaven and earth.
2. I believe in Jesus Christ, his only Son, our Lord.
3. He was conceived by the power of the Holy Spirit and born of the Virgin Mary.
4. He suffered under Pontius Pilate, was crucified, died, and was buried.
5. He descended into hell. On the third day he rose again.

6. He ascended into heaven and is seated at the right hand of the Father.
7. He will come again to judge the living and the dead.
8. I believe in the Holy Spirit,
9. the holy catholic Church, the communion of saints,
10. the forgiveness of sins,
11. the resurrection of the body,
12. and the life everlasting.
Amen.

Christ says:

> **[John 12:31]** Sentence is now being passed on this world; now is the time when the prince of this world is to be cast out. **[32]** Yes, if only I am lifted up from the earth, I will attract all men to myself. **[33]** (In saying this, he prophesied the death he was to die.)

Teilhard's concept of evolution in Christ is built upon this, for if evolution is true, and Teilhard, as a scientist, knew that it is; and if Christ is true, and Teilhard as a Jesuit and son of the Church, knew that he is, then Christ is at the center of and animating evolution.

Teilhard's call to bring into alignment science and faith was part of the impetus for Vatican II, and much good has come from that council, but there are still central aspects that have not, and the status of women in the Church still reeks of centuries-old ideas which have indeed, caused the Church to lose something quite valuable.

After years as Catholic, years of constant study of the theology and practice of the Church, the theology stands radiant and sure, but the practice suffers from contradiction, unreasonableness, and even, I am sad to say, harmfulness.

For the first eight or so years of being Catholic, my study remained in orthodox fields, but once practice cracks opened up allowing a more subtle light to enter, I ventured into the writings of the unorthodox and even those sanctioned by the Church, writing from the perspective of the woman's ordination movement.

I studied scriptures, not only the canonical, but the non-canonical and the gnostic.

The world thus opened up to me posed no threat to the essential theology of the Church represented by her ancient Apostle's Creed, which still, and always will, hold my heart within its bond.

Yes, as we have seen from the sexual abuse scandal, evidence tragically points to a Catholic Church supporting a culture of pederasty, from the Vatican to the parish; a Catholic Church deeply misogynistic; a Catholic Church deeply conflicted about its past and future.

Yes, the Catholic Church on earth has been and is now, corrupted by the works of men; but her supernatural, eternal reality: the communion of saints, the deep holiness of so many of her popes—Pius XII stands so clear to me as an example within memory of what is great and holy about Peter—is not corrupted nor can it ever be; and yet, the earthly, corrupted, and pilgrim Catholic Church, is still the widest and most illuminated of the many narrow gates to heaven.

Chapter 10: The Lampstand

Foundation

The Lampstand Foundation is a 501 c (3) nonprofit corporation I founded in Sacramento, California in 2003 as a lay apostolate built on the social teaching of the Catholic Church, to provide leadership development tools for community & prison apostolates, managed by reformed criminals working to reform criminals.

Vision, Mission, Beliefs, Goals

Our Vision

Inspiring criminals who have transformed their lives, secured college degrees, and returned home to Rome; to show others the transformative path, and how the pain of suffering can become the power of teaching.

Our Mission

To transform the repentant criminal, suffering from his distance from God, into a deep knowledge leader who can teach other criminals the path to redemption through the Catholic Church.

Our Core Beliefs

Suffering transformed builds souls. Just as the muscle tissue tearing that leads to greater physical muscle growth resulting from body building, suffering is soul tearing which, through redemption, allows soul growth.

1) Deep knowledge leadership: college-educated, transformed criminals professionally trained to manage

criminal transformative organizations; will dramatically improve the effectiveness of criminal transformation.

2) Catholic social thought forms the intellectual and spiritual foundation of criminal transformation.

3) Grassroots criminal transformation organizations need ongoing access to capacity building services.

4) Business and professional leadership, working to create community social capital through the transformation of criminals, will benefit from gaining knowledge about Catholic social thought.

Our Goals

We want to facilitate the leadership development of penitential criminals whose personal transformation, education, and reconciliation or conversion to Catholicism has inspired them to seek graduate degrees, professional organizational training, social teaching training, and assume a leadership role in the community helping other criminals transform their lives.

1) To inspire educated and transformed criminals who are baptized Catholics and want to help others, gain a graduate college education and professional training.

2) To provide capacity building tools to criminal transforming organizations about Catholic social teaching, start-up planning, strategic planning, fund development, board development, communications & marketing, and for profit business development.
3) To educate the business and professional community about the leadership capability of educated, transformed criminals and the use of Catholic social teaching as a transformative tool.

Our Apostolate Principles

1) We will defend innocent human life in all that we do.

"**80.** Reason attests that there are objects of the human act which are by their nature "incapable of being ordered" to God, because they radically contradict the good of the person made in his image. These are the acts which, in the Church's moral tradition, have been termed "intrinsically evil" (*intrinsece malum*): they are such *always and per se,* in other words, on account of their very object, and quite apart from the ulterior intentions of the one acting and the circumstances. Consequently, without in the least denying the influence on morality exercised by circumstances and especially by intentions, the Church teaches that "there exist acts which *per se* and in themselves, independently of circumstances, are always seriously wrong by reason of their object". The Second Vatican Council itself, in discussing the respect due to the human person, gives a number of examples of such acts. "Whatever is opposed to life itself, such as any type of murder, genocide, abortion, euthanasia, or wilful self-destruction, whatever violates the integrity of the human person, such as mutilation, torments inflicted on body or mind, attempts to coerce the will itself; whatever insults human dignity, such as subhuman living conditions, arbitrary imprisonment, deportation, slavery, prostitution, the selling of women and children; as well as disgraceful working conditions, where people are treated as mere instruments of gain rather than as free and responsible persons; all these things and others like them are infamies indeed. They poison human society, and they do more harm to those who practise them than to those who suffer from the injury. Moreover, they are a supreme dishonour to the Creator." (Pope John Paul II, 1993,*Veritatis Splendor* #80)

2) We will work for social justice in all that we do.

"**1928.** Society ensures social justice when it provides the conditions that allow associations or individuals to obtain what is their due, according to their nature and their vocation. Social justice is linked to the common good and the exercise of authority.

"**1929.** Social justice can be obtained only in respecting the transcendent dignity of man. The person represents the ultimate end of society, which is ordered to him:

"What is at stake is the dignity of the human person, whose defense and promotion have been entrusted to us by the Creator, and to whom the men and women at every moment of history are strictly and responsibly in debt.

"**1930.** Respect for the human person entails respect for the rights that flow from his dignity as a creature. These rights are prior to society and must be recognized by it. They are the basis of the moral legitimacy of every authority: by flouting them, or refusing to recognize them in its positive legislation, a society undermines its own moral legitimacy. If it does not respect them, authority can rely only on force or violence to obtain obedience from its subjects. It is the Church's role to remind men of good will of these rights and to distinguish them from unwarranted or false claims." (*Catechism of the Catholic Church*, #1928-1930)

3) We know that our work is with, and through, the community.

"In our time, *the role of human work* is becoming increasingly important as the productive factor both of non-material and of material wealth. Moreover, it is becoming clearer how a person's work is naturally interrelated with the work of others. More than ever, *work is work with others* and *work for others*: it is a matter of doing something for someone else." (Pope John Paul II, 1991, *Centesimus Annus*, #31)

456

4) We know that Catholic social thought is a transformative social force.

"2419   "Christian   revelation...promotes   deeper understanding of the laws of social living." The Church receives from the Gospel the full revelation of the truth about man. When she fulfills her mission of proclaiming the Gospel, she bears witness to man, in the name of Christ, to his dignity and his vocation to the communion of persons. She teaches him the demands of justice and peace in conformity with divine wisdom.

"2420 The Church makes a moral judgment about economic and social matters, "when the fundamental rights of the person or the salvation of souls requires it." In the moral order she bears a mission distinct from that of political authorities: The Church is concerned with the temporal aspects of the common good because they are ordered to the sovereign Good, our ultimate end. She strives to inspire right attitudes with respect to earthly goods and in socio-economic relationships.

"2421 The social doctrine of the Church developed in the nineteenth century when the Gospel encountered modern industrial society with its new structures for the production of consumer goods, its new concept of society, the state and authority, and its new forms of labor and ownership. The development of the doctrine of the Church on economic and social matters attests the permanent value of the Church's teaching at the same time as it attests the true meaning of her Tradition, always living and active.

"2422 The Church's social teaching comprises a body of doctrine, which is articulated as the Church interprets events in the course of history, with the assistance of the Holy Spirit, in the light of the whole of what has been revealed by Jesus Christ. This teaching can be more easily accepted by men of good will, the more the faithful let themselves be guided by it." (*Catechism of the Catholic Church* 2419-2422)

5) We know that corporal works of mercy are essential to comfort the suffering, and that spiritual works of mercy are essential to stop the suffering.

"**2447** The *works of mercy* are charitable actions by which we come to the aid of our neighbor in his spiritual and bodily necessities. Instructing, advising, consoling, comforting are spiritual works of mercy, as are forgiving and bearing wrongs patiently. The corporal works of mercy consist especially in feeding the hungry, sheltering the homeless, clothing the naked, visiting the sick and imprisoned, and burying the dead. Among all these, giving alms to the poor is one of the chief witnesses to fraternal charity: it is also a work of justice pleasing to God:

> He who has two coats, let him share with him who has none and he who has food must do likewise. But give for alms those things which are within; and behold, everything is clean for you. If a brother or sister is ill-clad and in lack of daily food, and one of you says to them, "Go in peace, be warmed and filled," without giving them the things needed for the body, what does it profit? (*Catechism of the Catholic Church* 24)

Our Criminal Justice Principles

1) *Broken windows policing works.* Allowing even the minor violation of a broken window in an area helps create the impression of an environment where law and order does not prevail and where crime flourishes. Responding quickly and efficiently to all crimes, regardless of the perceived state of seriousness or other local community concerns, is the foundation of good police work.

458

2) *The response to crime should be timely, balanced, and just.* When justice is for sale, either through wealth, influence, or ideology, a fertile soil is created from which crime grows. The training and education of professionals in the criminal justice system is built on a foundation of traditional and well-reasoned concepts of justice and it needs continual reinforcement to remain an effective response to crime.

3) *Prison is an appropriate criminal sanction to protect society and punish the criminal, while allowing the opportunity for criminal reformation.* Prison is an effective sanction for crime which has been used by human beings since ancient times. It serves to protect the public from predatory crime, acts as a deterrence and as incapacitation, and allows the penitential criminal the opportunity—while removed from the community—to reflect upon and correct his criminal behavior.

4) *Capital punishment is an appropriate response to the criminal evil of murder, rape, and pedophilia.* Capital punishment is often the only effective social method available to protect the innocent and applied with dispatch after legal review of the crimes charged and determining the fitness of its application, should be considered an appropriate sentence for murderers, rapists and pedophiles; who, knowing the time of their death, are able, with certainty of their remaining time to do so, seek God's forgiveness. Lane (2010) notes: "During the decade beginning in 1997, five states enacted the death penalty for rape of a child--though the Supreme Court struck those laws down in 2008." Lane, C. (2010). *Stay of execution: Saving the death penalty from itself.* New York: Rowman & Littlefield Publishers. (p. 66)

5) *Repentant criminals deserve a second chance.* Excepting those cases of serious predatory behavior deserving the death penalty or natural life in prison, repentant criminals, once they have clearly shown—over a ten year period after being released from criminal justice supervision—that they have transformed their life by becoming a productive member of their family, their church, their work, and their community, should be allowed to apply for a complete pardon in a simple straightforward process.

6) *It takes a reformed criminal to reform criminals.* For generations the ability of non-criminals—even those with the highest professional and academic credentials—to effectively rehabilitate criminals has proven, based on sound evaluations, to be virtually non-existent. Recruiting reformed criminals who have, through education, training, and the development of a deep knowledge leadership approach to criminal transformation, may well succeed where others have failed. Considering the current recidivism rate of 70-80%, and with the consensus that peer-based help does, at the very least, attract those who want help to transformative programs, it is time to try this approach in a substantial enough way, over time and properly evaluated, to discover if we can rely on it as a valuable tool for large-scale implementation.

7) *In the work of criminal reformation, it is vital to keep in mind that the criminal—not society, capitalism, or the criminal justice system—is the problem.* Some criminal justice advocates take the position that among the people connected with the carceral world, the good guys are the criminals and the police, district attorneys, prison guards, and the legislators who support stringent criminal sanctions, are the bad guys.

This is the absolutely wrong position, for in virtually any carceral population in America it is the criminals who are the indisputable bad guys, while the good guys are the ones protecting the public from the depredations of criminals. Those who parlay the myths of Hollywood or Marxism into an intellectual stance that fails to understand this basic fact, does everyone a disservice—in particular the penitential criminal—who may find little reason for proper expiation within a culture defining criminality as somehow admirable.

Program & Publications

Our Program

Lampstand's direct teaching work is supplemented by a monthly e-letter, quarterly newsletter, nine policy primer research reports, eleven (including this one) books from Chulu Press, a Lampstand imprint, Articles, and periodic monographs.

Our Publications

Books

(Book One) *The Criminal's Search for God: Criminal Transformation, Catholic Social Teaching, Deep Knowledge Leadership, and Communal Reentry*, **by David H. Lukenbill (2006)** This book is about a criminal life, personal transformation through education and deep spiritual work, the principles of Catholic social teaching, and the type of leadership needed to develop and manage effective criminal transformation programs. **Paperback & E-Book, Free to members, or the paperback can be ordered through Amazon.**

(Book Two) *Carceral World, Communal City*, **by David H. Lukenbill (2007)** "The criminal world in the United States, with the carceral shaping of it, has become a coherent entity and within that entity it is the criminal world leadership to whom we must look for transformative leadership who have already transformed the pain of their suffering into the power of teaching others." (p. 8). **Paperback & E-Book, Free to**

members, or the paperback can be ordered through Amazon.

(Book Three) *The Criminal, The Cross & The Church: The Interior Journey*, by David H. Lukenbill (2008) "The penitential criminal working to reform other criminals, wisely spends the rest of his life atoning for the harm he has done during his criminal life; not because the world requires it, but because the eternal balance requires it, his immortal soul requires it, and God wishes it." (Frontpiece) **Paperback & E-Book, Free to members, or the paperback can be ordered through Amazon.**

(Book Four) *Capital Punishment & Catholic Social Teaching: A Tradition of Support*, by David H. Lukenbill (2009) "This book is a defense of the scriptural and traditional Catholic position of support for capital punishment as expressed in the two universal catechisms, the *Catechism of the Council of Trent*, published by Pope Pius V in 1566, and the *Catechism of the Catholic Church*, published by Pope John Paul II in 1992 & 1997 (First and Second Edition), in response to calls for its abolition." (p. 9) **Paperback or E-Book is free to members, or the paperback can be ordered through Amazon.**

(Book Five) *Invictus: The Way of the Apostolate*, by David H. Lukenbill (2010) "This book is for penitential professional criminals whose involvement in the criminal/carceral world is of long duration and commitment. Professional criminals commit crimes for money and live by the ancient criminal way that precludes betrayal of partners or hurting women and children. To professional criminals, crime is their profession and way of life. To those professional criminals who are very good—and lucky—at what they do and never get caught, my work will have little value. It is for those professional criminals who do get caught and

462

serve time in prison, comprising approximately 70 – 80% of the prison population; and who, at some point, may enter a penitential state." (pp. 11-12) **Paperback or E-Book is free to members, or the paperback can be ordered through Amazon.**

(Book Six) *The Lampstand Prison Ministry: Constructed On Catholic Social Teaching & the History of the Catholic Church,* **by David H. Lukenbill (2011)** "The foundational ideas animating the Lampstand prison ministry—that it takes a reformed criminal to reform criminals and that the conversion approach must be intellectual—are ideas I have been working with since the beginning of my reformation from criminality at age thirty five, as I began seeing the world from the perspective of a college education (leading to a successful criminal rehabilitative college-based educational program I developed and managed) and continuing to the final washing from my spirit the last remnants of a lifetime of criminal thinking twenty years later, in the waters of baptism. The peer relationship is where the impact this apostolate may have on future criminal activity lies, and it will be seen most dramatically within the Lampstand prison ministry where the apostolate work will *only* be optimized by conversions of the criminal/carceral elite— the professional criminal—whose history within rehabilitative work is virtually nil, because for him, the rewards of deep immersion within the criminal/carceral culture are too great, and other than as a ruse, rehabilitation is considered a tragic fool's errand." (p. 11) **Paperback or E-Book is free to members, or the paperback can be ordered through Amazon.**

(Book Seven) *The Criminal's Search for God: Sources,* **by David H. Lukenbill (2012)** "This book is a reflection on the collection of ideas within a group of books—sources—that played such a large role in the development of my thinking; initially to deepen my criminality, but eventually becoming the soil from which my transformation and conversion to Catholicism grew.

Most of my exploration of the ideas in these books occurred in prison or shortly after release and as such, they were works from which I drew ideas that largely supported and expanded the underlying narrative of the criminal/carceral world within which I lived, and are largely congruent with its driving ethos. When I was in prison I read whatever books were available in the prison library or those I could get mailed in with my very limited budget. (p. 9) **Paperback or E-Book is free to members, or the paperback can be ordered through Amazon.**

(Book Eight) *Catholicism, Communism & Criminal Reformation,* **by David H. Lukenbill (2013)** "What is important—in the context of our apostolate work through The Lampstand Foundation—is not the theory of Communism, "to each according to need", which many may support; but the influence on criminals from the system of government and its practice under Lenin and Stalin in Russia, Mao in China, and the lessor monsters of our world; practice continuing largely unchanged today except as modified within the constrictions created by the ability of global communications about governmental atrocities making it much more difficult to keep such atrocities hidden now than during the last century; and a governing practice diametrically opposed to the sacred doctrine of the Catholic Church, who Communism sees as its most dangerous enemy." (p. 13) **Paperback or E-Book is free to members, or the paperback can be ordered through Amazon.**

(Book Nine) *The Lampstand Foundation: It Takes a Reformed Criminal to Reform Criminals,* **by David H. Lukenbill (2014)** "This book is a compilation of the organizational elements of Lampstand; including: Vision, Mission, Beliefs, Goals, Apostolate Principles, Criminal Justice Principles, Program and Publications, Published Articles about Lampstand, and Published Articles by Lampstand. **Paperback or E-Book is free to**

members, or the paperback can be ordered through Amazon.

(Book Ten) *Women in the Church: St. Catherine of Siena, Fr. Teilhard de Chardin & Criminal Reformation,* by David H. Lukenbill (2014) "The Church stands in the world as a sign of contradiction and as the world since time immemorial excluded women from full personhood; the Church *must* ensure that within her embrace, woman's full personhood is deeply rooted and complete; which can only be accomplished by priestly ordination and full equality with men in the leadership of the Church on earth as that equality is certainly so in Heaven.

"I have come to believe, fully and completely, that the institutional Church has been wrong in not ordaining women to be priests; just as the Church was wrong for centuries in seeing the earth as the center of the solar system, and slavery as acceptable and usury not; and this wrongness, in the treatment of women, will become obvious to criminals being evangelized, for they know, better than most, the pain and sorrow of being marginalized, even though their marginalization is self-imposed while that of the women in the Church comes from the Vatican and twisted history." (pp. 9-10)

Papers

St. Dismas Day Policy Primer #1: Terms-Thesis-Policy, (March 25, 2007) E-Report (Free to members only)

Summary: A criminal, as we use the term, is a professional criminal. Our thesis is that it takes a reformed criminal to reform criminals, and the policy we suggest is that of providing financial support for a model reentry program managed by a reformed criminal.

St. Dismas Day Policy Primer #2: Catholic Social Teaching & Capital Punishment: A Tradition of Support, (March 25, 2008) E-Report (Free to members only)

Summary: One of the strongest statements from Christ concerning capital punishment is Matthew 18:6. The magisterium of the Catholic Church supports the use of capital punishment. Those within the social science field informed by Catholic teaching, with professional knowledge of criminal justice issues and an understanding of how evil is expressed within the criminal world, embrace that tradition. Research clearly indicates that capital punishment deters crime and saves lives.

St. Dismas Day Policy Primer #3: Justice, Theology, Criminal Transformation & Pope Pius XII, (March 25, 2009) E-Report (Free to members only)

Summary: Justice informed by the theology of the Church, expressed through the social teaching, and responding to the call of Pope Pius XII, can transform criminals. These stated principles, when coupled with the work of the Church through its saints, through its Popes, and the entire history of two thousand years of standing against the gates of hell, is a concrete story of standing on principle, speaking truth to power, walking the talk, proclaiming the truth to man; that will resonate with the criminal—when presented by another who shares the depth of experience represented by the criminal/carceral world—like none other.

St. Dismas Day Policy Primer #4: Unpacking the Lampstand Catholic Reentry Program Model, (March 25, 2010) E-Report (Free to members only)

Summary: The purpose of the Lampstand reentry model program is to evangelize criminals--those who are not Catholic and those who are--bringing them the truths of the social teaching of the Church, from a transformed criminal who has become a deep-knowledge leader, as it will lead to the leaving of their criminal life and conversion to communal life. The truths of the Catholic Church trump the truths of the criminal/carceral world, and as important to the criminal--as it is to all men--is the drive to know the truth; which the criminal already thinks he knows and has been living--the truths of the world--taught and learned under the influence of the prince of the world.

St. Dismas Feast Day Policy Primer #5: The Prison Ministry: A Lampstand Policy Primer, **(March 25, 2011) E-Report (Free to members only)**

Summary: The prison ministry in this policy primer is designed for an individual Catholic parish working with a maximum security prison, through a ministry community of at least four parishioners, in conjunction with the prison's Catholic priest, and supported by prison officials. In order for a Catholic parish to effectively provide a prison ministry that can lead to conversion, a new paradigm in thinking about the criminal world is required rather than the Hollywood dramas or Marxist fantasies too often animating many undertaking this most valuable of ministries called for by Christ in his final teaching to the apostles.

St. Dismas Feast Day Policy Primer #6: The Criminal's Search for God, Sources, **(March 25, 2012) E-Report (Free to members only)**

Summary: The collection of source books and the seminal ideas within them, that have played a large role in the development of my thinking—initially to deepen my criminality, but eventually became the soil from which my transformation grew—is a potential transformative tool that can be used as a guide for those criminals seeking to restructure their lives who are not yet prepared to embrace Catholic works. Most of my exploration of the ideas within these books occurred in prison or shortly after release, and as such, they are influences that supported and expanded the underlying narrative of the criminal/carceral world within which I lived and are largely congruent with its driving ethos. This literature largely emanates from the 1940's to the 1970's—though the ideas are ancient—when the social adulation of the outsider, the outlaw, and the criminal, came into full flower, and it was during the latter decade, that the carceral world was beginning to shape the criminal world.

St. Dismas Feast Day Policy Primer #7: Catholicism, Communism & Criminal Reformation, (March 25, 2013) (Free to members only)

Summary: Communism, and its socialistic method of government, its Marxist method of historical criticism, its violent form of revolution, its state control of religion, and its deep atheism, is a powerful enemy of the Church. We are specifically focusing on Russian Communism, as that is what the Holy Mother of God warned us about at Fatima, and that is the Communism that is the intellectual father of all of the others, deeply engaged since its founding on spreading its revolution worldwide; a revolution that has led, in Russia itself, to the criminal corruption endemic to atheistic governments. The Church has gone from a clear denunciation of Russian Communism by Peter during the 19th and the early 20th century to an accommodation with it immediately prior to and since Vatican II.

St. Dismas Feast Day Policy Primer #8: Women in the Church, Teilhard de Chardin, & Criminal

Reformation, (March 25, 2014) (Free to members only)

Summary: The Church stands in the world as a sign of contradiction, and as the world does, and has since time immemorial, excluded women from full personhood, the Church must ensure that within her embrace, woman's full personhood is deeply rooted and complete; which can only be accomplished by priestly ordination. I have come to believe, fully and completely, that the institutional Church is, and has been, wrong, in not ordaining women to be priests; just as the Church was wrong for centuries in seeing the earth as the center of the solar system, and slavery as acceptable.

St. Dismas Feast Day Policy Primer #9: Judaism, Knights Templar, & Criminal Reformation: A Lampstand Policy Primer (March 25, 2015) E-Report (Free to members only)

Summary: This paper is a summary response to the ancient argument of being, in the Church, pacifist or warrior. Today, as it was in the 12th Century, the response should be, defend the People of God, defend the Church, be a warrior, not a pacifist. The call now is for the Church, for the People of God, and for their leaders, to be warriors, spiritually and martially, and, in their essence, are they not the same. This is a paper calling on transformed professional—excluding rapists, pedophiles and informers—criminals who have done time in maximum security prisons, who have gained graduate degrees from the Academy and an in-depth knowledge of Catholic Social Teaching, to take to the city streets and country byways of this world to defend, spiritually and martially, Catholics being persecuted, and thus to evangelize in the toughest and most dangerous mission fields they can find; for the Church needs you, the People of God need you, and you need to do this for you are among the few who can do this without fear; for who can remain fearful who has survived and thrived on the main yards of America's maximum security prisons.

Articles

Here is a sampling of articles published up to date of publication, (June 2016).

1) This excerpt is from the book review of Andrew Skotnicki's book *"Criminal Justice and the Catholic Church"* by David H. Lukenbill

Published in the *Journal of Markets & Morality* Volume 11, Number 1, Spring 2008 (pp. 118-119)

Criminal Justice and the Catholic Church, Andrew Skotnicki, Lanham, Maryland: Rowman & Littlefield, 2007 165 pp.

Working in the criminal justice system and having read many of the writings of Andrew Skotnicki, I approached his new book with a certainty that I would be rewarded with well-researched and eloquent expressions of those things which I already agree to be true about an effective criminal justice system, which are: that punishment for crimes is important in a spiritual and temporal sense; that prisons are an appropriate ground for punishment while protecting the public from the criminal in the process; and that the essential impetus for reformation comes from the criminal, not from any external influence applied to him.

There are essentially two criminal justice narratives; one from the academy and many nonprofit advocacy organizations which is primarily sociological and rests on the assumption that we need less of everything involved in criminal justice—crimes, arrests, convictions, prisons—and one from the practitioners (the police, district attorneys, judges and prison guards) who make the case for strengthening the existing system or more of everything.

Dr. Skotnicki's work, as expected from work based on the universal faith of the Catholic Church and her social teaching principles, bridges those two narratives in a way no other perspective can.

2) This excerpt is from a paper published in the *Social Justice Review*, Vol. 100, No. 11-12 November-December, 2009, (pp.150-154)

Catholic Punishment and the Constancy of Catholic Social Teaching, by David H. Lukenbill

The experience of individuals in the world shares certain consistent realities, and among those shared realities is response to institutional constancy. We all share the experience of receiving promises that are not kept, from individuals representing institutions. When this becomes a continual experience, then our response to those promises will often be different than it otherwise would have been. And while we may still embrace the institution, we will become more deeply exasperated by its lack of constancy. While an institution's failure to deliver on promises may merely make some people cynical, it can have disastrous results upon individuals seeking the truth if the institution in question is the Church herself, the custodian of Truth.

When promises are kept and faith is congruent with practice, particularly over a long period of time, constancy is maintained and the level of trust and respect engendered rises proportionately. We have this wonderful gift in our well-informed knowledge of the history of the Church, her great constancy to the ancient truths that are congruent with what she still teaches. Many of these are embodied in the simple, visible movement of the priests and the faithful through the sacraments, but it is in the teaching—built on the stones of Sinai, the ministry, death and resurrection of Christ, and the rock of Peter—that there shines a light in the eternal cathedral of time and memory, embracing us all in the immortal truths.

This constancy is sometimes not easily perceived. The world has attempted to destroy the Church from her very beginning, often with the conscious or unconscious help of her members, and the smoke of Satan's war against the Church has always swirled about the corners of the sanctuary, often as close to us as Cain was to Abel. But the record of the thousand battles of this war during the thousands of years it has been waged, and the great triumphs of Holy Mother Church, are resounding still; even within the darkest heart of a sinner they may resound—and when a penitent soul discovers the mark of this triumph written across the heavens and through the centuries, it can be efficacious in bringing that soul to redemption.

3) This excerpt is from a paper published in the *Social Justice Review*, Vol. 101, No. 11-12 November-December, 2010, (pp.172-175)

The Prison Ministry, by David H. Lukenbill

The prison ministry is one of the most dangerous of ministries but also one of the most valuable. This article will examine the issues involved in developing and sustaining a prison ministry, while making sure that the ministers themselves become proficient and remain protected.

The prison first enters Western consciousness through Genesis and the story of Joseph, sold by his brothers into slavery and became, for a while, a prisoner in Egypt.

Joseph's prison was the "Great Prison," the hnrt wr at Thebes, present-day Luxor, whose existence is unrecorded before the period of the Middle Kingdom. [2050-1786 B.C.]

In the New Testament, Christ Himself teaches us to regard visiting those in prison as a work of corporal mercy: "...I was in prison and you came to me." (Matthew 25: 36)

Our prisons have root deriving from Catholic Church history, says Andrew Skotnicki:

> My own conclusion is that the prison as we know it in the West originated in the penitential practice of the early church and in primitive monastic communities. With some reservations, I argue that it thus bears a meaning as valid and necessary as penance and monasticism themselves. Perhaps a more restrained way of phrasing it would be that since the contemporary prison is in many ways a Catholic innovation, whatever hope it may have as a locus and vehicle of criminal justice lies within the history we are about to survey. 2

The Catechism of the Catholic Church has more to say about the works of mercy:

> The works of mercy are charitable actions by which we come to the aid of our neighbor in his spiritual and bodily necessities. Instructing, advising, consoling, comforting are spiritual works of mercy, as are forgiving and bearing wrongs patiently. The corporal works of mercy consist especially in feeding the hungry, sheltering the homeless, clothing the naked, visiting the sick and imprisoned, and burying the dead. 3

Let us keep in mind the four elements I have just mentioned: the prison as an ancient institution; prison visits as a work of mercy; the prison in the modern West as Catholic- inspired; and works of mercy being how we aid one another. The prison ministry that I present in this article is a spiritual work of mercy directed to prisoners in maximum security prisons, for the purpose of evangelization and the development of transformative criminal/carceral leadership to help other prisoners.

At the end of 2009 there were 1,613,656 prisoners in American federal and state prisons. 4 The population in maximum security prisons hovers around 40% of the total—including the 1-2% in super-maximum security prisons.

In 1974, about 44% of the inmates in state confinement facilities were housed in maximum security prisons; by 2000, this percentage declined to about 38%. 5

The reason for focusing on maximum security prisoners is because they are "the point of the spear", able, if converted, to lead others to conversion. Christ calls us to extend our evangelical reach to the greatest sinners, whose conversion creates the greatest joy in Heaven, revealed in the parable of the prodigal son and in the compassion Christ felt for the two criminal saints, Dismas and Mary of Magdala. Maximum security prisoners are mostly professional criminals—those who commit crimes for money and as a profession—with a strong commitment to the carceral/criminal world, but in the roots of that commitment lies the possibility of a commitment to conversion.

4) This excerpt is from a paper published in the *Social Justice Review*, Vol. 102, No. 11-12 November-December, 2011, (pp.167-171)

The Hierarchy of Evil in the Criminal/Carceral World, by David H. Lukenbill

Within the criminal/carceral world there exists a hierarchy of evil. Professional criminals occupy the upper echelons; informants, rapists and paedophiles occupy the lower. The hierarchy is inverted, as those at the lower end are considered the most evil and those at the top the least evil. This hierarchy plays a crucial rôle for pastoral work related to the rehabilitation or conversion of criminals; the present article examines the hierarchy and its implications for work in the prison ministry.

The work of my apostolate to help reform professional criminals through exposure to the history and social teaching of the Catholic Church can only be as effective as my love for the professional criminal—those who commit crimes for money, and are not informants, paedophiles, or rapists. That love is built on the knowledge of the criminal world that I absorbed during twenty years as a criminal, including twelve years spent in maximum-security state and federal prisons.

Though it has been decades since I was in prison or lived as a criminal among criminals, my love for them continues today, and it manifests itself in the pleasure and joyful anticipation I still feel when I have the opportunity to venture into a maximum-security prison to speak with prisoners. The love I came to know in the criminal/carceral world for professional criminals of both sexes is built upon shared experience and many shared perspectives on the world. It has grown as a result of my deep immersion in Catholicism, which began during the months leading up to my entering the Rite of Christian Initiation for Adults, and has deepened in many ways since my baptism and the founding of the apostolate.

I am no longer a criminal, yet I retain a deep respect and quiet love for some of the cultural artefacts of the criminal/carceral world and the moral principles that have marked criminals since before the criminal saint Dismas hung at Christ's side on Golgotha. This love informs the work of my apostolate—as love of neighbour should always inform the criminal-ministry work undertaken by other Catholics acting in the spirit of the charitable love which Pope Benedict XVI reminds us is at the heart of the Church:

> The Church's deepest nature is expressed in her three-fold responsibility: of proclaiming the word of God (kerygma-martyria), celebrating the sacraments (leitourgia), and exercising the ministry of charity (diakonia). These duties presuppose each

other and are inseparable. For the Church, charity is not a kind of welfare activity which could equally well be left to others, but is a part of her nature, an indispensable expression of her very being. (p. 167)

Leadership Resources

Resources for Leaders of Criminal Transformation Programs (An annotated listing of professional associations, books, journals, newspapers, websites, reports and other resources for grassroots leaders.) **E-Booklet (Free to members only)**

A Catholic Grassroots Organization Model (A workbook about a model reentry community program, staffed by one transformed criminal, helping 60-70 reentering prisoners annually on an annual budget of $70,000.00) **E-Booklet (Free to members only)**

Annotated Catholic Criminal Justice Bibliography (A resource that can help guide study, research, and reference around the issues that intersect with Catholicism and criminal justice.) **E-Booklet (Free to members only)**

Lampstand Leader's Circle: Definitions, Experiential Requirements, Daily Practice, & Resources (A workbook defining the professional criminals our work is directed to, their life benchmarks, and the daily practice necessary to become a member of the Lampstand Leader's Circle. **E-Booklet (Free to members only)**

Praying the Rosary for the Criminal (A resource that is useful for penitential criminals who pray the rosary, incorporating prayers and brief histories of five great penitential criminal saints: St. Mary Magdalen, St. Dismas, St. Pope Callistus, St. Mary of Egypt, & St. Paul Hanh.) **E-Booklet (Free to members only)**

Periodic Monographs

Lampstand Monograph #1: *Capital Punishment & Matthew 18:6*, E-Paper (Free to members only)

Abstract: Matthew 18:6 is perhaps the clearest expression of support for capital punishment spoken by Christ. The Catholic & Protestant commentaries about this verse and the teaching of the entire chapter reveal the vigorous sanctions - capital punishment and banishment - Christ taught as applying to the members of the church community who violate its teachings. Matthew 18 has long been acknowledged as a *Discourse on the Church*, but not enough attention has been devoted to its support for capital punishment; and the historic support of the magisterium for capital punishment, and the corrosive direction taken by some segments of Catholic leadership in the United States to abolish capital punishment, all of which are the subject of this monograph.

Lampstand Monograph #2: *The Way of the Saints & Doing Life*, E-Paper (Free to members only)

Abstract: Becoming a true soldier of Christ, fighting to gain entry to heaven, fighting the evil one; this is a call of substance, depth, and honor, which penitential professional criminals imprisoned for life can respond to if the teaching and history of the Church is presented with potency by deeply orthodox Catholics. An unusual cultural aspect of criminal/carceral world culture is the power and influence the elder exerts—almost tribal like in its potency—due to the simple fact that no criminal/prisoner hardly ever retires due to age. I have seen men well into their seventies and eighties who retain the physicality and intellectual heft of men decades younger. The benefits to the criminal/carceral world from the intercessory abilities of a prison saint would be immeasurable.

How Others See Us

There have been several articles published and interviews conducted about Lampstand. Here is a sampling published up to date of publication, (June 2016).

1) These excerpts are from the 2009 article, By the Secret Ladder: Christian Mysticism and Liberation of the Imprisoned, by Dr. Andrew Skotnicki in the journal *Theology Today* (66) 33-44:

In a recent autobiographical account, David Lukenbill writes of the thin line separating the frequently distorted values of penal environments and those in which most of us live: "The cruelty and brutality of the prison is classically evil in the sense that the prisoners are being cruel and brutal consciously. That is the paradigm that works. It is not that there is that much in the prison that doesn't happen on the outside, it's just that in prison it is so much more concentrated." (n. 13, David H. Lukenbill, The Criminal's Search for God (Sacramento, CA: Chulu, 2006), p. 19) (p. 36)

David Lukenbill discovered Thomas Merton in one of his many institutional commitments and similarly writes that there is "much of the monastery in prison." (n. 23, Lukenbill, Criminal's Search for God, p. 18.) Furthermore, he narrates the powerful religious experience he has while on a hunger strike in solitary confinement. In words that recall the self-surrender type of conviction found in the work of William James, he calls it a "break down": "I prayed to God to forgive and protect me and He came to me. I felt such peace and rapture. I felt I was lifted out and walked with Him in a beautiful mountain meadow." (n. 24 Ibid., p. 20.) (pp. 38-39)

2) The following article excerpt is from an interview by Scott Alessi for the In Focus Prison Ministry special in the May 23, 2010 Issue of *Our Sunday Visitor News Weekly.* (pp. 9-12):

Ex-prisoner uses Catholic teaching to break 'criminal world culture'

There's an old adage when dealing with criminals that it takes a thief to catch a thief. But David Lukenbill believes that saying can be taken one step further: It takes a reformed criminal to reform a criminal.

Lukenbill knows firsthand how difficult it can be for a professional criminal to turn his or her life around.

Many years ago, Lukenbill was drawn into a life of crime by the lure of monetary gains, which ultimately landed him inside a maximum security prison. And even though he started to experience some internal rehabilitation during a year in solitary confinement, it didn't hold once he was back among the other inmates.

"Once I got back out into the prison population, I pretty much reverted," Lukenbill said. "The criminal world culture is so dominant in there, and it is pretty hard to counteract that."

3) The following article excerpt is from the January 11, 2011 Catholic Culture website.

Reforming Criminals, By Dr. Jeff Mirus, January 11, 2011

The only daily paper we get in our household is the local paper which covers our town and county in Northern Virginia, or about 375,000 souls. Despite this modest population, nearly every day there is a new local disaster on the front page, very often a crime—burglary, armed robbery, assault, child pornography, even murder. Some of the reports are perversely humorous, as in the recent robbery of a convenience store in which the perpetrator used a six-foot broken branch as a weapon; or the effort to steal a van while the owner was busy in the back. But we've had a string of over twenty burglaries in nearby neighborhoods in recent weeks, there have been some unprovoked gang attacks, and today we learned about the first murder of the new year.

Crimes of passion—and the violent use of an available knife or hand gun in a sudden quarrel—are to some degree understandable, as is the increased incidence of random violence in a crumbling society which is increasingly incapable of nurturing well-adjusted and fundamentally happy people. But consistent criminal activity is a trickier subject; one wonders about the causes that lead someone down that path. A great deal of ink has been spilled over the past fifty years on the sociology of crime, and in particular the degree to which the criminal is himself a victim who cannot be held completely responsible for his actions. Among various attempts to identify root problems, we have seen indictments of society as a whole, of capitalism in particular, and even of the criminal justice system itself.

One man who works directly in this area of assessing criminal responsibility believes that such analyses are fundamentally unproductive. David H. Lukenbill, himself a former 20-year criminal and founder of The Lampstand Foundation, puts the matter succinctly: "In the work of criminal reformation, it is vital to keep in mind that the criminal is the problem." Lukenbill now devotes his life to criminal reformation, and to recruiting other former criminals who have gone on to convert or come back to their Catholic faith (as Lukenbill did) to work directly to touch and transform others.

(4) The following article excerpt is from an interview by Brian Fraga from the June 2012 *US Catholic* magazine.

Crime Fighter

David Lukenbill bears witness to the fact that living outside the law doesn't have to be a life sentence.

A knock on the door introduced David Lukenbill to a life of crime. "My real dad got out of prison when I was 12," recalls Lukenbill. "He showed up on our door one day and my mother said, 'This is your real father'" His dad, a member of the infamous Pendergast gang in Kansas City, Missouri, had spent 10 years behind bars at Fort Leavenworth, Kansas.

Father and son quickly bonded. "I admired my father," says Lukenbill, admitting that he was drawn to his dad's criminal past. Within a couple of years Lukenbill began following in his father's footsteps, stealing and committing armed robberies. He spent 12 of the next 20 years in prison.

"When I was a criminal, I believed that I was acting according to what the truth of the world was," he says. "Rather than working for somebody and enslaving myself for money, I was just taking it, which was what I believed the most powerful people in the world did."

Chapter Eleven
Theology & Practice of
Criminal Reformation

Believing in God incorporates belief in the symphony of God's creation and all that I have written in this book is part of coming to that belief and in the process, a new theology of ancient root emerges; though only in the shadow of the only true theology of Christ.

To the criminal, the real is the dark, the more real, the darker and moving from the dark to the light involves revealing the path to the reality of the Catholic Church, the supernatural Catholic Church, the Catholic Church that has walked the talk for over two thousand years; has been a sign of contradiction in the world even when the institutional church staggers drunkenly, the supernatural Catholic Church walks the clear path; and it is this path that must be revealed to the criminal if transformation is to occur.

In this book all of the theological and practical positions of the Church that play a role in criminal transformation, that I am aware of, have been examined and where the Church stumbles—in my opinion—I offer the supernaturally real as I understand it based on my prayer, my study, and my experience.

It is a theology from the Teilhardian heart of matter, from the heart of the Church, from Christ and those closest to him, as much influenced by Magdalene's penitential depth as from the organizational genius of Peter, the evangelical genius of Paul, and the great leap of faith from Dismas.

It is also a theology of paganism, wherein the king of the wood was killed so that his successor could reign, foreshadowing the transfer of power in criminal gangs, and criminal states.

It is a theology centered on sinners, those who are materially poor who must work harder, to those who are materially rich who must give more.

It is a theology of penance marked by Magdalene and Dismas.

From the penitential criminal who once walked with Satan, within prison and without, a theology of criminal transformation is the spiritual root which the penitential criminal must discover to complete the transformation from the criminal/carceral world to the Catholic communal world.

Before we examine the theology of criminal transformation we must review the theology of the criminal; a theology built on murder, theft, deception, so clearly marked in the actions of Cain, the first criminal since the expulsion from the Garden.

The central element is that the criminal is the archetype of modern worldly man.

Criminals loved the Beats because they wanted to be criminals and in their own halting way were; their lives moving about an axis of sex, drugs and pseudo-intellectual ravings while under the influence, which they proclaimed as blindingly new and as great cosmic insights; but it was just the same old criminal glamor worship of angel headed hipsters, in the body and spirit of the hopelessly helpless sometime criminal inspiring them.

The human mind is hard wired to seek absolute truth and that always, ultimately, involves the study of theology—for the seeking of absolute truth is a search for God—and the criminal, like others on the margins, will resonate most fully to a theology, to a seeking for God, constructed on his vision of reality in which the criminal/carceral world is the axis.

Many say Christ was born a criminal but this is absurd as he was born to perform a mission that he did not know would have been responded to and I assume he hoped the Jews would respond to him as the Messiah he was.

Reality is not a programmed bit of exercise where everything is predetermined, that is the Protestant myth which denies free will.

Each must grow towards the Cosmic Christ through their own path, their own way, their own knowing and being thyself.

We have seen so dramatically during the time of the Beat and the movements following it during the chaos of those times, the degradation accompanying the wearing of the selves of others as the sons and daughters, or order assumed the identities of disorder, deadening their natural response to bring order to chaos, with intoxicants, driving them deeper into chaos.

The avatars, so many having a moment of clarity, taking their own life rather than continue the drama for which they—who were raised to build—spent their precious time destroying.

The theology of the criminal is a pagan theology woven around sensation, exaltation, lust, blood, appetite, and poetry.

In the strikingly original poetics of the criminal/carceral world, Stagger Lee, Blue Velvet Band, and the rap calls to witness the sacredness and vitality of street life, of wonder, and deep night passion; and death.

The eternal mission of the reformed criminal, the formerly evil person, as seen through the perspective of the teachings of Pierre Teilhard de Chardin, is to bring their knowledge of the power of evil and their courage to confront it directly, to the great war, fighting on the side of God and all the angels and saints against Satan and all his demons.

The role of the reformed criminal is to challenge the naivety of the non-criminal, the good person, in order to bring them to fuller integration; while the role of the human good is to absorb evil and change it to the fullness of saintly good.

If you do not understand the reality of Satan, how can you possibly know the reality of God?

Forgetting Satan in our thought and action is a wishful returning to the Garden of Eden, from which we were driven out because we listened to Satan.

If you do not understand evil you cannot be good, for good conquers evil, good drives evil from the field; but if you do not understand evil, its first approach, which may be clothed in glamor, will capture you, rendering you helpless.

In the Telhardian convergence, the reformed criminal will eternalize human knowledge of evil so that Satan will stand naked before humans, no longer shrouded in glamor and the mists of confusion he has hid behind for so long, under the legion of isms of time and history.

The role of the reformed criminal is to share that which has helped shape his soul from the criminal/carceral world where death, violence and the brutality of active evil rule each waking hour.

The value of a reformed criminal to God is much more valuable than a corrupted saint to Satan, because whereas

God does not know evil; Satan, having been an angel, knows good.

This is told many times by Christ: the prodigal son, the one sheep lost, and it forms the axis of the theology of criminal transformation.

It is sad to see Peter walk away from Catholic tradition as he calls for the abolition of capital punishment in opposition to the Catechism; but he merely joins the mass of shepherds who, rather than protecting the flock from the wolves, too often, become protectors of wolves or wolves themselves.

It has always been so, just as it has always been so that saints walk among us—and who was the first saint if not Dismas the Good Thief hanging next to Christ who Christ canonized that very day—and witness with their lives the truth of our faith as the sign of contradiction rather than the go along to get along with the world so characteristic of the majority of Church leaders to whom giving money is wasting money which should be saved to provide for your family.

Walk with Peter of the ages—the saintly popes of blessed memory and sanctified power; to Christ, the true center, God-Man, of all life; through his Mother, Our Holy Mother Mary, the perfect human.

I once proclaimed a daily practice regime of Mass, Rosary and Prayer, which I lived for three years. As my studies deepened into a fuller knowledge of the truth of the Catholic Church founded by God-Man on earth, I realized it was not the rituals we perform that connect us to heaven but the daily life we live comporting with the simple teachings of scripture, tradition, and a sure guide in all is the Angelic Doctor.

Pray for Church leaders to develop spine and witness.

Catholic truth is a golden rod of the hardest steel folded and fired through the blood of saints until it is divinely sharpened and held in the hand of God stretching into the future of the world.

It is warm to the touch, straight and true, cutting through the chaos of the world battering it always, and those who grasp it, live lives sheltered in its golden glow.

It is only grasped by the seeking soul immersed in the ancient Catholic orthodoxy from Christ through Augustine, Saint Thomas Aquinas, Saint Catherine of Sienna and the other Doctors of the Church, the sainted popes and the two Universal Catechisms of Trent and Vatican II.

For liberals it is good to be good. It is good, when speaking of crime and prisons to put the blame on a faceless, irresponsible 'society' rather than directly confront individual evil and in this path lies madness—the madness of incomprehension, of a denial, in the tragic and ultimately insane belief that everything can be worked out if we will but reason with one another.

This is not the path Our Lord walked on earth—when he put Peter behind him, when he drove the moneychangers from the Temple, when he pronounced Judas would have been better had he not been born, and when he said the scandalous need be thrown into the sea with a millstone about their neck.

Our Lord confronted evil directly, clearly, for he knew some human actions must be put behind us, some of the greedy and corrupt must be driven out, some should not have been born, and some should die.

Chapter Twelve
Concluding Thoughts

After many years of studying the Catholic Church—my wife and I converted and were baptized in 2004—I realized the complete difference between the institutional Catholic Church, which operates in public, and the supernatural Catholic Church, which operates in the hearts of the faithful.

My conversion was to the supernatural Church explained so beautifully by its Saints and Doctors of the Church.

My physical interaction with the institutional Church slowly capitulated to the spiritual interactions with the supernatural Church as I learned how vile and corrupt much of the institutional Church has been, is now, and always will be, as long as fallen men lead her.

In a world where women have led nations since antiquity, the failure of the institutional Church to recognize this in its operation speaks deeply of its failure.

I hold fast to the Apostle's Creed, to Aquinas, Catherine of Sienna, Jacques and Raissa Maritain, Teilhard de Chardin, Pius XII, Benedict XVI and the great galaxy of Catholic thinkers who structure and maintain our faith as it was founded and ratified by Christ, captured in the Creed.

Becoming Catholic continues to be the most significant event in my life after my marriage and having a child; and Catholicism provides an endless source of deep knowledge that I keep studying and which I feel is continuing my conversion, though it is now far from the down-the-line conservative Catholicism embraced after baptism.

While researching and writing the eleven (including this one) books which form the body of transformational material useful within Catholic ministry to criminals, I learned many things which have broadened and deepened my faith and brought me to a personal path—embracing both conservative and liberal Catholicism within—that I have come to understand is the real methodology Catholic faith calls us to.

The Apostle's Creed—each one of the 12 Apostles contributing a line—still forms my foundation, and it bears repeating, from the *Catechism* (pp.49-50):

1. I believe in God, the Father Almighty, creator of heaven and earth.

2. I believe in Jesus Christ, his only Son, our Lord.

3. He was conceived by the power of the Holy Spirit and born of the Virgin Mary.

4. He suffered under Pontius Pilate, was crucified, died, and was buried.

5. He descended into hell. On the third day he rose again.

6. He ascended into heaven and is seated at the right hand of the Father.

7. He will come again to judge the living and the dead.

8. I believe in the Holy Spirit,

9. the holy catholic Church, the communion of saints,

10. the forgiveness of sins,

11. the resurrection of the body,

12. and the life everlasting.

Amen.

All the rest is the creation of the institutional church, the creation of men, and so much is so closely entwined with the ways of this world; which clearly is under the sway of Satan, as to be suspect; pray, pay, and obey is the mantra of a tyrant, not that of Holy Mother Church.

And it is gospel, it is the interior truth we all live by, whether divine or profane, and the move, the transformative move, from an interior truth of criminality, of the truth of the world and of the truth of the Prince of the world; to the eternal truth of Catholicism; is a major transformation which can only be accomplished by criminals in concert and under the direction and teaching of a transformed criminal.

My first ten books were somewhat academic, replete with extended quotes from the *Catechism*, Early Church Fathers, the Holy Father, and Catholic scholars; providing a formal introduction to my essential premise: 'It takes a reformed criminal to reform criminals', and helping direct the penitential criminal to further study.

Those books were intended specifically for criminals in prison and transformed criminals who had become deep-knowledge leaders.

This book is a compilation and refinement of those by removing the quotes, revising the narrative, presenting my reflections on the criminal transformative work and the apostolate of the Lampstand Foundation within the social teaching principles of the Catholic Church.

Deep knowledge leaders—who are entrepreneurial—often can make the transformation from a criminal/carceral life to a communal life through textual resources alone, without personal mentoring but through the spiritual mentoring great books can provide.

Fear of transformation on the part of the criminal, fear of becoming a fool—which is how criminals see non-criminals—is something only a respected former, transformed criminal can relieve and even realize it as a fear; for certainly the non-criminal, who tends to see the criminal as foolish, will not see this as an inhibition to rehabilitation or conversion.

This truth which is generally a very minor part of national rehabilitation efforts is continually validated by the 70% recidivist rate representing the failure of rehabilitation.

This high a rate hasn't always been true as recidivism rates of as low as 10% (noted by the works of Dr. Andrew Skotnicki) were reported during the early days of rehabilitation efforts in America which were primarily driven by religion.

However, once the criminal/carceral world became deeply internalized and the over-arching narrative saw outlaws, the outlaw life and getting over, as values in themselves; the ability of the non-criminal to reform criminals vanished.

This glamorization, or theologyfication to be more precise, occurred throughout history but it only became overt and part of the aboveworld culture through the works of the Beat Generation where writers like Allen Ginsburg and William Burroughs virtually created theological grounds for drug addiction, criminality, and immorality in general as the only way to attain freedom from the oppressiveness of modern life.

Another aspect of criminalization are criminogenic communities, which play a largely unpublicized role in the current trend around mass incarceration. Within criminogenic communities—and this has been true for centuries—the police are seen as an occupying army and criminals are seen as positive role models who should be protected from the police; hence, informing on criminals is taboo.

In relation to the ethnic arguments around mass incarceration, the criminogenic communities populated largely by minority ethnics, because they see criminals as positive role models, and because they see police and the society they represent, as the enemy, it is reasonable that the results are much higher crime rates leading to a much higher prison representation; much of which was foretold by the 1965 Moynihan Report.

The specific practices used by the reformed criminal to reform other criminals is oral—deep one on one conversations—mouth to heart, presenting a world view-trumping that of the criminal/carceral world; similar to those utilized by the Didache community transforming Gentiles into Christians, written about by Aaron Milavec in his book, *The Didache: Faith, Hope & Life of the Earliest Christian Communities, 50-70 C.E.* (2003).

The only world-view capable of leading to a productive, communal life from the predatory, destructive life of the criminal is Catholicism, supernatural Catholicism, buttressed by the institutional Church, warts and all.

This is because the criminal is only attracted to absolutes, truth of a clarity and depth, undiluted by worldly lures in contrast to the criminal/carceral truth completely congruent with those lures.

The criminal—and it is important to remind you, dear reader, that the criminal I am referring to is the professional criminal, who commits crimes for money; not the pedophile, serial rapist, serial killer, or informer—as the professional criminal lives by a code of honor that is as perversely ancient as that of the first criminal and as modern as that portrayed by Hollywood in such moral tales as *Thief,* starring James Caan, *Thick as Thieves,* starring Alec Baldwin, and undergirded by the *Godfather* saga starring Marlon Brando and Al Pacino.

Only the way of God trumps the way of Satan and we come close to God with Peter, to Christ, through Mary.

About the Author

David H. Lukenbill is a former criminal—thief and robber—who has transformed his life through education—an Associate of Arts degree in Administration of Justice from Sacramento City College, a Bachelor of Science degree in Organizational Behavior from the University of San Francisco, and a Master of Public Administration degree from the University of San Francisco—several years developing, managing, and consulting with criminal transformative organizations, a conversion to Catholicism and a strong marriage and family life.

He is married to his wife of 32 years and they have one child. They live by the American River in California with two cats, and all the wild critters they can feed.

Contact information:

David H. Lukenbill, President
The Lampstand Foundation
Post Office Box 254794
Sacramento, CA 95865-4794

E-mail: Dlukenbill@msn.com

496

Prayer for Prisoners, Pope Pius XII

⊕ Divine Prisoner of the sanctuary, Who for love of us and for our salvation not only enclosed Yourself within the narrow confines of human nature and then hid Yourself under the veils of the Sacramental Species, but also continually live in the tabernacle! Hear our prayer which rises to You from within these walls and which longs to express to You our affection, our sorrow, and the great need we have of You in our tribulations - above all, in the loss of freedom which so distresses us.

For some of us, there is probably a voice in the depths of conscience which says we are not guilty; that only a tragic judicial error has led us to this prison. In this case, we will draw comfort from remembering that You, the most August of all victims, were also condemned despite Your innocence.

Or perhaps, instead, we must lower our eyes to conceal our blush of shame, and beat our breast. But, even so, we also have the remedy of throwing ourselves into Your arms, certain that You understand all errors, forgive all sins, and generously restore Your grace to him who turns to You in repentance.

And finally, there are those among us who have succumbed to sin so often through the course of our earthly lives that even the best among men mistrust us, and we ourselves hardly know how to set out on the new road of regeneration. But despite all this, in the most hidden corner of our soul a voice of trust and comfort whispers Your words, promising us the help of Your light and Your grace if we want to return to what is good.

May we, O Lord, never forget that the day of trial is an opportune time for purifying the spirit, practicing the highest virtues, and acquiring the greatest merits. Let not our afflicted hearts be affected by that disgust which dries up everything, or by that distrust which leaves no room for brotherly sentiments and which prepared the road for bad counsel. May we always remember that, in depriving us of the freedom of our bodies, no one has been able to deprive us of freedom of the soul, which during the long hours of our solitude can rise to You to know You better and love You more each day.

Grant, O Divine Savior, help and resignation to the dear ones who mourn our absence. Grant peace and quiet to this world which has rejected us but which we love and to which we promise our co-operation as good citizens for the future.

Grant that our sorrows may be a salutary example to many souls and that they may thus be protected against the dangers of following our path. But above all, grant us the grace of believing firmly in You, of filially hoping in You, and of loving You: Who, with the Father and the Holy Spirit, live and reign forever and ever.

Amen.

O Sacred Heart of Jesus, make us love Thee more and more!
Our Lady of Hope, pray for us!
Saint Dismas, the Good Thief, pray for us!

Pius XII, April 1958

Prayer to St. Dismas

Glorious Saint Dismas, you alone of all the great Penitent Saints were directly canonized by Christ Himself; you were assured of a place in Heaven with Him *"this day"* because of the sincere confession of your sins to Him in the tribunal of Calvary and your true sorrow for them as you hung beside Him in that open confessional; you who by your love and repentance did open the Heart of Jesus in mercy and forgiveness even before the centurion's spear tore it asunder; you whose face was closer to that of Jesus in His last agony, to offer Him a word of comfort, closer even than that of His Beloved Mother, Mary; you who knew so well how to pray, teach me the words to say to Him to gain pardon and the grace of perseverance; and you who are so close to Him now in Heaven, as you were during His last moments on earth, pray to Him for me that I shall never again desert Him, but that at the close of my life I may hear from Him the words He addressed to you: "This day thou shalt be with Me in Paradise." Amen.

Prayer to St. Michael for Protection of the Catholic Church and Her Members

℣ **Glorious St. Michael,** Guardian and Defender of the Church of Jesus Christ, come to the assistance of the Church, against which the powers of Hell are unchained. Guard with thy special care her august visible head, and obtain for him and for us that the hour of triumph may speedily arrive.

℣ **Glorious Archangel St. Michael,** watch over us during life, defend us against the assaults of the demon, assist us especially at the hour of death, obtain for us a favorable judgment and the happiness of beholding God face to face for endless ages. Amen

www.ingramcontent.com/pod-product-compliance
Lightning Source LLC
Chambersburg PA
CBHW052117270326
41930CB00012B/2664